Fodor's 99
The Bahamas

The complete guide, thoroughly up-to-date

Packed with details that will make your trip

The must-see sights, off and on the beaten path

What to see, what to skip

Mix-and-match vacation itineraries

City strolls, countryside adventures

Smart lodging and dining options

Essential local do's and taboos

Transportation tips, distances and directions

Key contacts, savvy travel tips

When to go, what to pack

Clear, accurate, easy-to-use maps

Background essays

Fodor's Travel Publications, Inc.
New York • Toronto • London • Sydney • Auckland
www.fodors.com

Fodor's The Bahamas

EDITORS: Rebecca Miller Ffrench, Christina Knight

Editorial Contributors: Jenner Bishop, David Brown, Gordon Lomer, Rich Rubin, Helayne Schiff, M. T. Schwartzman (Gold Guide editor)
Editorial Production: Nicole Revere
Maps: David Lindroth, *cartographer;* Steven K. Amsterdam, *map editor*
Design: Fabrizio La Rocca, *creative director;* Guido Caroti, *associate art director;* Jolie Novak, *photo editor*
Production/Manufacturing: Robert Shields
Cover Photograph: Wayne Levin
Database Production: Phebe Brown, Janet Foley, Mark Laroche, Victoria Lu, Andrea Pariser, Priti Tambi, Julie Tomasz, Martin Walsh, Lucy Wu, Alexander Zlotnick

Copyright

Special Sales

Fodor's Travel Publications are available at special discounts for bulk purchases for sales promotions or premiums. Special editions, including personalized covers, excerpts of existing guides, and corporate imprints, can be created in large quantities for special needs. For more information, contact your local bookseller or write to Special Markets, Fodor's Travel Publications, 201 East 50th Street, New York, NY 10022. Inquiries from Canada should be directed to your local Canadian bookseller or sent to Random House of Canada, Ltd., Marketing Department, 2775 Matheson Boulevard East, Mississauga, Ontario L4W 4P7. Inquiries from the United Kingdom should be sent to Fodor's Travel Publications, 20 Vauxhall Bridge Road, London SW1V 2SA, England.

PRINTED IN THE UNITED STATES OF AMERICA

10 9 8 7 6 5 4 3 2 1

CONTENTS

Maps and Plans

ON THE ROAD WITH FODOR'S

WE'RE ALWAYS THRILLED to get letters from readers, especially one like this:

It took us an hour to decide what book to buy and we now know we picked the best one. Your book was wonderful, easy to follow, very accurate, and good on pointing out eating places, informal as well as formal. When we saw other people using your book, we would look at each other and smile.

Our editors and writers are deeply committed to making every Fodor's guide "the best one"—not only accurate but always charming, brimming with sound recommendations and solid ideas, right on the mark in describing restaurants and hotels, and full of fascinating facts that make you view what you've traveled to see in a rich new light.

About Our Writers

Our success in achieving our goals—and in helping to make your trip the best of all possible vacations—is a credit to the hard work of our extraordinary writers.

Rich Rubin is a New York–based freelance writer. He has written about the Bahamas and other locales for *Bride's, Saveur, Woman's Day, Genre, Endless Vacation, The Los Angeles Times, Boston Globe,* and many other publications. He may be in the Bahamas right now; if he's not, he wishes he were.

Gordon Lomer, a senior editor with Dupuch Publications in Nassau and a certified diving instructor, has spent 10 years in the Bahamas reporting on diving, fishing, and yachting events for the Bahamas News Bureau. He updated our Grand Bahama chapter this year.

Yoked between wanderlust and writer's cramp, Out Islands correspondent **Jenner Bishop** sallies forth once again for Fodor's; when she's not sussing out prime skindiving sites, sampling spicy conch salads, or evaluating the ideal hammock slack, Jenner traipses through the Southwest in search of majestic desert vistas

for Fodor's Arizona guide. She is a freelance-writer based in Los Angeles.

We'd also like to thank a number of people and organizations: Aileen Zerrudo at Bozell Public Relations; Charity Armbrister and Maxine Williamson at the Bahamas Ministry of Tourism (New Providence Island); Carmeta Miller at the Grand Bahama Island Tourism Board; Deborah Simorne at Grand Bahama Beach Hotel; Chris Allison at UNEXSO on Grand Bahama Island; and Keith Fox at Solomon's Wholesale Club in Freeport.

New This Year

We're proud to announce that the American Society of Travel Agents has endorsed Fodor's as its guidebook of choice. ASTA is the world's largest and most influential travel trade association, operating in more than 170 countries, with 27,000 members pledged to adhere to a strict code of ethics reflecting the Society's motto, "Integrity in Travel." ASTA shares Fodor's devotion to providing smart, honest travel information and advice to travelers, and we've long recommended that our readers consult ASTA member agents for the experience and professionalism they bring to the table.

On Fodor's Web site (www.fodors.com), check out the new Resource Center, an online companion to the Gold Guide chapter of this book, complete with useful hot links to related sites. In our forums, you can also get lively advice from other travelers and more great tips from Fodor's experts worldwide.

How to Use This Book

Organization

Up front is the **Gold Guide,** an easy-to-use section divided alphabetically by topic. Under each listing you'll find tips and information that will help you accomplish what you need to in the Bahamas. You'll also find addresses and telephone numbers of organizations and companies that offer destination-related services and detailed information and publications. We've also included a special Up-Close box titled

"Boating in the Abacos," which is packed with tips on sailing in Bahamian waters.

The first chapter in the guide, **Destination: The Bahamas,** helps get you in the mood for your trip. "A Country Built on Water: The Alluring World of the Bahamas" gives some colorful insight of the island country, New and Noteworthy cues you in on trends and happenings, What's Where gets you oriented, Pleasures and Pastimes describes the activities and sights that really make the Bahamas unique, Great Itineraries help you make the most of your time, Fodor's Choice showcases our top picks, and Festivals and Seasonal Events alerts you to special Bahamian events you'll want to seek out.

Chapters on New Providence and Grand Bahama islands are divided into sections on exploring, dining, lodging, nightlife and the arts, outdoor activities and sports, and shopping, and the chapters end with sections called A to Z, which tell you how to get there and get around and provide important contacts and resources. The Out Islands and the Turks and Caicos Islands chapters cover these smaller islands (and groups of islands) individually in alphabetical order.

At the end of the book you'll find Portraits of the Bahamas. The first essay, "In the Wake of Columbus," provides a short history of the island country. In the second essay, inveterate traveler William G. Scheller follows the path of Columbus through the Bahamian islands. Lastly, our Casino Gambling Primer is a mini-guide to gambling.

Icons and Symbols

★   Our special recommendations
✕   Restaurant
🏨   Lodging establishment
✕🏨   Lodging establishment whose restaurant warrants a special trip
☝   Good for kids (rubber duckie)
☞   Sends you to another section of the guide for more information
✉   Address
☎   Telephone number
🕐   Opening and closing times
💷   Admission prices (those we give apply to adults; substantially reduced fees are almost always available for children, students, and senior citizens)

Numbers in white and black circles that appear on the maps, in the margins, and within the tours correspond to one another.

Dining and Lodging

The restaurants and lodgings we list are the cream of the crop in each price range.

Hotel Facilities

We always list the facilities that are available—but we don't specify whether they cost extra: When pricing accommodations, always ask what's included. In addition, assume that all rooms have private baths unless otherwise noted.

Throughout the Bahamas, there are numerous meal plans offered: **European Plan** (EP, with no meals), **Full American Plan** (FAP, with all meals), **Modified American Plan** (MAP, with breakfast and dinner daily), **Continental Plan** (CP, with a Continental Breakfast daily), or **All-inclusive** (all meals and most activities). At the end of each review, we have listed the meal plans the hotel offers. If no plan is mentioned, assume that the hotel operates on the European Plan, with no meals included in the rate.

A Full American Plan may be ideal for travelers on a budget who don't want to worry about additional expenses, but travelers who enjoy a different dining experience each night will prefer to book rooms on the European Plan. Since some hotels insist on the Modified American Plan, particularly during the high season, you might want to find out whether you can exchange dinner for lunch or for meals at neighboring hotels.

Restaurant Reservations and Dress Codes

Reservations are always a good idea; we note only when they're essential or when they are not accepted. Book as far ahead as you can, and reconfirm when you get to town. Unless otherwise noted, the restaurants listed are open daily for lunch and dinner. We mention dress only when men are required to wear a jacket or a jacket and tie. Look for an overview of local habits in the Gold Guide.

Credit Cards

The following abbreviations are used: **AE,** American Express; **DC,** Diners Club; **D,** Discover; **MC,** MasterCard; and **V,** Visa.

Please Write to Us

You can use this book in the confidence that all prices and opening times are based on information supplied to us at press time; Fodor's cannot accept responsibility for any errors. Time inevitably brings changes, so always confirm information when it matters—especially if you're making a detour to visit a specific place. In addition, when making reservations be sure to mention if you have a disability or are traveling with children, if you prefer a private bath or a certain type of bed, or if you have specific dietary needs or other concerns.

Were the restaurants we recommended as described? Did our hotel picks exceed your expectations? Did you find a museum we recommended a waste of time? If you have complaints, we'll look into them and revise our entries when the facts warrant it. If you've discovered a special place that we haven't included, we'll pass the information along to our correspondents and have them check it out. So send us your feedback, positive *and* negative: e-mail us at editors@fodors.com (specifying the name of the book on the subject line) or write the Bahamas editor at Fodor's, 201 East 50th Street, New York, NY 10022. Have a wonderful trip!

Karen Cure
Editorial Director

The Bahamas

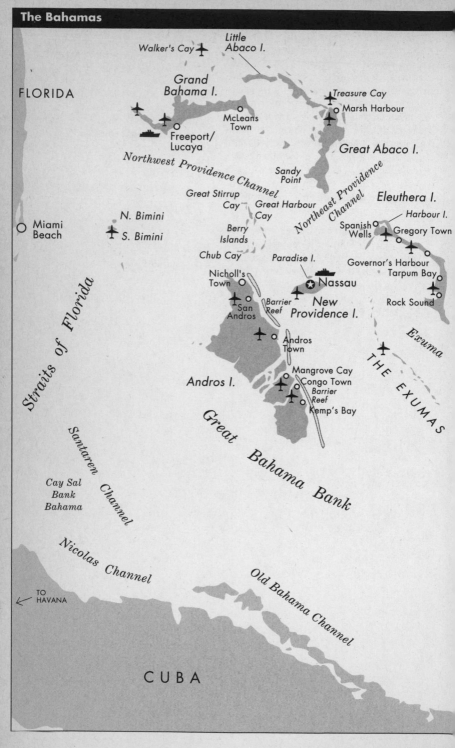

FLORIDA

Walker's Cay ✈

Little Abaco I.

Grand Bahama I.

Treasure Cay ✈
○ Marsh Harbour

✈
✈
○ McLeans Town
○ Freeport/Lucaya

Great Abaco I.

Northwest Providence Channel

Sandy Point

Great Stirrup Cay
Great Harbour Cay

Northeast Providence Channel

Eleuthera I.

N. Bimini

Berry Islands

Spanish Wells ○
Harbour I.
✈ Gregory Town
✈

○ Miami Beach

✈ S. Bimini

Chub Cay

Paradise I.

Governor's Harbour
Tarpum Bay

Nicholl's Town ◯

Nassau ☆

New Providence I.

Rock Sound

Straits of Florida

✈
San Andros ○

Barrier Reef

✈

Exuma

✈

○ Andros Town

Andros I.

Mangrove Cay ○
Congo Town
Barrier Reef
✈
Kemp's Bay

THE EXUMAS

Great Bahama Bank

Santaren Channel

Cay Sal Bank Bahama

Nicolas Channel

Old Bahama Channel

TO HAVANA
←

C U B A

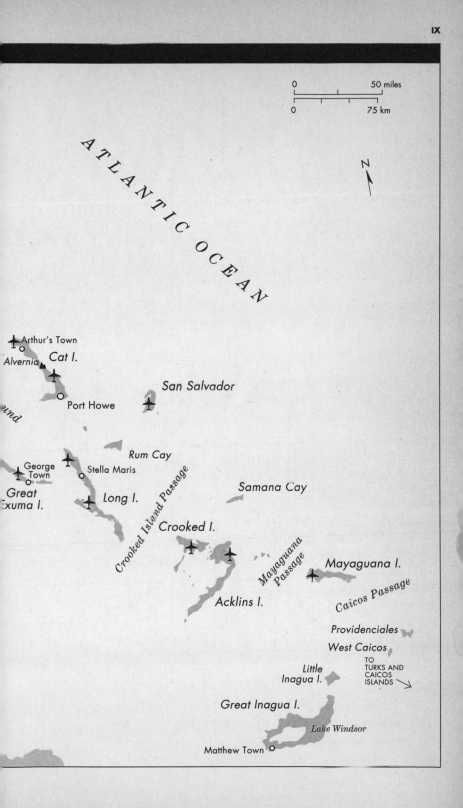

Island Finder

	Cost of Island	Number of rooms	Nonstop flights (from the U.S.)	Cruise ship port	U.S. dollars accepted	Historic sites	Natural beauty	Lush	Arid	Mountainous	Rain forest	Beautiful beaches	Good roads	
New Providence	$$$	7,460	●	●	●	●	●					●	●	
Grand Bahama	$$	3,179		●	●		●					●	●	
The Abacos	$$$	656	●		●		●	●				●	●	
Andros	$$	200	●		●		●	●				●	●	
The Berry Islands	$$$	44	●		●		●	●				●	●	
The Biminis	$$	193	●		●	●	●	●				●	●	
Cat Island	$$	113			●	●	●	●				●	●	
Crooked & Acklins Islands	$$	17			●		●					●		
Eleuthera	$$$	595	●		●	●	●	●				●	●	
The Exumas	$$	147	●		●	●	●	●				●	●	
Inagua	$	23			●		●							
Long Island	$$$	41	●		●	●	●	●				●	●	
San Salvador	$$$	328	●		●	●	●	●				●	●	
Turks & Caicos	$$$	1,205		●	●				●			●		

	Public transportation	Fine dining	Local cuisine	Shopping	Music	Casinos	Nightlife	Diving and Snorkeling	Sailing	Golfing	Hiking	Ecotourism	Villa rentals	All-inclusives	Luxury resorts	Secluded getaway	Good for families	Romantic hideaway
	●	●	●	●	●	●	●	●	●	●		●	●	●	●		●	
	●	●	●	●	●	●	●	●	●	●	●	●	●	●	●		●	
		●	●	●	●		●	●	●	●		●		●	●	●	●	●
			●					●	●			●	●	●	●	●	●	●
		●	●						●	●		●			●			●
		●	●	●	●		●		●			●					●	●
			●					●	●		●	●	●				●	●
			●					●						●		●		
		●	●	●	●		●		●			●		●	●		●	●
		●	●		●		●		●	●		●	●	●	●		●	●
			●					●				●	●			●		
		●	●		●		●	●	●			●			●	●	●	●
		●	●					●	●			●		●	●		●	●
			●			●		●		●		●	●		●	●		●

SMART TRAVEL TIPS A TO Z

Basic Information on Traveling in the Bahamas, Savvy Tips to Make Your Trip a Breeze, and Companies and Organizations to Contact

AIR TRAVEL

BOOKING YOUR FLIGHT

Price is just one factor to consider when booking a flight: frequency of service and even a carrier's safety record are often just as important. Major airlines offer the greatest number of departures. Smaller airlines—including regional and no-frills airlines—usually have a limited number of flights daily. On the other hand, so-called low-cost airlines usually are cheaper, and their fares impose fewer restrictions, such as advance-purchase requirements. Safety-wise, low-cost carriers as a group have a good history—about equal to that of major carriers.

Most flights to the Bahamas—to Nassau, Freeport, and the Out Islands alike—connect through cities in Florida or Atlanta, depending on the airline. There are no direct flights to Freeport from Europe; most make a quick stop in Miami. If you are flying to the Out Islands, consider whether you would rather make one connection through a Florida city, or two—through a Florida city and Nassau.

When you book, **look for nonstop flights** and **remember that "direct" flights stop at least once.** Try to **avoid connecting flights,** which require a change of plane. Two airlines may jointly operate a connecting flight, so ask if your airline operates every segment—you may find that your preferred carrier flies you only part of the way. International flights on a country's flag carrier are almost always nonstop; U.S. airlines often fly direct.

Ask your airline if it offers electronic ticketing, which eliminates all paperwork. There's no ticket to pick up or misplace. You go directly to the gate and give the agent your confirmation number—a real blessing if you've lost your ticket or made last-minute changes in travel plans. There's no worry about waiting on line at the airport while precious minutes tick by.

CARRIERS

When flying internationally, you must usually choose between a domestic carrier, the national flag carrier of the country you are visiting, and a foreign carrier from a third country. National flag carriers have the greatest number of nonstops. Domestic carriers may have better connections to your home town and serve a greater number of gateway cities. Third-party carriers may have a price advantage.

➤ MAJOR AIRLINES: **Delta** (☎ 800/221–1212) flies to Nassau and Freeport. **Continental** (☎ 800/525–0280) and **US Airways** (☎ 800/428–4322) fly to Nassau only. From Canada, **Air Canada** (☎ 800/676–7725) flies to Nassau and Freeport.

➤ SMALLER AIRLINES: **American Eagle** (☎ 800/433–7300) flies to Nassau, Freeport, Governor's Harbour, Marsh Harbour, and George Town; **Bahamasair** (☎ 800/222–4262) connects through Miami, Orlando, and Fort Lauderdale to Nassau, Freeport, Treasure Cay, George Town, Eleuthera (North Eleuthera and Governor's Harbour airports), and Stella Maris on Long Island, and through Nassau to Marsh Harbour, Acklins, Crooked Island, Andros, Cat Island, Eleuthera (North Eleuthera, Governor's Harbour, and Rock Sound), Great Exuma, Inagua, Long Island, and San Salvador; **Comair** (☎ 800/354–9822) flies to Nassau and Freeport; **Carnival Airlines** (☎ 800/824–7386) and **Paradise Island Airlines** (☎ 800/786–7202) fly only to Nassau; and **Pan Am Air Bridge** (☎ 800/424–2557) flies to Paradise Island (New Providence) and to Bimini.

➤ FROM THE U.K.: **British Airways** (☎ 0345/222–111) flies twice weekly to Nassau from London Gatwick. There is an even wider choice of flights via Miami—on **British West Indian Airways** (☎ 0181/570–5552), **Caledonian** (✉ Golden Lion Travel, ☎ 01293/567–800), and **Virgin Atlantic** (☎ 01293/747–747)—with competitive prices. Contact **American Airlines** (☎ 0345/789–789) or **Bahamasair** (☎ 0171/437–8766 or 0171/437–3542) for flights to the islands from Miami.

➤ WITHIN THE BAHAMAS: **Bahamasair** (☎ 242/377–5505), the national airline, has interisland routes; its schedule to some of the islands is limited. To reach the remoter islands, charter a plane at Nassau International Airport: **Cleare Air** (☎ 242/377–0341), **Congo Air** (☎ 242/377–8329), **Sandpiper Air** (☎ 242/377–5751), **Sky Unlimited** (☎ 242/377–8993), **Taino Air Service** (☎ 242/327–5336). Some Out Island lodgings charter their own planes for guests, so see Chapter 4 as well.

CHARTERS

Charters usually have the lowest fares but are the least dependable. Departures are infrequent and seldom on time, flights can be delayed for up to 48 hours or can be canceled for any reason up to 10 days before you're scheduled to leave. Itineraries and prices can change after you've booked your flight.

In the U.S., the Department of Transportation's Aviation Consumer Protection Division has jurisdiction over charters and provides a certain degree of protection. The DOT requires that money paid to charter operators be held in escrow, so if you can't pay with a credit card, **always make your check payable to a charter carrier's escrow account.** The name of the bank should be in the charter contract. If you have any problems with a charter operator, contact the DOT (☞ Airline Complaints, *below*). If you buy a charter package that includes both air and land arrangements, remember that the escrow requirement applies only to the air component.

➤ CHARTER CARRIERS: *See* A to Z section within the chapter that covers your destination.

CONSOLIDATORS

Consolidators buy tickets for scheduled international flights at reduced rates from the airlines, then sell them at prices that beat the best fare available directly from the airlines, usually without restrictions. Sometimes you can even get your money back if you need to return the ticket. Carefully read the fine print detailing penalties for changes and cancellations, and **confirm your consolidator reservation with the airline.**

➤ CONSOLIDATORS: **Cheap Tickets** (☎ 800/377–1000). **Up & Away Travel** (☎ 212/889–2345). **Discount Travel Network** (☎ 800/576–1600). **Unitravel** (☎ 800/325–2222). **World Travel Network** (☎ 800/409–6753).

COURIERS

When you fly as a courier, you trade your checked-luggage space for a ticket deeply subsidized by a courier service. It's all perfectly legitimate, but there are restrictions: You can usually book your flight only a week or two in advance, your length of stay may be set for a certain number of days, and you probably won't be able to book a companion on the same flight.

CUTTING COSTS

The least-expensive airfares to the Bahamas are priced for round-trip travel and usually must be purchased in advance. It's smart to **call a number of airlines, and when you are quoted a good price, book it on the spot**—the same fare may not be available the next day. Airlines generally allow you to change your return date for a fee. If you don't use your ticket, you can apply the cost toward the purchase of a new ticket, again for a small charge. However, most low-fare tickets are nonrefundable. To get the lowest airfare, **check different routings.** Compare prices of flights to and from different airports if your destination or home city has more than one gateway. Also price off-peak flights, which may be significantly less expensive.

When flying within the U.S., **plan to stay over a Saturday night and travel** during the middle of the week to get the lowest fare. These low fares are usually priced for round-trip travel and are nonrefundable. You can, however, change your return date for a fee ($75 on most major airlines).

Travel agents, especially those who specialize in finding the lowest fares (☞ Discounts & Deals, *below*), can be especially helpful when booking a plane ticket. When you're quoted a price, **ask your agent if the price is likely to get any lower.** Good agents know the seasonal fluctuations of airfares and can usually anticipate a sale or fare war. However, waiting can be risky: The fare could go *up* as seats become scarce, and you may wait so long that your preferred flight sells out. A wait-and-see strategy works best if your plans are flexible. If you must arrive and depart on certain dates, don't delay.

CHECK IN & BOARDING

Airlines routinely overbook planes, assuming that not everyone with a ticket will show up, but sometimes everyone does. When that happens, airlines ask for volunteers to give up their seats. In return these volunteers usually get a certificate for a free flight and are rebooked on the next flight out. If there are not enough volunteers, the airline must choose who will be denied boarding. The first to get bumped are passengers who checked in late and those flying on discounted tickets, so **get to the gate and check in as early as possible,** especially during peak periods.

Although the trend on international flights is to drop reconfirmation requirements, many airlines still ask you to reconfirm each leg of your international itinerary. Failure to do so may result in your reservation being canceled.

Always **bring a government-issued photo ID to the airport.** You may be asked to show it before you are allowed to check in.

ENJOYING THE FLIGHT

For better service, **fly smaller or regional carriers,** which often have higher passenger-satisfaction ratings. Sometimes you'll find leather seats, more legroom, and better food.

For more legroom, **request an emergency-aisle seat.** Don't sit in the row in front of the emergency aisle or in front of a bulkhead, where seats may not recline.

If you don't like airline food, **ask for special meals when booking.** These can be vegetarian, low-cholesterol, or kosher, for example.

Many carriers have prohibited smoking on all of their international flights; others allow smoking only on certain routes or certain departures, so **contact your carrier regarding its smoking policy.**

HOW TO COMPLAIN

If your baggage goes astray or your flight goes awry, complain right away. Most carriers require that you **file a claim immediately.**

➤ AIRLINE COMPLAINTS: U.S. Department of Transportation **Aviation Consumer Protection Division** (⊠ C-75, Room 4107, Washington, DC 20590, ☎ 202/366–2220). **Federal Aviation Administration Consumer Hotline** (☎ 800/322–7873).

AIRPORTS

The major gateways to the Bahamas include **Nassau,** on New Providence Island, and **Freeport,** on Grand Bahama Island. There are also some direct flights from Florida to Out Island airports like Marsh Harbour and Treasure Cay in the Abacos. See the A to Z sections in the Out Islands chapter for more airports.

➤ AIRPORT INFORMATION: **Nassau** (☎ 242/377–7281). **Freeport** (☎ 242/352–6020).

BIKE TRAVEL

Biking is fairly easy on these flat islands. Some hotels offer bikes as amenities to their guests, or rent them out, as do general stores. On the Out Islands and Turks and Caicos, bikes are often the most logical way to get around on land and match the laid-back pace of life.

BIKES IN FLIGHT

Most airlines will accommodate bikes as luggage, provided they are dismantled and put into a box. Call to see if your airline sells bike boxes (about

$5; bike bags are at least $100) although you can often pick them up free at bike shops. International travelers can sometimes substitute a bike for a piece of checked luggage for free; otherwise, it will cost about $100. Domestic and Canadian airlines charge a $25–$50 fee.

BOAT & FERRY TRAVEL

If you're of an adventurous frame of mind, you can revert to the mode of transportation that islanders used before the advent of air travel: ferries and the traditional mailboats, which regularly leave Nassau from **Potter's Cay,** under the Paradise Island bridge. You may find yourself sharing company with goats and chickens, and making your way on deck through piles of lumber bound for Cat Island. Fares vary from $20 to $70 each way, depending on the destination. **Don't plan to arrive or depart punctually;** the flexible schedules can be thrown off by bad weather. Remember, too, that they operate on Bahamian time, which is an unpredictable measure of tempo. You cannot book ahead. In Nassau, check details with the dock master's office at Potter's Cay. You can purchase tickets from the dock master or from the captain or mate just before departure.

If you're setting sail yourself, note that cruising boats must clear customs at the nearest port of entry before beginning any diving or fishing (you must have a permit for sports fishing, which costs $20 per trip). *See* A Mariner's Guide to the Bahamas *in* Chapter 4 for more information on boating in the Abacos.

BUS TRAVEL

Buses on New Providence Island and Grand Bahama are called jitneys, and are actually vans. Exact change of 75¢ or $1 is required and while there are established stops, you can sometimes hail a jitney. You should also let the driver know where you would like to get off.

BUSINESS HOURS

BANKS

Banks are open Monday–Thursday 9:30–3 and Friday 9:30–5. Principal banks are Bank of the Bahamas, Bank of Nova Scotia, Barclays Bank, Canadian Imperial Bank of Commerce, Chase Manhattan Bank, Citibank, Commonwealth Bank, and Royal Bank of Canada.

SHOPS

Shops in the Bahamas are open Monday–Saturday 9–5. Bahamian stores are permitted to open on Sunday, but most choose to remain closed. **Best shopping times are in the morning,** when streets are less crowded. Remember that when you're shopping in Nassau, Freeport, and Port Lucaya, you'll be competing with the hordes of passengers that pour off cruise ships daily.

CAMERAS & COMPUTERS

EQUIPMENT PRECAUTIONS

Always **keep your film, tape, or computer disks out of the sun.** Carry an extra supply of batteries, and **be prepared to turn on your camera, camcorder, or laptop** to prove to security personnel that the device is real. Always **ask for hand inspection of film,** which becomes clouded after successive exposure to airport X-ray machines, and **keep videotapes and computer disks away from metal detectors.**

TRAVEL PHOTOGRAPHY

➤ PHOTO HELP: Kodak Information Center (☎ 800/242–2424). *Kodak Guide to Shooting Great Travel Pictures,* available in bookstores or from Fodor's Travel Publications (☎ 800/533–6478; $16.50 plus $4 shipping).

CAR RENTAL

➤ MAJOR AGENCIES: **Avis** (☎ 800/331–1084, 800/879–2847 in Canada, 008/225–533 in Australia). **Dollar** (☎ 800/800–4000; 0990/565656 in the U.K., where it is known as Eurodollar). **Hertz** (☎ 800/654–3001, 800/263–0600 in Canada, 0345/555888 in the U.K., 03/9222–2523 in Australia, 03/358–6777 in New Zealand).

CUTTING COSTS

To get the best deal, **book through a travel agent who is willing to shop around.**

THE GOLD GUIDE / SMART TRAVEL TIPS

Also **ask your travel agent about a company's customer-service record.** How has the company responded to late plane arrivals and vehicle mishaps? Are there often lines at the rental counter? If you're traveling during a holiday period, does a confirmed reservation guarantee you a car?

INSURANCE

When driving a rented car you are generally responsible for any damage to or loss of the vehicle. You also are liable for any property damage or personal injury that you may cause while driving. Before you rent, **see what coverage you already have** under the terms of your personal auto-insurance policy and credit cards.

REQUIREMENTS

In the Bahamas your own driver's license is acceptable for up to three months. An International Driver's Permit is a good idea; it's available from the American or Canadian automobile association, and, in the United Kingdom, from the Automobile Association or Royal Automobile Club. These international permits are universally recognized, and having one in your wallet may save you a problem with the local authorities.

SURCHARGES

Note that some rental agencies charge extra if you return the car before the time specified in your contract. To avoid a hefty refueling fee, **fill the tank just before you turn in the car,** but be aware that gas stations near the rental outlet may overcharge.

CAR TRAVEL

AUTO CLUBS

➤ IN AUSTRALIA: **Australian Auto-mobile Association** (☎ 06/247–7311).

➤ IN CANADA: **Canadian Automobile Association** (CAA, ☎ 613/247–0117).

➤ IN NEW ZEALAND: **New Zealand Automobile Association** (☎ 09/377–4660).

➤ IN THE U.K.: **Automobile Associa-tion** (AA, ☎ 0990/500–600), **Royal Automobile Club** (RAC, ☎ 0990/

722–722 for membership, 0345/121–345 for insurance).

➤ IN THE U.S.: **American Automobile Association** (☎ 800/564–6222).

GASOLINE

Gas costs approximately $2.50 per gallon.

RULES OF THE ROAD

Remember, like the British, Bahami-ans **drive on the left side of the road,** which can be confusing because most cars are American with the steering wheel on the left. As a pedestrian, this means that you should **look right before crossing the street** instead of left, as those of us learned who grew up in the States. Be aware, however, that many streets in Downtown Nassau are one way.

CASINO GAMBLING

For tips on how to gamble, see Cashing In: A Casino Gambling Primer in Chapter 8.

CHILDREN & TRAVEL

CHILDREN IN THE BAHAMAS

Be sure to plan ahead and **involve your youngsters** as you outline your trip. When packing, include things to keep them busy en route. On sightsee-ing days try to schedule activities of special interest to your children. If you are renting a car don't forget to **arrange for a car seat** when you reserve. Most hotels in the Bahamas allow children under a certain age to stay in their parents' room at no extra charge, but others charge them as extra adults; be sure to **ask about the cutoff age for children's discounts.** Club Med, Breezes, Sandals and some small inns discourage or don't permit children; be sure to ask.

FLYING

If your children are two or older, **ask about children's airfares.** As a general rule, infants under two not occupying a seat fly at greatly reduced fares or even for free.

In general the adult baggage allowance applies to children paying half or more of the adult fare. When booking, **ask about carry-on allowances for those traveling with infants.** In general, for babies charged

10% of the adult fare you are allowed one carry-on bag and a collapsible stroller, which may have to be checked; you may be limited to less if the flight is full.

Experts agree that it's a good idea to use safety seats aloft for children weighing less than 40 pounds. Airlines, however, can set their own policies: U.S. carriers allow FAA-approved models but usually require that you buy a ticket, even if your child would otherwise ride free, since the seats must be strapped into regular seats. Airline rules vary, so it's important to **check your airline's policy about using safety seats during takeoff and landing.** Safety seats cannot obstruct the movement of other passengers in the row, so get an appropriate seat assignment as early as possible.

When making your reservation, **request children's meals or a free-standing bassinet** if you need them; the latter are available only to those seated at the bulkhead, where there's enough legroom. Remember, however, that bulkhead seats may not have their own overhead bins, and there's no storage space in front of you—a major inconvenience.

CONSUMER PROTECTION

Whenever possible, **pay with a major credit card** so you can cancel payment or get reimbursed if there's a problem, provided that you can provide documentation. This is the best way to pay, whether you're buying travel arrangements before your trip or shopping at your destination.

If you're doing business with a particular company for the first time, **contact your local Better Business Bureau and the attorney general's offices** in your state and the company's home state, as well. Have any complaints been filed?

Finally, if you're buying a package or tour, always **consider travel insurance** that includes default coverage (☞ Insurance, *below*).

➤ LOCAL BBBs: **Council of Better Business Bureaus** (✉ 4200 Wilson Blvd., Suite 800, Arlington, VA 22203, ☎ 703/276–0100, ℻ 703/525–8277).

CRUISE TRAVEL

➤ CRUISE LINES: **Carnival Cruise Lines** (✉ 3655 N.W. 87th Ave., Miami, FL 33178 ☎ 800/327–9501) offers three-day trips to Nassau and four-day trips to Nassau and Freeport. The *Fantasy,* which holds 2,044 passengers, leaves from Port Canaveral on Thursday and Sunday. The 2,040-passenger *Ecstasy* leaves from the Port of Miami on Friday and Monday.

Celebrity Cruises (✉ 5201 Blue Lagoon Dr., Miami, FL 33126, ☎ 800/437–3111) stops in Nassau with their 1,750-passenger cruise ship *Century,* which leaves every other Saturday from Port Everglades on a seven-night eastern Caribbean cruise.

Discovery Cruises (✉ 1850 Eller Dr., Suite 402, Fort Lauderdale, FL 33316, ☎ 800/937–4477) has one-day trips to Freeport. The *Discovery I,* which holds 1,250 passengers, leaves from the Port of Fort Lauderdale every Sunday, Monday, and Wednesday, and from the Port of Everglades on Friday. The *Discovery Sun,* which holds 1,050 passengers, leaves from the Port of Miami on Tuesday, Thursday, and Saturday.

Dolphin & Majesty Cruise Line (✉ 901 South America Way, Miami, FL 33132, ☎ 800/222–1003 or 800/532–7788) offers three- and four-day cruises to Nassau aboard the *Ocean-Breeze,* with room for 776 passengers, and three-day trips to Nassau aboard the *Royal Majesty,* which can take 1,056 passengers. The 588-passenger *SeaBreeze* stops in Nassau on its seven-day eastern Caribbean cruise. All cruises depart from the Port of Miami.

Norwegian Cruise Line (✉ 9655 Center Dr., Miami, FL 33126, ☎ 800/327–7030) has three-day cruises to Nassau, departing every other Friday. The liner is the *Leeward,* which holds 764 passengers and operates out of Miami.

Premier Cruises (✉ Box 573, 400 Challenger Rd., Cape Canaveral, FL 32920, ☎ 800/515–7890) sends its Big Red Boats, the 1,098-passenger *Atlantic* and the 1,180-passenger *Oceanic,* on three- or four-day loops to Nassau and Port Lucaya from Port Canaveral. The three-night cruises depart Thursday and Friday; the four-night cruises, Sunday and Monday.

Royal Caribbean International (✉ 1050 Caribbean Way, Miami, FL 33132, ☎ 800/327–6700) offers three- and four-day cruises aboard the 2,276-passenger **Sovereign of the Seas,** departing every Monday and Friday from Miami. Three-day cruises sail to Nassau and Coco Cay; four-day cruises sail to Nassau, Coco Cay, and Freeport.

New SeaEscape Cruises (✉ 140 S. Federal Hwy., Dania, FL 33004, ☎ 800/327–2005) offers one-day cruises to Freeport. The 1,170-passenger *SeaEscape* departs from Fort Lauderdale on Monday, Wednesday, Friday, and Sunday.

CUSTOMS & DUTIES

When shopping, **keep receipts** for all of your purchases. Upon reentering the country, **be ready to show customs officials what you've bought.** If you feel a duty is incorrect, appeal the assessment. If you object to the way your clearance was handled, get the inspector's badge number. In either case, first ask to see a supervisor, then write to the appropriate authorities, beginning with the port director at your point of entry.

IN THE BAHAMAS

Customs allows you to bring in 50 cigars or 200 cigarettes or 1 pound of tobacco and a quart of liquor and 1 quart of wine in addition to personal effects and all the money you wish. But **don't even think of smuggling** in marijuana or any kind of narcotic. Justice is swifter in the Bahamas than in the United States. Expect conviction and severe punishment within three days, which could certainly put a damper on your vacation.

You would be well advised to **leave pets at home,** unless you're considering a prolonged stay in the islands. An import permit is required from the **Ministry of Agriculture and Fisheries** (✉ Box N 3028, Nassau, ☎ 242/325–7413) for all animals brought into the Bahamas. You'll also need a veterinary health certificate issued by a licensed vet within 24 hours of

embarkation. The permit is good for 90 days from the date of issue.

IN AUSTRALIA

Australia residents who are 18 or older may bring back $A400 worth of souvenirs and gifts (including jewelry), 250 cigarettes or 250 grams of tobacco, and 1,125 ml of alcohol (including wine, beer, and spirits). Residents under 18 may bring back $A200 worth of goods.

➤ INFORMATION: **Australian Customs Service** (Regional Director, ✉ Box 8, Sydney, NSW 2001, ☎ 02/9213–2000, FAX 02/9213–4000).

IN CANADA

Canadian residents who have been out of Canada for at least 7 days may bring in C$500 worth of goods duty-free. If you've been away less than 7 days but more than 48 hours, the duty-free allowance drops to C$200; if your trip lasts 24–48 hours, the allowance is C$50. You may not pool allowances with family members. Goods claimed under the C$500 exemption may follow you by mail; those claimed under the lesser exemptions must accompany you. Alcohol and tobacco products may be included in the 7-day and 48-hour exemptions but not in the 24-hour exemption. If you meet the age requirements of the province or territory through which you reenter Canada, you may bring in, duty-free, 1.14 liters (40 imperial ounces) of wine or liquor *or* 24 12-ounce cans or bottles of beer or ale. If you are 16 or older you may bring in, duty-free, 200 cigarettes and 50 cigars.

You may send an unlimited number of gifts worth up to C$60 each duty-free to Canada. Label the package UNSOLICITED GIFT—VALUE UNDER $60. Alcohol and tobacco are excluded.

➤ INFORMATION: **Revenue Canada** (✉ 2265 St. Laurent Blvd. S, Ottawa, Ontario K1G 4K3, ☎ 613/993–0534, 800/461–9999 in Canada).

IN NEW ZEALAND

Although greeted with a "Haere Mai" ("Welcome to New Zealand"), homeward-bound residents with goods to declare must present themselves for inspection. If you're 17 or older, you may bring back $700 worth of souvenirs and gifts. Your duty-free allowance also includes 4.5 liters of wine or beer; one 1,125-ml bottle of spirits; and either 200 cigarettes, 250 grams of tobacco, 50 cigars, or a combo of all three up to 250 grams.

➤ INFORMATION: **New Zealand Customs** (✉ Custom House, 50 Anzac Ave., Box 29, Auckland, New Zealand, ☎ 09/359–6655, ☎ 09/309–2978).

IN THE U.K.

From countries outside the EU, including the Bahamas, you may import, duty-free, 200 cigarettes or 50 cigars; 1 liter of spirits or 2 liters of fortified or sparkling wine or liqueurs; 2 liters of still table wine; 60 milliliters of perfume; 250 milliliters of toilet water; plus £136 worth of other goods, including gifts and souvenirs.

➤ INFORMATION: **HM Customs and Excise** (✉ Dorset House, Stamford St., London SE1 9NG, ☎ 0171/202–4227).

IN THE U.S.

Non-U.S. residents ages 21 and older may import into the United States 200 cigarettes or 50 cigars or 2 kilograms of tobacco, 1 liter of alcohol, and gifts worth $100. Prohibited items include meat products, seeds, plants, and fruits.

U.S. residents may bring home $400 worth of foreign goods duty-free if they've been out of the country for at least 48 hours (and if they haven't used the $400 allowance or any part of it in the past 30 days).

U.S. residents 21 and older may bring back 1 liter of alcohol duty-free. In addition, regardless of your age, you are allowed 200 cigarettes and 100 non-Cuban cigars. Antiques, which the U.S. Customs Service defines as objects more than 100 years old, enter duty-free, as do original works of art done entirely by hand, including paintings, drawings, and sculptures.

You may also send packages home duty-free: up to $200 worth of goods for personal use, with a limit of one parcel per addressee per day (and no alcohol or tobacco products or perfume worth more than $5); label the package PERSONAL USE, and attach a list of its contents and their retail value. Do not label the package UNSOLICITED GIFT, or your duty-free exemption will drop to $100. Mailed items do not affect your duty-free allowance on your return.

➤ INFORMATION: **U.S. Customs Service** (Inquiries, ✉ Box 7407, Washington, DC 20044, ☎ 202/927–6724; complaints, Office of Regulations and Rulings, ✉ 1301 Constitution Ave. NW, Washington, DC 20229; registration of equipment, Resource Management, ✉ 1301 Constitution Ave. NW, Washington DC 20229, ☎ 202/927–0540).

DISABILITIES & ACCESSIBILITY

ACCESS IN THE BAHAMAS

Downtown Nassau took into account wheelchair accessibility when it underwent redevelopment in 1995. The Bahamas Association for the Physically Disabled has a van for hire that can pick you up from the airport or provide other transportation. Reservations must be made well in advance. The Association can also provide temporary ramps and other portable facilities.

➤ LOCAL RESOURCES: **Bahamas Association for the Physically Disabled** (☎ 242/322–2393).

LODGING

Most major hotels throughout the Bahamas have special facilities for people with disabilities, in the way of elevators, ramps, and easy access to rooms and public areas. Here are some suggestions based on a survey conducted by the Bahamas Association for the Physically Disabled:

➤ NASSAU: **Best Western British Colonial Beach Resort** (✉ Box N 7148, ☎ 242/322–3301), **Nassau Marriott Resort & Crystal Palace Casino** (✉ Box N 8806, ☎ 242/327–6200), **Nassau Beach Hotel** (✉ Box N 7756, ☎ 242/327–7711), **Radisson Cable Beach Casino & Golf Resort** (✉ Box N 4914, ☎ 242/327–6000), and **Little Orchard Cottage** (✉ Box N 1514, ☎ 242/393–1297).

➤ PARADISE ISLAND: **Atlantis, Paradise Island** (✉ Box N 4777, ☎ 242/363–

3000), **Bay View Village** (✉ Box SS 6308, ☎ 242/363–2555), **Pirate's Cove Beach Resort** (✉ Box SS 6214, ☎ 242/363–2100), and **Radisson Grand Resort** (✉ Box SS 6307, ☎ 242/363–2011).

➤ GRAND BAHAMA: **Bahamas Princess Resort & Casino** (✉ Box F 40207, ☎ 242/352–9661).

➤ LONG ISLAND: **Stella Maris Marina Inn & Estate** (✉ Box SM 30105, ☎ 242/338–2050 or 800/426–0466).

MAKING RESERVATIONS

When discussing accessibility with an operator or reservations agent, **ask hard questions.** Are there any stairs, inside *or* out? Are there grab bars next to the toilet *and* in the shower/tub? How wide is the doorway to the room? To the bathroom? For the most extensive facilities meeting the latest legal specifications, **opt for newer accommodations,** which are more likely to have been designed with access in mind. Older buildings or ships may have more limited facilities. Be sure to **discuss your needs before booking.**

TRANSPORTATION

➤ COMPLAINTS: **Disability Rights Section** (✉ U.S. Department of Justice, Civil Rights Division, Box 66738, Washington, DC 20035–6738, ☎ 202/514–0301 or 800/514–0301, TTY 202/514–0383 or 800/514–0383, FAX 202/307–1198) for general complaints. **Aviation Consumer Protection Division** (☞ Air Travel, *above*) for airline-related problems. **Civil Rights Office** (✉ U.S. Department of Transportation, Departmental Office of Civil Rights, S-30, 400 7th St. SW, Room 10215, Washington, DC 20590, ☎ 202/366–4648, FAX 202/366–9371) for problems with surface transportation.

TRAVEL AGENCIES & TOUR OPERATORS

As a whole, the travel industry has become more aware of the needs of travelers with disabilities. In the U.S., the Americans with Disabilities Act requires that travel firms serve the needs of all travelers. Note, though, that some agencies and operators specialize in making travel arrange-ments for individuals and groups with disabilities.

➤ TRAVELERS WITH MOBILITY PROBLEMS: **Access Adventures** (✉ 206 Chestnut Ridge Rd., Rochester, NY 14624, ☎ 716/889–9096), run by a former physical-rehabilitation counselor. **CareVacations** (✉ 5019 49th Ave., Suite 102, Leduc, Alberta T9E 6T5, ☎ 403/986–6404, 800/648–1116 in Canada) has group tours and is especially helpful with cruise vacations. **Flying Wheels Travel** (✉ 143 W. Bridge St., Box 382, Owatonna, MN 55060, ☎ 507/451–5005 or 800/535–6790, FAX 507/451–1685), a travel agency specializing in customized tours and itineraries worldwide. **Hinsdale Travel Service** (✉ 201 E. Ogden Ave., Suite 100, Hinsdale, IL 60521, ☎ 630/325–1335), a travel agency that benefits from the advice of wheelchair traveler Janice Perkins.

DISCOUNTS & DEALS

Be a smart shopper and **compare all your options** before making any choice. A plane ticket bought with a promotional coupon may not be cheaper than the least expensive fare from a discount ticket agency. For high-price travel purchases, such as packages or tours, keep in mind that what you get is just as important as what you save. Just because something is cheap doesn't mean it's a bargain.

CLUBS & COUPONS

Many companies sell discounts in the form of travel clubs and coupon books, but these cost money. You must use participating advertisers to get a deal, and only after you recoup the initial membership cost or book price do you begin to save. If you plan to use the club or coupons frequently, you may save considerably. Before signing up, find out what discounts you get for free.

➤ DISCOUNT CLUBS: **Entertainment Travel Editions** (✉ 2125 Butterfield Rd., Troy, MI 48084, ☎ 800/445–4137; $20–$51, depending on destination). **Great American Traveler** (✉ Box 27965, Salt Lake City, UT 84127, ☎ 801/974–3033 or 800/548–2812; $49.95 per year).

Moment's Notice Discount Travel Club (✉ 7301 New Utrecht Ave., Brooklyn, NY 11204, ☎ 718/234–6295; $25 per year, single or family). **Privilege Card International** (✉ 237 E. Front St., Youngstown, OH 44503, ☎ 330/746–5211 or 800/236–9732; $74.95 per year). **Sears's Mature Outlook** (✉ Box 9390, Des Moines, IA 50306, ☎ 800/336–6330; $19.95 per year). **Travelers Advantage** (✉ CUC Travel Service, 3033 S. Parker Rd., Suite 1000, Aurora, CO 80014, ☎ 800/548–1116 or 800/648–4037; $59.95 per year, single or family). **Worldwide Discount Travel Club** (✉ 1674 Meridian Ave., Miami Beach, FL 33139, ☎ 305/534–2082; $50 per year family, $40 single).

CREDIT-CARD BENEFITS

When you use your credit card to make travel purchases you may get free travel-accident insurance, collision-damage insurance, and medical or legal assistance, depending on the card and the bank that issued it. American Express, MasterCard, and Visa provide one or more of these services, so **get a copy of your credit card's travel-benefits policy.** If you are a member of an auto club, always **ask hotel and car-rental reservations agents about auto-club discounts.** Some clubs offer additional discounts on tours, cruises, and admission to attractions.

DISCOUNT RESERVATIONS

To save money, **look into discount-reservations services** with toll-free numbers, which use their buying power to get a better price on hotels, airline tickets, even car rentals. When booking a room, always **call the hotel's local toll-free number** (if one is available) rather than the central reservations number—you'll often get a better price. Always ask about special packages or corporate rates.

When shopping for the best deal on hotels and car rentals, **look for guaranteed exchange rates,** which protect you against a falling dollar. With your rate locked in, you won't pay more, even if the price goes up in the local currency.

➤ AIRLINE TICKETS: ☎ **800/FLY–4–LESS.**

PACKAGE DEALS

Packages and guided tours can save you money, but don't confuse the two. When you buy a package, your travel remains independent, just as though you had planned and booked the trip yourself. Fly/drive packages, which combine airfare and car rental, are often a good deal.

ELECTRICITY

Electricity is 120 volts/60 cycles, which is compatible with all U.S. appliances.

GAY & LESBIAN TRAVEL

➤ GAY- AND LESBIAN-FRIENDLY TOUR OPERATORS: **Olivia** (✉ 4400 Market St., Oakland, CA 94608, ☎ 510/655–0364 or 800/631–6277, FAX 510/655–4334), for cruises and resort vacations for lesbians.

➤ GAY- AND LESBIAN-FRIENDLY TRAVEL AGENCIES: **Corniche Travel** (✉ 8721 Sunset Blvd., Suite 200, West Hollywood, CA 90069, ☎ 310/854–6000 or 800/429–8747, FAX 310/659–7441). **Islanders Kennedy Travel** (✉ 183 W. 10th St., New York, NY 10014, ☎ 212/242–3222 or 800/988–1181, FAX 212/929–8530). **Now Voyager** (✉ 4406 18th St., San Francisco, CA 94114, ☎ 415/626–1169 or 800/255–6951, FAX 415/626–8626). **Yellowbrick Road** (✉ 1500 W. Balmoral Ave., Chicago, IL 60640, ☎ 773/561–1800 or 800/642–2488, FAX 773/561–4497). **Skylink Travel and Tour** (✉ 3577 Moorland Ave., Santa Rosa, CA 95407, ☎ 707/585–8355 or 800/225–5759, FAX 707/584–5637), serving lesbian travelers,

HEALTH

DIVERS' ALERT

Do not fly within 24 hours after scuba diving.

MEDICAL PLANS

No one plans to get sick while traveling, but it happens, so **consider signing up with a medical-assistance company.** Members get doctor referrals, emergency evacuation or repatriation, 24-hour telephone hot lines for medical consultation, cash for emergencies, and other personal and legal assistance. Coverage varies by plan, so **review the benefits of each carefully.**

THE GOLD GUIDE / SMART TRAVEL TIPS

THE GOLD GUIDE / SMART TRAVEL TIPS

➤ MEDICAL-ASSISTANCE COMPANIES: **International SOS Assistance** (✉ 8 Neshaminy Interplex, Suite 207, Trevose, PA 19053, ☎ 215/245–4707 or 800/523–6586, FAX 215/244–9617; ✉ 12 Chemin Riantbosson, 1217 Meyrin 1, Geneva, Switzerland, ☎ 4122/785–6464, FAX 4122/785–6424; ✉ 10 Anson Rd., 14-07/08 International Plaza, Singapore, 079903, ☎ 65/226–3936, FAX 65/226–3937).

SUNBATHING

Basking in the sun is one of the great pleasures of a Bahamian vacation; but because the sun is closer to the earth the farther south you go, it will burn your skin more quickly, so take precautions against the ravages of sunburn and sunstroke. On a hot, sunny day, even people who are not normally bothered by strong sun should **cover up with a long-sleeve shirt, a hat, and pants or a beach wrap.** These are essential for a day on a boat but are also advisable for midday at the beach. **Carry some UVA/UVB sunblock** (with a sun protection factor, or SPF, of at least 15) for nose, ears, and other sensitive areas such as eyelids, ankles, and so forth; if you're engaging in water sports, be sure the sunscreen is waterproof. Wear sunglasses because eyes are particularly vulnerable to direct sun and reflected rays. Be sure to **drink enough liquids—water or fruit juice preferably**—and avoid coffee, tea, and alcohol. Above all, limit your sun time for the first few days until you become accustomed to the heat. Do not be fooled by an overcast day. Quite often you will get the worst sunburns when you least expect it. The safest hours for sunbathing are 4–6, but even then it is wise to limit exposure to 15–20 minutes.

VACCINATIONS

A vaccination against yellow fever is required if you're arriving from an infected area. Otherwise, no special shots are required before visiting the Bahamas.

INSURANCE

Travel insurance is the best way to **protect yourself against financial loss.** The most useful plan is a comprehensive policy that includes coverage for trip cancellation and interruption, default, trip delay, and medical expenses (with a waiver for preexisting conditions).

Without insurance, you will lose all or most of your money if you cancel your trip, regardless of the reason. Default insurance covers you if your tour operator, airline, or cruise line goes out of business. Trip-delay covers unforeseen expenses that you may incur due to bad weather or mechanical delays. It's important to compare the fine print regarding trip-delay coverage when comparing policies.

For overseas travel, one of the most important components of travel insurance is its medical coverage. Supplemental health insurance will pick up the cost of your medical bills should you get sick or injured while traveling. U.S. residents should note that Medicare generally does not cover health-care costs outside the United States, nor do many privately issued policies. Residents of the United Kingdom can buy an annual travel-insurance policy valid for most vacations taken during the year in which the coverage is purchased. If you are pregnant or have a preexisting condition, make sure you're covered. British citizens should buy extra medical coverage when traveling overseas, according to the Association of British Insurers. Australian travelers should buy travel insurance, including extra medical coverage, whenever they go abroad, according to the Insurance Council of Australia.

Always **buy travel insurance directly from the insurance company**; if you buy it from a cruise line, airline, or tour operator that goes out of business you probably will not be covered for the agency or operator's default, a major risk. Before you make any purchase, **review your existing health and home-owner's policies** to find out whether they cover expenses incurred while traveling.

➤ TRAVEL INSURERS: In the U.S., **Access America** (✉ 6600 W. Broad St., Richmond, VA 23230, ☎ 804/285–3300 or 800/284–8300). **Travel Guard International** (✉ 1145 Clark St., Stevens Point, WI 54481, ☎ 715/345–

0505 or 800/826–1300). In Canada, **Mutual of Omaha** (✉ Travel Division, 500 University Ave., Toronto, Ontario M5G 1V8, ☎ 416/598–4083, 800/268–8825 in Canada).

➤ INSURANCE INFORMATION: In the U.K., **Association of British Insurers** (✉ 51 Gresham St., London EC2V 7HQ, ☎ 0171/600–3333). In Australia, the **Insurance Council of Australia** (☎ 613/9614–1077, FAX 613/9614–7924).

LANGUAGE

Bahamians speak English with a lilt influenced by their Scottish, Irish, and/or African ancestry. The official language of the Turks and Caicos is also English.

LODGING

Beachfront resort hotels—on Cable Beach and Paradise Island on New Providence Island, and in Lucaya on Grand Bahama Island—are among the most expensive. They also have the widest range of sports facilities, including tennis courts and sailboats. High room rates in many hotels in winter season (slightly less on Grand Bahama than on New Providence) are cut by as much as 30% during the slower May–December period, when managements try to outdo one another with attractive three-day or one-week packages. Prices at hotels away from the beach tend to be considerably lower and are often a better deal because accessible beaches are never far away.

In addition to the apartment suggestions *below*, Out Islands' lodging includes cottages that come with fully equipped kitchens.

➤ RESERVATION SERVICE: For the Turks and Caicos Islands, contact the **Turks & Caicos Reservation Service** (☎ 800/282–4753).

APARTMENT & VILLA RENTALS

If you want a home base that's roomy enough for a family and comes with cooking facilities, **consider a furnished rental.** These can save you money, especially if you're traveling with a large group of people. Home-exchange directories list rentals (often second homes owned by prospective house swappers), and some services

search for a house or apartment for you (even a castle if that's your fancy) and handle the paperwork. Some send an illustrated catalog; others send photographs only of specific properties, sometimes at a charge. Up-front registration fees may apply.

➤ RENTAL AGENTS: **At Home Abroad** (✉ 405 E. 56th St., Suite 6H, New York, NY 10022, ☎ 212/421–9165, FAX 212/752–1591). **Europa-Let/Tropical Inn-Let** (✉ 92 N. Main St., Ashland, OR 97520, ☎ 541/482–5806 or 800/462–4486, FAX 541/482–0660). **Hometours International** (✉ Box 11503, Knoxville, TN 37939, ☎ 423/690–8484 or 800/367–4668). **Property Rentals International** (✉ 1008 Mansfield Crossing Rd., Richmond, VA 23236, ☎ 804/378–6054 or 800/220–3332, FAX 804/379–2073). **Rental Directories International** (✉ 2044 Rittenhouse Sq., Philadelphia, PA 19103, ☎ 215/985–4001, FAX 215/985–0323). **Rent-a-Home International** (✉ 7200 34th Ave. NW, Seattle, WA 98117, ☎ 206/789–9377 or 800/488–7368, FAX 206/789–9379). **Vacation Home Rentals Worldwide** (✉ 235 Kensington Ave., Norwood, NJ 07648, ☎ 201/767–9393 or 800/633–3284, FAX 201/767–5510). **Villas International** (✉ 950 Northgate Dr., Suite 206, San Rafael, CA 94903, ☎ 415/499–9490 or 800/221–2260, FAX 415/499–9491). **Hideaways International** (✉ 767 Islington St., Portsmouth, NH 03801, ☎ 603/430–4433 or 800/843–4433, FAX 603/430–4444; membership $99) is a club for travelers who arrange rentals among themselves.

MAIL

POSTAL RATES

Airmail postcards to the United States, Canada, the United Kingdom, Europe, and South America require a 40¢ stamp. If you're sending an airmail letter, it costs 55¢ per half ounce to the United States and Canada, 60¢ to the United Kingdom, Europe, and South America. The stamps must be Bahamian. Prices from the Turks and Caicos are comparable. Whether or not the term "snail mail" was coined in the Bahamas, you're likely to find that you arrive home long before your postcards do.

SMART TRAVEL TIPS / THE GOLD GUIDE

MONEY

COSTS

Generally, prices in the Bahamas reflect the exchange rate: They are about the same as in the United States, less expensive than in the United Kingdom, and more expensive than in Canada. A hotel can cost anywhere from $35 a night (for cottages and apartments in downtown Nassau and in the Out Islands) to $165 and up (at the ritzier resorts on Cable Beach and Paradise Island and in Freeport and Lucaya), depending on the season. Add $35 to $50 per person per day for meals. Four-day/three-night and eight-day/seven-night package stays offered by most hotels can cut costs considerably. On the Out Islands, you'll notice that meals and simple goods can be expensive; this is due to the remoteness of the islands and the costs of importing.

CREDIT & DEBIT CARDS

Should you use a credit card or a debit card when traveling? Both have benefits. A credit card allows you to delay payment and gives you certain rights as a consumer (☞ Consumer Protection, *above*). A debit card, also known as a check card, deducts funds directly from your checking account and helps you stay within your budget. When you want to rent a car, though, you may still need an old-fashioned credit card. Although you can always *pay* for your car with a debit card, some agencies will not allow you to *reserve* a car with a debit card.

Otherwise, the two types of plastic are virtually the same. Both will get you cash advances at ATMs worldwide if your card is properly programmed with your personal identification number (PIN). (You will not need to alter your PIN number for use in the Bahamas). Both offer excellent, wholesale exchange rates. And both protect you against unauthorized use if the card is lost or stolen. Your liability is limited to $50, as long as you report the card missing. Be aware that there are few ATMs on the islands: There is one at the Princess Casino on Grand Bahama Island, and **there are no ATM machines on the Out Islands** so be sure to have credit cards and ample cash handy to cover your expenses.

➤ ATM LOCATIONS: **Cirrus** (☎ 800/424–7787). **Plus** (☎ 800/843–7587) for locations in the U.S. and Canada, or visit your local bank.

CURRENCY

The U.S. dollar is on par with the Bahamian dollar and is accepted all over the Bahamas; the U.K. pound sterling compares at about 75 pence, and the Canadian dollar at around $1.20. If someone offers you a $3 bill, don't think you're being conned. Bahamian money runs in bills of a half dollar, $1, $3, $5, $10, $20, $50, and $100. The rare 50¢ and $3 bills make unusual souvenirs.

EXCHANGING MONEY

In the Bahamas, only U.S. cash will be exchanged freely in hotels, stores or restaurants, and since the U.S. currency is accepted throughout, there really is no need to change to Bahamian.

For the most favorable rates, **change money through banks.** Although fees charged for ATM transactions may be higher abroad than at home, Cirrus and Plus exchange rates are excellent, because they are based on wholesale rates offered only by major banks. You won't do as well at exchange booths in airports or rail and bus stations, in hotels, in restaurants, or in stores, although you may find their hours more convenient.

➤ EXCHANGE SERVICES: **Chase *Currency To Go*** (☎ 800/935–9935; 935–9935 in NY, NJ, and CT). **International Currency Express** (☎ 888/842–0880 on the East Coast, 888/278–6628 on the West Coast). **Thomas Cook Currency Services** (☎ 800/287–7362 for telephone orders and retail locations).

TRAVELER'S CHECKS

Do you need traveler's checks? It depends on where you're headed. If you're going to the Out Islands and small towns, go with cash; traveler's checks are best used in cities. Lost or stolen checks can usually be replaced within 24 hours. To ensure a speedy refund, buy your own traveler's checks—don't let someone else pay for them: irregularities like this can cause delays. The person who bought the checks should make the call to request a refund.

NEWSPAPERS

You'll get all the Bahamian news and a good idea of what's going on internationally in the *Tribune* and the *Nassau Guardian* on New Providence and in the *Freeport News* on Grand Bahama. But if you want up-to-date news on what's happening around the world, you can also get the locally printed, satellite-generated *Miami Herald,* the *Wall Street Journal,* and the *New York Times* daily at newsstands.

PACKING

LUGGAGE

How many carry-on bags you can bring with you is up to the airline. Most allow two, but the limit is often reduced to one on certain flights. Gate agents will take excess baggage—including bags they deem oversize—from you as you board and add it to checked luggage. To avoid this situation, make sure that everything you carry aboard will fit under your seat. Also, get to the gate early, and request a seat at the back of the plane; you'll probably board first, while the overhead bins are still empty. Since big, bulky baggage attracts the attention of gate agents and flight attendants on a busy flight, make sure your carry-on is really a carry-on. Finally, a carry-on that's long and narrow is more likely to remain unnoticed than one that's wide and squarish.

If you are flying internationally, note that baggage allowances may be determined not by piece but by weight—generally 88 pounds (40 kilograms) in first class, 66 pounds (30 kilograms) in business class, and 44 pounds (20 kilograms) in economy.

Airline liability for baggage is limited to $1,250 per person on flights within the United States. On international flights it amounts to $9.07 per pound or $20 per kilogram for checked baggage (roughly $640 per 70-pound bag) and $400 per passenger for unchecked baggage. You can buy additional coverage at check-in for about $10 per $1,000 of coverage, but it excludes a rather extensive list of items, shown on your airline ticket.

Before departure, **itemize your bags' contents** and their worth, and label the bags with your name, address, and phone number. (If you use your home address, cover it so that potential thieves can't see it readily.) Inside each bag, **pack a copy of your itinerary.** At check-in, **make sure that each bag is correctly tagged** with the destination airport's three-letter code. If your bags arrive damaged or fail to arrive at all, file a written report with the airline before leaving the airport.

PACKING LIST

The reason you're going to the Bahamas is to get away from all of that suit-shirt-and-tie turmoil, so your wardrobe should reflect the informality of the experience. Aside from your bathing suit, which will be your favorite uniform, take lightweight clothing (short-sleeve shirts, T-shirts, cotton slacks, lightweight jackets for evening wear for men; light dresses, shorts, and T-shirts for women). If you're going during the high season, between mid-December and April, toss in a sweater for the occasional cool evening. Cover up in public places for downtown shopping expeditions, and save that skimpy bathing suit for the beach at your hotel.

Only some of the more sophisticated hotels require jackets for men and dresses for women at dinner. But there are no such dress rules in any of the Bahamas' casinos.

In your carry-on luggage **bring an extra pair of eyeglasses or contact lenses** and **enough of any medication you take** to last the entire trip. You may also want your doctor to write a spare prescription using the drug's generic name, since brand names may vary from country to country. **Never put prescription drugs or valuables in luggage to be checked.** To avoid customs delays, carry medications in their original packaging. And don't forget to copy down and carry addresses of offices that handle refunds of lost traveler's checks.

PASSPORTS & VISAS

When traveling internationally, **carry a passport even if you don't need one** (it's always the best form of I.D.), and make **two photocopies of the data page** (one for someone at home and another for you, carried separately from your passport). If you lose your passport, promptly call the nearest embassy or consulate and the local police.

ENTERING THE BAHAMAS

For your specific questions, contact the Bahamas Immigration Department (☎ 242/322–7530) or the nearest consulate.

U.S. CITIZENS

For a stay of up to eight months, a passport and visa are not required of tourists with onward/return tickets; a birth certificate with a raised seal and two forms of photo identification are sufficient. However, bringing a passport is the best option. Even an expired passport, if it expired less than five years ago, is a valid form of identification.

CANADIANS

For stays of three weeks or less, Canadian travelers with onward/return tickets do not need a valid passport; a certified birth certificate with a raised seal and two forms of photo identification are sufficient. You do need a valid passport to enter the Bahamas for stays from three weeks to eight months.

U.K. CITIZENS

For stays up to eight months, it's best for citizens of the U.K. to have valid passports along with onward/return tickets.

AUSTRALIANS AND NEW ZEALANDERS

Australian and New Zealand citizens should bring a valid passport for entry to the Bahamas along with onward/return tickets.

TURKS AND CAICOS

U.S. citizens need some proof of citizenship, such as a birth certificate with a raised seal, plus a photo ID or a current passport. British subjects are required to have a current passport.

All visitors must have an ongoing or return ticket.

PASSPORT OFFICES

The best time to apply for a passport or to renew is during the fall and winter. Before any trip, be sure to check your passport's expiration date and, if necessary, renew it as soon as possible. (Some countries won't allow you to enter on a passport that's due to expire in six months or less.)

➤ AUSTRALIAN CITIZENS: **Australian Passport Office** (☎ 131–232).

➤ CANADIAN CITIZENS: **Passport Office** (☎ 819/994–3500 or 800/567–6868).

➤ NEW ZEALAND CITIZENS: **New Zealand Passport Office** (☎ 04/494–0700 for information on how to apply, 0800/727–776 for information on applications already submitted).

➤ U.K. CITIZENS: **London Passport Office** (☎ 0990/21010), for fees and documentation requirements and to request an emergency passport.

➤ U.S. CITIZENS: **National Passport Information Center** (☎ 900/225–5674; calls are charged at 35¢ per minute for automated service, $1.05 per minute for operator service).

RELIGION

Bahamians are church-going people, and you'll find churches representing most faiths on New Providence and the other islands: Anglican, Assembly of God, Baptist, Church of Christ, Church of God, Christian Science, Greek Orthodox, Lutheran, Free Evangelical, Methodist, Presbyterian, Islamic, Jehovah's Witness, Baha'i, and Roman Catholic. For times of services, consult the "What-to-Do" guide available at your hotel desk. Also look for church suppers, which can be a good way to mix with Bahamians.

SAFETY

Crime against tourists is relatively unheard of, and, unlike some of the Caribbean countries, the Bahamas has little pan-handling. But take the precautions you would in any foreign country: Be aware of your wallet or handbag at all times, and keep your jewelry in the hotel safe.

SENIOR-CITIZEN TRAVEL

To qualify for age-related discounts, **mention your senior-citizen status up front** when booking hotel reservations (not when checking out) and before you're seated in restaurants (not when paying the bill). Note that discounts may be limited to certain menus, days, or hours. When renting a car, **ask about promotional car-rental discounts,** which can be cheaper than senior-citizen rates.

➤ EDUCATIONAL PROGRAMS: **Elder-hostel** (✉ 75 Federal St., 3rd floor, Boston, MA 02110, ☎ 617/426–8056).

SHOPPING

There's enough of a savings over U.S. prices (30%–50%, in many cases) to make duty-free shopping enjoyable on New Providence and Grand Bahama. On both islands, be sure to visit the straw markets, where you can bargain for low-priced hats, baskets, place mats, and other handcrafted items.

STUDENT TRAVEL

TRAVEL AGENCIES

To save money, **look into deals available through student-oriented travel agencies.** To qualify you'll need a bona fide student I.D. card. Members of international student groups are also eligible.

➤ STUDENT I.D.s & SERVICES: **Council on International Educational Exchange** (✉ CIEE, 205 E. 42nd St., 14th floor, New York, NY 10017, ☎ 212/822–2600 or 888/268–6245, FAX 212/822–2699), for mail orders only, in the United States. **Travel Cuts** (✉ 187 College St., Toronto, Ontario M5T 1P7, ☎ 416/979–2406 or 800/667–2887) in Canada.

TAXES

There is no sales tax in the Bahamas. There is a $15 departure tax ($18 from Grand Bahama Island) for all travelers over 6 years of age. United States visitors can take home $600 worth of duty-free goods; the next $1,000 is taxed at 10%.

TAXIS

As in the United States, there are taxis waiting at every airport, all along Bay Street in Nassau and outside all of the main hotels and cruise ship docks. At press time, on Grand Bahama and New Providence, the stipulated rates were $2.20 for two passengers for ¼ mi, 30¢ for each additional ¼ mi. Cabs can also be hired by the hour for $20, and $10 for every additional half hour. In the Out Islands rates are negotiated, and you might find that renting a car is more economical. Upon arriving, you're likely to find that Bahamian taxi drivers are more loquacious than their U.S. counterparts, so by the time you've reached your hotel, points of interest will have already been explained.

TELEPHONES

BATELCO (Bahamas Telecommunications Corporation), ☎ 242/323–4911, is the phone company in the Bahamas.

COUNTRY CODES

The area code for the Bahamas is 242; you can dial the Bahamas from the U.S. as you would make an interstate call.

DIRECTORY & OPERATOR INFORMATION

Dial 916 for directory information and 0 for operator assistance. From outside the Bahamas, dial ☎ 242/555-1212 for information.

INTERNATIONAL CALLS

From outside the U.S. and Canada, the country code for the Bahamas is 1. After dialing the appropriate international access code (00 in the U.K.), you dial 1 followed by the 242 Bahamas area code.

LOCAL CALLS

Within the Bahamas, to make a local call from your hotel room, dial 9, then the number. If your party doesn't answer before the fifth ring, hang up or you'll be charged for the call. Most 800 numbers cannot be called from the Bahamas. You can call 880, a charged call.

LONG-DISTANCE CALLS

To place a call using your own calling card, dial 0 for the operator, who will then place the call using your card number.

THE GOLD GUIDE / SMART TRAVEL TIPS

THE GOLD GUIDE / SMART TRAVEL TIPS

PUBLIC PHONES

Pay phones cost 25¢ per call; Bahamian and U.S. quarters are accepted as are BATELCO phonecards. Cards are sold at BATELCO locations.

TIPPING

The usual tip for service, whether from a taxi driver or a waiter, is 15%. Some hotels and restaurants automatically add a 15% gratuity to your bill.

TOUR OPERATORS

Buying a prepackaged tour or independent vacation can make your trip to the Bahamas less expensive and more hassle-free. Because everything is prearranged, you'll spend less time planning.

Operators that handle several hundred thousand travelers per year can use their purchasing power to give you a good price. Their high volume may also indicate financial stability. But some small companies provide more personalized service; because they tend to specialize, they may also be more knowledgeable about a given area.

BOOKING WITH AN AGENT

Travel agents are excellent resources. In fact, large operators accept bookings made only through travel agents. But it's a good idea to **collect brochures from several agencies,** because some agents' suggestions may be influenced by relationships with tour and package firms that reward them for volume sales. If you have a special interest, **find an agent with expertise in that area**; ASTA (☞ Travel Agencies, *below*) has a database of specialists worldwide.

Make sure your travel agent knows the accommodations and other services. Ask about the hotel's location, room size, beds, and whether it has a pool, room service, or programs for children, if you care about these. Has your agent been there in person or sent others you can contact?

Do some homework on your own, too: Local tourism boards can provide information about lesser-known and small-niche operators, some of which may sell only direct.

BUYER BEWARE

Each year consumers are stranded or lose their money when tour operators—even very large ones with excellent reputations—go out of business. So **check out the operator.** Find out how long the company has been in business, and ask several travel agents about its reputation. If the package or tour you are considering is priced lower than in your wildest dreams, **be skeptical.** Try to **book with a company that has a consumer-protection program.** If the operator has such a program, you'll find information about it in the company's brochure. If the operator you are considering does not offer some kind of consumer protection, then ask for references from satisfied customers.

In the U.S., members of the National Tour Association and United States Tour Operators Association are required to set aside funds to cover your payments and travel arrangements in case the company defaults. It's also a good idea to choose a company that participates in the American Society of Travel Agent's Tour Operator Program (TOP). This gives you a forum if there are any disputes between you and your tour operator; ASTA will act as mediator.

➤ TOUR-OPERATOR RECOMMENDATIONS: **American Society of Travel Agents** (☞ Travel Agencies, *below*). **National Tour Association** (✉ NTA, 546 E. Main St., Lexington, KY 40508, ☎ 606/226–4444 or 800/755–8687). **United States Tour Operators Association** (✉ USTOA, 342 Madison Ave., Suite 1522, New York, NY 10173, ☎ 212/599–6599 or 800/468–7862, ℻ 212/599–6744).

COSTS

The more your package or tour includes, the better you can predict the ultimate cost of your vacation. Make sure you know exactly what is covered, and **beware of hidden costs.** Are taxes, tips, and service charges included? Transfers and baggage handling? Entertainment and excursions? These can add up.

Prices for packages and tours are usually quoted per person, based on two sharing a room. If traveling solo, you may be required to pay the full double-occupancy rate. Some operators eliminate this surcharge if you agree to be matched with a roommate of the same sex, even if one is not found by departure time.

PACKAGES

Like group tours, independent vacation packages are available from major tour operators and airlines. The companies listed below offer vacation packages in a broad price range.

➤ AIR/HOTEL: **American Airlines Vacations** (☎ 800/321–2121). **Certified Vacations** (☎ 954/522–1440 or 800/233–7260). **Delta Vacations** (☎ 800/872–7786). **US Airways Vacations** (☎ 800/455–0123).

THEME TRIPS

➤ FISHING: **Anglers Travel** (✉ 1280 Terminal Way, #30, Reno, NV 89502, ☎ 702/324–0580 or 800/624–8429, FAX 702/324–0583). **Cutting Loose Expeditions** (✉ Box 447, Winter Park, FL 32790, ☎ 407/629–4700 or 800/533–4746, FAX 407/740–7816). **Fishing International** (✉ Box 2132, Santa Rosa, CA 95405, ☎ 707/539–3366 or 800/950–4242, FAX 707/539–1320). **Rod & Reel Adventures** (✉ 566 Thomson Ln., Copperopolis, CA 95228, ☎ 209/785–0444, FAX 209/785–0447).

➤ GOLF: **Stine's Golftrips** (✉ Box 2314, Winter Haven, FL 33883-2314, ☎ 813/324–1300 or 800/428–1940, FAX 941/325–0384).

➤ LEARNING: **Earthwatch** (✉ Box 9104, 680 Mount Auburn St., Watertown, MA 02272, ☎ 617/926–8200 or 800/776–0188, FAX 617/926–8532) for research expeditions. **Natural Habitat Adventures** (✉ 2945 Center Green Ct., Boulder, CO 80301, ☎ 303/449–3711 or 800/543–8917, FAX 303/449–3712). **Naturequest** (934 Acapulco St., Laguna Beach, CA 92651, ☎ 714/499–9561 or 800/369–3033, FAX 714/499–0812). **Oceanic Society Expeditions** (✉ Fort Mason Center, Bldg. E, San Francisco, CA 94123-1394, ☎ 415/441–1106 or 800/326–7491, FAX 415/474–3395).

➤ SCUBA DIVING: **Rothschild Dive Safaris** (✉ 900 West End Ave., #1B, New York, NY 10025-3525, ☎ 212/662–4858 or 800/359–0747, FAX 212/749–6172).

➤ YACHT CHARTERS: **Alden Yacht Charters** (✉ 1909 Alden Landing, Portsmouth, RI 02871, ☎ 401/683–1782 or 800/662–2628, FAX 401/683–3668). **Cat Ppalu Cruises** (✉ Box 661091, Miami, FL 33266, ☎ 305/888–1226 or 800/327–9600, FAX 305/884–4214). **Huntley Yacht Vacations** (✉ 210 Preston Rd., Wernersville, PA 19565, ☎ 610/678–2628 or 800/322–9224, FAX 610/670–1767). **Lynn Jachney Charters** (✉ Box 302, Marblehead, MA 01945, ☎ 617/639–0787 or 800/223–2050, FAX 617/639–0216). **The Moorings** (✉ 19345 U.S. Hwy. 19 N, 4th floor, Clearwater, FL 33764, ☎ 813/530–5424 or 800/535–7289, FAX 813/530–9747). **Ocean Voyages** (✉ 1709 Bridgeway, Sausalito, CA 94965, ☎ 415/332–4681, FAX 415/332–7460). **Russell Yacht Charters** (✉ 404 Hulls Hwy., #175, Southport, CT 06490, ☎ 203/255–2783 or 800/635–8895, FAX 203/255–3426). **SailAway Yacht Charters** (✉ 15605 S.W. 92nd Ave., Miami, FL 33157-1972, ☎ 305/253–7245 or 800/724–5292, FAX 305/251–4408).

TRAVEL AGENCIES

A good travel agent puts your needs first. Look for an agency that has been in business at least five years, emphasizes customer service, and has someone on staff who specializes in your destination. In addition, **make sure the agency belongs to a professional trade organization,** such as ASTA in the United States. If your travel agency is also acting as your tour operator, *see* Buyer Beware in Tour Operators, *above*).

➤ LOCAL AGENT REFERRALS: **American Society of Travel Agents** (ASTA, ☎ 800/965–2782 24-hr hot line, FAX 703/684–8319). **Association of Canadian Travel Agents** (✉ Suite 201, 1729 Bank St., Ottawa, Ontario K1V 7Z5, ☎ 613/521–0474, FAX 613/521–0805). **Association of British Travel Agents** (✉ 55–57 Newman St., London W1P 4AH, ☎ 0171/637–2444, FAX 0171/637–0713). **Australian Federation of Travel**

Agents (☎ 02/9264–3299). Travel Agents' Association of New Zealand (☎ 04/499–0104).

TRAVEL GEAR

Travel catalogs specialize in useful items, such as compact alarm clocks and travel irons, that can **save space when packing.** They also offer dual-voltage appliances, currency converters, and foreign-language phrase books.

➤ CATALOGS: **Magellan's** (☎ 800/962–4943, FAX 805/568–5406). **Orvis Travel** (☎ 800/541–3541, FAX 540/343–7053). **TravelSmith** (☎ 800/950–1600, FAX 800/950–1656).

VISITOR INFORMATION

TOURIST INFORMATION

For general information contact these tourist offices before you go. The Bahamas Ministry of Tourism also has a web site on the Internet, featuring maps, photos, and interactive activities that enable you to communicate directly with the ministry. The address is http://www.interknowl-edge.com/bahamas.

Bahamas Tourist Office (☎ 800/422–4262; ✉ 8600 W. Bryn Mawr Ave., Suite 820, Chicago, IL 60631, ☎ 773/693–1500, FAX 773/693–1114; ✉ Box 581408, 2050 Stemmons Fwy., Suite 116, World Trade Center, Dallas, TX 75258, ☎ 214/742–1886, FAX 214/741–4118; ✉ Bahama Out Islands Promotion Board, 1100 Lee Wagener Blvd., #204, Fort Lauderdale, FL 33315, ☎ 305/359–8099 or 800/688–4752, FAX 305/359–8098; ✉ 3450 Wilshire Blvd., Suite 208, Los Angeles, CA 90010, ☎ 213/385–0033, FAX 213/383–3966; ✉ 19495 Biscayne Blvd., Aventura, FL 33180, ☎ 305/932–0051, FAX 305/682–8758; ✉ 121 Bloor St. E, Suite 1101, Toronto M4W 3M5, ☎ 416/968–2999, FAX 416/968–6711; ✉ 3, The Billings, Walnut Tree Close, Guildford, Surrey G1 4UL, U.K., ☎ 01483/448–900, FAX 01483/448–990).

Grand Bahama Tourism Board (✉ 19495 Biscayne Blvd., Suite 809, Aventura, FL 33180, ☎ 305/935–9461, FAX 305/935–9464). **Nassau/Paradise Island Promotion Board** (✉ 19495 Biscayne Blvd., Suite 804, Aventura, FL 33180, ☎ 305/931–1555, FAX 305/931–3005). **Bahamas Tourism Center** (✉ 150 E. 52nd St., New York, NY 10022, ☎ 212/758–2777, FAX 212/753–6531). **Caribbean Tourist Organization** (✉ 20 E. 46th St., New York, NY 10017, ☎ 212/682–0435, FAX 212/697–4258). **Morris-Kevan International Ltd.** (✉ International House, 47 Chase Side, Enfield, Middlesex EN2 6NB, ☎ 0181/364–5188, FAX 0181/367–9949).

U.S. GOVERNMENT

Government agencies can be an excellent source of inexpensive travel information. When planning your trip, **find out what government materials are available.**

➤ PAMPHLETS: **Consumer Information Center** (✉ Consumer Information Catalogue, Pueblo, CO 81009, ☎ 719/948–3334 or 888/878–3256) for a free catalog that includes travel titles.

WHEN TO GO

The Bahamas is affected by the refreshing trade-wind flow generated by an area of high atmospheric pressure covering a large part of the subtropical North Atlantic, so the climate varies little during the year. The most pleasant time is between December and May, when the temperature averages 70°–75°F. It stands to reason that hotel prices during this period are at their highest—around 30% higher than during the less popular times. The rest of the year is hot and humid and prone to tropical storms; the temperature hovers around 80°–85°F.

Whether you want to join it or avoid it, be advised that Spring Break takes place between the end of February and mid-April. This means lots of vacationing college students, beach parties, sports events and entertainment. When making hotel reservations, inquire whether your hotel expects to be hosting plenty of festive 20-year-olds.

CLIMATE

What follows are average daily maximum and minimum temperatures for Nassau. Freeport's temperatures are nearly the same: a degree or two cooler in the spring and fall, and a degree or two warmer in the summer.

Climate in the Bahamas

NASSAU

Jan.	77F	25C	May	85F	29C	Sept.	88F	31C
	62	17		70	21		74	23
Feb.	78F	26C	June	87F	31C	Oct.	85F	29C
	63	17		73	23		72	22
Mar.	80F	27C	July	89F	32C	Nov.	82F	28C
	64	18		75	24		68	20
Apr.	82F	28C	Aug.	89F	32C	Dec.	79F	26C
	66	19		75	24		64	18

➤ FORECASTS: **Weather Channel Connection** (☎ 900/932–8437), 95¢ per minute from a Touch-Tone phone.

1 Destination: The Bahamas

A COUNTRY BUILT ON WATER: THE ALLURING WORLD OF THE BAHAMAS

BAHAMIANS LIKE TO tell the story—whether real or apocryphal—that American astronauts returning from orbit declared that they could recognize only two sights from space: the Great Wall of China and the waters of the Bahamas. It wouldn't be surprising, for the sea is the prevailing feature of this country of more than 700 islands—approximately 75% of the country lies underwater, and its shores are rimmed by some of the world's great barrier reefs. The sea is geography, attraction, livelihood, and inspiration all in one. Talk to a painter, diver, boatbuilder, fisherman, or chef, and they'll all likely agree: without the sea the Bahamas would lose its raison d'être.

The nation's existence is based largely on tourism. Even though you can reach it in less than an hour's flight from the Florida coast, the Bahamas' singular natural beauty and exotic appeal make it seem more like a far-flung outpost. Picture a tiny cay (pronounced "key") ringed by lacy casuarina pines, stately palms, and silken sands that meet the startlingly hued sea. The water ranges from pale aqua to deep sapphire, the spectrum changing hourly as the relentless Bahamian sun sweeps across the island sky. As you lie on the beach, a distant boat plies the calm waters; a lonely gull swoops by overhead, surprised to see that he has company. A single set of footprints—yours—crosses the strand. In many ways, you realize, things have changed very little since Christopher Columbus arrived here in 1492.

Venture inland to a lush world of tropical foliage: hibiscus of watery apricot, brilliant scarlet, and jaunty yellow; bougainvillea of shocking pink or fluorescent lavender; poinciana trees inflaming the sky with their bright orange flowers. Pineapples and guavas grow in profusion here, as do mangoes, breadfruit, guineps, papayas, sugar apples, and sapodillas. Surprisingly, all of these were imports; no fruit-bearing plant is indigenous to the Bahamas.

Tiny villages known as "settlements," often consisting of New England–style cottages dressed up in vibrant tropical hues, dot the verdant landscape. Underwater more delights await. Beneath the 100,000 square miles of Atlantic Ocean across which the Bahamas are scattered (the country is not, as many believe, in the Caribbean) lies a wonderland waiting to delight experienced divers and novice snorkelers. Drift on the surface of the crystal sea, noticing how the colors so striking from a distance fade to transparency when you're out in the water. Gaze through fantasies of frilly fan coral and phantasmagoric sponges to the sea floor below as a smiling blue tang and a phosphorescent parrotfish float past your eyes. A school of tiny silversides darts by, engulfing you in a glittering wall of motion.

Should you prefer to park yourself on a hammock strung between pines overlooking the deserted shores for a daylong nap, no one would think it odd—the favorite activity of many tourists is no activity at all. There's something about the atmosphere here—the steamy sun, the picture-perfect vistas, the alluringly slow-paced local life—that beckons even the most active types to a shocking indolence. It's a magic that works subtly but effectively. Harried executives suddenly find that their most pressing business is watching the waves beat against the shore, and bankers with type-A personalities discover their commerce dwindling to the collection of sand dollars from a deserted beach.

You may even find, to your surprise, that you ventured out of your resort without wearing your watch. Congratulations! You've discovered "Bahamian time," where 20 minutes could mean an hour and a half, and days stretch endlessly in patterns of fabulous idleness, rendering the concept of time flexible, if not downright meaningless. Ask five Bahamians how long it takes to get to a certain place; you're guaranteed to get five different answers. Tell someone self-importantly that you need something done "yesterday," and you'll be met with an unfailing, all-knowing, and sympathetic smile. You can try to fight it if you like, but there's really no point. Things just don't move too fast down here. Get used to that fact, and you'll have come a long way toward appreciating these laid-back and leisurely isles.

Life in the Bahamas is not all about glorious laziness. Nassau, the country's capital, is a bustling town on New Providence Island with shops, nightclubs, and an enviable array of restaurants, glitzy casinos, and posh hotels. Even in Nassau, though, there are quiet byways and shady lanes where you can escape the tumult of the main tourist drags. Shop till you drop or wander past colonial buildings that reveal the capital's fascinating history. Dine on elegant French cuisine in a hotel restaurant or rub shoulders with Bahamians in a down-home friendly eatery. Drop your dollars in a clangorous casino or escape to the seclusion of Paradise Island's Versailles Gardens. Boogie the night away in a rowdy club or stroll along quiet Cable Beach—the daytime hubbub just a memory.

O F COURSE, YOU CAN FLEE the hurly-burly altogether and head straight for one of the Out Islands (the term refers to everything except New Providence Island and Grand Bahama Island). The most exciting development in the Out Islands is usually the results of last night's domino game, the most pressing news the size of the wave that crashed onto the shore that afternoon. In contrast to the modernity of Nassau and Freeport resorts, you'll find intimate inns here where you can escape from the world entirely.

But it would be a shame to escape too completely, for the Bahamians are about as wonderful a group of people as you're likely to meet. This is a country where children stop on their bicycles to say hello and to ask, in a distinctive, not-quite-Caribbean lilt, "Everyt'ing OK?" A country where the drugstore cashier is the mother of your hotel manager, where a stranger you meet on the Nassau–to–Paradise Island bridge turns out to be the brother of a straw-weaver you encountered on Exuma. Where your waitress, discovering she's run out of iced tea, heads to the back of the bar for her thermos and pours you a glass of her private supply. In response to your effusive thanks, she looks at you, a smile on her face but surprise in her eyes that you'd consider this at all unusual. "Well, it's no problem," she declares, "no problem at all. That's what friends are for."

Everyone's a friend in the Bahamas; strike up a conversation with the person next to you at the bar or strolling down along the harbor wall. If there's one thing Bahamians enjoy, it's talking. Take advantage of this garrulousness; you might find that you come away with new and fascinating insights.

You may, for instance, find out about bush medicine, a time-honored use of the plants that grow in such profusion throughout the islands. On some islands, you can even take a bush-medicine tour; your guide will point out the swelling bush (good for back problems) or love vine (not surprisingly used in many romance-involved concoctions). Have a headache? Try some breadfruit leaves, beaten with warm water. You may be surprised at the results.

Strike up another conversation; it's getting easier, isn't it? Is that because you've finally opened up to the amicable Bahamian style, or could it be the potent rum drinks you've been downing while listening to your newfound friends? Whichever it may be, you've done well, for there's a wealth of information waiting in this many-layered culture. Perhaps you'll hear about the renaissance of Bahamian painting and vow to discover for yourself the works of Eddie Minnis, Walter Bethel, or Alton Lowe, or listen to local music, which ranges from old-time gospel and calypso to Bahamian rake 'n' scrape, played on cowbells and other uncommon instruments. You might be regaled with stories of local church activities—these establishments are so important to Bahamian society that one Paradise Island resort offers a church visit at its activities desk, and tiny Man-O-War Cay, in the Abacos, boasts three churches in as many blocks. If you're lucky, you'll be invited to a church supper or afternoon fish fry.

Maybe you'll discover some of the engrossing history that gives the country its multicultural heritage, which in turn makes for enviably easy relations among races.

The islands are full of historians, both amateur and professional, and if you can sort out the facts from the embroidery you'll come away truly enlightened. At the very least, you'll hear a long, complicated, and undeniably vivid saga. Pull up a bar stool as the story begins. Order another Goombay Smash from the smiling bartender—you'll undoubtedly need it before the tale is over.

It's a colorful story, beginning with the Lucayan Indians—the first residents of the islands—who gave our language such words as iguana, potato, guava, and (interesting for such a peace-loving people) cannibal. It continues with Spanish invaders led by the likes of Columbus and Ponce de León; the Spanish virtually wiped out the indigenous population by 1520 and gave their own name to these islands surrounded by a "Baja Mar," or shallow sea—a term that later became corrupted into "Bahama." It tells of English settlers escaping from religious repression (the islands were claimed by England in 1629 and remained under its control, except for brief periods, for almost three-and-a-half centuries), of British Loyalists fleeing the Carolinas and New England after the Revolutionary War; a tale of marauding pirates from Edward Teach (better known as Blackbeard) and Henry Morgan to Calico Jack Rackham and his notorious female cohorts, Anne Bonney and Mary Read. It's a tale of slaves and former slaves, some freed at sea and transported to Bahamian shores to form their own settlements without ever knowing the shackles of servitude, some emancipated only with the ending of slavery here in the 1830s. You can still see the effects of slavery in the names of many residents, who often took on the surnames of their former owners; this is why, for instance, every other resident of Exuma seems to be named Rolle.

Above all, it's a story of intriguing characters. There's Captain Woodes Rogers, the first royal governor of the Bahamas, a former privateer himself, who's widely credited with ending the 40-plus-year reign of piracy by, among other things, hanging eight offenders on the site of what was to become Nassau's British Colonial Hotel. There's Sir Harry Oakes, a rough-and-ready Canadian who made his fortune in gold during the 1940s built the Bahamas Country Club and developed the Cable Beach Golf Course. On July 8, 1943, his battered and badly charred body was found in his bed; the mystery remains unsolved to this day.

There's that famous pair of lovebirds, the Duke and Duchess of Windsor, who arrived in the Bahamas in 1939 for the duke's stint as governor. The Bahamians were impressed; a calypso ballad, "Love Alone," was composed in honor of the couple's fairy-tale romance. Sentimental? Perhaps. Unfailingly romantic? Of course. But then there's always been a romantic streak here; live your life among such beauty and see if you don't develop a bit of a tender touch yourself. An evening on a quiet Out Island bluff is enough to bring out the softhearted underside of even the most confirmed cynic.

I N THE END it comes back to the sea, as it always has in this country surrounded by, and built upon, the water. The Bahamas is progressing faster than ever, especially since the current Prime Minister, Hubert Alexander Ingraham, has set the country on a forward-moving course since coming into power in 1992. Independent from Britain since 1973, the Bahamas has come a long way toward restoring prosperity and stability. Tourism is booming, and new construction is relentless, at least in the major resort areas. Head to the Out Islands, though, or even to many corners of the bigger towns, and you'll still discover a feeling of being lost in time, transported to a different, more relaxed era.

Like the sea, the changes ebb and flow, but also like the sea, the things that make the Bahamas what they are—and have been—are little changed: the overwhelming natural beauty, the extraordinary progression of cultures, and above all the steadfastly congenial Bahamian people themselves. With a warmth that seems to flow directly from the unceasing tropical sun, with the constancy of the inexorable sea itself, they welcome the ever-increasing numbers of visitors who come to spend a few days, or weeks, or perhaps (stranger things have happened) the rest of their lives in this little corner of paradise.

— Rich Rubin

NEW AND NOTEWORTHY

Those who remember the Bahamas from college spring-break trips might be surprised on a return visit. Both the Bahamian government and the private sector have been investing time and money to enhance the tourism infrastructure, and the islands' advertising slogan, "It just keeps getting better," is that rare publicity motto that actually has a ring of truth to it. Service standards have been raised through training programs for those who interact with visitors, including police and immigration officers, taxi drivers, tour operators, and hotel workers.

Nassau's still a popular cruise ship destination and there's a resurgence of visits by a more upscale crowd. A sophistication here that belies the city's rowdy and dowdy reputation, with hotels upgrading, dining possibilities expanding, and a slew of coffeehouses opening—the ultimate sign of '90s chic. Construction of a second bridge linking Nassau and Paradise Island is underway to alleviate the heavy traffic between the two areas. The dock area has been spruced up; but progress in the new phase of renovation has been slow.

The biggest Bahamas news is in the hotel sector, where construction and refurbishment proceed at an astounding rate. Sun International continues to expand its Atlantis, Paradise Island, with the construction of The Palace, twin towers that will more than double the size of the resort, several restaurants, a 50,000-sq-ft casino, water attractions, and "The Dig," a representation of the lost city of Atlantis. The project, scheduled to open by 1999, will stretch the megaresort across the width of the island, from Cabbage Beach to Nassau Harbour.

In downtown Nassau, an ambitious project is in the works for the historic but run-down British Colonial Beach Hotel that will restore this once-glamorous dowager to its former splendor and provide a luxury option for the business market. RHK Capital, a Canadian company, plans to convert the newer wing into a banking and business center housing Nassau's Stock Market and other financial institutions; the project culminates in upscale condominiums and a marina on the tiny downtown beach.

Many Providence Island resorts have been or will soon be undergoing far-reaching renovations, and some smaller properties are making improvements as well. When making reservations anywhere, ask if the property is being renovated; if so, request a renovated room or try to ascertain whether on-going renovations will detract from your comfort (ie, will your brand new room be next to a construction site).

And it's not only in Nassau and on Paradise Island that changes are in motion. On Grand Bahama Island, a major facelift is in progress for the resorts of Freeport and Lucaya. Hutchinson Ports Properties has acquired several properties along the beach and will be redeveloping the entire Lucayan strip; the project, scheduled for completion in 2000, will include a new luxury hotel, casino, convention facilities, and refurbishment of the existing hotel rooms and the Bahama Reef Golf Course.

The Out Islands, too, are seeing several new projects, the largest-inscale being Castaway Cay, Disney's new project on the former Gorda Cay in the Abacos; this 1,000-acre private island will be used by Disney Cruise Line for day-long excursions. On Eleuthera, hotel openings are revitalizing tourism, including two properties in Tarpum Bay: homey Ingraham's Beach Inn and the Italian-run all-inclusive Venta Club Eleuthera. Palmetto Point is another area of Eleuthera seeing some action. Unique Village has acquired new neighbors: Atlantic Suites, an apartment complex offering efficiencies, and Ocean Beach Villas, with day- or week-long luxury condo rentals. Ground has also been broken in Palmetto Point for a 200-room hotel under the auspices of Sunset Development.

WHAT'S WHERE

The Bahamian Islands—with their exquisite golden- and pink-sand beaches, lush tropical landscapes, unsullied waters, and year-round sunshine—couldn't have sprung from the sea in more perfect shape for 20th-century vacationers. The archipelago begins 55 mi off the Florida coast and contains more than 700 islands, approximately 30 of them inhabited, scattered over 100,000 sq mi of the Atlantic.

New Providence Island

Many travelers make New Providence Island—more specifically Nassau, the nation's capital and something of a tourist mecca—their principal stop in the Bahamas. Discover the nation's past in the island's historic buildings, forts, gardens, and monuments. Two resort areas, Cable Beach and Paradise Island, are chockablock with luxurious resorts, upscale restaurants, groomed beaches, water sports aplenty, and a busy nightclub scene.

Grand Bahama Island

Grand Bahama's twin cities, Freeport and Lucaya, may not have the colonial charm of Nassau, but if you want to shop, gamble, or just hang out at the beach—at a slightly lower cost than in the capital—there's no need to go elsewhere. Freeport, which was built in the '60s, has a much-visited International Bazaar, where you'll find imported goods at reduced prices. In Lucaya, adjacent to Freeport, you can swim with dolphins or learn to dive at a world-renowned scuba school. Resorts are split between the two: Freeport's have the best access to shopping, gambling, and golf; Lucaya's sit directly on the beach.

The Out Islands

To escape the crowds and the glittering modernity of New Providence and Grand Bahama, hop a plane, boat, or even helicopter to one of the Out Islands, where life progresses at a slower pace, and the landscape is still largely unaffected by major development. In fact, many seasoned Bahamas travelers skip the more-populated islands altogether and head straight for these unspoiled isles, usually called the Family Islands by locals (it's the rare Bahamian who doesn't have roots here). Wander uncluttered beaches and narrow, sand-strewn streets, or lunch in a village where fishermen's tidy homes are painted in soft pastel shades and shrouded in brilliantly colored vegetation. The Out Islands' common traits—an abundance of natural beauty and small-town atmosphere—should not disguise

their differences, however. You may be surprised by the variety of sites and activities the islands have to offer.

The Abacos

The Abacos, a center for boatbuilding, have attracted sailing and yachting fans over the years with their translucent waters and excellent marina facilities. If you come without a yacht, you can still enjoy a look at Elbow Cay's famous striped lighthouse and strap on your fins to explore Pelican Cay, an underwater national park. Marsh Harbour, the third-largest city in the country, is well stocked with restaurants and shops (as well as the only stoplight in the Abacos, a source of great local pride).

Andros

Andros, the largest Bahamian island, is flanked by the world's third-largest coral reef—a spectacular, 140-mi-long haunt for underwater creatures, making it a favorite for diving enthusiasts. On land, the appeal is equally wild, with the little-explored island of forests and swamps having none of the buildup of the more touristed spots. This is also where Androsia fabric, a Bahamian version of batik, is made, as well as some of the country's finest straw work.

The Berry Islands

The tiny cays of the Berry Islands are virtually uninhabited but for seabirds and big-game fishers, who appreciate the proximity to the Tongue of the Ocean and the excellent marinas on Chub and Great Harbour cays.

The Biminis

Deep-sea anglers find bliss in Bimini, for in its waters roam great warriors such as marlin, swordfish, giant tuna, wahoo, sailfish, dolphin, and bonefish. Literary aficionados can follow in the footsteps of Papa himself: In the '30s, Ernest Hemingway chose the Biminis as his favorite getaway, and both the bar he frequented and one of his homes are accessible to visitors.

Cat Island

Lush, hilly, and unspoiled, shrouded in an air of mysticism, this is a tranquil isle of small farms and fishing villages. Father Jerome's crumbling hilltop hermitage dominates the landscape. Its isolation makes it a perfect getaway for honeymooners, modern-day Robinson Crusoes, or anyone in search of natural beauty and blessed seclusion. A few resorts have sprung up to take advantage of a coast ringed with stunning—and usually deserted—beaches.

Crooked and Acklins Islands

Divers, snorkelers, and bonefishers find plenty to keep them busy on these adjoining, very undeveloped islands. Miles of virgin barrier reef seem, so far, to be a well-kept secret, far off the beaten path.

Eleuthera

Eleuthera, notable for beaches, surfing, and excellent diving, is also an agricultural center where crops, from pineapples and mangoes to okra and peas, are grown. This 100-mi-long island is sparsely populated, with just a handful of small, friendly settlements scattered throughout its bounteous landscape. Just off the north coast of Eleuthera lies tiny Harbour Island. With its renowned 3-mi pink-sand beach, some of the Bahamas' most distinctive small hotels, and the New England–style village of Dunmore Town, it's one of the best-known Out Islands, but tourist activity hasn't ruined its low-key appeal. Also off Eleuthera is Spanish Wells, which thrives on fishing; while residents can seem a little closed to outsiders, particularly in contrast to Harbour Island's tourism-based existence, it nonetheless makes an interesting expedition.

The Exumas

These hundreds of little cays are prime cruising ground for yachters, but you might also come to enjoy the charms of several attractive towns, welcoming small hotels, Exuma Land and Sea Park (a favorite with snorkelers and bird-watchers), and a 7-mi beach fabled for its seashells. Tourist activity is centered in the capital of George Town, on Great Exuma, whose residents are reputed to be the friendliest in this country known for friendliness, and whose lovely Elizabeth Harbour fills with boats during regatta time.

Inagua

Bird-watchers marvel at the flock of more than 60,000 flamingos that resides in a national park on Inagua, the southernmost of the Bahamian islands. Hundreds of other bird species also make their home in the island's salt flats, which provide much of the raw material for the Morton Salt Company, whose processing plant is located here.

Long Island

Two contrasting coastlines make Long Island one of the most scenic Out Island destinations: While the western coast has soft, sandy beaches, the eastern side (never more than 4 mi away on this stretched, skinny strip) falls down to the ocean in dramatic rocky cliffs.

San Salvador

History may have been made on this little island, the legendary landfall of Christopher Columbus—though the claim is open to dispute. You can visit the marker commemorating the event or dive, snorkel, and fish in the surrounding waters.

The Turks and Caicos Islands

The Turks and Caicos, two groups of islands that lie to the southeast of the Bahamas, are nearly unknown to all but avid divers and seekers of untrodden beaches. While there's talk of developing the islands along the lines of some Bahamian destinations, for now you'll find all of the beauty but very little glitz.

PLEASURES AND PASTIMES

Beaches

You're standing in water so clear you can see straight down to your toes; in the distance, the sea becomes the patchwork of emerald, aqua, and sapphire that you thought existed only in postcards. The torrid Bahamian sun beats inexorably down, and golden sands stretch toward infinity. As you look around, you realize there's only one thing you don't see: other people. And that—sun, sea, sand—is the appeal of the Bahamas in a nutshell. Best of all, the concept of private beaches doesn't apply here; all beaches in the Bahamas are public up to the high-water mark. Of course, land access can be restricted, so you may need to boat into that unspoiled Eden—but if you can get there, it's yours—for the afternoon, anyway.

In Nassau, the major Cable Beach and Paradise Island hotels sit right on the water, while hotels on the outskirts are always near beaches such as Love Beach and Saunders Beach on the north shore, and Adelaide Beach on the south. On Grand Bahama, only the Lucaya hotels are beachside, but if you're staying in Freeport you'll have access to public beaches like Xanadu Beach, Taino Beach, and the long strip at Williams Town, all local favorites. The Out Islands are similarly brimming with beautiful beaches. One of the most intriguing is the pink-sand beach at Harbour Island, off Eleuthera.

The calm, leeward, western sides of most islands have the safest and most popular swimming beaches. There are no big waves, little undertow, and the buoyant salt water makes staying afloat almost effortless. The windward, or Atlantic, sides of islands are a different story, and even strong, experienced swimmers should exercise caution here. For novices, ocean waves are powerful and can be dangerous, and unseen currents, strong undertows, and uneven, rocky bottoms are only more perilous. Some beaches post signs or flags to alert swimmers to water conditions, but few—even those at the best hotels—are protected by lifeguards. Swim at your own risk.

Casinos

There are four glitzy casinos in the Bahamas: two on New Providence Island—the Crystal Palace Casino at the Nassau Marriott Resort on Cable Beach and the Paradise Island Casino on Paradise Island—and one on Grand Bahama—the Princess Casino in Freeport. All have the additional attractions of above-average restaurants, lounges, and colorfully costumed revues. Although a couple of Out Island resorts have received casino licenses, there are no immediate plans to bring gambling to these low-key locales.

Dining

Restaurants on New Providence (Nassau, Paradise Island, and Cable Beach) and Grand Bahama (Freeport and Lucaya) range from Indian and Chinese to upscale French and Italian. Until recently, what was harder to find in the tourist centers was, ironically, Bahamian cuisine; but the Ministry of Tourism's "Taste of the Bahamas" program, which encourages the use of local ingredients, is thankfully changing this. One night you might be

munching conch (pronounced *kahnk*) fritters and panfried grouper at an out-of-the-way local spot, and the next you might be savoring a Grand Marnier soufflé in a fancy French bistro. On the Out Islands, Bahamian food predominates, but international fare is gaining ground, particularly at resorts.

Most Bahamian cuisine looks to the sea, which provides a cornucopia of fresh products; meat, on the other hand, is often imported and consequently expensive. The islands' signature seafood is the conch; this slow-moving creature abounds in the shallow waters of the Bahamas, and consequently finds its way onto many a menu; its widely touted aphrodisiacal qualities don't hurt its popularity either. (The shiny pink interior of its shell appears in pendants, bracelets, earrings, brooches, and other ornaments, and you can even find the occasional conch pearl.) The meat turns up in a variety of incarnations, including cracked conch (pounded until tender and fried in seasoned batter), conch salad (raw, marinated in lime juice, with onions and peppers), conch chowder, conch fritters, even conch burgers. You can find stands selling fresh conch salad throughout the islands, and you might see fishermen on docks preparing scorched conch, which is eaten straight from the shell after being spiced with hot peppers—said to cure hangovers—salt, and lime.

Grouper is the headline fish, and you can feast on it and other fish from dawn to dusk if you so desire. For breakfast, you might try "boil fish," cooked with salt pork, onions, peppers, and spices, or "stew fish," in a rich brown gravy—both are usually served with grits or mildly sweet johnnycake. For lunch you might move on to steamed fish, cooked with a fragrant tomato base, then sample panfried grouper for dinner. Bahamian lobster, clawless and somewhat toothier than its cousins from Maine, is another delicious option. Order minced lobster, and the meat will come shredded and cooked with tomatoes, green peppers, and onions.

At lunch and dinner, your entrée will likely be flanked by a generous mound of peas 'n' rice, potato salad, coleslaw, baked macaroni and cheese, or fried plantains. Some other local specialties, easier to find in the Out Islands, include turtle steak, wild boar, mutton, okra soup, "peas soup" and dough (dumplings), and the morning eye-opener known as souse—pigs' feet, chicken parts, sheep's tongue, or other bits of meat simmered with onions and potatoes in a spicy broth. Salads and other greens are scanty on most local menus, but fruit is abundant. Walk by a neighborhood fruit stand and you're likely to see such alluring offerings as mangoes, pineapples, breadfruit, sugarplums, hog plums, sapodillas, sea grapes, coco plums, soursops, avocados, tangerines, tamarinds, and papayas.

For many, beer is the thirst quencher of choice. Be sure to try locally brewed Kalik, a beer named for the sound of the cowbells played in indigenous Junkanoo music. When you're in the mood for a fruity, rum-based concoction, sip a Goombay Smash, a Bahama Mama, or a Yellowbird.

Bring your meal to a sweet close with guava duff, made by slathering guava jelly on a strip of dough, rolling and boiling it, then pouring a cream, rum, and egg-based sauce onto warm slices. Bahamians also love benny cake, created by cooking sesame seeds with sugar; and coconut jimmy— chewy dumplings in coconut sauce.

For the most inexpensive local treats, stop in on one of the fund-raising cookouts or parties periodically hosted on beaches and in Nassau and Freeport churches. The staff at your hotel or local newspapers can provide details.

Fishing

This country is an angler's dream. Light tackle, heavy tackle, fly-fishing, deep-sea fishing, reef fishing, fishing for blue marlin, bonefishing—you name it. Fishing in the Bahamas starts in the waters of Bimini off the Florida coast and ends at the southernmost island, Inagua, on the northern edge of the Caribbean. Tournaments pop up all over the Out Islands during the year—Bimini alone has a dozen.

Golf

Golfers will find some enticing courses, most of them with refreshing sea views. The 18-hole, par-72, championship courses on New Providence and Paradise islands are all spectacularly beautiful and will put your swing to the test. Cable Beach Golf Club is on West Bay Street in Nassau,

across the boulevard from Breezes. The course at South Ocean Beach & Golf Resort, an elegant spot on the island's south coast, is secluded and scenic. A third course, Paradise Island Golf Club, covers most of the east end of Paradise Island. All three courses are open to the public, and instruction is available. A fourth course, at the Lyford Cay Golf Club, is only available to members and their guests. There are also three courses on Grand Bahama. Paradise Island and Freeport host tournaments annually. PGA championship golf returned to the Bahamas in November 1995, with the initiation of the annual Paradise Island Invitational Pro-Am Tournament.

Although your choices for teeing off on the Out Islands are more limited, you'll still find some appealing courses: one in Treasure Cay, Great Abaco; another at the Cotton Bay Club in Rock Sound, Eleuthera (the once-upscale hotel is closed, but the golf course is open to the public); and a nine-holer on Great Harbour Cay, Berry Islands.

Junkanoo

Much of the Bahamians' music carries echoes of African rhythms, Caribbean calypso, English folk songs, and its own hearty beat. Nowhere is the Bahamians' zest for life more exuberantly expressed than in the Junkanoo celebrations held yearly on Boxing Day (the day after Christmas) and New Year's Day.

The origin of the word "Junkanoo" is hazy and might be linked to a legend about an African chieftain named John Canoe who loved to indulge in wild parties. Whatever its provenance, Junkanoo can be likened in its uninhibited and frenzied activities to Carnival in Rio de Janeiro and Mardi Gras in New Orleans. Although festivals occur throughout the islands, the biggest celebrations are in Nassau.

Beginning at 2 AM, the darkened streets come alive with raucous revelers dressed in costumes representing everything from kaleidoscopic dragons to eye-poppingly bright fish. Competing groups carry elaborately adorned floats fashioned from cardboard fastened to aluminum rods and decorated with glitter and crepe paper. The results of a year's worth of fiercely secret preparations, the most ornate of these floats can weigh up to 400 pounds. The music, too, is distinctly Bahamian and indisputably clamorous, filling the breezy night with the sounds of goatskin drums, clanging cowbells, and shrieking whistles. The celebration gets more imaginative, more colorful, and noisier every year.

People-to-People Programme

The free People-to-People Programme, a popular social event in the islands, gives visitors a more intimate glimpse of Bahamian life. The most extensive programs are on New Providence and Grand Bahama Islands, where coordinators match visitors with Bahamians who have similar interests. Your hosts may show you around their town, invite you to attend a church service or community event, or even ask you into their home for a meal. People-to-People also sponsors an afternoon tea at Government House on the last Friday of each month (January–August) and arranges tropical weddings that, at 50 to 60 each month, have become one of the most successful aspects of the program. They'll take care of all the paperwork necessary for Americans to marry in the Bahamas—they even find the minister and photographer—and can arrange everything from a shipboard service to "I do's" in stunning Versailles Gardens. People-to-People events in the Out Islands consist mainly of monthly teas, fashion shows, barbecues, dances, and other gatherings; check with the local tourist office to see if anything's been scheduled during your stay.

Coordinators ask that potential participants contact the **People-to-People Unit** (☎ 242/ 326–0435) or a Bahamas tourist office in the United States two to three weeks before their visit. However, arrangements can sometimes be made with short notice, so if you're already in the islands, go to a Nassau or Freeport Tourist Information Centre or ask at your hotel's events desk.

Sailing and Seafaring

Crystal seas tinted every color from deep sapphire to pale aqua are dotted with tiny, palm-fringed cays that beckon the weary sailor to step ashore for a brief respite; with more than 700 to visit, the best and only way to reach many of the isles is by ship. And with such pleasures as diving and snorkeling of prime quality here, it would be a shame not to get off the islands for some exploration. Boat rentals are scattered through the islands, making it easy to procure your own craft for a seafaring adventure (most also offer crews for the sailing-challenged); sheltered waters, protected by offshore cays and undersea coral reefs, make navigating relatively easy, and plentiful marinas (many Out Islands hotels offer facilities to boaters) means you're never far from a spot to tie up for the night.

Scuba

Few places in the world offer a wider variety of diving opportunities than the Bahamas—wrecks and reefs, blue holes and drop-offs, sea gardens and shallow shoals can all be found here. In fact, one of the most famous scuba schools and NAUI (National Association of Underwater Instructors) centers in the world is UN-EXSO (Underwater Explorers Society), in Lucaya, Grand Bahama. For the most stunning peek at the watery underworld, head to the less crowded Out Islands, where many hotels offer economical dive packages.

With hundreds of islands, the Bahamas has literally thousands of dive sites within its crystal-clear waters. Local dive shops are geared for regularly scheduled dives or personalized custom diving, and are generous in offering correct and precise directions to many dive sites. In some cases, they will even give you the coordinates of a location. Unless you and your navigational equipment are extremely sharp, however, you could miss a site by 100 yards or so, which would still give you a lot of seabed to search. Some sites, of course, are obvious; you won't need a local guide to show you a sunken ship that stands 25 ft out of the water, and drop-offs aren't that hard to spot. Local experts, however, will know the best places to dive, the drop-offs, the safest places to drop an anchor, and even the best time of day for the dive.

Tennis

New Providence has more than 80 courts, Grand Bahama has about 40, and many of the Out Islands, including Eleuthera, Exuma, and the Abacos, are also in on the racket. Each year, Paradise Island sponsors the Bahamas International Tennis Open, and the Freeport Tennis Open is held on Grand Bahama.

GREAT ITINERARIES

The most important thing to decide is what kind of vacation you want: a quiet getaway or an action-packed excursion. If you want shopping, dining, and nightlife, head straight for Nassau on New Providence, where's there's plenty to do and lots to see. If it's a tranquil trip you're seeking, go to the Out Islands. Below are suggested itineraries for both areas. See the Exploring sections in each chapter for more information about individual sights.

If You Have 3 Days

If you've opted for a lively three days on New Providence, spend your first morning in **downtown Nassau** visiting historical sights. Have a leisurely lunch and spend the afternoon shopping—be sure to check out the **Straw Market.** Day or night, you can test your luck in the two **casinos** (one on Cable Beach, one on Paradise Island). On day two, begin by exploring the sights on the eastern side of the island, including **St. Augustine's Monastery** and **Blackbeard's Tower.** Continue west around the island, perhaps taking time to tour the **Bacardi Distillery** or the **Commonwealth Brewery.** Head back towards Nassau and spend the afternoon at **Crystal Cay,** exploring the marine theme park's sealife displays. **Arawak Cay** is near the entrance and is a nice spot for a quick, local-style lunch. If you have any energy left after this, dance the night away in a club or see one of the glittery extravaganzas offered by the resorts. Spend your last day on Paradise Island wandering through the **Atlantis, Paradise Island resort,** visiting **Cabbage** or **Paradise beaches,** and spending a few minutes in lovely **Versailles Gardens.** If you're still in search of more activity, water sports abound and, of course, there's lounging on the beach to occupy the rest of your time.

If you've decided to head for the Out Islands, **Exuma** is a good choice if your time is limited; you can fly straight into George Town airport, outside Great Exuma's main town. On your first day, wander through the village of **George Town,** stopping to chat with the ladies in the tiny straw market. On day two, pick up some goodies at Mom's Bakery, a roadside van right in the center of town, be-fore catching the ferry to picture-postcard **Stocking Island,** just a few minutes away and good for a half-day's worth of shelling and tanning. If you're feeling adventurous, rent a car and see some of this enticing island, from the tiny settlements of **Barreterre** and **Rolleville** in the north all the way down to **Williams Town** at the southern tip of Little Exuma, connected to Great Exuma by a bridge. On your last day, you may want to try bonefishing, diving, or snorkeling. There are operators in town (check with the local tourist office) who will gladly set you up. Another half-day possibility: a bush medicine tour with a local flora expert, who will show you how various island plants are used medicinally.

A word on the Out Islands: It is hard to recommend the best island for a three-day trip because, of course, choosing the right destination depends upon your interests. If you're a dedicated angler, Bimini or the Berry Islands are where you should head; birdwatchers should choose Inagua; devotees of island architecture should try Elbow Cay in the Abacos (or, for that matter, Nassau); those enamored of a more modern look should consider Freeport and Lucaya on Grand Bahama Island. And if you're interested in doing nothing at all, consider Cat Island.

If You Have 5 Days

If you're traveling to Nassau, follow the first three-day itinerary above, and spend your fourth day on a day excursion to the **Exuma Cays,** reached by powerboat or seaplane. You can also take a day-trip via boat or helicopter to quaint **Harbour Island.** In either case, you can make it back to Nassau in time for dinner. Spend your last day in the water—swim for a few hours or sign up for a guided tour. With Dolphin Encounters, for example, you can actually swim with dolphins. If this seems too tame, consider the shark dive available in South New Providence, which is suited for more experienced underwater types.

If traveling to the Out Islands, follow the Exuma three-day itinerary above, and on the fourth day, fly to **Marsh Harbour** in the Abacos. Start your explorations in **Elbow Cay**—be sure to visit charming Hope Town with its vibrant Cape Cod–style houses and peppermint-striped lighthouse. If you can arrange to rent a boat for the rest of your stay, you'll discover endless possibilities for exploring the cays. But even on the infrequent ferry service, you can manage a day trip to **Man-O-War Cay,** home of the Abacos's boatbuilding industry. Visit **Albury's Sail Shop,** where several generations of women fashion luggage and other products from brightly colored sail canvas, or wander some of the most isolated beaches in the country. Spend your final day on **Green Turtle Cay** (it's a ferry, cab, and ferry ride from Elbow Cay, but doable), relaxing on tranquil **Coco Beach** or the wilder ocean shores, visiting the charming village of **New Plymouth,** or arranging a snorkeling expedition through **Brendal's Dive Shop** on the Green Turtle Club grounds. Then, it's time to head home: the best place to fly out of from here is Treasure Cay.

If You Have 10 Days or More

See the best of both worlds, spending half your time in Nassau and the rest in one of the Out Islands, just a short flight away. If you're determined, you could manage to see three destinations: spend four days in Nassau, and split the rest of your days between, for instance, Exuma and Cat Island. You could fly directly to George Town, Exuma, catch a flight back to Nassau from there, and head out a few days later to Cat, returning home on a flight out of Cat Island International Airport by way of Nassau. But that gets a little complicated. Maybe you're best plunking yourself down on an untrodden patch of Exuma, Eleuthera, Cat, Long Island, Andros, or any of the scores of other islands in the archipelago, and learning to live (for 10 days, at least) on Bahamian time.

FODOR'S CHOICE

Best Beaches

★ **Elbow Cay.** Hugging the Atlantic for about 3 semideserted mi, the stark white sand of the beach in Hope Town in the Abacos is a gorgeous sight.

★ **Great Guana Cay.** The 7-mi-long western coast of this cay in the Abacos is a deserted stretch of white sand bordered by palms.

★ **Great Harbour Cay.** Along the length of this 7½-mi strip, you may find your only company to be seabirds.

★ **Harbour Island.** Perhaps the most famous beach in the Bahamas, this 3-mi Eleutheran beach is covered in pink sand, colored by pulverized coral and shells.

★ **Long Island.** Extremely fine, bright white sand edges brilliantly blue water on Cape Santa Maria Beach, on the island's western shore.

★ **Stocking Island.** This delightful little cay off Great Exuma is known for its shelling.

Fun for Kids

★ **Glass-bottom boat trips.** At Prince George Wharf in Nassau, even children who don't swim can take a peek at the underwater world.

★ **Horseback riding.** Ride along Grand Bahama's coast on mounts from the Pinetree Stables in Freeport.

★ **Snorkeling.** Many facilities offer instruction and expeditions for all levels; at some Out Islands spots, children can discover the underwater wonderlands just a few feet off the beach, in less than 2 ft of water.

★ **Swimming with dolphins.** The Dolphin Experience in Lucaya, Grand Bahama, and on Blue Lagoon Island near Nassau, can put kids (even the adult variety) in close contact with the sensitive marine mammals.

Great Golf

★ **Cable Beach Golf Club.** This par-72, 7,040-yard course on Cable Beach, in New Providence, is the oldest and most highly regarded course in the Bahamas. It has ponds and small lakes among the back nine holes.

★ **Cotton Bay Club.** This par-72, 7,068-yard course at Rock Sound, Eleuthera, was designed by Robert Trent Jones, who placed two holes on narrow spits of land that effectively turn the Atlantic into a water trap.

★ **Emerald Golf Course.** One of two courses at the Bahama Princess Resort on Grand Bahama (the other is called the Ruby), the par-72, 6,679-yard Emerald was designed by Dick Wilson.

★ **Lucaya Golf and Country Club.** The other Dick Wilson course on Grand Bahama, this 6,824-yarder is the oldest on the island and requires more precision than power. The resort is closed for renovation, but the golf course remains open.

★ **Paradise Island Golf Club.** This stunning course on the far eastern tip of Paradise Island is surrounded on three sides by the ocean. Designed by Dick Wilson, it clocks in at 6,805 yards and par 72.

★ **South Ocean Golf Course.** The rolling hills of this 6,707-yard Joe Lee course, considered the best on New Providence Island, are unusual for the Bahamas.

Memorable Dining

★ **Buena Vista.** This Nassau institution is housed in one of city's gracious colonial mansions. $$$$

★ **Pink Sands.** Creative Bahamian dishes are served in a tropical garden paradise at this elegant Harbour Island resort. $$$$

★ **Runaway Hill Club.** Local chefs whip up culinary masterpieces at this homey inn on beautiful Harbour Island, off Eleuthera. $$$$

★ **The Sun and . . .** French cuisine with a Bahamian twist makes this Nassau restaurant a perennial favorite with locals and vacationing celebrities alike. $$$$

★ **Luciano's.** Enjoy Italian and French specialties at this spot overlooking the water in Lucaya. $$$

★ **Wally's.** Enjoy creative versions of Bahamian classics at this favorite spot in Marsh Harbour, Great Abaco. $$$

★ **Eddie's Edgewater.** Eddie's is the *in* spot for seafood and other Bahamian specialties in the Exuman capital of George Town, particularly during the weekly "Rake 'n' Scrape" music performances. $$

★ **Angela's Starfish.** A Harbour Island institution it's known as much for the down home friendly atmosphere as for the mouthwateringly fresh Bahamian food. Be sure to bring a business card for Angela to add to her display. $

Hideaways in the Out Islands

★ **Fernandez Bay Village.** Oceanfront villas hewn from native stone front one of Cat Island's prettiest crescents of sand at this friendly resort, indisputably Cat's finest and a perfect spot to escape the daily bustle. $$$$

★ **Pink Sands.** Chris Blackwell's latest recreation of an old Harbour Island resort on one of the prettiest pink-sand beaches in the Bahamas is truly fabulous—and expensive. $$$$

★ **Cape Santa Maria Beach Resort.** On a stunning, 4-mi arc of white sand on Long Island, this is just about as remote as luxury gets. $$$–$$$$

★ **Coconut Cove Hotel.** This intimate inn just outside George Town, Great Exuma, has the feel of a private home—not surprising, since that's what it was until the owners converted it to a casually refined hostelry. $$$

★ **Small Hope Bay Lodge.** This dive resort on Andros is a busy, popular place, but rustic private cottages—as well as the easygoing atmosphere on little-touristed Andros—let you get away from it all. $$$

★ **Bluff House Beach Hotel.** The vistas are spectacular, the welcome effusive, and the private villas a delight at this laidback Green Turtle Cay (Abacos) resort. $$–$$$

Top Resort Hotels

★ **Club Med Columbus Isle.** This deluxe all-inclusive resort sprawls along a luscious beach on the virtually undeveloped island of San Salvador, believed to be Columbus's first landfall in the New World. $$$$

★ **Atlantis, Paradise Island.** This ever expanding resort has everything from elaborate waterscapes to the area's largest casino. $$$

★ **Bahamas Princess Resort & Casino.** Two golf courses, a giant casino, and proximity to the International Bazaar shopping arcade make the twin resorts on this property among the most popular in Freeport. $$$

★ **Club Fortuna Beach.** This European-owned resort east of Lucaya on Grand Bahama is the island's only all-inclusive. $$$

★ **Radisson Cable Beach Casino & Golf Resort.** At the center of Cable Beach action, and connected to Cable Beach's casino by a shopping arcade, this property has a wide variety of water sports and a well-designed golf course. $$$

FESTIVALS AND SEASONAL EVENTS

WINTER

DECEMBER➤ The **Sun International Bahamas Open,** an event attracting some of the world's highest-ranked tennis players, is held at the Ocean Club on Paradise Island.

DECEMBER➤ **Christmas Day,** December 25, and **Boxing Day,** December 26, are both public holidays. Boxing Day coincides with the first of the **Junkanoo** parades.

DECEMBER➤ The **Waterford Crystal Lucaya Golf and Country Club Pro-Am Golf Tournament** is a week of meets at Grand Bahama's Lucaya Golf & Country Club that draws a roster of professional and amateur golfers almost as long as the tourney's name.

DECEMBER➤ Other annual December doings include the **Beaux Arts Masked Ball** and **Night of Christmas Music on Paradise Island,** and Nassau activities such as **Christmas at Government House festivities,** the **Police Band Annual Christmas and Classical Concert, Junior Junkanoo Parade,** and **Renaissance Singers Concert.**

JANUARY➤ **Junkanoo** continues its uniquely Bahamian (Mardi Gras–style) festivities welcoming the New Year. Less extensive celebrations take place in the Out Islands—also on January 1, a public holiday.

JANUARY➤ Pomp and pageantry take over when the **Supreme Court** opens in Nassau, a quarterly event.

JANUARY➤ The **New Year's Day Sailing Regatta** at Montagu Bay, Nassau, features competition among Bahamian-built sloops, as well as onshore entertainment.

JANUARY➤ The annual **New Year's Day Festival** is celebrated at Staniel Cay in the Exumas.

JANUARY➤ The **Bahamas Wahoo Tournament** draws anglers in great number to the waters around several Out Islands for a series of competitions that continue into February.

JANUARY➤ The **Bahamas Princess Resort & Casino Crystal Pro-Am Golf Tournament,** on Grand Bahama Island, is one of the area's most prestigious, bringing amateurs and professionals (who play together on teams) to the Princess' Ruby and Emerald golf courses.

JANUARY➤ The Bahamas National Trust, the major agency of environmental preservation in the Bahamas, holds an annual **open house** that includes children's activities, garden tours, and a display of indigenous snakes and birds at The Retreat, on Village Road in Nassau.

FEBRUARY➤ The **Farmer's Cay Festival** is held the first Friday on this tiny cay in the Exumas.

FEBRUARY➤ The **Pepsi Cola Classic** draws amateur golfers to New Providence's South Ocean Golf & Beach Resort.

FEBRUARY➤ The **Bahamas Wahoo Tournament** continues on several Out Islands.

SPRING

MARCH➤ The annual **Red Cross Fair** in the gardens of Nassau's Government House rounds off the winter social season, while the **Grand Bahama Red Cross Ball,** held at the Princess Resort, provides a bit of elegance on that island.

MARCH➤ The annual **George Town (All Exuma) Cruising Regatta** is a popular sailing event attracting more than 500 visiting yachts for a week of fun and festivities.

MARCH➤ Hope Town, Elbow Cay, comes alive with a **Heritage Day** featuring games, a raffle, treasure hunt, and of course lots of food.

MARCH➤ The week-long **Bacardi Rum Billfish Tournament** on Bimini is one of the most prestigious events of the year for deep-sea sportfishers.

MARCH➤ The annual **International Dog Show & Obedience Trials** are held at the Nassau Botanical Gardens.

APRIL➤ **Easter, Good Friday** and the following **Easter Monday** are public holidays.

APRIL➤ George Town, Exuma, hosts the **Out Islands Regatta,** the most important yachting event of the year in the Bahamas.

APRIL➤ The **Bimini Sailing Regatta** is at North Beach,

while competition is fierce during the **Bimini Break Blue Marlin Rendezvous.**

APRIL➤ The **South Eleuthera Homecoming Festival** livens up the Rock Sound area with celebrations, while the tiny Eleuthera settlement of James Cistern comes alive with food, drink, parties, and cultural events during the **James Cistern Heritage Affair Gala Fair,** held April 9–13.

MAY➤ The Abacos are the spot for anglers this month, with **billfish tournaments** at Treasure Cay and Marsh Harbour and the annual **Green Turtle Club Invitational Fishing Tournament** on Green Turtle Cay. The **Bimini Festival** is yet another in that island's lineup of fishing tournaments.

MAY➤ The **Long Island Sailing Regatta,** Salt Pond, Long Island, features sloop races, a yacht parade, and lots of activity both on and off the water.

MAY➤ The **Barreterre Festival** livens up this settlement on the north end of Great Exuma.

MAY➤ The **Rolex Classic** is played at the Paradise Island Golf & Country Club.

MAY➤ The **South Caicos Regatta** is held at Cockburn Harbour, South Caicos.

SUMMER

JUNE➤ **Labour Day,** the first Friday of the month, and **Whit Monday** (June 8) are public holidays.

JUNE➤ Yes, more **deep-sea fishing tournaments:** the Bimini Big Five Tournament and the Bahamas Billfish Tournament (Abaco) are major ones this month.

JUNE➤ Golfers tee off at the **Bahamas U.K. Paris Challenge** at the Radisson Cable Beach Casino & Golf Resort.

JUNE➤ Gregory Town is the scene of the **Eleuthera Pineapple Festival,** featuring a Junkanoo parade, crafts displays, tours of pineapple farms, and sports events.

JULY➤ The Bahamas' most important public holiday falls on July 10— **Independence Day,** which was established in 1973 and marks the end of 300 years of British rule. **Independence Week** is celebrated throughout the Bahamas with regattas, boat races, fishing tournaments, and a plethora of parties.

JULY➤ Eleuthera offers two **Homecoming Festivals,** in Savannah Sound and Bluff; both are great ways to mingle with locals over food, drink, games, and general partying.

AUGUST➤ **Emancipation Day,** which marks when the English freed Bahamian slaves in 1834, is a public holiday celebrated on the first Monday in August.

AUGUST➤ The annual 10-day **Fox Hill Festival** in Nassau pays tribute to Emancipation with an early morning Junkanoo Rushout (dancing in the streets), music, cookouts, games, and other festivities.

AUGUST➤ The **Paradise Island Amateur Golf Championship** is played at the Paradise Island Golf Club, while a very different Paradise Island competition can be seen at the annual **Miss Bahamas Beauty Pageant,** held at Atlantis.

AUGUST➤ Annual **regattas** take place at, Eleuthera and two Exuma locations (Rolleville and Black Point).

AUGUST➤ The Turks and Caicos islands hold their **carnival** during the last days of the month.

AUTUMN

AUGUST➤ Guess what, Bimini has another fishing competition, the **Bimini Native Fishing Tournament.**

SEPTEMBER➤ The **Ladies Futures Pro-Am Golf Tournament** takes place at the Paradise Island Golf Club, while the **Finco Open** is held at South Ocean Golf & Beach Resort.

SEPTEMBER➤ Three legs of the small **B.O.A.T. Tournament,** a (try to hide your surprise) Bimini fishing contest for boats of less than 27 ft, take place this month.

OCTOBER➤ The first Wednesday marks the fourth and final opening of the year for the **Supreme Court** in Parliament Square.

OCTOBER➤ The **Annual McLean's Town Conch Cracking Contest,** which includes games and entertainment along with good eating, takes place on Grand Bahama Island on October 12.

OCTOBER➤ **Discovery Day,** commemorating the landing of Columbus in the islands in 1492, is observed on October 12, a public holiday.

OCTOBER➤ The **North Andros Community Awareness and Discovery Regatta** is a weeklong event, while the **North Eleuthera Sailing Regatta** and the **San Salvador Sailing Regatta** each occupy five days of busy sailing.

2 New Providence Island

The exquisite white-and-pink sand beaches, lush tropical landscapes, unsullied waters, and year-round sunshine make this island the perfect vacation haven. Nassau and Paradise Island are the big hitters in the Bahamian lineup. However, there's plenty more to do than doze in the sun, from shopping to snorkeling, exploring forts to sampling conch—and don't forget the casinos, which are always open (or so it seems). And, after dark, Nassau's nightlife hops.

Updated by
Rich Rubin

NEW PROVIDENCE ISLAND, home to two-thirds of all Bahamians, is a study in contrasts: glitzy casinos and quiet, shady lanes; trendy, up-to-date resorts and tiny settlements that recall a distant, simpler age; land development unrivaled elsewhere in the Bahamas; and vast stretches of untrodden territory. In the course of its history, the island has weathered the comings and goings of lawless pirates, Spanish invaders, slave-holding British Loyalists who fled the United States after the Revolutionary War, Civil War–era Confederate blockade-runners, and Prohibition rumrunners. Despite this polyglot past, New Providence remains most influenced by England, which sent its first royal governor to the island in 1718. Although Bahamians won control of the government in 1967 and independence six years later, the British influence continues to this day.

Nassau is the nation's capital and transportation hub, as well as the banking and commercial center. While businesspeople take advantage of bank secrecy laws that rival Switzerland's and enjoy the absence of inheritance, income, and sales taxes, most visitors need look no farther than Nassau's many duty-free shops for proof of the island's commercial vitality. The fortuitous combination of tourist-friendly enterprise, tropical weather, and island atmosphere with a European overlay has not gone unnoticed: each year more than a million cruise-ship passengers arrive at Nassau's Prince George Wharf, on short trips from Florida or as the final stop on Caribbean cruises.

Exploring Nassau's Bay Street shops and its busy Straw Market is a vivid experience—and a joy for hard-bargaining shoppers. Be advised, though, that very few Bahamian-made goods are sold here, as you may discover when the occasional vendor embarrassingly forgets to remove the "Made in the Philippines" tag. A mile or so east of town, under the Paradise Island Bridge, Potter's Cay Dock is another colorful scene: sloops bring catches of fish and conch (pronounced *kahnk*), open-air stalls carry fresh fruit and vegetables, and street vendors sell local foods—freshly-made conch salad predominates. If the daytime bustle isn't enough, the nighttime action at the island's nightclubs and casinos can take you into the wee hours of the morning.

You'll find most hotels either on Cable Beach or Paradise Island; both areas are just outside downtown Nassau and have plush hotels, unfettered beach access, and proximity to casinos. Cable Beach, so named because the Bahamas' first transatlantic telephone cable was laid here, is a crescent-shaped stretch of sand west of Nassau, rimmed by resorts and the Crystal Palace Casino. While by no means secluded, Cable Beach is nevertheless one of New Providence's prettiest stretches.

Paradise Island lies across a high, arched bridge from the east end of downtown Nassau (a second bridge is under construction to handle the heavy traffic). Long considered the unspoiled alternative to Cable Beach's glitz, Paradise Island has been reinvented, and although you'll still find quiet corners, upscale dining, and elegant lodgings, the island is now home to the area's largest casino and a slew of mega-resorts. It's still a little quieter than Cable Beach, but just barely. Most credit the beginnings of this new era to Atlantis, Paradise Island, which continues to expand across the island, changing the very face of P.I. (as locals call the island). Many residents fear that new development threatens the island's placid existence, but for now Paradise Island still lives up to its name. Clear, blue-green, sheltered waters appeal to yachters, anglers, divers, water-skiers, parasailers, and windsurfers. Landlubbers will find plenty to do, too, from golf to tennis to lying on one of the beaches.

EXPLORING NEW PROVIDENCE ISLAND

Tourist action is concentrated on the northeastern side of New Providence. If you have time, you can make your way around the rest of this 7-by-21-mi island in a day, including occasional stops. The terrain is flat, and getting around is easy. Renting a car is your best bet—or pick up a scooter for a more adventurous ride. Either way, drive on the left-hand side of the road. Remember to pick up a copy of a New Providence map at your hotel desk. Wear comfortable shoes, and try to do most of your walking before the sweltering Bahamian sun reaches its full midday force.

Numbers in the text correspond to numbers in the margin and on the Nassau and Paradise Island, and New Providence Island maps.

A Good Tour

In a day, you can take in most of the markets, gardens, and historical sites of **Nassau** ①–⑭ and **Paradise Island** ⑮–⑱. Most of the historic sites can be reached on foot, bicycle, scooter, or horse-drawn carriage. Set aside a half-day or more for an excursion to Lake Nancy for a few hours of canoeing; a trip to the **Commonwealth Brewery** ㉝ or the **Bacardi Distillery** ㉟; or a spin through the largely-residential east end of the island, stopping at the gardens of **The Retreat** ㉑.

A good starting point is **Rawson Square** ①, which opens off the north side of Bay Street in the heart of downtown Nassau. Pick up brochures and maps at the Ministry of Tourism information booth on the northern side of the square, then head west along the north side of famous Bay Street. While there are stores galore on this broad, palm-lined boulevard, save your shopping for later, as your newfound treasures will prove cumbersome during your explorations. Continue west to the **Pompey Museum** ④ for an educational excursion into the slave days of old Nassau and a glimpse of the islands' best contemporary art. Follow the bend at Navy Lion Road past the historic **British Colonial Hotel** ⑤, at the entrance to Bay Street, which curves around the hotel to become West Bay Street.

Continue along West Bay, up along the Western Esplanade beach for a spectacular view of the ocean and the harbor.

If you've packed a sense of adventure, stray west for lunch and a bite of culture at **Arawak Cay** ㉘, which lies a few minutes farther along West Bay Street on the north side; it's quite a long walk.

Head back east along West Bay Street to West Street, then turn right and take in the typical Bahamian houses lining the street. Stop in at **St. Francis Xavier Church,** and then turn left onto West Hill Street. Walk across Blue Hill Road as West Hill Street angles around to turn into Duke Street. Here you can snap a picture with Christopher Columbus, whose likeness graces the entrance to the stately **Government House** ⑥.

Head north onto George Street (it begins at Government House) and on the right, at the corner of Marlborough Street, is the regal **Christ Church Cathedral** ⑦. From the cathedral, turn east on King Street then south along Market Street, where you'll see the pink **Balcony House** ⑧, typical of late-18th-century Bahamian architecture. Check whether local artists' work is on display at the **Central Bank of the Bahamas** ⑨ across the street, then continue east until you reach Frederick Street. Trinity Methodist Church is on the corner. On Shirley Street, head east,

Nassau and Paradise Island

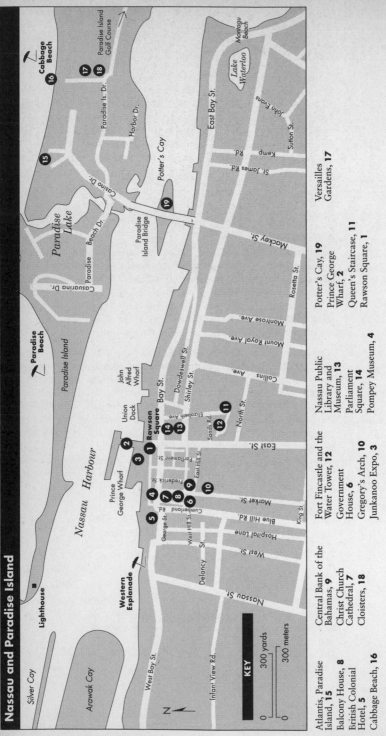

Atlantis, Paradise
Island, **15**
Balcony House, **8**
British Colonial
Hotel, **5**
Cabbage Beach, **16**

Central Bank of the
Bahamas, **9**
Christ Church
Cathedral, **7**
Cloisters, **18**

Fort Fincastle and the
Water Tower, **12**
Government
House, **6**
Gregory's Arch, **10**
Junkanoo Expo, **3**

Nassau Public
Library and
Museum, **13**
Parliament
Square, **14**
Pompey Museum, **4**

Potter's Cay, **19**
Prince George
Wharf, **2**
Queen's Staircase, **11**
Rawson Square, **1**

Versailles
Gardens, **17**

past Charlotte and Parliament streets, to the **Nassau Public Library and Museum** ⑬.

Follow Shirley Street farther east until you reach Elizabeth Avenue. Head south, and you'll find the **Queen's Staircase** ⑪—hand-cut out of limestone—and **Fort Fincastle and the Water Tower** ⑫, the highest point on the island.

When you're finished at the fort, backtrack along Elizabeth Avenue and Shirley Street to Bank Lane. Stop to take in the buildings at **Parliament Square** ⑭, then return to Rawson Square and nearby **Woodes Rogers Walk** to get a close look at the cruise ships, horse-drawn surreys, and the stylists at work in the **hair braiding pavilion.**

From here you can catch a cab to Paradise Island, where you can take in **Atlantis, Paradise Island** ⑮, **Versailles Gardens** ⑰, and the **Cloisters** ⑱; then spend some time relaxing on the beach.

Try to leave time for the **Straw Market,** on the western end of Market Street, if only to check out the vibrant scene—more authentically Bahamian goods can be found at small shops such as East Bay Street's **The Plait Lady** (☞ Shopping, *below*). Remember that Straw Market vendors expect you to barter for goods, and that the best bargains are often found in the late afternoon.

TIMING

This tour will take up the better part of a day. If Arawak Cay seems too far, or you seek more commodious surroundings for lunch, consider the countless good restaurants along the route. You can always save Arawak Cay for another day, perhaps combining it with a visit to nearby **Crystal Cay** ㉙, or with **Fort Charlotte** ㉕, **Ardastra Gardens and Conservation Centre** ㉖, and the **Nassau Botanic Gardens** ㉗, all within an easy shot across West Bay Street. To keep your bearings, remember that Bay Street and Shirley Street run east–west, and streets linking them run north–south. Heading in the direction of Cable Beach means traveling west; the harbor (or should we say, "harbour") is on the north edge of downtown.

Nassau

Nassau's sheltered harbor bustles with cruise ship hubbub, while a block away, broad, palm-lined Bay Street is alive with commercial activity. Shops angle for tourist dollars with fine imported goods at duty-free prices while Straw Market vendors bargain for the same dollars with straw work of doubtful origin, T-shirts, and jewelry. However, you will find a handful of shops overflowing with authentic Bahamian crafts, food supplies, and other delights. Nassau's historic sites are centered around downtown.

With its thoroughly revitalized downtown, Nassau is recapturing some of its past glamour. However, a distinct '90s flavor has taken hold: chic cigar bars, fancy restaurants, suave clubs, and trendy coffeehouses are popping up everywhere. This is partly due to the upper-crust crowd supplementing the spring-breakers and cruise-passengers who have traditionally flocked to Nassau.

The face of the city began to improve with Atlantis, Paradise Island, which set a new standard for hotel upkeep, forcing other neglected properties to follow suit, and with record mogul Chris Blackwell's Compass Point, which began to draw celebrities. Today the seedy air of the town's not-so-distant past is almost unrecognizable. Petty crime is no greater than in other towns of this size, and the streets not only look cleaner but feel safer. Of course, you can still find a wild club or a rowdy bar, but you can also sip cappuccino while viewing contemporary Bahamian art or dine by candlelight among prints of Old Nassau, serenaded by the soft, island-inspired sounds of a gentle calypso tune. Culture and glamour abound: coffeehouses advertise poetry readings, fashion shows, and bistro nights, and along the streets you'll find elegant stores that many bigger towns would be lucky to have. It's exciting to watch the city come into its own again.

Sights to See

★ ⑧ **Balcony House.** This charming 18th-century landmark—a pink two-story house named aptly for its freestanding balcony—is the oldest wooden residential structure in Nassau. Originally, the house was constructed with American cedar; its architecture suggests that it was built by ship's carpenters. Later, a mahogany staircase, believed to have been salvaged from a ship during the last century, was installed. The furnishings and design of Balcony House recapture the elegance of a bygone era. Note: the museum has been closed for renovation and may reopen by the end of 1998; call to check its status. ⊠ *Market St. and Trinity Pl.,* ☎ *242/322–2193.* ⊡ *Donation recommended.* ☉ *Mon., Wed., Fri. 10–1 and 2–5.*

⑤ **British Colonial Hotel.** The imposing building at the corner of Bay and Cumberland streets is the island's oldest hostelry and downtown's most convenient reference point; such phrases as "it's just a block east of the British Colonial" are common in Nassau. As the name implies, it was once an outpost of the British Empire. The original structure, built in 1899 on the old Fort Nassau site, was destroyed by fire in 1921 and rebuilt and reopened in 1923 as the New Colonial Hotel. An ambitious renovation of this major downtown landmark was begun in 1997 and is slated for completion in early 1999. ⊠ *1 Bay St.,* ☎ *242/322–3301.*

⑨ **Central Bank of the Bahamas.** The Central Bank of the Bahamas functions as the government's official arm monitoring and regulating the country's financial institutions. The cornerstone of the building was laid by Prince Charles on July 9, 1973, during the country's Independence celebrations, and the bank was opened by Queen Elizabeth II in February 1975 (you can find commemorations of these events at the back of the building). Throughout the year, exhibits on two floors of the lobby display the work of emerging Bahamian artists. ⊠ *Market St. and Trinity Pl.,* ☎ *242/322–2193.*

★ ⑦ **Christ Church Cathedral.** It's worth the short walk off the main thoroughfare to see the stained-glass windows of this cathedral, which was built in 1837. The white pillars of the church's spacious, airy interior support ceilings beamed with dark wood. The east windows depict the Crucifixion in the center panel and the Empty Tomb and the Ascension in the two side panels. Be sure to take a leisurely stroll through the small Gardens of Remembrance, where roses bloom and tombstonelike plaques adorn the walls. ⊠ *George St. near Marlborough St.,* ☎ *242/322–4186.* ☉ *Daily 8:30–4.*

⑫ **Fort Fincastle and the Water Tower.** Shaped like a paddle-wheel steamer and perched at the top of the **Queen's Staircase** (☞ *below*), Fort Fincastle—named for Royal Governor Lord Dunmore (Viscount Fincastle)—was completed in 1793 to serve as a lookout post for marauders trying to sneak into the local harbor. It served as a lighthouse in the early nineteenth century. The fort's 126-ft-tall water tower, which is more than 200 ft above sea level, is the highest point on the island. From here, the panorama of Nassau and the harbor is spectacular. ⊠ *Top of Elizabeth Ave. hill, south of Shirley St.* ☉ *Fri.–Wed. 8–5.*

★ ❻ **Government House.** The official residence of the governor-general of the Bahamas since 1801 is an imposing pink-and-white building on Duke Street, appropriate since its most notable occupants were the Duke and Duchess of Windsor, who lived here during World War II. This distinguished mansion is an excellent example of the mingling of Bahamian-British and American Colonial architecture. Its graceful columns and broad, circular drive recall the styles of Virginia or the Carolinas; but its pink color and distinctive white quoins are typically Bahamian. (Quoins are cross-laid cornerstones reaching to the full height of a building's walls. Notice, too, the shutters—wooden louvers that completely enclose the large upper and lower verandas—which are designed to keep out the tropical sun and appear typically on well-preserved old mansions in Nassau. Halfway up the white steps that lead to the entrance is an 1830 statue of Christopher Columbus. Here you can also catch the crisply disciplined but beautifully flamboyant **Changing of the Guard ceremony,** which takes place every other Saturday morning at 10. The star of the pomp and pageantry is the Royal Bahamas Police Force Band, the members of which are decked out in white tunics, red-striped navy trousers, and spiked, white pith helmets with red bands; the drummers sport leopard skins. ⊠ *Duke St. and George St.,* ☎ *242/ 322–7500 for changes in ceremony schedule.*

❿ **Gregory's Arch.** Named for John Gregory (royal governor from 1849 to 1854), this arch, at the intersection of Market and Duke streets, separates downtown from the "over-the-hill" neighborhood of **Grant's Town,** where much of Nassau's population lives. Grant's Town was laid out in the 1820s by Governor Lewis Grant as a settlement for freed slaves. Visitors once enjoyed late-night mingling with the locals in the small, dimly lit bars of Grant's Town. Nowadays, tourists should exhibit the same caution they would if they were visiting impoverished areas of a large city; nevertheless, it's a vibrant section of town. Here you can rub shoulders with Bahamians at a funky take-out food stand or down-home restaurant, while catching a glimpse of local life.

❸ **Junkanoo Expo.** Handmade floats and costumes used by revelers during the annual Bahamian Junkanoo celebration are exhibited in an old customs warehouse at the entrance to the wharf. Visiting the Expo is the next best thing to seeing festivities in person. The accommodating staff will tell you everything you want to know about Junkanoo—and the colorful displays speak for themselves. Junkanoo parades, similar to those that take place elsewhere during Mardi Gras or Carnival, are held in the early morning hours on Boxing Day (the day after Christmas) and on New Year's Eve. Note: the Expo has been closed for renovation; call or stop by to make sure they've reopened. ⊠ *Prince George Wharf,* ☎ *242/356–2731.* ▧ *$1.* ☉ *Daily 9–5:30.*

⓭ **Nassau Public Library and Museum.** This octagonal building near Parliament Square was the Nassau Gaol (a British spelling for *jail*), circa 1797. You're welcome to pop in and browse. The small prison cells are now lined with books. The museum has an interesting collection of historic prints and old colonial documents. ⊠ *Shirley St., between Parliament St. and Bank La.,* ☎ *242/322–4907.* ▧ *Free.* ☉ *Mon.– Thurs. 10–8, Fri. 10–5, Sat. 10–4.*

★ ⓮ **Parliament Square.** Nassau is the seat of national government. The Bahamian Parliament comprises two houses—a 16-member Senate (Upper House) and a 40-member House of Assembly (Lower House)—and a ministerial cabinet headed by a prime minister. Parliament Square's pink, colonnaded government buildings were constructed during the early 1800s by Loyalists who came to the Bahamas from North Carolina. The buildings were patterned after the southern Colonial architecture of New Bern, the early capital of North Carolina. The Square is dominated by a statue of a slim young Queen Victoria that was erected on her birthday, May 24, in 1905. In the immediate area are a half-dozen magistrates' courts (open to the public). Behind the House of Assembly is the **Supreme Court;** its four-times-a-year opening ceremonies (held the first weeks of January, April, July, and October) recall the wigs and mace-bearing pageantry of the Houses of Parliament in London. The Royal Bahamas Police Force Band is usually on hand for the event. ⊠ *Bay St.,* ☎ *242/322–7500 or 242/356–7591 for information on Supreme Court ceremonies.* ⊡ *Free; obtain pass at door to view session.* ⊙ *Weekdays 10–4.*

❹ **Pompey Museum.** Housed in a building where slave auctions were held in the 1700s, this museum is named for a rebel slave who lived on the Out Island of Exuma in 1830. Exhibits focus on the issues of slavery and emancipation and highlight the works of local artists, such as Amos Ferguson, one of the country's best-loved artists; his folk-art canvases depict a wide variety of themes from religious to natural. ⊠ *Bay and George Sts.,* ☎ *242/326–2566 or 242/326–2568.* ⊡ *$1.* ⊙ *Weekdays 10–4:30, every other Sat. 10–1.*

❷ **Prince George Wharf.** The wharf that leads into Rawson Square is the first view that cruise passengers encounter after they tumble off the ships. Up to a dozen gigantic cruise ships call on Nassau at any one time. They stop here either on short jaunts from Miami or during weeklong cruises to Caribbean islands. The wharf received a $2.5 million facelift in 1996, and phase II—completion date not yet announced—will add island shops, an audiovisual information center, and a footbridge from the Straw Market on Bay Street to the wharf. ⊠ *Waterfront at Rawson Sq.*

⑪ **Queen's Staircase.** These 65 steps are thought to have been carved out of a solid limestone cliff by slaves in the 1790s. The staircase was later named to honor the 65-year reign of Queen Victoria; recent innovations include a waterfall cascading from the top, and an ad hoc straw market along the narrow road that leads to the sight.⊠ *Top of Elizabeth Ave. hill, south of Shirley St.*

❶ **Rawson Square.** Many locals congregate at this square that connects Bay Street to the Prince George Wharf. Note the statue of Sir Milo Butler, the first post-independence (and first native Bahamian) Governor-General, and walk by (or perhaps stop inside) the **Hairbraiding Pavilion,** where women work their magic at prices ranging from $2 for a single strand to $100 for an elaborate do. You can see horse-drawn surreys waiting for passengers in nearby **Woodes Rogers Walk.** ⊠ *Bay St.*

Paradise Island

The graceful, arched Paradise Island Bridge ($2 toll for cars and motorbikes; free to bicyclists and pedestrians), 1 mi east of Nassau's Rawson Square, leads to the extravagant, tranquil world of Paradise Island, which is such a popular destination that a second bridge is now being built to handle the heavy traffic.

Until 1962, Paradise Island was largely undeveloped and known as Hog Island. A&P heir Huntington Hartford changed the name when he built the island's first resort complex. Although several huge high-rise resorts have been erected since—as have many million-dollar houses—you can still find several quiet getaway spots. The north shore is lined with white-sand beaches, and the protected south shore, directly across the harbor from Nassau, is a haven for yachts. Aptly renamed, the island *is* a paradise for beach lovers, boaters, and fun lovers.

Flat and compact, Paradise Island is conducive to walking and bicycling. A free casino shuttle bus makes frequent rounds, picking up passengers at major hotels as well as anywhere along the route—a good way to get around on hot days.

Sights to See

⑮ Atlantis, Paradise Island. Just across the Paradise Island Bridge, Casino Drive leads directly to the Atlantis with its surrounding 14 acres of unparalleled waterscape. The huge complex is home to restaurants, glitzy shopping malls, a cabaret theater, and an outdoor aquarium complete with an underwater tunnel and sharks looming above. At press time, expansion plans—scheduled for completion in late 1998—included a 50,000-sq-ft casino, and a slew of new water parks and themed attractions. ⊠ *Casino Dr.,* ☎ *242/363–3000.* ☉ *Daily 24 hrs.*

⑯ Cabbage Beach. This stretch of white sand along the north side is one of the prettiest on New Providence. Though resorts line much of its length, several minutes' stroll to the east will bring you to a nearly uninhabited span of beach overlooking emerald waters and tiny offshore cays.

★ **⑱ Cloisters.** At the top of the **Versailles Gardens** (☞ *below*) stand the remains of a 14th-century French stone monastery that were imported to the United States in the 1920s by newspaper baron William Randolph Hearst. (The cloister is one of four that have ever been removed from French soil.) Forty years later, grocery-chain heir Hartford bought the Cloisters and had them installed on their present commanding site. At the center is a graceful, contemporary white marble statue called *Silence,* by U.S. sculptor Dick Reid. Daily, tourists take or renew wedding vows under the delicately wrought gazebo overlooking Nassau Harbour. The Cloisters are owned by the Ocean Club, but visitors are welcome to look around. ⊠ *Paradise Island Dr.*

⑲ Potter's Cay. Here, beneath Paradise Island Bridge, you can watch sloops bring in and sell loads of fish and conch. Many locals and hotel chefs come here to purchase the fresh catches, which they clean on the spot. Vegetables, herbs, and such condiments as fiery Bahamian peppers preserved in lime juice are sold at nearby stalls, along with locally grown pineapples, papaya, and bananas. If you don't have the know-how to handle the preparation of the tasty conch—getting the diffident creature out of its shiny pink shell requires boring a hole at the right spot to sever the muscle that keeps it entrenched—you'll find a stall selling local delicacies such as conch salad. Empty shells are sold as souvenirs.

⑰ Versailles Gardens. Fountains and statues of luminaries and legends (such as Napoléon and Josephine, Franklin Delano Roosevelt, David Livingstone, Hercules, and Mephistopheles) adorn Versailles Gardens, the terraced lawn at the Ocean Club (☞ Lodging, *below*), which was once the private hideaway of Huntington Hartford. **Cloisters** (☞ *above*) brought over from France grace the top of the gardens. Although the property is owned by the Ocean Club, visitors are welcome to stroll through. ⊠ *Ocean Club, Paradise Island Dr.,* ☎ *242/363–3000.*

Eastern New Providence

The eastern end of New Providence Island is residential, although there are some interesting historical sites and fortifications here. From East Bay Street, just beyond Paradise Island Bridge, it's a short, scenic drive along Eastern Road, which is lined with gracious homes, to East End Point—about 20 minutes, depending on traffic.

Sights to See

㉔ Blackbeard's Tower. On a hill near the easternmost point of New Providence, this edifice is dismissed by the more pragmatic people of Nassau as the remains of an old stone water tower. The more romantic insist it was used by the piratical Edward Teach, a.k.a. Blackbeard, as a lookout for Spanish ships ripe for plundering. The best thing about the place is its view of Nassau and its harbor. ⊠ *Eastern Rd.*

⑳ Fort Montagu. The oldest of the island's three forts, Montagu was built in 1741 of local limestone to repel Spanish invaders. The only action it saw, though, was when it was occupied for two weeks by rebel American troops—among them a lieutenant named John Paul Jones—seeking arms and ammunition during the Revolutionary War. The fortification is well maintained, and though there are no guided tours, you are welcome to wander around. A broad public beach stretching for more than a mile beyond the fort looks out upon Montagu Bay, where many international yacht regattas and Bahamian sloop races are held annually. ⊠ *East of Bay St., on Eastern Rd.* 🖼 *Free.*

㉒ Fox Hill. Settled by freed slaves who were given land grants, which they paid for either in cash or labor, this residential area was originally four smaller settlements. Today there's not much here of touristic interest—except on the second Tuesday of August, when the community holds its annual Fox Hill Day celebration. It falls a week after the rest of the island celebrates Emancipation Day (some say that's because it took a week back in 1834 for the original news of freedom from slavery to reach the community here). Festivities include music, home-cooked food, and arts-and-crafts booths. Call the Ministry of Tourism (☎ 242/322–7500) for more information.

㉑ The Retreat. Nearly 200 species of exotic palm trees (more than half the genera of this tree in existence), grace the 11 verdant acres appropriately known as the Retreat, which serves as the headquarters of the Bahamas National Trust. Stroll in blessed silence through the lush grounds, past smiling Buddhas, and under stone arbors overhung with vines. It's a perfect break on a steamy Nassau day. ⊠ *Village Rd.,* ☎ *242/393–1317.* 🖼 *$2.* ☉ *Weekdays 9–5.*

㉓ St. Augustine's Monastery. This Romanesque home of the Bahamas' Benedictine brothers was built in 1946 by a monk named Father Jerome, who is also famed for his carvings of the Stations of the Cross on Cat Island's Mt. Alvernia. The St. Augustine buildings, home to a college as well as the religious complex, overlook beautiful gardens, and the monks are pleased to give tours of their home, including the tiny chapel. Their famed bakery, sadly, is now closed due to the passing of the brother who used to supervise it. ⊠ *Bernard Rd., west of Fox Hill Rd.*

Western New Providence and South Coast ·

Starting from downtown Nassau, West Bay Street follows the coast west past the glamorous resorts and posh residential neighborhoods of Cable Beach, then past popular Love Beach to Northwest Point. Just beyond is Lyford Cay, the most exclusive residential area on the island. Old-money pioneers started settling the cay four decades ago, and along with its 200-odd houses there is a private golf course for residents. Your experience of Lyford Cay is likely to be voyeuristic at best—an entrance gate wards off all but residents and friends.

Much of the interior and southwestern coast of New Providence is undeveloped, and the coastal scenery and long, low stretches of palmetto and pine forest are picturesque. The loop around the west and south

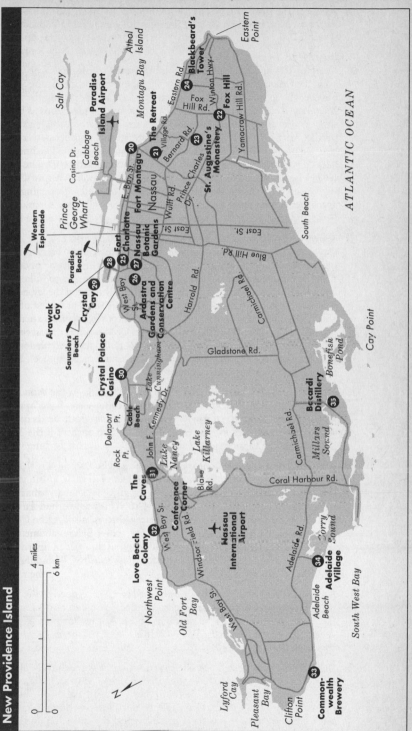

New Providence Island

ATLANTIC OCEAN

4 miles
6 km

Salt Cay
Athol Island
Montagu Bay Island
Blackbeard's Tower
Eastern Point
Paradise Island Airport
Cabbage Beach
Casino Dr.
Prince George Wharf
Western Esplanade
Paradise Beach
Saunders Beach
Arawak Cay
Crystal Cay
Crystal Palace Casino
Cable Beach
Delaport Pt.
Rock Pt.
The Caves
Northwest Point
Old Fort Bay
Love Beach Colony
Conference Corner
Nassau International Airport
Lyford Cay
Pleasant Bay
Clifton Point
Commonwealth Brewery
Adelaide Beach
Adelaide Village
South West Bay
Gorry Sound
Millars Sound
Carmichael Rd.
Bacardi Distillery
Bonefish Pond
Cay Point
South Beach
Gladstone Rd.
Coral Harbour Rd.
Blue Hill Rd.
Harrold Rd.
Lake Killarney
Lake Nancy
John F. Kennedy Dr.
Cunningham Dr.
West Bay St.
Windsor Field Rd.
Blake Rd.
Adelaide Rd.
East St.
Wulff Rd.
Prince Charles Dr.
St. Augustine's Monastery
Yamacraw Hill Rd.
Winton Hwy.
Fox Hill Rd.
Fox Hill
Eastern Rd.
Bernard Rd.
Village Rd.
The Retreat
Fort Montagu
Nassau Botanic Gardens
Fort Charlotte
Ardastra Gardens and Conservation Centre
Nassau

20 21 22 23 24 25 26 27 28 29 30 31 32 33 34 35

coasts of the island can be done in a couple of hours by car or scooter; however, you may wish to take time out for lunch and a swim along the way.

Sights to See

㉞ Adelaide Village. This small community on the southwestern coast of New Providence sits placidly, like a remnant of another era, between busy Adelaide Road and the ocean. It was first settled during the early 1800s by Africans who had been captured and loaded aboard slave ships bound for the New World. They were rescued on the high seas by the British Royal Navy, and the first group of liberated slaves reached Nassau in 1832. Today, only a few dozen families live in Adelaide. They raise vegetables and chickens and inhabit well-worn, pastel-painted wooden houses, sheltered in bougainvillea and other vegetation. The village has a primary school, some little grocery stores, and a locally popular restaurant-bar called Avery's Restaurant and Bar (℡ 242/362–1547). ✉ *Adelaide Rd.*

㉘ Arawak Cay. Known to Nassau residents as "The Fish Fry," Arawak Cay is one of the best places to knock back a Kalik beer (brewed right on New Providence Island), chat with the locals, play a game of dominoes, or sample Bahamian fare. You can get small noshes to full meals at one of the pastel-colored shacks lining the perimeter of the large fairgrounds. Order up a cracked conch (beaten, breaded, and fried), fresh conch salad (diced with onions, cucumbers, tomatoes, and a touch of hot pepper in lime marinade), or fried fish. Goldies Enterprises, on the western side of the cay, is one of the most popular stalls; try the mixed grill (shrimp, conch, and fish) and Goldie's famous Sky Juice (a potent gin and coconut-water concoction).

To reach Arawak Cay, head west along Bay Street, follow the main road around the British Colonial Hotel, and continue west. Pass Western Esplanade beach on the north shore, then Fort Charlotte on the south side of the street, and the cay is on the north side of the T-junction of West Bay and Chippingham Road.

㉖ Ardastra Gardens and Conservation Centre. The flamingo is the national bird of the Bahamas, and you'll see plenty of them at these gardens, renowned for the parade of pink, spindly legged, marching birds that perform daily at 11:10, 2:10, and 4:10. This zoo, with more than 5 acres of tropical greenery and flowering shrubs, also has an aviary of rare tropical birds, tame boa constrictors, native Bahamian creatures such as rock iguanas, and a global collection of animals ranging from caimans to lemurs. ✉ *Chippingham Rd., just south of W. Bay St.,* ℡ *242/323–5806.* 🎟 *$10.* ☉ *Daily 9–5.*

㉟ Bacardi Distillery. This factory, established in 1962, is open to the public for tours (reservations are recommended); you can also sample a range of its well-known rum products at the Visitors Pavilion. ✉ *Bacardi and Carmichael Rds.,* ℡ *242/362–1412.* 🎟 *Free.* ☉ *Mon.– Thurs. 9:30–4, Fri. 9:30–3.*

㉛ The Caves. These large limestone caverns that the waves have sculpted over the aeons are said to have sheltered the early Arawak Indians. An oddity perched right beside the road, they're worth a glance—though in truth, there's not much to see, as the dark interior doesn't lend itself to exploration. Just a short drive beyond the caves, on an island between traffic lanes, is **Conference Corner,** where U.S. President John F. Kennedy, Canadian Prime Minister John Diefenbaker, and British Prime Minister Harold MacMillan planted trees on the occasion of their summit in Nassau. ✉ *W. Bay St. and Blake Rd.*

③③ Commonwealth Brewery. Kalik, Nassau's own tasty beer, is brewed here. The local beverage—by far the most popular among locals—is named for the sound of the cowbells used in the Junkanoo Parade. Free tours are given by appointment only. ✉ *Clifton Pier and Southwest Rd.,* ☎ *242/362–4789.*

㉙ Crystal Cay. To say that you must see Crystal Cay (it used to be called Coral Island) is an understatement. This 16-acre marine extravaganza occupies an entire island, which is linked to Arawak Cay and the mainland by a bridge; its observation tower soars 100 ft above the ocean surface. You can descend a winding staircase to a depth of 20 ft below sea level to observe such denizens of the deep as turtles, stingrays, moray eels, and starfish. In the adjacent **Marine Park,** the Reef Tank is the world's largest man-made living reef, where you have a 360° view of coral, sponges, tropical fish, and other sea life. You can observe predators native to the Caribbean in the nearby Shark Tank. All together, the Marine Gardens Aquarium has 24 exhibits that tell the story of life on the reef. Flamingos occupy another area of the park. Shark-, turtle-, and other feeding times are posted daily. The boat to Crystal Cay shuttles visitors between Woodes Rogers Dock (near the Straw Market) in Nassau and Silver Cay several times a day. Call for exact times. ✉ *Silver Cay,* ☎ *242/328–1036.* 🎟 *$16.* ◷ *Mon.– Sat. 9–5:30.*

㉚ Crystal Palace Casino. You can try your luck at baccarat, blackjack, roulette, craps, and Caribbean stud poker or simply settle for the slots—there's plenty to keep you entertained, including a sports book, where you can place bets on all your favorite sports—professional and collegiate. When you've had enough gaming, stroll through the shopping malls connecting the casino with neighboring hotels. ✉ *Nassau Marriott Resort, Cable Beach, Nassau,* ☎ *242/327–6200.* ◷ *Daily, tables 9 AM–4 AM, slots 24 hrs.*

★ ㉕ Fort Charlotte. This imposing fort was built during the late 18th century and comes complete with a waterless moat, drawbridge, ramparts, and dungeons. Lord Dunmore, who built it, named the massive structure in honor of George III's wife. At the time, some called it Dunmore's Folly because of the staggering expense of its construction—it cost eight times more than was originally planned. (Dunmore's superiors in London were less than ecstatic with the high costs, but he managed to survive unscathed.) Ironically, no shots were ever fired in battle from the fort. It is about 1 mi west of central Nassau. ✉ *W. Bay St., at Chippingham Rd.* 🎟 *Free.* ◷ *Local guides conduct tours daily 8–4.*

㉜ Love Beach Colony. One of the loveliest stretches of beach on the island is near the northwestern corner of New Providence. About 1 mi off Love Beach are 40 acres of coral and sea fan, with forests of fern, known as the **Sea Gardens.** The clear waters are a favorite with snorkelers. Glass-bottom boats with guides make frequent excursions to the Sea Gardens from Prince George Wharf. 🎟 *Boat fare $10 per person.*

㉗ Nassau Botanic Gardens. Six hundred species of flowering trees and shrubs, a small cactus garden, and two freshwater ponds with lilies, water plants, and tropical fish cover 18 acres. The many trails that wind through the gardens are perfect for leisurely strolls. The Botanic Gardens are across the street from Ardastra Gardens and Conservation Centre, home of Nassau's zoo. (☞ *above*). ✉ *Chippingham Rd., just south of W. Bay St.,* ☎ *242/323–5975.* 🎟 *$1.* ◷ *Weekdays 8–4:30.*

BEACHES

New Providence is blessed with stretches of white sand studded with palm and sea-grape trees. Some of the beaches are small and crescent shape, while others stretch for miles. Right in downtown Nassau, you'll find the **Western Esplanade.** It sweeps west from the British Colonial Hotel on Bay Street, and has a snack bar, rest rooms, and changing facilities. Just past the bridge that leads to Coral Island is **Saunders Beach,** a weekend rendezvous spot for locals. On Paradise Island, **Paradise Beach,** at the far western tip of the island, is a nice stretch of sand, but Paradise Island's real showpiece is 3-mi-long **Cabbage Beach,** which rims the entire north coast, from the Atlantis lagoon to Snorkelers Cove.

Cable Beach, is on the north shore of New Providence about 3 mi west of downtown Nassau. Luxury resorts line much of this beautiful, broad swath of white sand, and there is public access. Jet-skiers and beach vendors abound, so don't expect quiet isolation. Just west of Cable Beach is a rambling pink house on the Rock Point promontory, where much of the 1965 Bond film *Thunderball* was filmed. Tiny, crescent-shaped **Caves Beach** is beyond Cable Beach on the north shore, about 7 mi from downtown just before the turnoff on Blake Road that leads to the airport. **Love Beach** is a snorkeler's favorite, on the north shore beyond Caves Beach, about 9 mi from town (about a 20-minute drive). Access technically lies within the domain of Love Beach residents, but they aren't inclined to shoo anyone away. On the south shore, drive down to **Adelaide Beach,** at the end of Adelaide Village, for sand that stretches down to Coral Harbour. The people who live at the east end of the island flock to **South Beach,** at the foot of Blue Hill Road on the south shore.

DINING

With the escalation of Bahamian tourism the preparation of meals at the better dining spots has become as sophisticated as any leading U.S. city. European chefs brought in by the top restaurants have trained young Bahamians in the skills of fine cuisine. Chinese, Indian, Mexican, Creole, and Japanese fare have also become available on menus.

Oddly enough, one of the most difficult things to find on New Providence until recently was authentic Bahamian fare. Several spots now serve traditional dishes: peas 'n' rice, conch (chowder, fritters, and cracked), Bahamian lobster, "stew" or "boil" fish, grouper fingers, fresh local bread, and, for dessert, guava duff. These local restaurants offer lower prices, and restaurant-wide, because meats often have to be imported, fish is the most economical entree.

Coffeehouses have sprung up everywhere. Most serve light fare and desserts plus a variety of specialty coffees and teas; many also sponsor cultural events such as readings, music, or art displays. *See* Coffeehouses *in* Nightlife, *below,* for a list of favorites.

Cable Beach and Paradise Island resorts now offer special package rates that include meals. Many all-inclusives also offer meal plans for nonguests.

CATEGORY	COST*
$$$$	over $30
$$$	$20–$30
$$	$15–$20
$	under $15

*per person for a three-course meal, excluding drinks and 15% gratuity

Nassau

Bahamian

$$ ✕ **Cellar and Garden Patio.** You'll find two very different atmospheres at this lunch-only restaurant. The subdued, more traditional indoor dining room has Bahamian decor with a varnished wood bar and tables; the alfresco locale—a covered patio encircled with greenery—has lazily rotating ceiling fans suspended from beams of white latticework. Seafood is the specialty of both areas: conch chowder, grouper, lobster tail, grilled snapper, and cracked conch. Other items, which especially appeal to the local business crowd, include quiche and roast-beef sandwiches. ⊠ *2 Charlotte St. at Bay St.,* ☎ *242/322–8877. AE, MC, V. Closed Sun. No dinner.*

$$ ✕ **Crocodiles Waterfront Bar & Grill.** The deck of this informal grill, shaded by palms and adorned with signs from a plethora of Nassau establishments, including Sugar Reef (☞ *below*), the original restaurant of Crocodiles's owners, is a good spot to linger. It's relaxing to sit under the thatched umbrellas and take in harbor views. You can opt for a light bite—conch salad, burgers (both standard and conch varieties), calamari, spinach dip—or try one of the heartier choices like the mammoth T-bone steak. ⊠ *E. Bay St., just west of the Paradise Island Bridge,* ☎ *242/323–3341. AE.*

$$ ✕ **Poop Deck.** Coiled rope wraps around beams and railings, life pre-
★ servers hang on walls, and, port and starboard lights adorn the newel posts of this favorite locals' haunt. The restaurant, just east of the Paradise Island Bridge, is a quick eight-minute cab ride from the center of town. Tables on the large waterfront deck have a beautiful view of the harbor and bridge. Excellent Bahamian-style seafood, along with friendly service and a comfortable atmosphere, keeps regulars coming back. Expect spicy dishes with names like Mary's grouper and Rosie's chicken, and an extensive wine list. Save room for guava duff, that warm, layered Bahamian assemblage, and a calypso coffee spiked with secret ingredients. ⊠ *E. Bay St., near Nassau Yacht Haven Marina, ¼ mi east of bridge,* ☎ *242/393–8175. AE, MC, V.*

$ ✕ **Mama Lyddy's Place.** This old house just off the beaten tourist
★ track is the place for true Bahamian cooking. Start with a local-style breakfast of souse or "boil fish" and watch Nassau residents stream in for take-out or sit-down meals. For lunch and dinner you can try fried snapper, cracked conch, minced or boiled crawfish, pork chops, and chicken. All are served, of course, with peas 'n' rice or peas 'n' grits and other typical Bahamian side dishes. Notice the "No hats, plaits, muscle shirts, smoking, soliciting" signs at the entrance. ⊠ *Market St. at Cockburn St.,* ☎ *242/328–6849. No credit cards. No dinner Sun.*

$ ✕ **Shoal Restaurant and Lounge.** Saturday morning at 9 you'll find hordes of hungry Bahamians digging into boil fish and johnnycake, the specialty of the house. A bowl of this peppery local dish, filled with chunks of boiled potatoes, onions, and grouper, may keep you coming back to this dimly lit, basic, out-of-the-way "Ma's kitchen," where Bahamian dishes, including peas 'n' rice and cracked conch, are staples. Mutton can be hard to find locally, but if it suits your taste buds, try it here, curried. ⊠ *Nassau St., between Meadow St. and Poinciana Dr.,* ☎ *242/323–4400. AE, MC, V.*

Caribbean

$$$ ✕ **Sugar Reef Harbourside Bar and Grille.** You'll feel like you're on a
★ private yacht at this lovely restaurant built on a pier jutting into Nassau Harbour. Broken-glass mosaics, dark-blue lacquered tables, and flickering hurricane lamps echo the watery theme, as do the friendly staff's colorful tropical shirts. Starters such as rich seafood crepes or tangy crab cakes with black-bean salsa are among the many immacu-

32

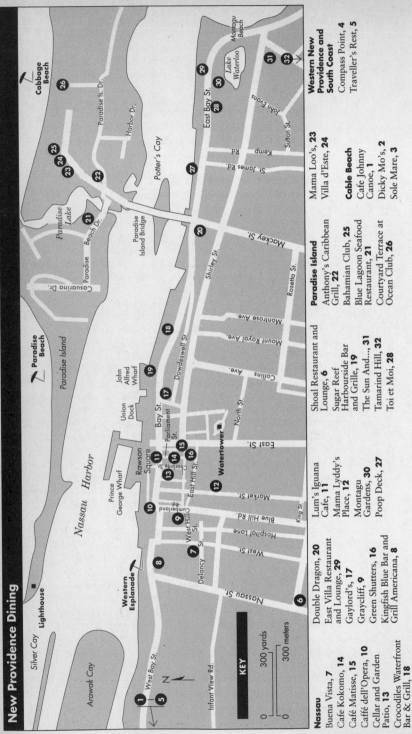

New Providence Dining

KEY

0 | 300 yards
0 | 300 meters

Nassau
Buena Vista, **7**
Café Kokomo, **14**
Café Matisse, **15**
Caffé dell'Opera, **10**
Cellar and Garden Patio, **13**
Crocodiles Waterfront Bar & Grill, **18**

Double Dragon, **20**
East Villa Restaurant and Lounge, **29**
Gaylord's, **17**
Graycliff, **9**
Green Shutters, **16**
Kingfish Blue Bar and Grill Americana, **8**

Lum's Iguana Cafe, **11**
Mama Lyddy's Place, **12**
Montagu Gardens, **30**
Poop Deck, **27**

Shoal Restaurant and Lounge, **6**
Sugar Reef Harbourside Bar and Grille, **19**
The Sun And..., **31**
Tamarind Hill, **32**
Toi et Moi, **28**

Paradise Island
Anthony's Caribbean Grill, **22**
Bahamian Club, **25**
Blue Lagoon Seafood Restaurant, **21**
Courtyard Terrace at Ocean Club, **26**

Mama Loo's, **23**
Villa d'Este, **24**

Cable Beach
Cafe Johnny Canoe, **1**
Dicky Mo's, **2**
Sole Mare, **3**

Western New Providence and South Coast
Compass Point, **4**
Traveller's Rest, **5**

lately prepared Bahamian-Caribbean specialties. The signature main course is pistachio-crusted grouper. Other festive dishes include tamarind-glazed mahimahi or grilled lobster with coconut rice, topped off by what the restaurant proudly (and accurately) calls "killer desserts." ⊠ *Bay and Deveaux Sts.,* ☎ *242/356–3065. AE, MC, V.*

$$ ✕ **Tamarind Hill.** Colorful Caribbean paintings and murals brighten this historic house originally built on the island of Eleuthera and brought to Nassau around 1920—the atmosphere is cheery and casual. The tasty fare includes such dishes as warm Cajun shrimp, mango chicken, or garlic shrimp fettuccine. There's often live music on weekends. ⊠ *Village Rd., near Shirley St.,* ☎ *242/393–1306. AE, MC, V. No lunch.*

Chinese

$$$ ✕ **East Villa Restaurant and Lounge.** Nassau residents declare that this dimly lit restaurant serves the best Chinese food in town. The Chinese-Continental menu includes such entrées as Canton lobster, *hung shew* (walnut chicken), and steak *kew* (cubed prime fillet served with baby corn, snow peas, water chestnuts, and vegetables). The New York Strip Steak is nirvana. A short taxi ride from Paradise Island or downtown Nassau, this is the perfect spot if you're seeking something a little different from the typical area restaurants. ⊠ *E. Bay St. near Nassau Yacht Club,* ☎ *242/393–3377. AE, MC, V. No lunch Sat.*

$ ✕ **Double Dragon.** Come to this informal spot for its array of Cantonese, Hunan, Szechuan, and Mandarin dishes. Try chicken with black bean sauce or, if you like it hot, shredded beef Szechuan style. You may want to go for one of the chef's specialties: shrimp and scallops or honey-garlic chicken. ⊠ *Bridge Plaza Commons, Mackey St., on the Nassau side of Paradise Island Bridge.* ☎ *242/393–5718. AE, MC, V. No lunch weekends.*

Continental

$$$$ ✕ **Buena Vista.** High on a hill above Nassau Harbour, this serene
 restaurant sits secure in its reputation as one of the city's dining institutions; it draws a loyal local clientele. Open for nearly 30 years, it occupies what was once a rambling private home built in the early 1800s. The tuxedoed waiters whisk about the dining room, where tables are set with china, crystal, and silver, and the light reflected in the windows off of the gracious chandeliers appears to emanate from the greenery outside. The menu has both Continental dishes and Bahamian seafood specialties. You may want to begin with escargot or cream of garlic soup, exemplary entrées include grouper and rack of spring lamb. Leave room for luscious cakes from the dessert trolley or Mrs. Hauck's Orange Pancakes, thick crepes baked in a Grand Marnier sauce—a house specialty since it was created several decades ago. ⊠ *W. Hill and Delancy Sts.,* ☎ *242/322–2811. AE, DC, MC, V. No lunch.*

$$$$ ✕ **Graycliff.** In a mid-18th-century Colonial mansion that was once the private home of a pirate are seven dining areas—among them the original dining room with a chandelier and an impressive mahogany table, the original library overlooking the garden, and an outdoor dining space. Antique furniture, French doors, and soft piano music set the mood for European cuisine with a Bahamian touch. One outstanding cold appetizer is Chiffonade Tiède: smoked goose, wild boar pâté, pickled papaya, thinly sliced truffles, and Bahamian chilies in coriander sauce. Other dishes are just as unusual. Rich and famous patrons frequent Graycliff, so don't be surprised that dinner for two might easily cost $300, not including wine (Graycliff is noted for its huge wine collection, and also for its large selection of hand-rolled cigars). ⊠ *W. Hill St. at Cumberland Rd.,* ☎ *242/322–2796. AE, DC, MC, V.*

\$\$\$\$ ✕ **The Sun and . . .** All the superlatives have long been exhausted for
★ this culinary oasis, one of Nassau's top restaurants. You may see Bahamian moguls wining and dining their clients here, and if you came
to Nassau hoping to catch sight of an international superstar, this is a
good place to look. Crossing the drawbridge of the converted 19th-
century estate brings you to an enclosed garden area with a rock pool
and fountain, where you dine under the stars. Try braised duckling with
raspberry sauce or sautéed grouper in puff pastry. Keep in mind while
feasting, though, that you'll be denying yourself heaven if you don't
end your meal with one of Belgian owner-chef Ronnie Deryckere's six
incomparable soufflés, which range from almond amaretto to guava.
The restaurant is nearly impossible to find by accident and almost as
difficult to find with directions; take a taxi or bring a map. ⊠ *Lake-
view Rd. and E. Shirley St.,* ☎ *242/393–1205. AE, D, MC, V. Closed
Aug., Sept., and Mon. No lunch.*

\$\$\$ ✕ **Montagu Gardens.** Certified 100% Angus beef and fresh native
seafood—flame-grilled and seasoned with home-mixed spices—are
the specialties at this romantic restaurant in an old Bahamian mansion
on Lake Waterloo. The dining room is surrounded by a walled courtyard and lovely gardens. Besides seafood and steak (carnivores love
the filet mignon smothered in mushrooms), menu selections include
chicken, lamb, lobster, pasta, and ribs. A favorite dessert is Mud Pie.
Montagu Gardens is next door to Club Waterloo (☞ Nightlife, *below*),
one of the town's trendy nightspots, making the restaurant a good place
to eat before going next door to boogie. ⊠ *E. Bay St., 1 mi east of
Paradise Island Bridge,* ☎ *242/394–6347. AE, MC, V. Closed Sun.*

Eclectic

\$\$\$\$ ✕ **Café Matisse.** Low-slung settees and arched walls set a casually re-
fined tone at this restaurant owned by a husband-and-wife team—he's
Bahamian, she's northern Italian. Consider starting with salmon carpac-
cio or crispy fried calamari, then dive into perennially popular curried
shrimp on jasmine rice, or the potato-crusted grouper with tangy onion
sauce. The pasta is freshly made, and if you're in the mood for pizza,
you won't go wrong with the *frutti di mare* (topped with fresh local
seafood). You can dine at candlelit tables inside or alfresco in the
ground-floor garden under lacy gazebos. Cigar smokers gravitate to
the second-floor veranda. The small tables up here also draw people
for after- and pre-dinner cocktails, particularly during the 5 to 7 PM
happy hour. ⊠ *Bank La. and Bay St., behind Parliament Sq.,* ☎ *242/
356–7012. AE, D, MC, V. Closed Sun.*

\$\$\$ ✕ **Cafe Kokomo.** You might just stumble upon this festive eatery while
strolling downtown. It's a colorful new incarnation of the former Pick-
a-Dilly, under the management of the Parliament Inn (☞ Lodging,
below). The best time to stop in is late afternoon, when the outdoor
daiquiri bar is jumping and locally famed bartender Demrist is doling
out these concoctions in mango, peach, banana, strawberry, and pineapple, and also creating the multicolored *Junkanoo Daiquiri.* One of these
drinks is sure to whet your appetite for the tasty dinner fare, from jerk-
chicken pizza or beef Wellington to crepes or fettuccine laden with tooth-
some seafood. There's usually live entertainment on weekends. ⊠
Parliament Inn, Parliament St. south of Bay St., ☎ *242/322–2836.
Reservations not accepted. AE, MC, V.*

\$\$ ✕ **Lum's Iguana Cafe.** The best thing about this restaurant is the second-story location on Bay Street; try to get a table on the upstairs bal-

cony, overlooking the bustle beneath you. The menu here is idiosyncratic, with a good variety of pastas, a few Greek entrées, and a fusion of Chinese and Bahamian cuisines; the latter may sound strange but yields such winning dishes as snapper in orange sauce, pork chops in spicy wine sauce, and fried fish sticks Peking-style. ⊠ *Prince George Plaza, Bay St. between Charlotte and Parliament Sts.,* ☏ *242/322–3119. AE, MC, V. Closed Sun.*

English

$$ ✕ **Green Shutters.** Shades of Fleet Street just two blocks south of Bay Street! This British-style pub, in a Bahamian house dating from 1782, is a cozy wood-paneled hangout beloved by locals. Traditional English fare—bangers and mash, fish-and-chips, shepherd's pie—shares the menu with such island favorites as cracked conch and Bahamian crayfish tail. Beer on draught is imported directly from England. ⊠ *48 Parliament St.,* ☏ *242/325–5702. AE, MC, V. Closed Sun.*

French

$$$$ ✕ **Toi et Moi.** Oddly found in a shopping center on East Bay Street, this upscale French restaurant is a new addition to Nassau's fine-dining scene. (There has been talk, though, that the menu may move away from haute cuisine, so if it's fancy French food you're after, give a call first.) You might start with either elegant Petrossian salmon or caviar, followed by succulent tenderloin or Bahamian fish both served in delicate French sauces. Will Nassau develop the palate to support such rarefied cuisine? See for yourself—and meanwhile pray that no matter what happens to the menu, the restaurant continues to sell its extensive selection of chocolates. ⊠ *Harbour Bay Shopping Center, E. Bay St.,* ☏ *242/394–7056. AE, MC, V. No lunch weekends.*

Indian

$$$ ✕ **Gaylord's.** This Indian restaurant is in a handsome historic building that dates back to the 1870s. The two dining areas are filled with decorative plates, sculpture, and other Indian works of art; draped silk adorns ceilings. Begin with a Gaylord Special, a cocktail made from tropical juice and rum, then try the tandoori chicken, vegetable curry, or a *roti* (nan bread stuffed with chicken or minced lamb). ⊠ *Dowdeswell and Bay Sts.,* ☏ *242/356–3004. AE, MC, V. No lunch weekends.*

Italian

$$$ ✕ **Caffè dell'Opera.** On the second floor of a converted church just opposite the British Colonial Hotel, this Italian restaurant specializes in pasta, made fresh daily. Pictures of composers establish an opera theme that's reflected in the names of dishes. Lasagne Donizetti, anyone? Other choices range from simple tortellini *Butterfly* (made with butter and sage) to fusilli *Orfeo* (with cream, orange, gin, butter, and parmesan cheese). And you'll dine to the sounds of—what else?—opera recordings. ⊠ *Bay St., across from the British Colonial Hotel,* ☏ *242/356–6118. AE, MC, V.*

Southwestern

$$$ ✕ **Kingfish Blue Bar and Grill Americana.** Nassau's first Southwestern-style restaurant is a winner, with friendly service and creatively spicy fare served in heaping portions. Choose a table in the pretty dining room—all slim black lines, soft lighting, and mellow music—or in the courtyard, lighted by old-fashioned gaslight fixtures. Start with a lob-

ster quesadilla or calamari rings tossed with sundried tomatoes and garlic; main courses include baked grouper Phoenix in a peppery potato crust; chicken sautéed in an ancho-chile sauce, or a wide variety of steaks. Try to save room for dessert, such as the decadent house specialty: Bacardi Rum cake served with homemade vanilla ice cream and hot rum sauce. ⊠ *W. Bay St., a few blocks west of the British Colonial,* ☎ *242/323–2236. AE, MC, V.*

Paradise Island

Caribbean

$$ ✕ **Anthony's Caribbean Grill.** The first thing you'll notice at Anthony's are the colors: bright red, yellow, and blue tablecloths spiked with multihued squiggles; yellow and green walls with jaunty cloths hanging from the ceilings; booths printed with bright sea-themes; and buoyant striped curtains. The lively spirit is reflected in the bouncy music and cheery service. The food is standard Caribbean fare: jerk chicken, ribeye seasoned with "Rasta" spices, or ribs served a multitude of ways—jerk, barbecue, or coconut-mango style. There's also a good selection of burgers and salads. ⊠ *Paradise Village Shopping Center,* ☎ *242/ 363–2152. AE, MC, V.*

Chinese

$$$$ ✕ **Mama Loo's.** Chinese delights are the order of the evening at this dinner-only restaurant in Atlantis. The tropical-Chinese atmosphere is enhanced with huge porcelain urns, carved wood ceilings, lush floral arrangements, and black-lacquer chairs. Pick seafood stir-fry, crispy duck, cashew chicken, or beef with garlic sauce. ⊠ *Atlantis, Paradise Island,* ☎ *242/363–3000. AE, MC, V. Closed Mon. No lunch.*

Continental

$$$$ ✕ **Bahamian Club.** A clubby British atmosphere prevails in this hand-
★   some restaurant, where walls are lined with dark oak and overstuffed chairs and banquettes are upholstered in leather. Impeccable table-side service heightens the experience. Starters include Dungeness crab cakes or a selection from the raw bar. Meat is the specialty of the house—grilled T-bone steak, veal chop, roast prime rib, and chateaubriand for two—but that is no reason to avoid the rest of the menu. Grilled swordfish steak, yellowfin tuna, salmon fillet, and other fresh seafood dishes are all prepared with finesse. And do leave room for a piece of homemade pecan pie with bourbon caramel sauce. Dinner is accompanied by soft piano music; between courses, couples can share a waltz on the small dance floor. ⊠ *Atlantis, Paradise Island,* ☎ *242/ 363–3000 ext. 6508. AE, DC, MC, V. No lunch.*

$$$$ ✕ **Courtyard Terrace at Ocean Club.** An elite clientele congregates here
★   to indulge in refined dining under the stars, accompanied by the music of a calypso combo. With its Wedgwood china, Irish linen napery, lighted fountains, and adjacent sculpture gallery, this garden setting is one of the most romantic in the Bahamas. The carefully orchestrated menu emphasizes the lighter side of Continental cuisine, with a distinct island touch. Sample the pecan-crusted snapper, served with orange butter sauce and ginger coconut rice, or the crab-stuffed shrimp, succulent beef tenderloin, and unique lobster and chicken roulade. Alfresco dining begins at twilight, and if the weather doesn't cooperate, dinner is served indoors. Service is superb. ⊠ *Ocean Club Dr.,* ☎ *242/363– 2501. Reservations essential. Jacket required. AE, DC, MC, V. No lunch.*

Italian

$$$$ ✕ **Villa d'Este.** Noble Italian cuisine is served in an Italianate room with dark wood, upholstered chairs, statuary, and an impressive fresco on the ceiling. The antipasti display is effective in whetting the appetite for such dishes as fettuccine with lobster, veal Marsala, or grouper fillet with plum tomatoes, peppers, and capers. Another favorite is the veal garnished with lobster and served with two sauces (basil and sun-dried tomato). The dessert pastries are delectable. ⊠ *Atlantis, Paradise Island,* ☎ *242/363–3000. AE, DC, MC, V. No lunch.*

Seafood

$$ ✕ **Blue Lagoon Seafood Restaurant.** This eatery at Club Land'Or (☞ *below*) specializes, as the name implies, in fish dishes. The decor tends to the nautical, with hurricane lamps, brass rails, hanging nets, and other seafaring memorabilia. Choose from such simply prepared possibilities as broiled Bahamian lobster tail or grouper, or such fancy selections as almond-fried shrimp and stuffed grouper au gratin. Even landlubbers will find some pleasing menu choices. ⊠ *Club Land'Or,* ☎ *242/346–8200. AE, DC, MC, V.*

Cable Beach

Bahamian

$ ✕ **Cafe Johnny Canoe.** Johnny Canoe is said to be the name of the first black man to set foot on the island after slavery was abolished. His name is the supposed origin of "Junkanoo," and a mini-Junkanoo show winds among the tables of this crowded restaurant on weekend nights. With a spacious outdoor seating area and a menu of traditional Bahamian fare—cracked conch and grouper fillet—as well as burgers, chicken, ribs, and tropical drinks, this has become a favorite casual hangout for locals (and tourists who have discovered it). Conch salad—a dish reputed to enhance a man's virility—is a spicy way to start your meal, and the grilled seafood entrées are also excellent. ⊠ *Next to the Nassau Beach Hotel,* ☎ *242/327–3373. AE, MC, V.*

Italian

$$$$ ✕ **Sole Mare.** The elegant setting, excellent service, and expertly pre-
★ pared entrées make this one of the best Italian restaurants on the island. Start off with imported meats and cheeses from the antipasti cart. Pasta and fresh Pecorino Romano cheese grated table-side, can be ordered in half or full portions. Entrées include tender veal scallopini alla marsala, grilled tenderloin of beef with green peppercorn sauce, lobster *fra diavolo,* and several other delicious possibilities. The best way to end? Tiramisu and a cup of espresso. ⊠ *Nassau Marriott Resort & Crystal Palace Casino, Cable Beach,* ☎ *242/327–6200 ext. 6861. AE, MC, V. Closed Mon. No lunch.*

Seafood

$$$ ✕ **Dicky Mo's.** The nautical decor lets you know that seafood is the star of the show at this Bahamian restaurant. With fishnets, glass buoys, and portholes, the indoor dining area resembles a ship; you can also dine outside. Dishes include conch fritters and conch chowder, stone crab claws, broiled or panfried grouper, minced lobster (cooked with herbs and spices in a tomato sauce), and a lightly fried seafood platter. Friendly staff and the live Bahamian music (every night except Monday) create a festive atmosphere. ⊠ *Next to the Radisson Cable Beach Casino & Golf Resort,* ☎ *242/327–7854. AE, MC, V.*

Western New Providence and South Coast

Bahamian

$$ ✕ **Traveller's Rest.** Traveller's Rest, across the street from Compass Point, has the reputation of serving some of the best seafood on the island. This relaxed family restaurant with a great ocean view opened in the early 1970s and is a favorite among Bahamians. A fresh seafood din-

ner served just steps from the beach is a real treat—conch, grouper, and crawfish are the big hitters. Try their "smudder fish" for a taste of heaven. Dine outside or in, and toast the sunset with a fresh-fruit banana daiquiri—a specialty of the house. Take-out service is available if you're on the road—or prefer eating at the beach. ⊠ *W. Bay St., Gambier,* ☎ *242/327–7633. AE, MC, V.*

Contemporary

$$$ ✕ **Compass Point.** The ocean view here is unparalleled both day and
★   night—surf literally laps against the seawall that supports the outdoor dining terrace. The indoor section is a den of cracked tile and colorful wall decor, a look that's carried outside to the terrace and the small but comfy bar. The menu mixes Bahamian, Caribbean, and Californian cuisines. Choose from Bahamian-style sushi, crab cakes, gourmet pizzas, or fuller meals, which you can see prepared in the open kitchen. Is that a fashion model or recording star next to you? No matter, everyone's treated like a celebrity at this customer-friendly spot; it's refreshingly free of attitude considering how chic it is. ⊠ *Compass Point Resort, W. Bay St., Gambier,* ☎ *242/327–4500. AE, MC, V.*

LODGING

New Providence Island is fortunate to have an extensive range of hotels, from quaint, family-owned guest houses to the megaresorts at Cable Beach and on Paradise Island.

The homey, friendly little spots will probably not be on the beach—and you'll have to go out to eat unless you have access to a kitchen (though some inns will prepare meals for you on request). On the flip side, your stay is likely to be relaxing, low-key, and less removed from everyday Bahamian life. The plush resorts are big and beautiful, glittering and splashy, but they can be overwhelming. In any case, these big, top-dollar properties generally have more amenities than you could possibly make use of, a selection of dining options, and a full roster of sports and entertainment. The battle for the tourist dollar rages unceasingly between Cable Beach and Paradise Island, where hotels are continually being developed and refurbished. The competition, of course, encourages a wide variety of vacation packages, with enticements such as free snorkeling gear, free scuba lessons, and free admission to Las Vegas–style revues.

If you're trying to choose between Cable Beach and Paradise Island accommodations, the latter, in general, has a broader choice of beaches and a less flashy atmosphere (though some P.I. resorts really are just pure flash). There are also more quiet lanes for strolling. Cable Beach hotels, on the other hand, tend to be noisier and more active, and as a guest, you are more likely to stick to you own hotel and beach; when you leave, it's usually to explore and shop in downtown Nassau.

A tax ranging from 8% to 10%, representing resort and government levies, is added to your hotel bill. Some hotels also add a gratuity charge of between $2.50 and $4 per person, per day, for the housekeeping or pool staff.

The prices below are based on high season (winter) rates. Expect to pay between 15% and 30% less off-season in most resorts. In general, the best rates are available through packages, which almost every hotel offers. Call the hotel directly or ask your travel agent.

CATEGORY	COST*
$$$	over $155
$$	$95–$155
$	under $95

All prices are for a standard double room during high season, excluding tax and service charge.

Nassau

$$$ 🏨 **Graycliff.** A prosperous retired pirate named Captain John Howard Graysmith built this Georgian Colonial landmark overlooking Nassau and the harbor over 250 years ago. Over the years, Graycliff has welcomed into its chambers the Duke and Duchess of Windsor, press baron Lord Beaverbrook, Aristotle Onassis, the Beatles, and King Olaf of Norway. Today, the small elegant hotel receives annual accolades from travel magazines for service and ambience. A genteel feel pervades the huge guest suites, which are individually decorated with turn-of-the-century pieces and modern amenities; thick terry robes, updated bathrooms, and bottles of springwater enhance comfort. The hotel's restaurant (☞ Dining, *above*) is one of the premier places to dine on the island. Though the grounds are not extensive, they are enveloped in tropical foliage, with graceful palms, small statues of cherubs, and a circular fountain. ⊠ *Box N-10246, W. Hill St.,* ☎ *242/322–2796 or 800/633–7411,* FAX *242/326–6610. 9 rooms, 5 suites. Restaurant, bar, air-conditioning, pool, sauna, health club. AE, DC, MC, V. CP.*

$$$ 🏨 **Villas on Crystal Cay.** Privacy-seekers and quiet-lovers are sure to ★ appreciate these one-level luxury villas on the small island of Silver Cay, which is easily reached by cab from downtown Nassau but is far enough from the city to cultivate a secluded atmosphere. The units, each with private swimming pool, overlook the sea. The interiors are light and airy with wicker furniture, pastel color schemes, large couches, track lighting, and ceiling fans. Buses and ferries make frequent runs from Silver Cay to Cable Beach, Paradise Island, and downtown Nassau. ⊠ *Box N-7797, Silver Cay,* ☎ *242/328–1036 or 888/662–7728,* FAX *242/323–3202. 20 one-bedroom villas, 2 two-bedroom villas. Restaurant, air-conditioning, kitchenettes, minibars, private pools, in-room VCRs. AE, MC, V.*

$$–$$$ 🏨 **British Colonial Beach Resort.** Massive changes are in store for this venerable old hotel. The dowdy dowager's getting a facelift—and it's about time, too. If completed as scheduled for early 1999, you'll find a gleaming, luxurious winner re-occupying the historical wing and aimed at the upscale business market. The newer wing will be turned into a business center with office space, luxury condominiums, and a brand-new marina. Check with your travel agent, or call the hotel directly for the latest information. ⊠ *Box N-7181, 1 Bay St.,* ☎ *242/322–3301 or 800/528–1234,* FAX *242/322–2286. 219 rooms. 2 restaurants, lounge, air-conditioning, pool, 3 tennis courts, basketball, volleyball, beach, snorkeling, windsurfing, boating, fishing. AE, D, DC, MC, V.*

$$ 🏨 **Buena Vista Hotel.** Surrounded by a beautiful 3-acre garden, this 19th-century plantation house is a half mile from downtown Nassau. The two-story building is better known for its restaurant (☞ Dining, *above*) but the rooms are spacious, individually decorated, and surprisingly affordable for such restrained elegance. Climb the aqua-hued staircase from the low-key, tasteful lobby, which is filled with tropical flowers. An antiques-filled hallway leads to the rooms, which are all but invisible to the restaurant guests. The public beach is just a 10-minute walk away. ⊠ *Box N-564, Delancy St.,* ☎ *242/322–2811,* FAX *242/322–2286. 5 rooms. Restaurant, bar, air-conditioning. AE, DC, MC, V.*

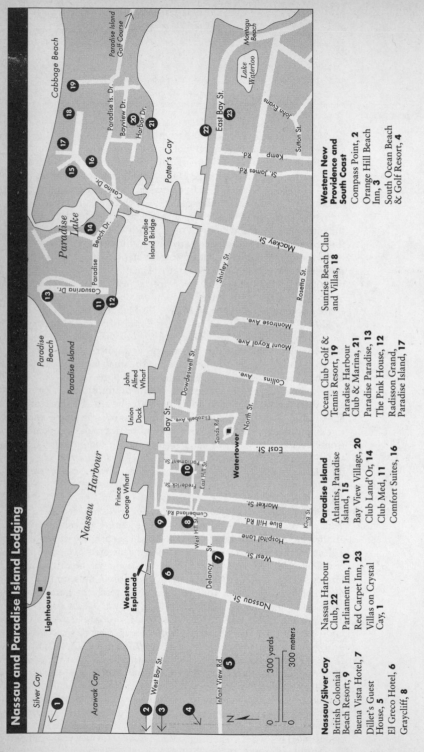

$$ ⊞ **Parliament Inn.** This guest house has a crisp look aimed at an up-scale business crowd that prefers the intimacy of a small inn. Island-style rooms come with computer and modem hookups, satellite television, and coffeemakers. The courtyard eatery, Cafe Kokomo (☞ Dining, *above*), is a great place to end a long business day, especially with one of bartender Demrist's daiquiris. She's well-known as the world's best concocter of these rum-laced treats. ⊠ *Parliament St.,* ☎ *242/322–2836,* FAX *242/326–7196. 10 rooms. Restaurant, bar, air-conditioning, in-room modem lines, laundry service, meeting room. AE, MC, V.*

$ ⊞ **Dillet's Guest House.** A model of Bahamian charm and friendliness,
★ this family-run guest house is operated out of the 60-year-old home in which the proprietress grew up. You know you're in for something special the minute you enter the lounge—the arched entry, ceiling fans, wicker furniture, caged birds, and massive flower arrangements exude Old Nassau charm. The large guest rooms are named after island fruits and are indicated by hand-painted pieces of driftwood on the doors, typical of the attention paid to detail and the profusion of Bahamian art throughout the house. Though unfancy, the place is spotlessly clean and furnished with true island flair. Five of the rooms have kitchenettes; guests in the other rooms are free to use the house's kitchen. The only regularly scheduled meal is a large Continental breakfast, but the staff will prepare others on request. The location near Ardastra Gardens and Conservation Centre (☞ Sightseeing, *above*) isn't for those who want to be at the center of the action—or on a long stretch of beach. You'll probably need a car, though it's possible to do without. ⊠ *Box N-204, Dunmore Ave. and Strachan St.,* ☎ *242/325–1133 or 800/742–4276,* FAX *242/325–7183. 7 rooms. Air-conditioning, kitchenettes, bicycles, parking. MC, V. CP, MAP.*

$ ⊞ **El Greco Hotel.** Pleasant Greek owners create an ambience here more in keeping with a cozy guest house than a hotel. While not fancy, large rooms, decorated in soothing, old-fashioned earth tones, surround a central courtyard and pool. The resulting atmosphere is quiet and appeals primarily to a European crowd. The El Greco is minutes from the center of town and is across the street from the public Western Esplanade beach. ⊠ *Box N-4187, W. Bay St.,* ☎ *242/325–1121. 26 rooms. Restaurant, air-conditioning, pool, baby-sitting. AE, MC, V.*

$ ⊞ **Nassau Harbour Club.** Long known for its restaurant, which feeds hungry mariners at all hours, this establishment is often mistakenly over-looked as a place to sleep. The Harbour Club is popular with international sailing aficionados and the hordes of students on spring break who make it their annual base. Though a convenient place to stay—it's on the main road into town—this is not a good choice for peace and quiet. Locals and tourists gather at the downstairs 'Cuda Bay bar (☞ Nightlife, *below*) to watch football and other sports or sit outside on the deck overlooking the harbor. On the hotel's main floor, up a spiral wooden staircase from the bar, is Passin' Jack's restaurant (it was closed for renovations in 1998, so call ahead to make sure it's reopened). ⊠ *Box SS-5755, E. Bay St.,* ☎ *242/393–0771,* FAX *242/393–5393. 44 rooms, 16 2-bedroom suites. Restaurant, bar, air-conditioning, pool, dock. AE, D, MC, V.*

$ ⊞ **Red Carpet Inn.** Passing the entrance to this hotel on busy East Bay Street (the white beaches of Paradise Island are a quick taxi ride away), you'd never know this haven of silence and relaxation existed. Two things are stressed here, cleanliness and quiet, which makes it one of the few area hotels in its price category not geared towards spring break-ers. The owners live on premises, which explains the devotion to spot-lessness and the agreeable atmosphere, and the hotel is far enough off the beaten path to provide a sense of island solitude. Rooms are simple; a few have kitchenettes with a microwave or stove and limited flatware. The Barn Bar and Restaurant serves Bahamian and American fare daily at breakfast and dinner, while the poolside El Rancho Restaurant and Bar serves barbecue with a distinctly Bahamian flavor. ⊠ *Box SS-6233, E. Bay St.,* ☎ *242/393–7981,* FAX *242/393–9055. 40 rooms. 2 restaurants, 2 bars, air-conditioning, kitchenettes, pool. AE, MC, V.*

Paradise Island

$$$ ★ 🏨 **Atlantis, Paradise Island.** Love it or hate it (and the overwhelming majority fit into the first category), the one thing you can't do is ignore it. The overriding theme here is water—for swimming, snorkeling, and observing marine life, as well as for mood and effect in lagoons, caves, waterfalls, a walk-through aquarium, and a variety of water rides. The Atlantis earned an immediate high profile upon opening in 1994, and at press time was undergoing major expansion slated for completion by the end of 1998. The renovation will more than double the number of rooms and add a slew of new attractions, including the largest casino in this part of the world, several new restaurants, and "The Dig," a re-creation of the lost island after which the resort is named. Most guest rooms in the original resort are in either the Coral Towers or the Beach Tower. The Reef Club is a VIP section of 92 luxurious rooms with concierge service. Sixty-four more one-bedroom suites are in four private low-rise villas facing the pool area. The twin towers of "The Palace," a part of the expansion, will house over 1,200 additional lodgings. A dine-around meal plan allows guests to eat breakfast and dinner at any of the resort's restaurants. The expansion will add five restaurants and more than a dozen bars. Numerous sporting activities are available, and there is plenty of nightlife on the premises. ⊠ *Casino Dr. (Box N-4777, Nassau),* ☎ *242/363–3000 or 800/321–3000,* FAX *242/363–3524. 1,083 rooms, 64 suites (1,041 rooms, 167 suites in Palace expansion). 12 restaurants, 12 bars, air-conditioning, 4 pools, beauty salon, 18-hole golf course, 9 tennis courts, health club, jogging, beach, snorkeling, windsurfing, boating, shops, casino, nightclub, baby-sitting, children's programs, travel services, car rental. AE, DC, MC, V. MAP, FAP.*

$$$ 🏨 **Bay View Village.** At this 4-acre condominium resort, you'll typically find guests socializing around the three pools (two for general use, one reserved for the villas). There's no restaurant—only a poolside snack bar and a minimarket (late new arrivals will be pleasantly surprised to find breakfast packages of eggs, coffee, jam, and other supplies awaiting them). The atmosphere is intimate and the lush tropical landscaping includes several varieties of hibiscus and bougainvillea. Choose among one- and two-bedroom apartments and two- and three-bedroom villas, all of which are spacious, clean, comfortable, and decorated in bright island style. Equipped with satellite TV, hair dryers, and a full kitchen with a microwave, all rooms have private balconies or garden terraces; penthouse apartments have roof gardens and a harbor view. Cabbage Beach is a 10-minute walk away. ⊠ *Bay View Dr. (Box SS-6308, Nassau),* ☎ *242/363–2555 or 800/757–1357,* FAX *242/363–2370. 30 units and villas. Bar, snack bar, air-conditioning, fans, kitchenettes, 3 pools, tennis court, baby-sitting, coin laundry. AE, MC, V.*

$$$ 🏨 **Club Land'Or.** Translating to "land of gold," this friendly time-share hotel has one-bedroom villas with full kitchens, bathrooms, living rooms, and patios or balconies that overlook the lagoon, the gardens, or the pool. The units are billed to accommodate four people, but they seem better suited to couples. The Blue Lagoon Seafood Restaurant is a favorite for locals and guests, even those staying at nearby Atlantis, Paradise Island. Many activities are planned throughout the week and guests here also have use of the Atlantis' facilities. ⊠ *Par-*

adise Beach Dr. (Box SS-6429, Nassau), ☎ *242/363–2400 or 800/446–3850,* FAX *242/363-3403. 72 suites. Restaurant, 2 bars, air-conditioning, pool, bicycles, baby-sitting, laundry service, activities desk. AE, DC, MC, V. FAP.*

$$$ **Club Med.** The originators of the all-inclusive concept have created another of their prototypical resorts on this island with myriad sporting options and a stunning setting. The 21-acre compound has a verdant look, with meandering paths bordered by swaying casuarina trees and graceful palms, a huge saltwater swimming pool set within a Gothic-style garden, and long stretches of green lawn. Forget Club Med's swinging singles reputation; guests are more likely to be parents traveling without their kids (children under 12 are not allowed), honeymooners, and other romantic sorts. The closely guarded gate ensures privacy and security but tends to keep the guests in a Frenchified world far removed from Bahamian culture and its people. ⊠ *Casuarina Dr. (Box N-7137, Nassau),* ☎ *242/363–2640 or 800/258–2633,* FAX *242/363–3496. 312 rooms. 3 restaurants, 2 bars, air-conditioning, 2 saltwater pools, 19 tennis courts, beach, nightclub. AE, MC, V. All-inclusive.*

$$$ **Comfort Suites.** This three-story pink-and-white hotel caters to honeymooners and others who seek a luxury at competitive rates. The cozy junior suites have sitting areas with sofa beds and are decorated in pinks, blues, and whites, with ceiling fans and wildlife prints. All units have coffeemakers, hair dryers, and in-room safes. Some suites also have refrigerators and microwaves. Guests can use pool and beach facilities, a health spa, tennis courts, and restaurant signing privileges at Atlantis, Paradise Island, across the street; kids can also enroll at Camp Paradise at Atlantis. There's also free Continental breakfast, a swim-up bar, and poolside lunch for those who want to stay amid the nicely landscaped grounds. Three-mi-long Cabbage Beach is just a hop, skip, and jump away. ⊠ *Casino Dr. (Box SS-6202, Nassau),* ☎ *242/363–3680 or 800/228–5150,* FAX *242/363–2588. 222 junior suites. Restaurant, air-conditioning, minibars, baby-sitting. AE, D, DC, MC, V. CP.*

$$$ **Ocean Club Golf & Tennis Resort.** Once the private hideaway of A&P
★   heir Huntington Hartford, and currently the secluded Bahamian getaway of the rich and famous, this resort provides the most understated elegance you'll find on Paradise Island. The Ocean Club resembles an exclusive country club, with manicured grounds, tennis courts, and a crystal-clear pool. A quiet, tasteful mood is apparent in the antiques-filled lounge, in the lovely courtyard with fountains, and in the 35-acre terraced Versailles Gardens and 14th-century French Cloister. The spacious and stylishly decorated rooms have private verandas, high ceilings, and a color scheme of soft green, peach, and gold. Each room is furnished with carved or hand-stenciled furniture, as well as a 27-inch TV. Sumptuous marble bathrooms have double sinks, bidets, irons and ironing boards, and terry towels and robes. Both rooms and verandas have ceiling fans. Guests lounging on the magnificent ocean beach are provided with small flags alongside their chaise lounges to signal watchful waiters that they would like a drink or a snack. Lunch is served at the Clubhouse and the Beach Bar and Grill. The open-air Courtyard Terrace (☞ Dining, *above*) is a particularly romantic dining spot in the evening, and the indoor restaurant is equally charming. ⊠ *Ocean Club Dr. (Box N 4777, Nassau),* ☎ *242/363–2501 or 800/321–3000,* FAX *242/363–2424. 49 rooms, 5 villas, and 4 suites. 3 restaurants, 3 bars, air-conditioning, pool, 18-hole golf course, 9 tennis courts, beach, snorkeling, windsurfing, boating, baby-sitting, laundry service. AE, DC, MC, V. MAP.*

$$$ **Radisson Grand, Paradise Island.** Having undergone a floor-by-floor overhaul in 1998, this hotel now has an airy and more appealing lobby, new plants in the entrance, and better furniture and fixtures in

guest rooms. Although still not as grand (or, at least, as showy) as the Atlantis, Paradise Island next door, the Radisson has easy access to its neighbor's casino as well as to a lovely stretch of beach. Near the Paradise Island bridge, the hotel is only about a mile from the restaurants and shops of Nassau proper. Every room overlooks the water from a small triangular balcony. Big spenders may opt for the enormous penthouse, with stained-glass windows, a wraparound terrace, two Jacuzzis, and a price tag of $5,000 per night. In summer and during the Easter and Christmas holidays, the Radisson's activity center organizes special children's events. The activities desk and water-sports center are among the busiest in town. ⊠ *Casino Dr. (Box SS-6307, Nassau),* ☎ *242/363–3500 or 800/333–3333,* ℻ *242/363–3193. 360 rooms. 4 restaurants, 3 bars, lounge, air-conditioning, minibars, pool, 4 tennis courts, beach, bicycles, nightclub, baby-sitting, meeting rooms, travel services. AE, DC, MC, V. MAP.*

$$$ ☆ **Sunrise Beach Club and Villas.** You'll feel like you're entering your own tropical wonderland when you arrive at this low-rise family resort, lushly landscaped with crotons, coconut palms, fragrant bougainvillea, and colorful hibiscus. The gardeners responsible for the glorious flora are co-owners Heinrich Kloihofer and his son, Heinz-Robert, who is also the Austrian consul to the Bahamas. Two pools sustain the ambience with statuary and tropical plantings, and the beach is accessible via a long flight of wooden stairs built right into the cliff. Paths wind through the floral arcadia, past trickling fountains, archways, and terra cotta tiles with color insets. It's no wonder the clientele, which is mostly European, is lured back year after year. Lodgings are an eclectic architectural mix— take your pick from one-bedroom townhouses with spiral staircases that lead to an upstairs bedroom; two-bedroom apartments; or three-bedroom villas. All have fully equipped kitchens or kitchenettes, king-size beds with floor-to-ceiling mirrored headboards, and a patios. On arrival, you'll find complimentary breakfast groceries in the refrigerator; shuttles can get you to food stores for groceries. ⊠ *Casino Dr. (Box SS-6519, Nassau),* ☎ *242/363–2234 or 800/451–6078,* ℻ *242/363–2308. 35 1-, 2-, and 3-bedroom units. Bar, snack bar, air-conditioning, fans, kitchenettes, 2 pools, baby-sitting, laundry service. AE, D, DC, MC, V.*

$$–$$$ ☆ **Paradise Harbour Club & Marina.** With a marina and an enviable location, this collection of oversized, comfortable apartments is a great choice for those who want the freedom of a private residence with the facilities of a large resort. A water taxi shuttles guests to the Straw Market across the harbor, and the club offers weekly trips to food stores. Full kitchens (complete with refrigerator, minibar, and dishwasher) lend a homey feeling to these somewhat characterless but very cushy lodgings. Commodious closet and sink space are among the extras. If you prefer a view, opt for the top-floor digs. Looking out over the harbor, you'll appreciate the waterside location. Construction on residential units does cut into the peace a bit, so ask about the progress of that project when booking. ⊠ *Harbour Dr., (Box SS-5804, Nassau),* ☎ *242/ 363–2992 or 800/742–4276 reservation service,* ℻ *242/363–2840. 22 units. Restaurant, bar, air-conditioning, kitchenettes, pool, hot tub, golf, tennis, boating, bicycles. AE, MC, V.*

$$ ☆ **Paradise Paradise.** Sun International's resort for the budget-minded fronts Paradise Beach and is a haven for those devoted to water and land sports. The busy (and complimentary) program includes everything from kayaking to volleyball—if that's not enough, consider the free use of the waterscape facilities at Atlantis, Paradise Island. The rooms, while a little worn and not fancy, are clean, and have wicker furniture and large potted plants; half have ocean views. There are also hammocks, ideal if you're worn out by all the activity—or for the occasional sedentary type who stumbles into Paradise Paradise, drawn by the beachside setting, low prices (for the Island, anyway), and friendly staff. ✉ *Casuarina Dr., (Box SS-6259, Nassau),* ☎ *242/363–3000 or 800/321–3000,* ☒ *242/363–2540. 100 rooms. 10 restaurants, 10 bars, air-conditioning, ping-pong, volleyball, kayaking, sailing, snorkeling, waterskiing, windsurfing, bicycling. AE, DC, MC, V. MAP.*

$$ 🏨 **The Pink House.** True to its colorful name, this charming pink guest house appears through a thicket of bamboo and palm trees. The Pink House, a throwback to colonial times, sits placidly on the grounds of Club Med but occupies an entirely different world. The two places have nothing to do with each other—Club Med just happens to own the land on which the Pink House stands. Pink House guests don't have special privileges for Club Med facilities, but must sign up and pay like other Club Med patrons. But, to many, this is the beauty of the place. You can use Club Med's sporting facilities, yet experience the personal attention of Pink House owner Minnie Wynn; she makes you feel like a resident, or a treasured family member. Rooms have a thrown-together, slightly worn look. However, the huge decks off a couple of the rooms more than compensate for any shabbiness. You can have breakfast on the front porch, shaded by huge trees and cool breezes, or lounge in the living room among eclectic furnishings, including a faux-marble fireplace, a Piedmontese painted chest from the mid-18th century, an ornate candelabra, and seating that's seen better days. Not for those craving luxury or anonymity, but if you're looking to sample old-time Nassau hospitality, you won't go wrong here. ✉ *Casuarina Dr. (Box SS-19157, Nassau),* ☎ *242/363–3363,* ☒ *242/377–3383. 4 rooms. Air-conditioning, beach. CP.*

Cable Beach

$$$ 🏨 **Nassau Beach Hotel.** Built in the 1940s, this venerable Cable Beach mainstay still exudes a cheerful, gracious air. Since being taken over in 1997 by the owners of the adjacent Nassau Marriott Resort & Crystal Palace Casino, the hotel has begun a thorough upgrade, with rooms receiving an overhaul and hallways emerging in sparkling condition. All rooms have balconies, but views vary: Some face the half-mile strip of sandy beach, and others overlook neighboring buildings. Mahogany furniture and bedspreads in deep colors give rooms an elegant look, particularly in the Club Premiere section, furnished with carved wooden chairs, armoires, and antique-style sconces. In case renovations aren't completed by fall 1998, be sure to ask for a newly redone room. Guests have use of all nonmotorized water sports equipment and tennis clinics are available. The hotel has indoor and outdoor restaurants on site, as well as a shopping arcade. The Crystal Palace Casino is next door, and the Cable Beach Golf Club is across the street. ✉ *W. Bay St. (Box N-7756, Nassau),* ☎ *242/327–7711 or 888/627–7282,* ☒ *242/327–7615. 411 rooms. 7 restaurants, 3 bars, air-conditioning, pool, 6 tennis courts, exercise room, snorkeling, windsurfing, boating, baby-sitting. AE, DC, MC, V. EP, MAP, FAP, all-inclusive.*

$$$ 🏨 **Nassau Marriott Resort & Crystal Palace Casino.** As soon as you see this hotel, the reason behind the name becomes, if you'll pardon the expression, crystal clear. The large structure, with memorable glistening windows, is unlike any other on the island. By night its five towers are illuminated, and each floor is lighted with a different color, making the entire hotel look like a giant rainbow reflecting off the ocean. The interior is equally glitzy, and a comprehensive sign system helps you to find your way around the massive resort. Eighty percent of the rooms overlook the water, and corner suites have as great as 180° ocean views. Guest rooms are furnished in light oak, with deep green and

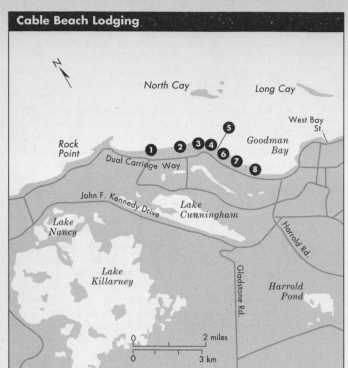

Cable Beach Lodging

white carpets, peach and tan floral comforters, and local art hanging on the walls. The Crystal Club, consisting of three concierge floors at the top of the Casino Tower, houses 30 spectacularly decorated supersuites—Galactica, Casablanca, Santa Fe, Kyoto, and others—available at spectacular rates ($550–$2,000 per night). The resort has its own palm-fringed beach and lagoon for swimming, sunbathing, and water sports. The health club has top-notch equipment and daily aerobics classes, youngsters are well taken care of in the Marriotter Kids Klub program, and the 35,000-sq-ft Crystal Palace Casino provides further adult diversion. There is also a 20-shop mall on site. ✉ *W. Bay St. (Box N-8306, Nassau),* ☎ *242/327–6200 or 800/222–7466,* ⅎ *242/327–6308. 870 rooms, 100 suites, 30 supersuites. 12 restaurants, 5 bars, air-conditioning, pool, 18 tennis courts, beach, dive shop, snorkeling, water slide, windsurfing, boating, shops, recreation room, theater, baby-sitting, children's programs, meeting rooms. AE, DC, MC, V. CP, MAP, FAP.*

$$$ 🏨 **Radisson Cable Beach Casino & Golf Resort.** This high-rise prop-
★ erty is ideal for those who want to be smack in the middle of Cable Beach action. Connected by a shopping arcade to Crystal Palace Casino, the hotel fairly buzzes with activity. In the lobby lounge there's usually live music or a happy hour in progress. Daytime options include dance lessons by the pool, beach volleyball, free scuba lessons, and plenty of activities for kids. Guests get special rates at the hotel's challenging 18-hole Cable Beach Golf Club. At night, choices range from a slew of dining possibilities to beach parties, revues and—of course—gambling at the adjoining casino. All rooms have balconies and face either the beach and pool or gardens. A recent overhaul resulted in renovated guest rooms, upgraded tropical landscaping, lagoons around the swimming pools, and much-improved dining facilities, making this one of the top resorts in the area. The resort offers a plan

that includes meals, beverages, activities, greens fees, tips, and taxes. ⊠ *W. Bay St. (Box N-4914, Nassau),* ☎ *242/327–6000 or 800/333–3333,* FAX *242/327–6987. 700 rooms. 6 restaurants, 3 bars, air-conditioning, pool, 18-hole golf course, 18 tennis courts, health club, racquetball, squash, beach, snorkeling, boating, bicycles, shops, babysitting, children's programs, meeting rooms. AE, DC, MC, V. EP, all-inclusive.*

$$$ ⊞ **Sandals Royal Bahamian Resort & Spa.** This all-inclusive luxury resort (for couples only) is spread over 13 beautifully landscaped acres on Cable Beach. Formerly Le Meridien Royal Bahamian, this regal spread centers around a pink-and-white Georgian-style manor with stately columns and Romanesque statues. It is the chain's first entry in its "Royal" collection of resorts, which present an elegant environment and spa facilities. Accommodations are in posh rooms with views of the ocean, garden, or pool. Each is opulently furnished with king-size, custom-crafted mahogany four-poster beds, separate sitting rooms, marble baths, and stocked bars. In addition to a "Wellness Clinic," the spa offers treatments such as massage for two—you and your partner can even learn to massage each other. There's a state-of-the-art fitness club, and multilingual concierge service assists foreign guests. You can dine in any of four gourmet restaurants, each of which offers spa cuisine. Nightly entertainment takes place in the resort's amphitheater. An expansion (which may be finished by 1999) will add 210 rooms, two restaurants (one Japanese and one Italian), a 12,000-sq-ft pool. ⊠ *W. Bay St. (Box CB 15005, Nassau),* ☎ *242/327–6400 or 800/726–3257,* FAX *242/327–1894. 196 rooms. 2 bars, pool, air-conditioning, 2 tennis courts, basketball, croquet, exercise room, volleyball, beach, dive shop, snorkeling, windsurfing, boating, waterskiing, dance club, recreation room, meeting rooms. AE, MC, V. All-inclusive.*

$$ ⊞ **Breezes Bahamas.** Right on Cable Beach, this SuperClubs property ★ offers couples and singles (guests must be age 17 or older) a moderately priced package that includes lodging, entertainment, all meals (even snacks) and unlimited beverages, a host of land and water sports, airport transfers, and taxes. This is not a place for the indolent, as a busy daily schedule, from trapeze and beach volleyball to body painting and a unique jousting game called "Off With Their Heads" keep guests hopping morning, noon, and night. If this is not enough for you, take advantage of the pool and Ping-Pong tables, fitness center, nightly entertainment, five freshwater pools (or, for the truly pampered, deck chairs planted right in a misting pool), and swim-up bar. The open-air lobby is bright and cheery, with a huge fish chandelier and multicolored tile floor. But it's not nearly as bright as the perky staff, who respond unflappably and cheerfully to any demands. And this in a place where tipping is not allowed! Large, modern rooms are pleasant but ordinary, and food is available in several locales 24 hours a day. Evening activities include local musical entertainment, beach parties, theme nights, toga parties, karaoke, pajama parties, dance contests, and cabaret. Guests must wear an identification wristband throughout their stay. ⊠ *W. Bay St. (Box CB-13049, Nassau),* ☎ *242/327–5356 or 800/859–7873,* FAX *242/327–5155. 400 rooms. 3 restaurants, 4 bars, snack bar, air-conditioning, 5 pools, 3 tennis courts, basketball, health club, jogging, volleyball, beach, windsurfing, boating, bicycles, billiards, dance club. AE, MC, V. All-inclusive.*

$$ ⊞ **Casuarinas of Cable Beach.** In 1977, Eleutheran native Nettica Symonette bought 1½ acres of land on the western edge of Cable Beach. This Bahamian entrepreneur parlayed her original investment into a seven-building hotel-restaurant—more rustic than most of the resorts in the area—which she named after the trees dotting the property. Lodgings vary wildly and are spread across both sides of the busy

road; although many could use an updating, it's the personalized attention and family atmosphere—enhanced by the fact that five of Nettie's daughters work here—that have built a loyal patronage over the years. The reasonable prices make this a spot for those more interested in savings and a laid-back Out Islands feel than luxury and amenities. There's a deck overlooking the beach and—depending on the tides—a tiny strip of sand beach. One of Nettie's sons redesigned Albion's restaurant with game tables, and an intimate, homey feel. A free casino shuttle runs every hour from 10 AM to 2 AM, and a public bus stop is located outside the front door. ⊠ *W. Bay St. (Box N-4016, Nassau),* ☎ *242/327–7921 or 800/327–3012. 78 rooms, some with kitchens. 2 restaurants, 2 bars, lounge, air-conditioning, 2 pools, tennis court, beach, baby-sitting. AE, D, DC, MC, V. EP, MAP.*

$$ 🏨 **Guanahani Village.** The substantial, well-furnished accommodations at this time-share resort are perfect for young families or groups of friends traveling together. Stucco units are spread across landscaped grounds; inside, the tiled three-bedroom luxury villas, oceanfront or gardenside, sleep six comfortably, up to eight using roll-aways. Each unit has oversize rooms filled with stylish glass and wicker furniture, a delightful secluded patio, a fully equipped kitchen, cable television, washers and dryers, and dishwashers. Room telephones connect through the hotel switchboard. The pool overlooks the ocean, though beaches are a bit of a walk. A snack bar serves chicken wings, conch fritters, and other light fare as well as a wide selection of tropical drinks, but there's no full restaurant on site. ⊠ *W. Bay St. (Box N CB-10977, Nassau),* ☎ *242/327–5193,* FAX *242/327–5059. 35 units. Snack bar, air-conditioning, kitchenettes, pool. MC, V.*

$$ 🏨 **West Wind II.** Privacy is the lure of these cozy time-share villas on the west end of Cable Beach, 6 mi from downtown. Two-bedroom, two-bath condominiums have wicker furniture, ceiling fans and air-conditioning, fully stocked kitchens, and comfortable (though not plush) living rooms with telephones and TVs. Balconies or patios overlook the gardens or the pools. The reasonable prices and relaxed atmosphere make it wonderful for families or groups on a budget, and the pleasant, quiet location—off the road amid manicured lawns and pruned gardens—gives children the freedom to play outdoors. The spectacular sea view somewhat compensates for the tiny and very windy beach. Lunch is the only meal served on premises, but a grocery store and myriad restaurants are nearby on the Cable Beach strip. A bus stop and taxi stand are right outside. A barbecue is held on Sundays, and the helpful staff can arrange excursions and other activities. ⊠ *W. Bay St. (Box N-10481, Nassau),* ☎ *242/327–7211 or 242/327–7019,* FAX *242/327–7251. 54 villas. Snack bar, air-conditioning, 2 pools, 2 tennis courts, beach, snorkeling, boating, baby-sitting, laundry service, travel services. MC, V.*

Western New Providence and South Coast

$$$ 🏨 **Compass Point.** Hotelier and recording-studio mogul Chris Blackwell has scored a hit with this cheerful beachfront property 20 minutes west of downtown Nassau. To call the accommodations colorful is an understatement: Designer Barbara Hulanicki used brilliant Junkanoo colors to transform the clapboards and architectural details of this tiny town of handcrafted wooden bungalows into a feast for the eyes. Since 1995, the hotel has attracted a trendy crowd of celebrities and those in search of the hippest that New Providence has to offer. But the staff, far from treating mere mortals with the haughtiness you might fear from such a modish spot, is as accommodating as you're likely to find—down to earth, welcoming, and pleasant. The seven one-

and two-bedroom cottages, four one-bedroom huts, and five air-conditioned cabanas are steps from sand and surf and connected by winding pathways. Some structures are duplexes on stilts, some are octagonal, some immediately face the ocean with decks where you can catch the morning sun or an evening breeze. All rooms have wood walls and furnishings covered in handmade batik, king- or queen-size beds, a personal sundeck, coffeemaker, fax machine, a range of bathroom amenities, and CD player with the stunning selection of CDs one should expect of a Blackwell property. Compass Point has its own stretch of sand, but stunning Love Beach—which is great for snorkelers—is right next door. ⊠ *W. Bay St., Gambier (Box CB-13842, Nassau)*, ☏ *242/327–4500 or 800/688–7678*, 𝖥𝖠𝖷 *242/327–3299. 21 rooms, 3-bedroom penthouse. Restaurant, bar, fans, kitchenettes, in-room VCRs, pool, tennis court, beach, dive shop, jet skiing, snorkeling, waterskiing, deep-sea fishing. AE, MC, V.*

$$$ 🏨 **South Ocean Golf & Beach Resort.** In a style reminiscent of a colo-
★ nial plantation, the main building of this most serene and secluded of New Providence getaways (40 minutes southwest of town), is dressed with white columns and ornate balconies. The casual, open-air-feeling interior is graced with wicker chairs, bright tropical prints, and plenty of mahogany. Guest rooms are cheerfully decorated with wicker valances and chairs, colorful bedspreads and paintings, and tile floors. Each unit has a patio that opens onto the gardens or a balcony that overlooks the pool. The finest accommodations are across the road on either side of the beach club. Called Great Houses (with such flowery appellations as Frangipani, Hibiscus, and Oleander), these oceanfront luxury rooms are filled with Queen Anne–style chairs, four-poster beds covered with cheerful country French bedspreads, bleached Mediterranean-tile floors, whirlpool baths, and three sets of fully screened mahogany doors that open onto a private beachfront patio or balcony. Pink jitneys drive you to the 18-hole PGA-rated golf course (the most challenging on the island), the four tennis courts (two lighted for night play), the beach club, and Stuart Cove's Dive South Ocean facility. You can take advantage of free tennis and golf clinics, an array of water sports activities, and dancing at the Flamingo Club; there is a nightly one-man calypso band. Public bus service runs into town for $1.75 round-trip, and another bus to Paradise Island costs $10 round-trip. ⊠ *Box N-8191, Nassau*, ☏ *242/362–4391 or 800/228–9898. 268 rooms. 2 restaurants, 3 bars, snack bar, air-conditioning, 2 pools, 18-hole golf course, 4 tennis courts, beach, dive shop, snorkeling, boating, baby-sitting, children's programs. AE, DC, MC, V. FAP.*

$ 🏨 **Orange Hill Beach Inn.** If you prefer down-home coziness over slick glamour, then this charming inn—laughingly dubbed "Fawlty Towers Nassau" by owner Danny and Judy Lowe—on the site of a former orange plantation is the place to stay. The Lowes make sure that guests are treated like family members, and the homey feel extends to the comfortably eclectic living room (equipped with stereo, television, VCR, video library, and jigsaw puzzles) and the daytime honor bar. Orange Hill has built a reputation as an inexpensive alternative for honeymooners and scuba divers. It's a half-hour drive from town and 15 minutes from the casino, but there are daily trips to the nearby grocery store, from which you can catch a jitney to the center of Cable Beach or downtown. A pleasant roadside beach is only 300 ft from the inn, which is perched on a hilltop overlooking the ocean. Rooms and apartments vary considerably in size; all have either a balcony or a patio with a view of the pool, ocean, or tropical gardens, and some have a kitchenette. The sea-themed dining room, where breakfast and dinner are served, has hanging multicolored fish, buoys, and nets; the international menu changes daily. None of the rooms has a phone, but guests are welcome to use one of several lines on the premises. ⊠ *Box N-8583, Nassau,* ☎ *242/327–7157,* FAX *242/327–5186. 32 rooms. Restaurant, bar, air-conditioning, pool. AE, MC, V. EP, MAP.*

NIGHTLIFE AND THE ARTS

The Arts

Dundas Center (☎ 242/393–3728) on Mackey Street, is Nassau's performing arts theater. Plays, musicals, ballets, and performances by local and out-of-town artists are staged throughout the year.

Casinos

Leave your black tie at home, for these are hardly intimate European gaming houses, and attire reflects the casual atmosphere. You have to be at least 21 years old to gamble; Bahamians and permanent residents are not permitted to indulge.

Crystal Palace Casino (⊠ Nassau Marriott Resort, Cable Beach, ☎ 242/327–6200) has 850 slot machines, craps, baccarat, blackjack, roulette, Big Six, and face-up 21. There's a Sports Book facility for sports betting, equipped with one 70-inch and eight 35-inch television screens, which air live sporting events. Both VIPs and low-limit bettors have their own areas. Casino gaming lessons are available for beginners. The casino is open from 10 AM to 4 AM weekdays, 24 hours on weekends; slots are open 24 hours daily.

Paradise Island Casino (⊠ Atlantis, Paradise Island, ☎ 242/363–3000) is a 30,000-sq-ft, world-class casino with more than 800 slots, as well as baccarat, blackjack, roulette, and craps tables. The Salon Privé is reserved for high-stakes players. Slot tournaments and complimentary gaming lessons are available daily. Tables are open from 10 AM to 4 AM daily, slots, 24 hours. Expansion plans (scheduled for completion in late 1998) include 50,000 sq ft of casino space incorporating views, sounds, and light of the Bahamas' tropical environment. The new casino is slated to have more than 1,100 slots and 70 gaming tables.

Coffeehouses

Most coffeehouses are open late into the evening, but note that a few listed below close at about 6 PM.

Caffè Caribe. This tiny spot in the Logos Bookstore has a simple, modern look with high tables and stools. Salads, quiches, and sandwiches supplement the coffee selection; there's a long list of flavors, perfect if you like your espresso with a fruity or nutty touch. It closes at 6 PM. ⊠ *Harbour Bay Shopping Centre,* ☎ *242/394–7040. Closed Sun.*

Cappuccino Café and Specialty Shop. Though it's a bit out of the way, and only open until 6:30 PM, this little upscale deli and coffeehouse has a bright, appealing look, with lots of greenery. There's an extensive selection of gourmet foods as well as coffeehouse standards. ⊠ *Royal Palm Mall, Mackey St.,* ☎ *242/394–6332. Closed Sun.*

Caripelago Bean and Berry Restaurant. You can sit at cracked-tile tables among bright paintings and soft island music at this cozy Cable Beach find, or on the small front porch. There's a wide selection of Bahamian-themed teas, from Junkanoo Jingle to Moonlight Over Nassau, as well as coffee drinks, pastries, and sandwiches. ⊠ *W. Bay St., across from Sandals Hotel,* ☎ *242/327–4750.*

Java Isle. In a shopping center just west of downtown Nassau, Java Isle actively promotes cultural affairs as well as caffeine consumption. Service can be a bit lackadaisical, but it's a pleasant spot nonetheless. ⊠ *W. Bay St., across from Saunders Beach,* ☎ *242/325–5271. Closed Sun.*

Jitters Cafe. This is definitely among the most comfortable places in town to relax over a magazine with a coffee drink or light meal. Sooner or later, most of Nassau's young and artsy types pass through; you'll also spot many chic international patrons. ⊠ *Bay St., two doors from Charlotte St.,* ☎ *242/356–9381. Closed Sun. No dinner Mon.–Wed.*

Le Bistro. A two-story European-style bistro in the heart of downtown Nassau, Le Bistro serves coffee, wine, bar drinks, and pastries, as well as Edy's ice cream. ⊠ *Charlotte St., just north of Bay St.,* ☎ *242/326–0206.*

Where There's Smoke . . . This coffee-and-juice bar/cigar dealer serves some of the best brews in town in a relaxing spot on the center of Bay Street. Sip your espresso or freshly squeezed drink on the balcony overlooking the scene. ⊠ *Bay and Charlotte Sts.,* ☎ *242/322–7891. Closed Sun.*

Nightlife

Cable Beach and Paradise Island resorts have their own flashy clubs, bistros, and discos where residents and visitors alike come to enjoy a variety of late-night entertainment. The attire for attending these soirees is typically as casual as the atmosphere, though some clubs require dressier duds.

Nassau

Club Waterloo (⊠ E. Bay St., ☎ 242/394–0163) is a popular disco, with five bars and nonstop dancing Monday through Saturday until 4 AM (no live band on Monday). Try the world-famous Waterloo Hurricane, a tropical mixture of rums and punches.

'Cuda Bay (⊠ Nassau Harbor Club, lower level, ☎ 242/393–0771) draws locals and visitors during happy hour and Monday night football games.

The Drop Off (⊠ Bay St., ☎ 242/322–3444), at the heart of downtown's Bay Street, is a downstairs pub with a variety of live entertainment in a sporty, noisy atmosphere.

601 Nightclub (⊠ E. Bay St., ☎ 242/322–3041), the most upscale club in town, recaptures the feel of old Nassau in its elegant environs with a doorman and dress code and the music of local celebrities, Baha Men.

Paradise Island

Atlantis Showroom (⊠ Atlantis, Paradise Island, ☎ 242/363–3000) has a late-night revue, Sunsation, a family entertainment spectacular with magic acts, acrobats, and an international cast. Shows are presented twice nightly. One night each week, a musical headliner substitutes for one of the shows. It's open Tuesday–Saturday.

Columbus Tavern (⊠ Paradise Harbour Club and Marina, ☎ 242/363–2534) is an oceanview bar with live entertainment on weekends.

Joker's Wild Comedy Club (⊠ Atlantis, Paradise Island, ☎ 242/363–3000) is just off the resort's casino floor. Mostly American comedians perform here; open Tuesday–Saturday.

Le Paon (⊠ Radisson Grand Resort, ☎ 242/363–2011) gets its groove on Friday and Saturday nights from about 7 to 3. Everybody boogies to the mix of oldies, calypso, and disco tunes. Thursday night is karaoke.

Oasis Lounge (✉ Club Land'Or, Paradise Island, ☎ 242/363–2400) presents live calypso music nightly 7 to midnight in a romantic setting overlooking the lake.

Cable Beach

King & Knights (✉ Nassau Beach Hotel showroom, ☎ 242/327–5321) is a native show featuring world-famous King Eric and his Knights. The show is the only one of its kind on the island, with steel drums, unbelievable limbo feats, fire dancing, Bahamian music, and song and dance. Dinner is at 7, followed by shows at 8:30 and 10:30 Tuesday–Saturday. One show is held Sunday and Monday at 8:30, and on Friday and Saturday after the show, you can stay and dance till the wee hours of the morning.

Palace Theater (✉ Nassau Marriott Resort, Cable Beach, ☎ 242/327–6200) presents a lavish Las Vegas–style revue that's as glitzy as you might expect of this flashy resort. The 800-seat dinner theater is open nightly except Mondays.

Rock N Roll Cafe (✉ Next to the Nassau Beach Hotel, Cable Beach, ☎ 242/327–7639) plays oldies, goodies, and karaoke daily from noon 'til 2 AM. The main bar is a favorite with entertainers who often stop by for a burger and brew. Walls are covered with rock memorabilia. Sporting events are shown on giant-screen and satellite TVs throughout the club.

Zoo Nightclub (✉ West Bay St. across from Saunders Beach, ☎ 242/322–7195) is Nassau's largest indoor nightclub. Five regular bars, a sports bar, and a VIP lounge keep the drinks coming while party animals dance the night away to top chart hits. Out back, reggae tunes flood the night, often performed live.

OUTDOOR ACTIVITIES AND SPORTS

Boating

From Chub Cay to Nassau, the sailing route goes across the mile-deep Tongue of the Ocean. The Paradise Island Lighthouse welcomes yachters to Nassau Harbour, which is open at both ends. The harbor can handle the world's largest cruise liners; sometimes as many as eight tie up at one time. The looming Paradise Island Bridge bisects the harbor connecting the resort island to Nassau; a second bridge is currently under construction. It has a high-water clearance of 70 ft, so sailboats with masts taller than this and heading for the marinas east of the bridge must enter the harbor from the east end. East of the bridge on the Nassau side of the harbor is the **Nassau Yacht Haven** (☎ 242/393–8173). **Bayshore Marina** (☎ 242/393–8232) and the **Nassau Harbour Club** (☎ 242/393–0771) are full-service marinas. **East Bay Yacht Basin** (☎ 242/394–1816) and **Hurricane Hole Marina** (☎ 242/363–3600) are boating facilities east of the bridge. Hurricane Hole has 61 slips and is on the Paradise Island side of the bridge. At the western end of New Providence, **Lyford Cay** (☎ 242/326–4267), a posh development for the rich and famous, has an excellent marina.

Kids love the concept of sitting in a row on a rubber banana and bouncing along behind a motorboat. The going rate is about $10 per person for a 15-minute banana-boat ride. Ride the big banana at **Sea & Ski Ocean Sports** at the Radisson Grand Resort (☎ 242/363–3500 ext. 6142), **Flash** at the Nassau Beach Hotel (☎ 242/327–7711 ext. 6590), and **Funsea** at the Radisson Cable Beach (☎ 242/327–6000 ext. 6315).

Bowling

There's an alley with 20 lanes called the **Village Lanes Bowling Club** (✉ Village Rd., ☎ 242/393–2277). A game costs $2.75 from 9 to 5; $3 after 5. You can rent shoes for $1, and there's a snack bar and lounge.

Canoeing

For a relaxing adventure, travel out to Lake Nancy for an afternoon of canoeing. Craig Ferguson rents two-person canoes for $10 per person, per hour. Lake Nancy is 700 ft wide by 2,100 ft long, and the brackish water is a mere 3 ft deep. A narrow opening in the mangrove thicks leads to the massive Lake Killarney, the largest lake in New Providence. Turtles, snapper, and tilapia swim around the canoes, and osprey, egrets, warblers, cranes, and white crown pigeons fly overhead. Afterward, traipse along the nature trail and obstacle course where flora and fauna are clearly identified, and obstacles offer a challenge at every turn. Beverages and snacks are served from a rustic green shack, and hamburgers, hot dogs, and steaks are cooked up on a barbecue. ✉ *Craig Ferguson, John F. Kennedy Dr.*, ☎ *242/356–4283.*

Fishing

The waters here are generally smooth and alive with many species of game fish, which is one of the reasons the Bahamas has more than 20 fishing tournaments open to visitors every year. A favorite spot just west of Nassau is the Tongue of the Ocean, so called because it looks like that essential organ when viewed from the air. The channel stretches for 100 mi. For boat rental, parties of two to six will pay $300 or so for a half day, $600 for a full day.

For fishing charters, try the **Charter Boat Association** (☎ 242/363–2335 or 242/393–3739), with 17 boats available, or one of the following: **Born Free Charters** (☎ 242/383–2003 or 242/393–4144); **Brown's Charters** (☎ 242/324–1215); **Chubasco Charters** (☎ 242/322–8148); and **Nassau Yacht Haven** (☎ 242/393–8173).

Fitness Clubs and Spas

Nassau has a number of health clubs and gyms for those in the mood for an indoor workout or some spa pampering—an energizing alternative to shopping on an overcast day. Most are stocked with the latest high-tech machinery, including stair climbers, treadmills, and exercise bikes, and offer aerobics and step classes. If you plan to stay in the area for a stretch, check into the several-day or weekly package rates available at many clubs.

Atlantis, Paradise Island Fitness Center (☎ 242/363–3000) has treadmills, exercise bikes, and saunas. Use of the facilities is free to guests. Massages are also available for a fee.

Gold's Gym (✉ Bridge Plaza, ☎ 242/394–4653) offers aerobics, step, and cardio-funk classes and has top-of-the-line fitness equipment, a juice bar, and a nursery. Fees start at $8 daily.

Palace Spa (☎ 242/327–6200) in the Crystal Palace complex and adjoining the Radisson Cable Beach is a full-service gym with all the amenities and aerobics classes. Exercise bikes face the water, and the spa has stair machines and excellent showers. Pamper yourself at the relaxing Jacuzzi and sauna. Fees are $8 daily and $30 weekly for Nassau Marriott and Radisson guests, $10 and $35 for nonguests.

Windermere (⊠ E. Bay St., ☎ 242/393–8788) offers a variety of luxurious, ultramodern spa treatments such as hydrotherapy and salt glows as well as top-quality facials, massages, manicures, and pedicures. There is also a small, exclusive training center. Daily rates for training equipment and steam, sauna, and shower facilities are $20.

Golf

Cable Beach Golf Club (7,040 yards, par 72) is the oldest and most highly regarded golf course in the Bahamas. Don't let the front nine here lull you into false complacency. If you do, the back nine will surprise you with longer holes and considerably more water hazards. The course is owned by the Radisson Cable Beach Casino & Golf Resort. ⊠ *Box N 4914, Nassau,* ☎ *242/327–6000.* ▦ *18 holes, Cable Beach–area guests $95, out of Cable Beach $100; 9 holes, $65/$70, carts included. Clubs $25.* ⊙ *Daily 7–5:30, summer; last tee-off at 3:30 in winter.*

Paradise Island Golf Club (6,805 yards, par 72), designed by Dick Wilson, has 70 sand traps and water hazards, among them the Atlantic Ocean. The championship course is surrounded by the ocean on three sides, which means that winds can get stiff. Staff pros are available for lessons and clinics. If you are not staying on Paradise Island, you should call ahead for reservations, since island guests get priority. ⊠ *Paradise Island Dr., next to airport (Box N-4777, Nassau),* ☎ *242/363–3925 or 800/321–3000 in the U.S.* ▦ *18 holes, guests $86, nonguests $135; 9 holes, guests $46, nonguests $70; carts included. Clubs $20.* ⊙ *Daily tee times 7–4, driving range daily 7:30–4:30.*

South Ocean Beach & Golf Resort (6,707 yards, par 72), on the secluded southern part of New Providence, is the newest course to surrender its divots to visiting players. Narrow fairways are a notable feature. ⊠ *Box N-8191,* ☎ *242/362–4391 or 800/223–6510.* ▦ *18 holes, guests $55, nonguests $90 carts included. Clubs $15.* ⊙ *Weekdays 7:30–5:30, weekends 7–5:30.*

Horseback Riding

Happy Trails Stables gives guided hour-long trail rides through remote wooded areas and beaches on the southwestern coast of New Providence. Courtesy round-trip bus transportation from hotels is provided (about an hour each way). Tours are limited to 10 persons, there is a 200-pound weight limit; and children must be at least eight years old. ⊠ *Coral Harbour,* ☎ *242/362–1820 or 242/323–5613.* ▦ *$50 per person.* ⊙ *Mon.–Sat.*

Parasailing

Atlantis, Paradise Island (☎ 242/363–3000) charges $45 for five to seven minutes of floating above the beach.

Ski & Ocean Sports at the Radisson Grand Resort (☎ 242/363–3500 ext. 6142) lets you jump off a platform and into the skies for five to seven minutes for $45.

Sailing

Funsea at the Radisson Cable Beach (☎ 242/327–6000 ext. 6315) rents Hobie Cats for $37 per hour, Sunfish $22 per hour, and gives hourly lessons for $25.

Sea & Ski Ocean Sports at the Radisson Grand Resort (☎ 242/363–3500 ext. 6142) on Paradise Island rents Hobie Cats for $35 per hour and Sunfish for $20 per hour.

Scuba Diving and Snorkeling

Diving operations are plentiful in Nassau. Most hotels have dive instructors who teach short courses, followed the next day by a reef trip. Many small operations have sprung up in recent years in which experienced divers with their own boats run custom dives for one to five people. A lot of these are one-person efforts. In many cases, the custom dive will include a picnic lunch with freshly speared lobster or fish cooked over an open fire on a private island beach.

New Providence Island has several popular dive sites and a number of dive operators who offer regular trips. The elusive (and thus exclusive) hole, **Lost Ocean Hole** (East of Nassau, 40–195 ft), is aptly named because it is difficult to locate. The rim of the 80-ft opening in 40 ft of water is dotted with coral heads and teeming with small fish—grunts, margate, and jacks—as well as larger pompano, amberjack, and sometimes nurse sharks. Divers will find a thermocline at 80 ft, a large cave at 100 ft, and a sand ledge at 185 ft that slopes down to 195 ft. The series of shallow reefs along the 14 mi of Rose Island is known as **Rose Island Reefs** (Nassau, 5–35 ft). The coral is varied, though the reefs are showing the effects of the heavy traffic. Plenty of tropical fish make these reefs home. The wreck of the steel-hulled ship *Mahoney* is just outside the harbor. **Lost Ocean Hole** is an 80-ft opening east of Nassau. **Gambier Deep Reef,** off Gambier Village about 15 minutes west of Cable Beach, goes to a depth of 80 ft. **Sea Gardens** is off Love Beach on the northwestern shore beyond Gambier. **Lyford Cay Drop-Off** (West of Nassau, 40–200+ ft). Starting from a 40-ft plateau, the cliff plummets almost straight into the inky blue mile-deep Tongue of the Ocean. The wall has endless varieties of sponges, black coral, and wire coral. Along the wall, grunts, grouper, hogfish, snapper, and rockfish abound. Off the wall are pelagic game fish, such as tuna, bonito, wahoo, and kingfish. The South Side reefs are great for snorkelers as well as divers because of the shallowness of the reefs.

Bahama Divers Ltd. (☎ 242/393–1466 or 800/398–3483) has two 42-ft custom dive boats that make separate trips for beginners and experienced divers. PADI certification courses are available, and there's a full line of scuba equipment for rent. Destinations are drop-off sites, wrecks, coral reefs and gardens, and an ocean blue hole. A video can be arranged. Three-hour "dive safaris" leave once a day; transportation is provided between hotels and the dock.

Dive Dive Dive, Ltd. (☎ 242/362–1143 or 242/362–1401) gives free scuba lessons at the Radisson Cable Beach pool. Resort courses, dives to walls and reefs, night dives, and shark dives are all available at this PADI facility. Transportation is provided.

Dive Nassau (☎ 242/356–5170), at Bay and Deveaux streets in Nassau, will teach you to dive in 80 minutes. They also offer specialty certification courses taught by PADI instructors. Dive trips explore magnificent reefs, walls, wrecks, and the Lost Blue Hole. Prices include equipment and transportation.

Diver's Haven (☎ 242/393–0869 or 242/393–3285), a five-star PADI facility, offers three daily dives, state-of-the-art equipment rental, classes at several area hotels, and a four-day scuba certification course. Two-tank dives run $65, or, for the more adventurous, dive trips to the Out Islands can be arranged. **Stuart Cove's Dive South Ocean** (☎ 242/362–4171), at the South Ocean Beach & Golf Resort on the island's south shore, offers scuba instruction, rents scuba and snorkel equipment, and runs dive trips to the south shore reefs twice a day, at 9:30 and 1:30. Shark dives and day trips to the Exuma Cays (where you dive the Highbourne Cay Wall, snorkel conch for lunch, and feed the iguanas on Allan's Cay), Andros (for the blue holes and shark dives), and the Berry Islands are also available, as well as a special shark dive.

Spectator Sports

Among other imperishable traditions, the British handed down to the Bahamians such sports as soccer, rugby, and cricket—that languid game whose players occupy such positions on the field as silly midon, third slip, long leg, and square leg. (It is absolutely essential that someone versed in the rules of the game and long on patience accompany you.) Cricket is played at Haynes Oval, baseball at Queen Elizabeth Sports Center, rugby at Winton Estates, and softball at Clifford Park. For information on spectator sports, call the **Ministry of Tourism** (☎ 242/322–7500) or check the local papers for sports updates and calendars to find out what's going on and when.

Squash

Village Squash Club (☎ 242/393–1580) charges $8 per hour, with a $1.50 charge for racket rental and $3.50 for balls.

Tennis

Fees quoted at hotel courts are for nonguests.

Atlantis, Paradise Island (☎ 242/363–3000 ext. 6118) has the largest tennis complex on the island. You can play on any of its 12 clay courts for $5 per hour.

Nassau Beach Hotel (☎ 242/327–7711) charges $5 per person for unlimited play on its six Flexipave courts.

Radisson Grand Resort (☎ 242/363–3500) on Paradise Island has four lighted asphalt courts and charges $15 per hour, with a $5 racket-rental fee. Lessons cost $20 per half-hour.

Waterskiing

Sea & Ski Ocean Sports at the Radisson Grand Resort (☎ 242/363–3500 ext. 6142) charges $30 for 3½ mi of riding the wake.

Windsurfing

Sea & Ski Ocean Sports at the Radisson Grand Resort (☎ 242/363–3500 ext. 6142) rents sailboards for $20 per hour.

SHOPPING

For many, shopping is one of Nassau's greatest delights. Wandering around Nassau's Straw Market, between Bay Street and the waterfront, is an experience in itself. Don't forget to look in the hotel arcades, which have many elegant shops. You can return home with a variety of handmade Bahamian goods or splurge at duty-free shops that offer such savings you simply have to load up. You'll find duty-free prices—generally 25% to 50% less than U.S. prices—on imported items such as crystal, linens, watches, cameras, sweaters, leather goods, and perfumes. Prices here rival those in other duty-free destinations.

Most of Nassau's shops are on Bay Street between Rawson Square and the British Colonial Hotel, and on the side streets leading off of Bay Street. However, some stores are beginning to pop up on the eastern end of the main shopping thoroughfare. You can bargain at the Straw

Market, but prices in shops are fixed. And do observe the local dress customs when you go shopping: Shorts are acceptable, beachwear is not.

Although a few shops will be happy to mail bulky or fragile items home for you, most won't even deliver purchases to your hotel, plane, or cruise ship.

Markets and Arcades

The **Straw Market,** midway along Bay Street, is a main attraction of old Nassau for good reason: It is one of the world's largest such markets. Hundreds of people, mostly women, hawk their wares—brightly colored, hand-decorated straw hats and bags, baskets and totes, mats and slippers, wall hangings, and dolls. You'll also find necklaces and bracelets strung with shells, sharks' teeth, and bright beans, berries, or pods; clothing; and original oils, prints, and wood carvings. Bargaining with vendors is part of the fun—all prices are negotiable. If you're looking for authenticity rather than entertainment, the market's not the best place to go, as many goods are imported from Taiwan, the Philippines, and other Asian sources; smaller specialty shops are generally a little more expensive but offer high-quality and truly Bahamian-made goods.

The **International Arcade,** a collection of shops under a huge, spreading bougainvillea, sells linens, souvenirs, and other offbeat items. The **Prince George Plaza,** which leads from Bay Street to Woodes Rogers Walk near the dock, has about two dozen shops with varied wares and a rooftop restaurant. The **Nassau Arcade** has the Bahamas' Anglo-American bookstore (☎ 242/325–0338), a tiny storefront with a smattering of interesting reading material, as well as a few other small stores and restaurants.

Specialty Shops

Antiques, Arts, and Crafts

Balmain Antiques and Gallery (⊠ Bay St., ☎ 242/323–7421) has a nice collection of Bahamian artwork and antique maps, prints, and bottles.

Charlotte's Gallery (⊠ Charlotte St., ☎ 242/322–6310), a small consignment shop, sells the work of local artists—everything from small prints and ceramic tiles to full-size original oil paintings.

Green Lizard (⊠ Prince George Plaza, Bay St., ☎ 242/356–5103) is home to a delightful cornucopia of handmade wind chimes and other native and imported gifts, including a specialty item you might be tempted to use during your stay: string hammocks.

Island Tings (⊠ Bay St., ☎ 242/326–1024) carries a variety of Bahamian and Caribbean items. Artwork includes prints by Eleutheran artist Eddie Minnis, Androsia fabric, and wood carvings; there's also a wide variety of food items, from pepper jelly and banana chutney to hot sauce and spices. And that's just the beginning of this eclectic store's offerings: Stock changes often as new treasures are discovered.

Kennedy Gallery (⊠ Parliament St., ☎ 242/325–7662) sells watercolors, oil, sculpture, and other art work by a wide variety of Bahamian artists, from the best-known to emerging young talent.

The Plait Lady (⊠ E. Bay St., ☎ 242/356–5726) is hands-down the best shop in town for authentic arts and crafts: Everything in the store is guaranteed made in the Bahamas. Owner Clare Sands has crisscrossed the Bahamas looking for interesting products, and her collection of straw weaves, or plaits, is the best around. You'll find bags, baskets, hats, briefcases, and even a water pitcher made of straw so tightly coiled it's leak-proof. Her staff, working from long coils of the woven goods, will custom-make straw items from bags to photo albums for a personalized, and unforgettable, souvenir.

Baked Goods

Kelly's Bakery (✉ Market St., ☎ 242/394–3283), steps away from the Straw Market, is a convenient place to stop for muffins, cakes, and other goodies.

Model Bakery (✉ Dowdeswell St., ☎ 242/322–2595), in Nassau's east end, is another great local bakery. Be sure to try their cinnamon twists.

Swiss Pastry Shop (✉ W. Bay St., ☎ 242/327–7601) is a haven of sweetness for those staying on Cable Beach. Choose from cakes, tarts, cheesecake, eclairs, and other treats. For a more Bahamian treat, try the beef and conch patties, as well as take-out versions of that glorious Bahamian dessert, guava duff.

China, Crystal, Linens, and Silver

Linen Shop (✉ Bay St., ☎ 242/322–4266) sells fine embroidered Irish linens and lace.

Little Switzerland (✉ Bay St., ☎ 242/322–8324) sells among other names, Waterford, Hummel, Lladró, Wedgwood, and Lenox.

Marlborough Antiques (✉ Bay St., ☎ 242/328–0502) specializes in English furniture and bric-a-brac. You can also find Bahamian art, rare books, European glassware, Victorian jewelry, and unusual greeting cards and notepaper.

Cigars

Cigars have become quite the rage in Nassau. And there is no doubt that the impressive displays of Cuban cigars, handpicked and imported by Bahamian merchants, lure aficionados to the Bahamas for cigar sprees. Beware, however, that some merchants on Bay Street and elsewhere in the islands are selling counterfeits—whether knowingly or not. If the price seems too good to be true, chances are it is. Check the wrappers, feel to ensure that there is a consistent fill before you purchase, and chances are you won't get burned. A number of stores along the main shopping strip do stock only the best authentic Cuban stogies.

Graycliff (✉ West Hill St., ☎ 242/322–2796), best known as an elegant restaurant (☞ Dining, *above*), also carries one of the finest selections of hand-rolled Cuban cigars in Nassau.

Pipe of Peace (✉ Bay St., ☎ 242/325–2022)—keep a lookout for the giant wooden pipe out front—is a conduit for a wide variety of cigars, pipes, and cigarettes, including all major Cuban cigars and a variety from other countries. While the cigar counter occupies just a small portion of the eclectic souvenir shop, it's well-known as a good source.

Tropique International Smoke Shop (✉ Nassau Marriott Resort & Crystal Palace Casino, ☎ 242/327–7292) carries a wide selection of products in its atmospherically controlled humidors. Their staff receives training in Havana, so you can count on knowledgable guidance.

Where There's Smoke . . . (✉ Bay and Charlotte Sts., ☎ 242/322–7891), on the second floor of Pink Flamingo Trading Company, has the best cigar bar in town. It stocks the world-renowned La Casa del Habano Cuban stogies as well as a variety of smokers' accessories.

Eclectic Bahamian

Animal Crackers (✉ Prince George Arcade, ☎ 242/325–1887) sells colorful Jams clothing, cool cards, and every kind of stuffed animal imaginable. It's a jungle inside.

Cody's Record and Video Store (⊠ Bay St., E. Bay St., and W. Bay St., ☎ 242/325–8834) has the best selection of tapes and CDs of island calypso, soca, reggae, and Junkanoo music in its three locations.

Island Shops (⊠ Bay St., ☎ 242/322–4183) sells travel guides, novels, paperbacks, gift books, and international magazines. Take a peek at the "Bahamian Books" section, where you'll find texts on everything from history to cookery.

Taste of the Islands (⊠ International Arcade, ☎ 242/356–7632) sells spices, jams, jerk seasoning, and other edibles from the Bahamas and Caribbean. It's the spot to pick up a bottle of hot sauce, a bag of Jamaican Blue Mountain coffee, some Cayman Islands rum cake, and even a cigar or two.

Fashion
Clothing is no great bargain in Nassau, but many stores sell fine English imports. Perhaps the best local buy is brightly batiked Androsia fabric—available by the yard or sewn into sarongs, dresses, and blouses.

Bonneville Bones (⊠ Bay St., ☎ 242/328–0804) is a handsome full-service men's store that sells everything from casual sportswear to fine Italian suits.

Fendi (⊠ Bay St., ☎ 242/322–6300) occupies a magnificent old building and carries the Italian house's luxury line of handbags, luggage, watches, jewelry, shoes, and more.

Girls From Brazil (⊠ Bay St., ☎ 242/356–9381) has a large selection of reasonably priced swimwear along with matching colorful wraps and casual evening wear at its Bay Street location.

Mademoiselle Ltd. (⊠ Bay St., ☎ 242/322–1530) has 17 shops throughout the Bahamas (many in hotel arcades) and stocks a variety of women's clothing; be sure to check out their Androsia fashions.

Jewelry, Watches, and Clocks
Coin of the Realm (⊠ Charlotte St., ☎ 242/322–4862) has Bahamian coins and native conch pearls in various jewelry settings.

Colombian Emeralds International (⊠ Bay St., ☎ 242/325–4083) is the local branch of this well-known jeweler carrying not only its signature gem but a variety of other fine jewelry.

Jewelry Box (⊠ Bay St., ☎ 242/322–4098) specializes in tanzanite jewelry—it's the largest Bahamian supplier of this gem mined in the foothills of Mt. Kilmanjaro—but also sells other precious and semiprecious stones and 14-carat gold jewelry.

John Bull (⊠ Bay St., ☎ 242/322–3328), established in 1929 and magnificently decorated in its latest incarnation behind a Georgian-style facade, fills its complex with Tiffany & Co., Cartier, and other boutiques that carry cultured pearls from Mikimoto and costume jewelry by Monet, Nina Ricci, and Yves Saint Laurent.

 Little Switzerland (⊠ Bay St., ☎ 242/322–8324) is the place to buy watches by Tag-Heuer, Omega, Borel, Swiss Army, and more. They also carry African diamonds, as well as Spanish pieces of eight in settings.

Perfumes
Body Shop (⊠ Bay St., ☎ 242/326–7068) sells the company's internationally acclaimed line of all-natural body lotions, shampoos and conditioners, and makeup.

John Bull (⊠ Bay St., ☎ 242/322–3328) is where you'll find fragrances by Chanel, Yves Saint Laurent, and Estée Lauder.

Little Switzerland (⊠ Bay St., ☎ 242/322–8324), one of the Caribbean's largest duty-free retailers, stocks French, Italian, and U.S. fragrances, skin-care products, and bath lines.

Perfume Bar (⊠ Bay St., ☎ 242/322–3785) exclusively carries the best-selling French fragrance, Boucheron, and the Clarins line of skin-care products, as well as products by Givenchy, Fendi, and other well-known designers.

Perfume Shop (⊠ Bay and Frederick Sts., ☎ 242/322–2375) is a landmark perfumery that has the broadest selection of imported perfumes and fragrances in the Bahamas.

NEW PROVIDENCE ISLAND A TO Z

Arriving and Departing

By Plane
AIRLINES

Flights listed below originate in the United States and Canada. If you are arriving from the United Kingdom, the best option is to fly to Miami and transfer to one of the numerous carriers listed below for the final leg to Nassau.

Air Canada (☎ 800/776–3000) flies from Montréal and Toronto.

American Eagle (☎ 800/776-3000), a subsidiary of American Airlines, flies into Nassau from Miami and also serves the Abacos, Exumas, and other destinations in the Out Islands.

Bahamasair (☎ 242/377–5505 or 800/222–4262), the national carrier, has daily flights from Miami, Fort Lauderdale, and West Palm Beach, as well as three flights weekly from Orlando. The airline also flies to all of the Out Islands.

Comair (☎ 800/354–9822), a Delta connection partner, flies from Orlando.

Delta (☎ 800/221–1212) is one of the busier carriers, with daily flights from Atlanta, Fort Lauderdale, New York City, and Orlando.

Gulf Stream International (☎ 242/377–4314 or 800/992–8532) has service from Fort Lauderdale and Miami.

Nassau–Paradise Island Express (☎ 242/377–2050 or 800/722–4262) is a charter service that uses Continental Airlines planes and staff for service out of Newark and Houston.

Paradise Island Airlines (☎ 242/394–8742 or 800/786–7202) flies daily from Miami, Fort Lauderdale, Orlando, and West Palm Beach into Paradise Island Airport. They also fly into Governor's Harbour on Eleuthera.

US Airways (☎ 242/377–8887 or 800/622–1015) flies in daily from Charlotte, NC; **US Airways Express** leaves from Fort Lauderdale, Miami, and West Palm Beach.

AIRPORTS

Nassau International Airport (☎ 242/377–7281), 8 mi west of Nassau by Lake Killarney, is served by an increasing number of airlines.

Paradise Island Airport (☎ 242/363–2845) is at the east end of Paradise Island and a very short drive from the island's resorts.

BETWEEN THE AIRPORT AND HOTELS

No bus service is available from Nassau International Airport to New Providence hotels, except for guests on package tours. A taxi ride from the airport to Cable Beach costs about $14; to Nassau, $16; and to Paradise Island, $23 (this includes the causeway toll of $2). In addition, drivers expect a 15% tip. (☞ Getting Around, *below,* for taxi companies.)

By Ship

Nassau is a port of call for a number of cruise lines, including **Carnival Cruise Lines, Disney Cruise Line, Dolphin/Majesty Cruise Lines, Kloster/Norwegian Cruise Line, Premier Cruise Lines,** and **Royal Caribbean Cruise Line** (☞ Cruise Travel *in* the Gold Guide). Ships dock at Prince George Wharf, in downtown Nassau.

Getting Around

By Bus

For the adventuresome, consider jitney (bus) service to get around Nassau and its environs. Rides in these vans, which careen along with windows open and music blaring, range from smooth-sailing to hair-raising. If you want to join locals on the jitney, these buses, which often carry the name of their owners painted in bold letters, can be hailed at bus stops, hotels, public beaches, and in residential areas. The fee is 75¢, exact change required. Call out to the driver as your stop approaches.

In downtown Nassau, you'll find jitneys on Navy Lion Road between Bay Street and Woodes Rogers Walk. Bus service runs throughout the day until 7 PM.

Guests staying at major hotels on Cable Beach can take the free **Cable Beach Casino Shuttle,** which starts at the Crystal Palace Casino every hour beginning at 6 PM and stops at every hotel along the beachfront. The last bus leaves the casino at 2 AM. A free **Atlantis, Paradise Island Casino Express Shuttle** takes a circular route around the island hourly starting at 8 AM and ending at the Paradise Island Casino. The shuttle stops at the major hotels en route or you can flag it down.

By Car

For exploring at your leisure, you'll want to have a car. Rentals are available at Nassau International Airport, downtown, on Paradise Island, and at some resorts. Plan to pay $45–$80 a day, $250–$480 a week, depending on the type of car. At press time, gasoline cost $2.50 a gallon. Remember to drive on the left.

Avis Rent-A-Car has branches at the Nassau International Airport (☎ 242/326–7121), on West Bay Street (☎ 242/322–2889), and downtown near the British Colonial Hotel (☎ 242/326–6380).

Budget has offices at the Nassau International Airport (☎ 242/377–9000) and the Paradise Island Airport (☎ 242/363–3095).

Dollar Rent-a-Car can be found at Nassau International Airport (☎ 242/377–7301), at the Radisson Cable Beach (☎ 242/377–6000 ext. 6220), on Paradise Island (☎ 242/325–3716), and downtown on Marlborough Street near Cumberland Street, (☎ 242/325–3716).

Hertz has branches at the airport (☎ 242/377–6231) and on East Bay Street, a block east of the Paradise Island bridge (☎ 242/393–0871).

Teglo Rental Cars (✉ Mt. Pleasant Village, ☎ 242/362–4361) is a local rental agency with offices near Cable Beach.

By Ferry

Ferries operate during daylight hours (usually 9–5:30) at half-hour intervals between Prince George Wharf and Paradise Island. The one-way cost is $2 per person

By Scooter

Two people can ride around the island on a motor scooter for $30 a half day or $40–$45 for a full day, plus a $10 deposit. Helmets for both driver and passenger and insurance are mandatory and are included in the rental price. Many hotels have scooters on the premises. You can also try **Fathia Investment** (☎ 242/326–8329) at Prince George Wharf. Once again, remember to drive on the left.

By Surrey

Beautifully painted horse-drawn carriages will take as many as four people around Nassau at a rate of $5 per person for a 25-minute ride; don't hesitate to bargain. Most drivers give a very comprehensive tour of the Bay Street area, giving an extensive history lesson.

By Taxi

Taxis are generally the best and most convenient way of getting around New Providence. Fares are fixed by the government at $2.20 for the first ¼ mi, plus 30¢ for each additional ¼ mi, though for longer trips it's a good idea to discuss price ahead of time. It is customary to tip taxi drivers 15%. You can also hire a car or small van for sightseeing for about $50 per hour or $13 per person.

Bahamas Transport (☎ 242/323–5111) has radio-dispatched taxis, as do **Li'l Murph & Sons** (☎ 242/325–3725) and the **Taxi Cab Union** (☎ 242/323–4555). There are stands at **Nassau Beach Hotel** (☎ 242/327–7865) on Cable Beach and **Paradise Taxi Co.** (☎ 242/363–3211) on Paradise Island.

Opening and Closing Times

Banks are open on New Providence Island Monday–Thursday 9:30–3 and Friday 9:30–5. They are closed on weekends. Principal banks on the island are Bank of the Bahamas, Bank of Nova Scotia, Barclays Bank, Canadian Imperial Bank of Commerce, Chase Manhattan Bank, Citibank, and Royal Bank of Canada.

Shops are generally open Monday–Saturday 9–5 (many stay open later); the Straw Market is also open on Sunday. By law, Bay Street shops are permitted to open on Sundays, but the main thoroughfare remains all but deserted.

Contacts and Resources

Embassies

U.S. Embassy Consular Section (✉ Mosmar Bldg., Queen St., ☎ 242/322–1181).

Canadian Consulate (✉ Shirley Street Shopping Plaza, Shirley St., ☎ 242/393–2123).

British High Commission (✉ Bitco Bldg., East and Shirley Sts., ☎ 242/325–7471).

Emergencies

Ambulance (☎ 242/322–2221).

Drug Action Service (☎ 242/322–2308) can provide prescription drugs.

Police or Fire (☎ 919).

Princess Margaret Hospital (⊠ Shirley St., ☏ 242/322–2861) is government-operated; **Doctors Hospital** (⊠ Shirley St., ☏ 242/322–8411) is private.

Guided Tours

More than a dozen local operators provide tours of New Providence Island's natural and commercial attractions. Some of the many possibilities include sightseeing tours of Nassau and the island; glass-bottom boat tours to Sea Gardens; and various cruises to offshore cays, all starting at $12. A full day of ocean sailing will cost around $60. In the evening, there are sunset and moonlight cruises with dinner and drinks ($35–$50) and nightlife tours to casino cabaret shows and nightclubs ($28–$45). Tours may be booked at hotel desks in Nassau, Cable Beach, and Paradise Island or directly through one of the tour operators listed below, all of which have knowledgeable guides, and a selection of tours in air-conditioned cars, vans, or buses.

CRUISES

Calypso I and II (⊠ Box N 8209, Nassau, ☏ 242/363–3577) offers cruises to a private island for swimming and snorkeling. The $45 cost includes lunch, two frozen daiquiris, and nonmotorized water sports.

❋ **Flying Cloud** (☏ 242/393–1957) runs half-day catamaran cruises at 9:30 and 2 that for $35 include two drinks, dry snacks, and snorkeling; for $30, sunset cruises include hors d'oeuvres. A five-hour Sunday cruise, departing at 10 AM, is $50 and includes rum punch and buffet lunch. All trips include complimentary round-trip transportation from hotels.

Topsail Yacht Charters' (☏ 242/393–0820 or 242/393–5817) *Wind Dance, Riding High,* and *Liberty Call* leave from the British Colonial Hotel Dock for a variety of sailing, snorkeling, and champagne cruises. All-day cruises cost $49; champagne-cocktail cruises $35.

EXCURSIONS

Commercial tour operators offering similar tours and prices include **Bowtie Tours** (⊠ Box N 8246, ☏ 242/325–8849), **Happy Tours** (⊠ Box N 1077, ☏ 242/323–5818), **Majestic Tours** (⊠ Box N 1401, ☏ 242/322–2606), **Playtours Ltd.** (⊠ Box N 7762, ☏ 242/322–2931), and **Richard Moss Tours** (⊠ Box N 4442, ☏ 242/393–2753).

HORTICULTURAL TOURS

The lofty casuarina trees that bend with the wind, the palms used to make umbrella-like thatched beach huts, yucca used in making hedges, sisal used in making rope, and jumbey trees, which have medicinal value—all are part of the Bahamian landscape. If you would like to know more about the island's flowers and trees, the **Horticultural Society of the Bahamas** meets at 10 AM at the homes of members on the first Saturday of each month. The Society can arrange field trips.

OUT ISLANDS TRIPS

Exuma Powerboat Adventures (☏ 242/327–5385 or 242/326–1936) offers full-day excursions to the Exuma Cays, with stops to feed iguanas, participate in a nature walk, and, of course, do some snorkeling in the Exumas' Land and Sea Park. It's a great way to experience some of the beauty of the less-developed islands outside Nassau. Lunch is included.

❋ **Seaplane Safaris** (☏ 242/393–2522 or 242/393–1179) utilize these low-flying craft for the Exuma Cays trip, allowing you to glide right over the surface of the water. You can swim right off the seaplane into Thunderball Grotto, an eerie natural formation (scenes from the James Bond movie bearing its name were filmed here) and enjoy some snorkeling, explore nature trails, or simply loll on the beach on Warderick Wells, the headquarters of the Land and Sea Park. Lunch is included, and the trip takes a full day.

SPECIAL-INTEREST TOURS

Dolphin Encounters (☎ 242/363–1653 or 242/363–1003) can be experienced on Blue Lagoon Island (Salt Cay), just east of Paradise Island. During the two-hour *Close Encounter* ($40 per person), you can sit on a platform with your feet in the water while dolphins play around you. Trainers are available to answer questions. If you wish, you can wade in the waist-deep water to get up close and personal with them.

Swim-with-the-Dolphins ($115 per person) actually allows you to swim with these friendly creatures for about 30 minutes. For more complete involvement, try the *Assistant Trainer for a Day* program ($195 per person) that teaches you about care and training and lets you feed them, prepare their food, and learn more about their environment. The Dolphin Encounters are very popular, so make reservations as early as possible. Programs are available daily, 8–5:30, and the cost includes transfers from your hotel and the boat ride to the island.

Hartley's Undersea Walk (☎ 242/393–8234) takes you for a stroll on the ocean floor. Special helmets protect hair, eyeglasses, and contacts while allowing you to see the fish and flora. Hartley's yacht, the *Pied Piper,* departs daily at 9:30 and 1:30 from the Nassau Yacht Haven on East Bay Street.

Pedal & Paddle Ecoventures (☎ 242/362–2772 or 800/331–5884) is a unique, full-day ecotourism adventure that combines rides through forests and along coastlines on an all-terrain bicycle with tours through mangrove creeks and sheltered waters in a two-person recreational kayak. Lunch is included in the full-day tours, which can be booked at most hotel desks. Half-day tours are also available.

Stingray City (☎ 242/363–3179) allows you to snorkel among a variety of sea life and feed a surprisingly friendly stingray or two.

WALKING TOURS

A walking tour around **Historic Nassau,** arranged by the Tourist Information Office at Rawson Square, is offered Monday through Saturday by advance arrangement. The cost is $2. Call ahead for information and reservations at 242/326–9781.

Visitor Information

The **Ministry of Tourism** (✉ Box N 3701, Nassau, ☎ 242/322–7500, FAX 242/328–0945) is on Bay Street. Its Tourism Help Line (☎ 242/325–4357 or 242/326–4357) is an information source that operates from 8:30 AM to 11:30 PM daily. The ministry also operates information booths at Nassau International Airport (☎ 242/377–6833), open daily from 8:30 AM to 11 PM, and at Rawson Square (☎ 242/326–9781 or 242/326–9772), open daily from 8:30 to 5. Ask about Bahamahosts, specially trained tour guides who will talk to you about island history and culture and pass on their individual and imaginative knowledge of Bahamian folklore.

The Ministry of Tourism's **People-to-People Programme** (☎ 242/326–0435) is designed to let a Bahamian personally introduce you to the Bahamas. By pre-arrangement through the ministry, you can spend a day with a Bahamian family with similar interests to learn local culture firsthand or enjoy a family meal. It's best if you make arrangements—through your travel agent or by calling direct—prior to your trip. (This is not a dating service!)

In case you want to see the world.

At American Express, we're here to make your journey a smooth one. So we have over 1,700 travel service locations in over 120 countries ready to help. What else would you expect from the world's largest travel agency?

do more

AMERICAN EXPRESS

http://www.americanexpress.com/travel

Travel

In case you want to be welcomed there.

We're here to see that you're always welcomed at establishments everywhere. That's why millions of people carry the American Express® Card — for peace of mind, confidence, and security, around the world or just around the corner.

do more

AMERICAN EXPRESS

Cards

In case you're running low.

We're here to help with more than 118,000 Express Cash locations around the world. In order to enroll, just call American Express before you start your vacation.

do more

AMERICAN EXPRESS

Express Cash

And just in case.

We're here with American Express® Travelers Cheques
and Cheques *for Two*® They're the safest way to carry
money on your vacation and the surest way to get a
refund, practically anywhere, anytime.
Another way we help you...

do more

AMERICAN
EXPRESS

**Travelers
Cheques**

3 Grand Bahama Island

Grand Bahama's twin cities, Freeport and Lucaya, may not have the colonial charm of Nassau, but if you want to shop, gamble, or just relax on the beach—at a slightly lower cost than in the capital—there's no need to go elsewhere. Beyond the ever-expanding Freeport-Lucaya region, most of the eastern and western parts of the 96-mi-long island remain invitingly remote— a seemingly endless, flat swath of casuarina, palmetto, and pine trees rimmed by long stretches of open beach and broken only by inlets and small fishing villages. Therein lies the charm, to the increasing delight of eco-sensitive visitors.

Updated by
Gordon Lomer

RAND BAHAMA, the fourth-largest island in the Bahamas after Andros, Eleuthera, and Great Abaco, lies only 55 mi off Palm Beach, Florida. The ever-warm waters of the Gulf Stream lap its western tip, and the Little Bahama Bank protects it from the northeast.

In 1492, when Columbus set foot on the Bahamian island of San Salvador, Grand Bahama was already well populated. Skulls found in caves here attest to the existence of the peaceable Lucayans, who were constantly fleeing the more bellicose Caribs. The skulls show that the Lucayans were flat-headed; parents flattened their babies' foreheads with boards to strengthen them, making them less vulnerable to the cudgels of the Caribs, who were cannibals.

Spanish conquistadors visited the island briefly in the early 16th century. They used the island as a watering hole but dismissed it as having no commercial value and went on their way. During the 18th century, Loyalists settled on Grand Bahama to escape the wrath of American revolutionaries who had just won the War of Independence. When Britain abolished the slave trade early in the 19th century, many of the Loyalists' former slaves settled here as farmers and fishermen.

Grand Bahama took on new prominence in the Roaring '20s, when the western end of the island, along with Bimini to the south, became convenient jumping-off points for rumrunners ferrying booze to Florida during Prohibition. But it was not until the 1950s, when the harvesting of pine trees was the island's major industry, that American financier Wallace Groves envisioned the grandiose future of Grand Bahama. Groves's dream was to establish a tax-free port for the shipment of goods to the United States, a plan that also involved building a city.

On August 5, 1955, largely due to Groves's efforts and those of British industrialist Sir Charles Hayward, the government signed an agreement, which set in motion the development of a planned city and established the Grand Bahama Port Authority to administer a 200-sq-mi area near the center of the island. Settlers were given tax concessions and other benefits. In return, the developers would build a port, an airport, a power plant, roads, waterways, and utilities. They would also promote tourism and industrial development.

What evolved are the cities of Freeport and Lucaya. They are separated by a 4-mi stretch of East Sunrise Highway, though no one is quite sure where one community ends and the other begins. A modern industrial park has developed west of Freeport and close to the harbor. Companies like Polymers Pharmaceuticals, Fine Chemicals SA, and Uniroyal have been attracted here because there are no corporate, property, or income taxes and no customs duties or excise taxes on materials used for export manufacturing. In return, these companies hire local workers and have become involved in community activities and charities.

Most of Grand Bahama's commercial activity is concentrated in Freeport, the country's second-largest city. On average, about one-third of the roughly 3.5 million people who come to the Bahamas visit Freeport and neighboring waterfront Lucaya. They are drawn by gambling, resort hotels, two large duty-free shopping complexes, and sea and land activities. Each day several thousand cruise-ship passengers arrive at Freeport Harbour from the Florida ports of Miami, Fort Lauderdale, Cape Canaveral, and Palm Beach. The harbor, now jointly owned by the Grand Bahama Port Authority and Hutchison Whampoa, the largest port owner in the world, accommodates up to 13 cruise ships at a time.

The container port has undergone an $88 million redevelopment and can now accommodate the largest cargo ships in the world. Expansion plans will double the port's container handling capacity. The port sits strategically astride the world's major shipping lanes between North and South America and between Europe and the Panama Canal. The port has generated millions of dollars of investment business, hundreds of jobs, and mushrooming residential development.

Despite the bustle of business and the influx of tourists, Grand Bahama has more than a half dozen opportunities to enjoy solitude and nature in the raw. Four places in and around Freeport shouldn't be missed: Hydroflora Gardens, the Garden of the Groves, the Bahamas National Trust's (BNT) Lucayan National Park, and the BNT Rand Nature Centre. Additionally, the worldwide trend toward eco-sensitivity has spawned ecotourism adventures, including kayak trips through mangrove flats, hiking trips through the national parks, adventure tours to the East End of the island, snorkeling tours of coral reefs, and horseback rides through pine forests and along ocean beaches. Surrounding waters lure anglers from around the world to compete in deepwater and bonefishing tournaments. The Second World International Invitational Bonefishing Championship tournament was held in Grand Bahama in late 1997. The island is also a mecca for scuba divers, and is home of the world famous scuba school, the Underwater Explorers Society (UNEXSO). Of course, there's more than just the water here: landlubbers flock to the island's golf courses year-round.

EXPLORING GRAND BAHAMA ISLAND

Numbers in the text correspond to numbers in the margin and on the Freeport-Lucaya and Grand Bahama Island maps.

A Good Tour

Grand Bahama is the only planned island in the Bahamas—this results in areas that are well-laid out, but quite a distance apart. Getting around in Freeport-Lucaya is very straightforward, and both the **International Bazaar** ② and the **Port Lucaya Marketplace** ⑦ can easily be explored on foot. But to get a look at some of the more remote areas, rent a car and spread out the sights over two days.

Start your day in the serene **Garden of the Groves** ⑪ on Midshipman Road. Photo opportunities greet you at each turn, and the quaint, little hilltop church is a must-see in Grand Bahama.

At this point, it's beach time. Turn onto the East Sunrise Highway to Casuarina Bridge. Continue along Casuarina Drive, turn right at the first roundabout and travel south until you hit Barbary Beach, so secluded that you'll rarely see another person.

Continue the adventure in the afternoon with a trip to **Lucayan National Park** ⑫, home of the wondrous Ben's Cave. To get to the park, return to Casuarina Drive and go right onto the Grand Bahama Highway and continue about 13 mi along the pine barren road. The park is on the left, and you'll find adequate parking. Across the road is a boardwalk trail that meanders about a mile to Gold Rock Creek.

To explore the western end of the island, start from the International Airport, take Airport Road to Queen's Highway and follow it until you get to Eight Mile Rock. The scenery is positively rural compared to the buzzing city of Freeport that you've left behind. Life moves at a slower pace. Find your way to a beach out here or strike up a conversation with locals. Relax—take out your camera for a few photographs while you're away from the city.

After taking all this in, head west on Queen's Highway to West End. It served as a base for gunrunners in the U. S. Civil War and for bootleggers during the days of Prohibition. You can continue out Queen's Highway and turn right onto Bayshore Road for a sundowner at the **Star Restaurant & Bar** (☞ Dining, *below*).

TIMING

To drive straight out to the farthest points on this tour, allow about 30 minutes to drive out to Lucayan National Park, east of Freeport, and 45 minutes to get to the Star Restaurant & Bar.

Freeport

Freeport is an attractive, planned city of broad boulevards, modern shopping centers, and convenient tourist facilities. The airport is just a few minutes from downtown, and the harbor not too much farther.

Sights to See

❸ Goombay Park Straw Market. Here dozens of Bahamian vendors display an endless selection of straw goods: handbags, place mats, hats, baskets, and more. You'll also find T-shirts, mahogany and native-pine carvings, and costume jewelry. Don't be shy about haggling over prices. The vendors will be surprised if you don't. ⊠ *Behind International Bazaar entrance, no phone.* ☉ *Daily 10–6.*

❻ Hydroflora Gardens. Plant enthusiasts and other nature lovers should plan to spend some time here, where a member of the Victor family takes you on "the most educational garden tour in Freeport," accompanied by classical music. Hydroflora Gardens was developed on the concept of hydroponics, plant cultivation without soil. The Bahamas' primarily limestone soil provides the perfect natural laboratory. Wander through trails blooming with native flora and learn about medicinal and biblical plants, especially as they pertain to Bahamian history and culture. If the fruit trees are bearing their seasonal crop, you might get to taste a mango or guava guaranteed to be bursting with homegrown flavor. ⊠ *E. Beach Dr. and E. Sunrise Hwy.,* ☎ *242/352–6052.* 🖼 *$5 for guided tour.* ☉ *Mon.–Sat. 9–5.*

★ ❷ International Bazaar. If the cobbled lanes and jumble of shops and restaurants in this 10-acre complex look like something from a Hollywood soundstage, that's not surprising: It was designed by special-effects artist Charles Perrin in 1967. At the entrance stands a 35-ft torii arch, a red-lacquered gate that is a traditional symbol of welcome in Japan. More than 100 shops, lounges, and restaurants representing goods and cuisines from 25 countries line the narrow walkways. You can purchase silver and emeralds from South America, French perfumes, Spanish leather, brass from India, Chinese jade, African carvings, tailored clothes from Hong Kong, Thai silks, Irish linens, English china, and caftans from Turkey—at 20% to 40% below U.S. prices. **Colombian Emeralds International** (☎ 242/352–5464), in the South American section of the bazaar, gives free three-hour tours of its jewelry factory, Mondays through Saturdays at 10 and 2. You can watch craftspeople fashion gold, silver, and gemstones into rings, bracelets, and pendants. Freeport is home base for this company, though you'll find its shops scattered throughout the Caribbean. A simple emerald set in a 14-karat-gold ring may cost about $100, but most pieces start at $300. The choice of ethnic restaurants is almost as varied as the shops. ⊠ *W. Sunrise Hwy. and Mall Dr., no phone* 🖼 *Free.* ☉ *Mon.–Sat. 10–6.*

❹ Perfume Factory. The quiet and elegant Perfume Factory is housed in a replica 19th-century Bahamian mansion—the kind built by Loyalists, who settled in the Bahamas after the American Revolution. The

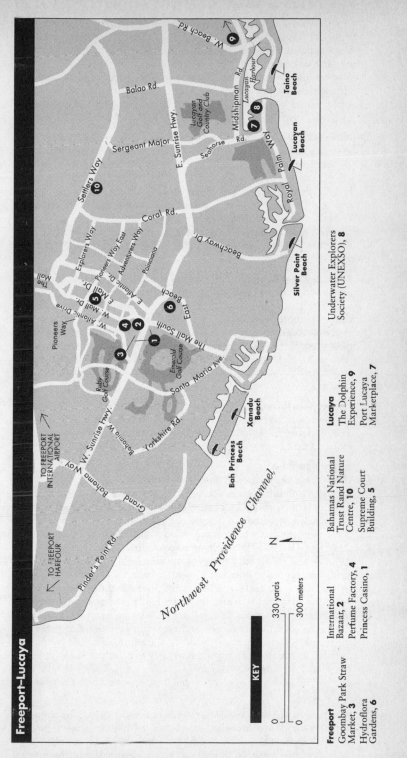

Freeport–Lucaya

KEY

0 — 330 yards
0 — 300 meters

Freeport
Goombay Park Straw Market, **3**
Hydroflora Gardens, **6**
International Bazaar, **2**
Perfume Factory, **4**
Princess Casino, **1**

Bahamas National Trust Rand Nature Centre, **10**
Supreme Court Building, **5**

Lucaya
The Dolphin Experience, **9**
Port Lucaya Marketplace, **7**
Underwater Explorers Society (UNEXSO), **8**

interior resembles a tasteful drawing room. This is the home of Fragrance of the Bahamas, a company that produces perfumes, colognes, and lotions using the scents of jasmine, cinnamon, gardenia, spice, and ginger. On a free tour of the mixology laboratory, you can blend your own creations from among 35 scents. You can sniff mixtures until they hit the right combination, then bottle, name, and take the personalized perfume home for a $30 charge. ⊠ *Behind International Bazaar, on access road,* ☎ *242/352–9391.* ☑ *Free.* ⊙ *Weekdays 10–5:30.*

★ **❶ Princess Casino.** Gamblers are attracted here in droves to try their hand at nearly 500 nickel, quarter, dollar and five-dollar slots; blackjack; and other gambling temptations (☞ Nightlife and the Arts, *below*). Place a bet on your favorite NFL, NBA, NHL, NCAA basketball, boxing, and baseball teams at the casino's Sports Book tucked at the rear of the bustling casino. The Princess Casino is part of the Bahamas Princess Resort & Casino, a Freeport landmark with a distinctive Moorish-style dome, adjacent to the International Bazaar. ⊠ *W. Sunrise Hwy.,* ☎ *242/352–6721 or 800/422–7466 in the U.S.* ⊙ *Daily 9 AM–3:30 AM.*

❺ Supreme Court Building. This striking building was completed in 1994 to honor the visit of Queen Elizabeth II. The design—bright pink stucco with white trim and green shutters—reflects the old British colonial architecture more common to Nassau than Freeport. The Bahamian legal system is based on British law; on workdays, you can catch a glimpse of lawyers in robes and wigs. Visitors are welcome to observe court in session. ⊠ *Mall Dr.,* ☎ *242/351–4275.* ⊙ *Weekdays 9–4:30.*

Lucaya

Lucaya, on the southern coast of Grand Bahama and just east of Freeport, was developed as the island's resort center. It has evolved into a comfortable residential area with large resort hotels, a fine sandy beach, marina facilities at Port Lucaya, and a championship golf course.

Sights to See

★ **❾ The Dolphin Experience.** A close encounter with a pod of Atlantic bottle-nosed dolphins awaits you in Sanctuary Bay at the world's largest dolphin facility, about 2 mi east of Port Lucaya. A ferry takes you from Port Lucaya to the bay to observe and photograph the animals. If you don't mind getting wet, you can sit on a partially submerged dock or stand waist deep in the water, and one of these friendly creatures will swim up and touch you. The program started in 1987, when five dolphins were trained to interact with people. Later, the animals were trained to head out to sea and swim with scuba divers on the open reef. A two-hour dive program is available. If you really get hooked on these affectionate animals, you can enroll in an all-day program and work with the trainers in different aspects of the dolphin program. Buy tickets for the Dolphin Experience and the dive program at UNEXSO (☞ *below*) in Port Lucaya; make reservations as early as possible. ⊠ *Dolphin Experience, Port Lucaya,* ☎ *242/373–1250 or 800/992–3483,* 𝖥𝖠𝖷 *242/ 373–8956.* ☑ *2-hr program $36, full day program $179, Dolphin dive $138.* ⊙ *Daily 9–5.*

★ **❼ Port Lucaya Marketplace.** The town of Lucaya's capacious shopping complex—a dozen low-rise, pastel-painted buildings with tropical colonial architecture influenced by traditional island homes—is on the waterfront 4 mi east of Freeport and across the street from several major hotels. Among the 100 or so establishments are waterfront restaurants and bars, and shops that sell clothes, crystal and china, watches, jewelry, and perfumes. Small wooden stalls dot the area, where vendors sell refreshing fresh-fruit drinks (with or without alcohol). Local artists hawk their wares, and you can watch wood-carvers hew animals and human faces out of native mahogany, ebony, and wild tamarind. The walkways have small, well-kept gardens of hibiscus and croton. An unwieldy straw market, once outside the marketplace, has been relocated inside: look for the tidy row of painted stalls at the east end of the complex. The centerpiece of the market is **Count Basie Square**, named after Freeport's own King of Jazz, Count Basie. Live bands, steel bands, and gospel singers often perform Bahamian music in its bougainvillea-covered bandstand. On balmy weekend evenings, families—locals and tourists—gather to make new friends and greet old. Kids of all ages form conga lines and dance around the square. ⊠ *Sea Horse Rd.,* ☎ *242/373–8446.* ⊘ *Mon.–Sat. 10–6.*

★ ⑧ **Underwater Explorers Society (UNEXSO).** One of the world's most respected diving facilities, UNEXSO welcomes more than 12,000 individuals each year and trains more than 3,000 of them in scuba diving. UNEXSO's facilities include an 18-ft-deep training tank with observation windows, and a recompression/decompression chamber. UNEXSO also has educational courses and specialized training for experienced divers seeking upgraded or specialized certification. Next door is an extensive dive shop, where you can talk to instructors, pick up brochures, and meet other divers. ⊠ *On the wharf at Port Lucaya Marketplace,* ☎ *242/373–1244 or 800/992–3483.* ⊠ *3-hr resort course and 1 dive $99, snorkeling trip (includes mask, fins, and snorkel) $18.* ⊘ *Daily 8–6.*

Beyond Freeport-Lucaya

Grand Bahama Island narrows at picturesque West End, once the capital of Grand Bahama and still home to many of the island's first settlers. Along the one main road, which runs just inches from the water, you'll see fishermen's boats moored opposite their colorful homes. Islanders come here to buy fresh fish; and if there's a hankering in the crowd for a conch salad, one of the fishermen will surely pop into his house for the necessary ingredients to whip one up. Local vendors also sell native meals, such as fried grouper and peas 'n' rice.

Little seaside villages, with houses painted in bright blue and pastel yellow, dot the landscape between Freeport and West End. Many of these settlements are more than 100 years old. Their names derive from the surnames of the original homesteaders, and most residents are descendants of these founders.

The East End is the "back-to-nature" side of Grand Bahama. The road east from Lucaya is long, flat, and straight. It cuts through endless pine forest to reach McLean's Town, the end of the road. Curly-tailed lizards, raccoons, pelicans, and other native creatures populate this part of the island.

Sights to See

★ ⑩ **Bahamas National Trust Rand Nature Centre.** On 100 acres just minutes from downtown Freeport, a half mile of trails show off 130 types of native plants, including many species of wild orchid. One variety, the *vanilla correlli,* is found nowhere else in the world. You might spot a Cuban emerald hummingbird sipping the nectar of a hibiscus, or an even tinier Bahama woodstar, or a raccoon, an animal introduced to the island during the rumrunning days of the 1920s and 1930s. In the learning and exhibit room, you can see three species of native boa constrictor, among other native and introduced animals. On the grounds themselves, don't miss the Lucayan Village Exhibit; this is a reconstruction of one of the small villages believed to have been inhabited by the original Lu-

Grand Bahama Island

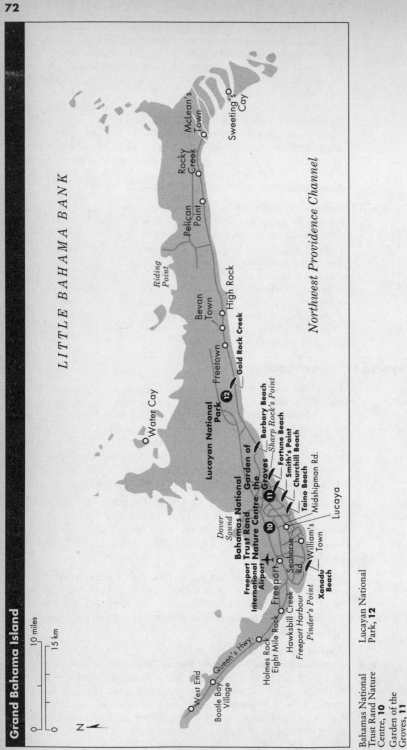

LITTLE BAHAMA BANK

West End
Boole Bay
Village
Queen's Hwy.
Holmes Rock
Eight Mile Rock
Hawksbill Creek
Freeport Harbour
Pinder's Point
Freeport
Seahorse
Rd.
Xanadu
Beach
William's
Town
Airport
Freeport
International
Nature Centre
Bahamas National
Trust Rand
10
Dover Sound
Garden of
the
Groves
11
Smith's Point
Churchill Beach
Taino Beach
Midshipman Rd.
Fortune Beach
Sharp Rock's Point
Barbary Beach
Lucaya

Lucayan National
Park
12
Gold Rock Creek
Freetown
Bevan
Town
High Rock
Riding Point
Water Cay

Pelican
Point
Rocky
Creek
McLean's
Town
Sweeting's
Cay

Northwest Providence Channel

10 miles
15 km

N

cayans. The reserve is named for philanthropist James H. Rand, the former president of Remington Rand, who donated a hospital and library to the island. ⊠ *E. Settlers Way, Freeport,* ☎ *242/352–5438.* ▣ *$5.* ⊙ *Mon.–Fri. 9–4, guided nature walk at 10; Sat. 9–1.*

★ ⑪ **Garden of the Groves.**There are some 10,000 varieties of Bahamian flora, including fruit trees, ferns, flowering plants, and exotic species at this lush, 12-acre botanical paradise, named for American financier and pioneer developer Wallace Groves and his wife, Georgette, the founders of Freeport. One path gives way to a picture-perfect chapel on a hill, a replica of Grand Bahama's first church. Beyond another pathway lies a hidden hibiscus garden—a favorite spot on the island for weddings. ⊠ *Midshipman Rd. and Magellan Dr.,* ☎ *242/352–4045.* ▣ *$7.95.* ⊙ *Mon.–Sat. 9–4, Sun. 10–4.*

★ ⑫ **Lucayan National Park.** Trails and elevated walkways wind through a natural forest of wild tamarind and gumbo-limbo trees, past an observation platform, a mangrove swamp, what is believed to be the largest explored underwater cave system in the world (it's 7 mi long), and sheltered pools containing rare marine species. This 40-acre seaside land preserve, some 20 mi east of Lucaya, contains examples of the island's five ecosystems: dunes, whiteland coppice, mangrove, blackland coppice, and pine forest. A sign near the entrance has a large map detailing the park's distinctive features, which enables you to find your way around. Expert divers who wish to explore beneath the caves (and who aren't put off by the horde of bats that visit en masse about once a year in August) should contact BNT Rand Nature Centre(☞ *above*). Across the road, a boardwalk winds through pine forest and mangrove swamp to Gold Rock Beach, an absolutely beautiful, usually deserted strand of white sand and aquamarine ocean. ⊠ *Grand Bahama Hwy.,* ☎ *242/ 352–5438.* ▣ *$3.* ⊙ *Daily 9–4.*

BEACHES

Some 60 mi of magnificent, uncluttered stretches of sand extend between Freeport-Lucaya and McLean's Town, the isolated eastern end of the island. Most are used only by people who live in adjacent settlements along the way. Lucaya hotels have their own beaches and watersports activities; guests at Freeport hotels are shuttled free to places like **Xanadu,** a mile-long stretch of white sand, and **Taino** beaches.

Local residents have their favorites. At **William's Town,** south of Freeport (off E. Sunrise Hwy. and down Beachway Dr.) and east of Xanadu Beach, the sandy solitude is broken only by the occasional passing of horseback riders from Pinetree Stables at the water's edge.

East of Port Lucaya, several delightful beaches run along the South Shore—**Taino Beach, Churchill Beach, Smith's Point, Fortune Beach,** and **Barbary Beach.** Farther east on the island, at the end of the trail from the Lucayan National Park, you'll find **Gold Rock Creek,** which is only a 20-mi drive from the Lucaya hotels. Locals drive here on the weekends for picnics.

DINING

In general, the restaurants on Grand Bahama Island cannot be rated as highly as those on New Providence; only a handful of establishments could be considered fine dining. However, a meal in Freeport usually costs less than a comparable one in Nassau.

You will find many options, though, in Freeport and Lucaya, from elegant hotel dining rooms and charming waterside cafés to local hangouts and familiar fast-food chains. Menus often combine Continental, American, and Bahamian fare. Freeport's International Bazaar offers exotic fare, such as Indian or Japanese. Wednesday evenings, there's a native fish fry at Smith's Point, east of Lucaya (taxi drivers know the way), where you can sample fresh seafood—conch, grouper, barracuda—cooked outdoors at the beach. It's a great opportunity to meet local residents, and at about $7 per person, it's also a bargain!

CATEGORY	COST*
$$$	over $30
$$	$20–$30
$	under $20

per person for a three-course meal, excluding drinks, service, and 15% tip

Freeport

Continental

$$$ ✕ **Crown Room.** Rose-colored, beveled-glass mirrors alternating with coral wall panels adorn this intimately lighted dining room in a corner of the Bahamas Princess Casino, away from the bustle of the gaming tables (celebrate a win here!). High-back French colonial–style chairs, tightly crowded tables, and white Italian smoked-glass chandeliers add to the cozy atmosphere—and soft jazz plays in the background. The fare is standard Continental; specialties include escargot ravioli, Caesar salad prepared table-side, and Caribbean seafood "Crown Room" (lobster, shrimp, and scallops in saffron cream sauce, on a bed of fettucine)—worth the splurge. The rack of lamb will more than satisfy meat lovers. ⊠ *Bahamas Princess Casino,* ☎ *242/352–7811 or 242/352–6721 ext. 54. Reservations essential. Jacket required. AE, MC, V. Closed Sun.–Mon. No lunch.*

$$$ ✕ **Ruby Swiss European Restaurant.** The extensive Continental menu here features 14 seafood dishes, more than 17 beef items, and an all-you-can-eat spaghetti bar; specialties include steak Diane (thinly sliced steak flavored with cognac), fondue bourguignonne (prepared with filet mignon), and desserts flambéed at the table. The wine list's 50-odd varieties cover six countries. Although you can have a nice evening here, the busy atmosphere and size aren't exactly conducive to romance; the dinnertime guitar music by Perry Gilbert does add a nice touch, however. Snacks are served until 5 AM, making this a good place to come after hitting the casinos. ⊠ *W. Sunrise Hwy. and Atlantic Dr., across from Bahamas Princess Tower,* ☎ *242/352–8507. Reservations essential. AE, DC, MC, V. No lunch weekends.*

$$–$$$ ✕ **Rib Room.** Come here when you hunger for a generous portion of prime rib, steak, or surf and turf. Some prices are high, but a good deal is the special three-course meal, served from 6 to 7, which includes appetizer, entrée, dessert, and coffee for $27.50. The interior resembles an English hunting lodge with its long narrow rooms, rough-hewn timber ceiling, wood and brick walls, red leather chairs, and tartan carpet. ⊠ *Princess Country Club, Bahamas Princess Resort & Casino,* ☎ *242/352–6721 ext. 59. Reservations essential. Jacket required. AE, DC, MC, V. Closed Tues.–Wed. No lunch.*

Italian

$$ ✕ **La Trattoria.** This bistro serves outstanding authentic northern Italian cuisine amid subdued lighting and stucco walls. The pizzas and pastas are especially good. ⊠ *Princess Tower, Bahamas Princess Resort & Casino,* ☎ *242/353-6721 ext. 59. AE, DC, MC, V. Closed Thurs. and Sun. No lunch.*

Freeport–Lucaya Dining

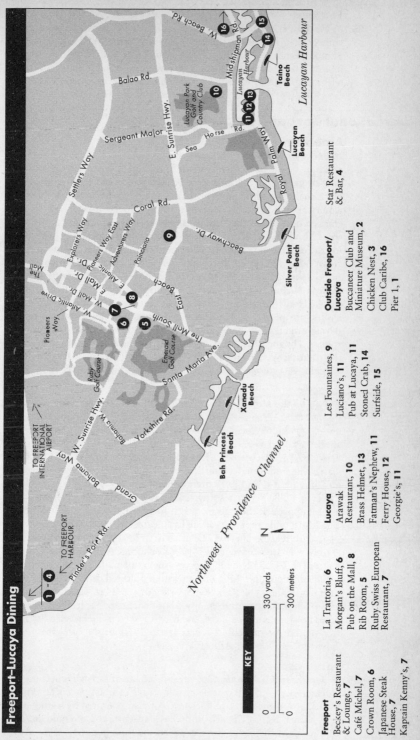

KEY

| 0 | 330 yards |
| 0 | 300 meters |

Lucayan Harbour

Taino Beach

Lucayan Beach

Silver Point Beach

Xanadu Beach

Bah Princess Beach

Northwest Providence Channel

TO FREEPORT INTERNATIONAL AIRPORT

TO FREEPORT HARBOUR

Freeport
Beccey's Restaurant & Lounge, **7**
Café Michel, **7**
Crown Room, **6**
Japanese Steak House, **7**
Kaptain Kenny's, **7**

La Trattoria, **6**
Morgan's Bluff, **6**
Pub on the Mall, **8**
Rib Room, **5**
Ruby Swiss European Restaurant, **7**

Lucaya
Arawak Restaurant, **10**
Brass Helmet, **13**
Fatman's Nephew, **11**
Ferry House, **12**
Georgie's, **11**

Les Fountaines, **9**
Luciano's, **11**
Pub at Lucaya, **11**
Stoned Crab, **14**
Surfside, **15**

Outside Freeport/ Lucaya
Buccaneer Club and Miniature Museum, **2**
Chicken Nest, **3**
Club Caribe, **16**
Pier 1, **1**

Star Restaurant & Bar, **4**

Seafood

$$ ✕ **Morgan's Bluff.** This relaxed family-style seafood restaurant is named for 17th-century pirate Sir Henry Morgan. The menu has tasty island specialties such as conch chowder, conch fritters, Bahamian lobster tail, blackened redfish, and fresh grouper sautéed in lemon, butter, and spices. ⊠ *Princess Tower, Bahamas Princess Resort & Casino,* ☎ *242/352–9661. AE, MC, V. Closed Mon.–Tues. No lunch.*

International Bazaar (Freeport)

American

$ ✕ **Beckey's Restaurant & Lounge.** This popular eatery opens at 7 AM and may be the best place in town to fuel up before a full day of shopping or gambling. Its diner-style booths and bright lighting provide a basic backdrop for the inexpensive menu of traditional Bahamian and American food, from conch salad and minced lobster tail to fried chicken or a BLT. Pancakes, eggs, and special Bahamian breakfasts— spicy "boil" fish, "stew" fish, or chicken souse (pickled), with johnnycake or grits—are served all day. In the afternoons, you'll find a mixed crowd enjoying drinks and people-watching on the buzzing patio. ⊠ *International Bazaar,* ☎ *242/352–8717. No credit cards.*

$ ✕ **Café Michel.** Stop by this unpretentious bistro for a light meal or snack. The 20-odd alfresco tables, with festive red umbrellas and tablecloths, are placed in an ideal people-watching location just off the Bazaar's main promenade. Indoors, there is a no-frills, coffee-shop atmosphere. The menu includes both American and Bahamian dishes, and the rotating specials menu always offers at least one tasty and filling bargain. ⊠ *International Bazaar,* ☎ *242/352–2191. AE, MC, V.*

Eclectic

$$ ✕ **Pub on the Mall.** You have four options here. **The Prince of Wales Lounge** (☎ 242/352–2700), an authentic English-style pub, serves fish-and-chips, kidney pie, and three types of draft ale; early and late-bird specials, served 5–7 and 10–11, include salad, entrée, dessert, and coffee for $7.95. **The Islander's Roost Restaurant** (☎ 242/352–5110) serves Caribbean and American dishes in a relaxed atmosphere with an open-air dining patio and live entertainment nightly. A brilliantly colored maccaw, Bella, screeches a welcome at you from her 20-ft-high cage as you approach the Pub from Ranfurly Circus. On 24 hours notice, The Roost will prepare its specialty, local fresh grouper baked in white wine with seasonal herbs. The price is $17.50 per person and the dish is only prepared on request for two or more. A third restaurant, **Silvano's** (☎ 242/352–5111), serves fine homemade cannelloni and fettuccine in a circular dining room with a bold red ceiling and paintings of Italian cities. The **Red Dog Sports Bar** (☎ 242/352–2700), on the ground floor, serves free happy hour snacks, has a friendly if sometimes boisterous atmosphere, and four TV screens including a 96″ monster screen for dedicated sports fans. ⊠ *Ranfurly Circus, opposite International Bazaar. AE, MC, V.*

Japanese

$–$$ ✕ **Japanese Steak House.** Experience a taste of Japan as chefs prepare chicken, seafood, and marbled Kobe steaks in a fast-paced, sizzling hibachi show right at your table. Two rooms, separated by sliding paper screens, are decorated with umbrellas, fans, and red and gold lanterns. In a room at the back, you can sit on the floor Japanese-style. At the front room's long tables, set for groups of 10 or more, you sit with other diners. All of the hibachi meals include soup, salad, vegetables, and rice with the entrée. The à la carte menu is more expensive, but you can save money by ordering the early bird dinner special—for $19.95

you can choose from among four complete hibachi meals. ☒ *International Bazaar,* ☎ 242/352–9521. *AE, MC, V. No lunch.*

Seafood

$$ ✕ **Kaptain Kenny's.** Lobster traps and hunks of driftwood hang from the ceiling and walls of this popular place to meet and eat. This is one of the oldest and most interesting buildings in Freeport and has been carefully remodeled to create a half-museum, half-Disney atmosphere—check out Freeport's Walk of Fame just outside the entrance, with imprints of such luminaries as Cliff Robertson, Hank Aaron, Lou Rawls, and a smattering of soap-opera stars who signed the names of their characters. Inside, gnarled-wood tables are inlaid with parchment treasure maps. Outside, on the spacious wood patio, diners and drinkers can listen to live music—and dancing is "always permissible." Despite all the trappings, however, this is not a form-over-content operation: Seafood is first-rate. Grouper, the house specialty, is prepared three ways—panfried, stuffed, and *papillote* (baked in parchment) with shrimp. Pizza with various toppings is also on the menu. ☒ *International Bazaar,* ☎ 242/351–4759. *AE, MC, V.*

Lucaya

Bahamian

$ ✕ **Fatman's Nephew.** Owner Stanley Simmons named his restaurant for the two rotund uncles who taught him the trade. One of the better spots to dine in Port Lucaya, this place serves substantial Bahamian fare. Watch for the seafood board's "catch of the day." The best seating is on the L-shaped outdoor terrace overlooking the waterway and marina. The menu is somewhat limited, but the value can't be beat. Try the Southern-style ham hocks, cracked conch, or curried beef. For the less adventurous, the menu also includes standard American burgers. ☒ *Port Lucaya Marketplace,* ☎ 242/373–8520. *AE, MC, V.*

$ ✕ **Georgie's.** Stop in at this pleasant, casual spot, in a quiet corner of Port Lucaya Marketplace, for happy hour and snacks or dinner. Conch fritters, lobster, and grouper are among the specialties. Get a table outside and watch the scene while you sip a fruity drink or a Kalik beer. The early bird special, 5–8 PM, offers lobster tails for $9.95 and grouper fingers or cracked conch for $7.95, and all dishes come with peas 'n' rice. ☒ *Port Lucaya Marketplace,* ☎ 242/373–8513. *AE, MC, V.*

Continental

$$$ ✕ **Luciano's.** This sophisticated Port Lucaya restaurant is one of the best
★ places on the island for upscale cuisine, which is prepared under the expert eye of owner Luciano Guindani, who formerly ran the Arawak Dining Room at the Lucaya Country Club. The large dining area overlooks the waterway; its modern decor uses halogen lamps and abstract paintings. You can't go wrong with the house specialty, veal Luciano, which is embellished with shrimp, lobster, and a spicy cream sauce. ☒ *Port Lucaya Marketplace,* ☎ 242/373–9100. *AE, MC, V.*

Eclectic

$ ✕ **Ferry House.** Manager Hanne Glud, a happy bubbling Dane, takes pride in never having served frozen vegetables at this restaurant; all the bread and Danish pastries served here are baked on the premises as well. You'll find both Danish and American dishes on the menu of this simple, bright and airy restaurant just inside Bell Channel. It has its own dock and serves as the main restaurant for nearby Pelican Bay at Lucaya and the Lucayan Marina Village, which is served by a ferry from 8 AM to 11 PM (the restaurant is open 7 AM to 10 PM). The dockside patio is a favorite with local businesspeople and visitors fortunate enough to find the place, just outside the Port Lucaya Marketplace.

The veal scallopini in a walnut sauce with grapes and sautéed celery is worth the search. ⊠ *Port Lucaya,* ☎ *242/373–1595. AE, MC, V.*

$ ✕ **Les Fountaines.** Arthur Fountain's unusual 24-hour restaurant on East Sunrise Highway serves an all-you-can-eat buffet from 11AM to midnight for $8.50. His flexible menu includes Bahamian, American, and vegetarian dishes; items from the jerk pit—pork ribs, chicken, snapper, and grunts (small panfish)—are served Wednesdays through Sundays. There are two 85-seat dining rooms and a 70-seat "tropical and celebrity lounge" with a 62" satellite TV. Out back is a state-of-the-art disco pavilion, Le Utopia, which is packed weekend nights. ⊠ *E. Sunrise Hwy.,* ☎ *242/373–9553. AE, V.*

English

$ ✕ **Pub at Lucaya.** Formerly Pusser's Pub, this amiable pub is right on the Port Lucaya waterfront. The nautical decor incorporates antique copper measuring cups and ersatz Tiffany lamps suspended from a wood-beam ceiling. Locals swap tall tales and gossip with tourists as they people-watch and drink Pusser's Painkillers, which are graded by strength from 2 to 4, depending on the quantity of Pusser's rum in the mix. The outside terrace is the most popular area for dining; a daiquiri bar there serves drinks and ice cream. Dependable English fare is favored, such as shepherd's and steak-and-ale pies. Other recommended dishes include double-cut lamb chops, Bahamian lobster tail, and strip sirloin. ⊠ *Port Lucaya Marketplace,* ☎ *242/373–8450. AE, DC, MC, V.*

French

$$$ ✕ **Arawak Restaurant.** This lovely restaurant at the Lucaya Golf & Country Club has a wall of windows overlooking the golf course and the Balancing Boulders of Lucaya waterfall. Fine French cuisine with a Bahamian flair is served at lunch and dinner. Jazz accompanies dinner weekend evenings and brunch on Sunday afternoons. ⊠ *Lucaya Golf & Country Club,* ☎ *242/373–1066 or 242/373–1067. Reservations essential. AE, DC, MC, V. No dinner Sun.*

Seafood

$$ ✕ **Stoned Crab.** A local favorite, this restaurant with a pyramid-shape roof faces one of the island's loveliest stretches of sand, Taino Beach. The scrumptiously sweet, fist-size stone crabs are locally caught, as are the lobsters. The broiled seafood platter *oreganato,* with lobster, grouper, shrimp, mussels, conch and blue crabs in garlic white wine with a sprinkling of bread crumbs, is delectable. Other specialties include swordfish, wahoo, and yellowfin tuna. In fair weather, you can enjoy a delightful ocean view from the outdoor patio. ⊠ *Taino Beach,* ☎ *242/373–1442. AE, MC, V. No lunch.*

$ ✕ **Brass Helmet.** The name is embodied in the timeworn metal diving helmet displayed on an aged wooden crate, amid other antique diving gear. To give you the feeling of being in the depths, colorful underwater videos play continually on a large-screen TV. Diners get a kick out of the fierce-looking life-size shark that has "burst" through one of the walls at this casual restaurant above the UNEXSO dive operation. The cracked conch is delicious here, along with Jamaican beef or chicken patties, and steak. Wash it all down with a Hammer'd, if you dare: It's made with both light and dark rum, apricot brandy, vodka, and fruit punch. ⊠ *Upstairs from UNEXSO, Port Lucaya Marketplace,* ☎ *242/373–2032. AE, D, MC, V.*

$ ✕ **Surfside.** This deceptively low-key restaurant sits on stilts atop Taino Beach (complimentary transportation is provided from your hotel). Its bare-bones decor—faded blue-and-gray color scheme—is more than made up for by its colorful clientele. The kitchen is somewhat unreliable, but the seafood and Bahamian dishes are popular staples. There is a daily happy hour from 5:30 to 6:30. ⊠ *Taino Beach,* ☎ *242/373–1814. MC, V.*

Outside Freeport-Lucaya

Bahamian

$$ ✕ **Club Caribe.** This small, attractive beachside haunt is an ideal spot to unwind. Relax with a Bahama Mama drink, or dine on the local fare, such as minced Bahamian lobster, grouper, or steamed pork chops. Free transportation is available to and from your hotel. ⊠ *Mather Town, off Midshipman Rd.,* ☎ *242/373–6866. Reservations essential. AE, MC, V.*

$$ ✕ **Pier 1.** You actually do walk the plank to get to this rustic, windswept
★ eatery on stilts, where you can observe the cruise-ship activity of Freeport Harbour or watch the sunset over cocktails. The pleasant dining area can become crowded with cruise passengers seeking a scrumptious sample of island seafood (including fresh oysters) and Bahamian cooking before returning to shipboard dining. Baby shark, prepared a half-dozen-plus ways—sautéed with garlic, stuffed with crabmeat and cheese, or over linguine with Provençale sauce are a few—is the specialty of the house; you can watch the denizens of the deep in the shark pool alongside the restaurant. Aquariums dot the restaurant, and when the sun goes down it's feeding time: Fish seem to appear out of nowhere to put on a show in which dozens of sharks and, if you're lucky, even a barracuda named Charlie appear. Uwe Nath, the German-born host, entertains guests with stories about sharks and other fish. ⊠ *Freeport Harbour,* ☎ *242/352–6674. AE, MC, V. No lunch Sun.*

$ ✕ **Chicken Nest.** About 6 mi west of the Buccaneer Club(☞ *below*), before West End, this is a simple, home-style place. Lovamae Nixon's no-nonsense menu includes fish, fritters, conch salad and homemade potato bread, and you can shoot pool while you wait for your order. ⊠ *Bayshore Rd.,* ☎ *242/346–6440. No credit cards. Closed Mon.*

$ ✕ **Star Restaurant & Bar.** An aging, two-story wooden building at the far western end of West End Village, looking for all the world like part of a ghost town, the Star is one of the oldest buildings on the island and is thought to be the first hotel. It saw lots of furtive action during the rumrunning days of Prohibition. The place hasn't had a stay-over guest in years, but you can still get a drink here and eat at the small restaurant. Proprietor Anne Grant caters to locals, boaters, and passing tourists with seafood, chicken and pigs feet souse, plus various American dishes. Wednesday night is fish fry night. ⊠ *Bayshore Rd., West End,* ☎ *242/346–6207. No dinner.*

Eclectic

$$$ ✕ **Buccaneer Club and Miniature Museum.** The oldest restaurant on the island—and the site of one of the most important Lucayan archaeological finds in the Caribbean—this festive place on the way to the West End, a 20-minute drive from Freeport, serves good Bahamian and Swiss cuisine in a rustic chalet setting. In June 1996, owners Heinz and Kitty Fischbacher started finding pieces of old pottery along their eroding beach. They reported their find to the Bahamas National Trust, and, since then, serious archaeological digging has unearthed more than 10,000 artifacts dating back to 14th-century Lucayan Indians. Heinz is planning to enlarge his restaurant to include a small museum featuring displays of the artifacts. You may wish to time your arrival to toast the sunset from the uncluttered 1 mi-long beach nearby. Beach parties—a "pirate's buffet" of salad, conch fritters, barbecued fish and ribs—take place Wednesday and Sunday evenings. The restaurant provides courtesy transportation. ⊠ *Deadman's Reef,* ☎ *242/349–3794. Reservations essential. AE, MC, V. Closed Mon.*

LODGING

Generally speaking, hotel rates are lower on Grand Bahama Island than in Nassau, Cable Beach, and on Paradise Island. You can choose from among Grand Bahama's approximately 3,500 rooms and suites, ranging from attractive one- and two-bedroom units in sprawling resort complexes to practical apartments with kitchenettes to comfortable rooms in economy-oriented establishments. The higher-price hotels in Freeport and Lucaya, some of which date back 30 years, have managed to maintain their appeal to guests through continual renovation. Small apartment complexes and time-sharing rentals are economical alternatives, especially if you're planning to stay for more than a few days. If being on the beach is important, Lucaya hotels and the Xanadu offer beach access, and UNEXSO—Freeport's scuba central—is within easy walking distance. If your priorities focus less on the beach and more on gambling, golf, and shopping, you will probably enjoy being right in Freeport, where hotels provide complimentary transportation to the beach.

The hotel strip along Lucaya Beach is in a state of flux: Hutchison Whampoa of Hong Kong bought the Lucayan Beach Hotel and Casino, the Grand Bahama Beach Hotel, and the Atlantik Beach Hotel—all to be transformed into the Lucayan, a 1,600-room resort with four hotel units. A casino, a spa, 18 bars and restaurants, two 18-hole championship golf courses, and a 2,000-seat convention center will complete the huge resort. The Grand Bahama Beach Hotel is undergoing renovations but is still open. The Lucayan Beach Hotel aims to re-open in February 1999. The casino is not slated for completion until December 1999.

All of the larger hotels offer honeymoon packages, and several offer special three-, four-, or seven-day money-saving packages to golfers, gamblers, scuba divers, and other vacationers. Families will find that almost every hotel, even the small economy type, offers baby-sitting services. Some also allow children under 12 to stay in a room for free and will even provide a crib or roll-away bed at no extra charge.

An 8% tax is added to your hotel bill, representing resort and government levies. Rates between April 15 and December 14 tend to be 25%–30% lower than during the rest of the year.

CATEGORY	COST*
$$$	over $125
$$	$85–$125
$	under $85

*All prices are for a standard double room, excluding tax and service charge.

Freeport

$$$ ⊞ **Bahamas Princess Resort & Casino.** Two sister resorts separated by
★   a boulevard—and sharing two 18-hole championship golf courses, a beach club, and a 20,000-sq-ft Moorish-style domed casino—make up this complex. Service, on the whole, is good. An activities hostess coordinates a daily schedule of events and games for both children and adults. Shoppers appreciate the fact that the International Bazaar is next door. Those who prefer the beach over a pool, however, must take a free shuttle bus (running every half hour) to the resort's beach club, which several other hotels use as well. There, you'll find waterskiing, parasailing, and the gamut of water sports—all of which can be arranged through the hotel. And you can elect a dining plan that provides charging privileges at nine restaurants. Special packages are available to honeymooners and to golfers—who show up in force

every January for the Waterford Crystal Pro-Am golf tournament. The resort also offers an all-inclusive package deal, which, for a fee added to standard room rates and airfare, provides three meals at any of seven wide-ranging restaurants, unlimited drinks all day long, a golf clinic, tennis lessons and other activities, admission to the resort's Las Vegas–style revue, and kids' enrollment in Camp Sea Shells.

Princess Tower. Next door to the casino, this 400-room, 10-story building is the quieter of the two properties because its guests are usually gambling. Its dramatic, Moorish-style design incorporates turrets, arches, and a dazzling white dome. Portuguese tiles in bright colors, soaring Moorish arches, and a 28-ft ceiling, give the lobby an exotic air. Despite the grand architecture, it's a casual hub of activity, especially at happy hour when a small band plays Bahamian music. The large guest rooms, however, are strictly contemporary—decorated in beige, mauve, and turquoise, with mirrored closets, framed watercolor prints, and oak-wash wood furniture. High rollers may want to opt for the lavish Princess Suite, for $950 a night, which comes with every conceivable amenity, including a baby grand piano.

Princess Country Club. This 565-room property, across the highway from the Princess Tower, attracts a lively, mixed crowd of serious golfers, families, and couples who enjoy sports. Tiered swim-through waterfalls cascade from a man-made rock formation that rises from the center of an enormous pool. Eight two- and three-story guest-room wings radiate outward like the spokes of a wheel from the circular deck around the pool area. The comfortable rooms in wings 2, 4, 7, and 9 have modern vanities and baths, emerald-green carpets, muted floral-print bedspreads and drapes, beige wallpaper, and oak-wash wood furniture. Wings 1, 3, and 8 offer rooms with plain wood furniture and tile floors instead of carpeting. Two full wings have been converted to time-share kitchen apartments under the name Princess Vacation Club International. ⊠ *Box F 2623, Freeport,* ☎ *242/352–9661, 242/352–6721, or 800/545–1300 in the U.S.,* ℻ *242/352–6842. 930 rooms, 35 suites. 9 restaurants, 6 bars, air-conditioning, room service, 2 pools, 2 beauty salons, hot tub, sauna, 2 18-hole golf courses, 9 tennis courts, exercise room, jogging, snorkeling, boating, dance club, theater, playground, travel services. AE, DC, MC, V. EP, FAP*

$$–$$$ 🔆 **Xanadu Marina and Beach Resort.** This high-rise is still best remembered as one of the final hideaways of billionaire Howard Hughes.
★ The resort—only a few minutes from town—has a pink exterior, with hot-pink trim and turquoise balconies overlooking either the small pool, marina, parking lot, or beach. Rooms are cheerful and tropical, with a soothing color scheme of sea-foam green and peach. The Escoffier Room, named after a 19th-century culinary genius, provides the perfect setting for a romantic dinner. The beach, a three-minute walk away, is dotted with coconut palms and flanked on both sides by thick stands of Australian pines. Here, water sports and beach volleyball are available. ⊠ *Box F 2438, Sunken Treasure Dr., Freeport,* ☎ *242/352–6782,* ℻ *242/352–5799. 189 rooms. Restaurant, 3 bars, air-conditioning, pool, beauty salon, 3 tennis courts, beach, dock, fishing, baby-sitting, meeting room. AE, MC, V.*

$$ 🔆 **Running Mon Marina & Resort.** Each room in this waterfront resort has a view of the 66-slip marina. Built in 1991, the two-story, pink stucco hotel with natural-wood decking is away from the action. Water quietly lapping against cabin cruisers docked at the marina punctuates the peaceful atmosphere. Guest rooms are decked out in soothing corals and aqua and island prints, light woods, wicker, and rattan. Boat owners will appreciate the haul-and-launch facility, on-site mechanics, and repair services. Deep-sea fishing charters can be arranged through the

Freeport-Lucaya Lodging

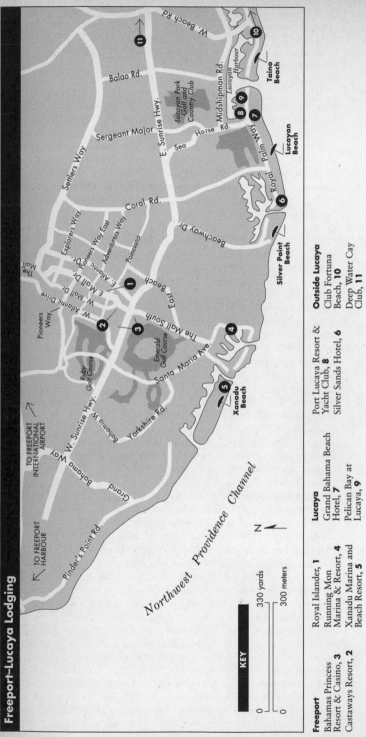

Freeport
Bahamas Princess
Resort & Casino, **3**
Castaways Resort, **2**

Royal Islander, **1**
Running Mon
Marina & Resort, **4**
Xanadu Marina and
Beach Resort, **5**

Lucaya
Grand Bahama Beach
Hotel, **7**
Pelican Bay at
Lucaya, **9**

Port Lucaya Resort &
Yacht Club, **8**
Silver Sands Hotel, **6**

Outside Lucaya
Club Fortuna
Beach, **10**
Deep Water Cay
Club, **11**

dockmaster. Mainsail, the resort's only restaurant (no lunch) and lounge, overlooks the marina channel. ⊠ *Box F 42663, 208 Kelly Ct., Freeport,* ☎ *242/352–6834,* FAX *242/352–6835. 32 rooms. Restaurant, bar, air-conditioning, refrigerators, pool, dive shop, fishing, meeting room, travel services. AE, MC, V. CP.*

$ 🖼 **Castaways Resort.** About as close to the action as you can get, this four-story budget hotel is next to the International Bazaar and a short walk away from the Bahamas Princess Casino. Kaptain Kenny's (☞ Dining, *above*), a popular (and often noisy) restaurant and nightspot, is just next door. This is not the most attractive hotel Freeport has to offer, but it has the basic amenities, is secure, and has a great location for shoppers and gamblers. The hotel's two buildings are connected by walkways over somewhat barren garden courtyards. Sun worshipers can find privacy on the large pool's sundeck or take the free shuttle to William's Town Beach. The average-size, motel-style rooms vary in price according to location; the most expensive, on the ground floor near the pool, have open decks. Furnishings are tropical against white, peach, or bright blue walls. Every night but Sunday, fire-eaters and limbo dancers perform in a popular "native" show at the hotel's Yellowbird nightclub. Monday-night manager's cocktail parties include free drinks, hors d'ocuvres, and prizes. The Flamingo Restaurant specializes in Bahamian and American food. ⊠ *Box F 2629, East Mall Dr., Freeport,* ☎ *242/352–6682,* FAX *242/352–5087. 130 rooms. Restaurant, 2 bars, air-conditioning, pool, volleyball, shops, nightclub, video games, playground. AE, MC, V.*

$ 🖼 **Royal Islander.** This motel-style property is near the International Bazaar and the Princess Casino, and provides free scheduled shuttle service to Xanadu beach. The rooms have light wood furnishings, framed pastel prints, and tile floors on the lower level or carpet upstairs, where no-smoking rooms are available. An inviting white-and-pastel lobby faces the spacious pool area, which has a performance space where "native" shows take place on Mondays, Wednesdays, and Fridays from 4 to 7 PM. Most native shows include live Bahamian Goombay and Junkanoo music, limbo dancers, a fire-eater, rake-and-scrape bands, and steel drums. There is also a show at the hotel's Royal Crown Restaurant at 6:30 on Tuesdays, Thursdays, and Saturdays. ⊠ *Box F 2549, West Mall Dr., Freeport,* ☎ *242/351–6000,* FAX *242/351–3546. 100 rooms. Dining room, bar, snack bar, air-conditioning, pool, Ping-Pong, travel services. AE, D, MC, V.*

Lucaya

$$$ 🖼 **Pelican Bay at Lucaya.** Pelican Bay opened its native mahogany lobby doors to its first guests in November 1996, and this Danish-style resort offers the romance of the Caribbean with European design and Bahamian hospitality. Earthy shades of green, gray, rust, and mustard distinguish one town house–type section of the resort from the next. The cozy reception area is furnished with a mahogany front desk, cushioned wicker seats, and paintings of Bahamian island scenery. Rooms come equipped with satellite TV, direct-dial phones, in-room safes, and coffeemakers. Stare endlessly at the ever-changing tides and sunsets from your room's full private wooden-railed balcony, which overlooks the pool and whirlpool area, canal, and marina. Pelican Bay is next door to UNEXSO, which makes it a popular stay for divers. Only steps away from the myriad shops, restaurants, and entertainment offered at Port Lucaya Marketplace, the resort is also across the street from magnificent beaches, and water-sports activities. A ferry runs between Pelican Bay and Lucayan Marina Village from 8 AM to 11 PM. ⊠ *Royal Palm Way (Box F 42654, Freeport),* ☎ *242/373–9550,* FAX *242/373–9551. 48 rooms. Restaurant, snack bar, air-conditioning, refrigerators, pool, hot tub, snorkeling, coin laundry. AE, MC, V.*

$$ 🏨 **Grand Bahama Beach Hotel.** This sprawling four-story resort, with its beautifully manicured grounds lined with coconut palms and seagrape trees, is part of the Hutchison redevelopment program. Ongoing renovations, which began in 1997, will incorporate a new pool, enhanced beach area, jogging and rollerblading tracks, lighted tennis courts, and a pavilion to be used for exhibitions and events. The large pool has an ocean view and is next to a kiddie pool and a bright, fun playground. Inside, rooms are spacious and tastefully decorated with soft, tropical teals and pinks, befitting an island getaway. Most rooms have a full-size private balcony—some with breathtaking ocean views—while others overlook tropical gardens. Quiet and simple, yet comfortable, this resort is across the street from the bustling activities of Port Lucaya. And it is ideal for ocean lovers and divers—right on the beach, and a short walk from UNEXSO. ⊠ *Royal Palm Way (Box F 2469, Freeport),* ☎ *242/373–1333, 800/622–6770, or 800–848–3315 in Canada,* FAX *242/373–2396. 200 rooms. Restaurant, bar, snack bar, air-conditioning, pool, 2 tennis courts, playground. AE, DC, MC, V.*

$$ 🏨 **Port Lucaya Resort & Yacht Club.** This full-service resort next door to the Port Lucaya Marketplace is equipped with its own 50-slip marina. Golf carts transport guests and luggage to its 10 pastel buildings, which are arranged in a decahedron around the Olympic-size swimming pool, Jacuzzi, restaurant, and garden. The rooms are styled as standard, superior, and deluxe and have garden, pool, or marina views. Decorated with rattan furniture, tile floors, large wall mirrors, and light tropical patterns, they are among the most appealing rooms in town. At night, the celebratory sounds of Port Lucaya Marketplace spill into buildings 7, 8, 9, and 10, and guests can enjoy the festivities from their balconies; those who prefer peace to partying should choose buildings 1–6, which are very quiet. Buildings 5 and 6 are strictly no-smoking. Marina activities are operated by the Port Lucaya Marina, and special rates are offered to hotel guests. Daily breakfast and dinner buffets at the restaurant are accompanied by Bahamian music. ⊠ *Box F 2452, Bell Channel Bay Rd., Freeport,* ☎ *242/373–6618 or 800/582–2921,* FAX *242/373–6652. 157 rooms, 3 suites. Restaurant, 2 bars, air-conditioning, pool, dock, laundry service. AE, D, MC, V.*

$–$$ 🏨 **Silver Sands Hotel.** This modest-looking hotel has more to offer than is apparent at first glance. The lobby is bright and cheerful, with a tile floor and bamboo furnishings, but the guest rooms are the most pleasant surprise: All have two full beds, a dining area, a full-size kitchen, and a private balcony. Upper-level rooms have dramatically slanting ceilings with skylights. Shades of beige and ivory, complemented by an island print, finish the look. Another plus is the beach—although you have to walk down a narrow path past a cesspool to get to it, this sandy stretch remains one of the nicest in the area. ⊠ *Box F 2385, Royal Palm Way, Freeport,* ☎ *242/373–5700,* FAX *242/373–1039. 78 studio apartments. Snack bar, air-conditioning, pool, 2 tennis courts, beach, snorkeling, meeting room. AE, MC, V.*

Outside Freeport-Lucaya

$$$ 🏨 **Club Fortuna Beach.** This all-inclusive Italian-run resort has been a
★   bit of a European secret since its 1992 opening. Recent years have brought more American vacationers, but you're still most likely to hear languages other than English as you stroll around the grounds. Popular with couples and families, the club provides a casual, low-stress, all-inclusive getaway—one price covers meals, unlimited drinks, taxes, tips, and activities, such as water sports, bicycling, tennis, boccie, volleyball, archery, table tennis, and aerobics. Club Fortuna Beach is a rather isolated enclave—4 mi from Port Lucaya—so to get around, you'll need to rent a car, take a taxi, or ride one of the hotel's bikes. A vast pri-

vate beach bustles with activity day and night. Golf, gambling excursions, and UNEXSO diving and dolphin experiences can be arranged through the hotel at extra cost. Meals are served buffet-style in the huge, natural wood, gazebo-style dining pavilion. The rooms are simple and pleasant, with unpainted pine furniture, clay tile floors, framed island prints, and small balconies that overlook the beach. ⊠ *Churchill Dr. and Bloom Rd. (Box F 42398, Freeport),* ☎ *242/373–4000,* FAX *242/ 373–5555. 276 rooms. Restaurant, pool, air-conditioning, 2 tennis courts, boccie, exercise rooms, beach, snorkeling, windsurfing, boating. AE, D, MC, V. All-inclusive.*

$$$ **Deep Water Cay Club.** Ideal if you want to get away from it all and
★ bonefish, this property has cottages scattered along the beach of a private island. Two cottages are two-bedroom, and all have their own bathrooms. Daily activities center on the main lodge, which houses the dining room, a self-service bar, and a tackle shop. The diversions here are beach lounging, diving, boating, and catch-and-release fishing—some of the best bonefishing in the Bahamas is here—and there's a 20-mi barrier reef nearby. The resort can arrange a charter flight from Florida, which lands at the property's own airstrip. ⊠ *Deep Water Cay (⊠ 1100 Lee Wagener Blvd., Suite 352, Fort Lauderdale, FL 33315),* ☎ *242/353– 3073 or 954/359–0488.* FAX *242/353–3095 or 954/359–9488. 9 units. Restaurant, bar, air-conditioning, pool, snorkeling, fishing, boating. No credit cards. All-inclusive.*

Time-Sharing

A number of condominiums in Freeport-Lucaya have become involved in time-sharing operations. Contact any of the following for information about rentals. For information about other time-share houses, apartments, and condominiums, check with the Grand Bahama Island Tourism Board (☞ Grand Bahama Island A to Z, *below*).

Bahama Reef (⊠ Box F 2695, Freeport, ☎ 242/373–1151). Eleven one-bedroom units and a three-bedroom penthouse face a canal 3½ mi from the beach. Visitors have access to bicycles and motorboats.

Coral Beach (⊠ Box F 2468, Freeport, ☎ 242/373–2468). A five-minute cab ride from the activity of Port Lucaya, these spacious, slightly weathered rooms are for budget-conscious travelers.

Freeport Resort & Club (⊠ Box F 2514, Freeport, ☎ 242/352–5371). The apartments here are in a woodsy setting close to the International Bazaar and the Bahamas Princess Casino.

Lakeview Manor Club (⊠ Box F 2699, Freeport, ☎ 242/352–2283). These one- and two-bedroom apartments are adjacent to the fairway of the fifth hole of the Ruby Golf Course.

Mayfield Beach and Tennis Club (⊠ Box F 458, Freeport, ☎ 242/352– 9776). The rentals here consist of apartments that share a pool and tennis court on Port-of-Call Drive at Xanadu Beach.

Ocean Reef Resort and Yacht Club (⊠ Box F 898, Freeport, ☎ 242/ 373–4661). These three-bedroom, three-bath apartments are midway between the International Bazaar and the Lucayan Beach hotels. The resort has a marina and a pool.

Princess Vacation Club International (⊠ Box F 684, Freeport, ☎ 242/ 352–3050). On the grounds of the Bahamas Princess Country Club, these converted time-shares are right in the middle of the action.

NIGHTLIFE AND THE ARTS

The Arts

Freeport Players' Guild (☎ 242/373–8400), a nonprofit repertory company, produces four plays a year at the 400-seat Regency Theatre during its September–June season.

Casinos

Whatever day and night activities are offered in Freeport and Lucaya, there's no doubt that the Princess Casino is among the island's top attractions. There is a dizzying array of slot machines, craps and blackjack tables, roulette, and baccarat to amuse novices and high rollers alike. Beginners can request a gaming guide, which explains the rules of each game, from the casino manager. There's usually nightly entertainment with live music and drinks are free to table or slots players; those not gaming have to pay. Slots are open from 9 AM until 3 AM or so; tables open at 10 AM. There's no specific dress code, although bathing suits and bare feet are not permitted. You must be at least 18 years of age to go into the casino, and residents of the Bahamas are not permitted to gamble. Photography is prohibited.

Princess Casino packs its 20,000 sq ft with 492 slot machines, 26 blackjack tables, seven craps tables, four roulette wheels, six Caribbean poker games, and one minibaccarat. A sports book for betting on sports enlivens the atmosphere a bit. An elevated circular bar is a great place from which to watch both casino action and live bandstand area entertainment. ⊠ *Bahamas Princess Resort & Casino, W. Sunrise Hwy.,* ☎ *242/352–6721 or 800/432–2294 in the U.S.* ☉ *Daily 8:30 AM–3:30 AM.*

Nightlife

For evening and late-night entertainment, Grand Bahama delivers calypso music, discos, live music for dancing at hotel lounges, and lavish Las Vegas–style sequins-and-feathers revues. Nightclubs are open generally from 8 or 9 PM until 3 AM. Major hotels organize their own late-night entertainment.

Bahamas Princess Country Club has the John B. outdoor lounge and disco every night but Sunday and a Goombay show, with live local music and dinner, on Saturday. ⊠ *Bahamas Princess Resort & Casino,* ☎ *242/352–6721.* ☉ *Lounge and disco nightly 9–2; doors open for Goombay show Sat. and Wed. at 6.*

Bahamas Princess Towers presents the Sultan's Tent, where singer and entertainer Marvin Henfield dazzles the hotel crowd with his glittering outfits, stunning impersonations, and expert all-request sets. ⊠ *Bahamas Princess Resort & Casino,* ☎ *242/352–9661.* ☉ *Shows Fri.–Wed. at 9.*

Casino Royale Show Room presents a twice-nightly extravaganza, with glamorous costumes, dancing, and novelty acts. ⊠ *Bahamas Princess Resort & Casino,* ☎ *242/352–6721.* ☉ *Shows at 8:30 and 10:45. Closed Mon.*

Joker's Wild Supper & Show Club features an exciting "native" show that includes limbo dancing, a fire-eater, island dancers, steel drum music, and a climactic Junkanoo finale. Dinner (choose from steak and lobster, Bahamian grouper, or a seafood platter) and the show cost $39; the show alone is $20. You can also boogie down on alternate nights, when $10 will get you a live Bahamian band and a free drink. ⊠ *Midshipman Rd., Lucaya,* ☎ *242/373–7765.* ☉ *Show Sun., Mon., Wed.; dinner at 7, show at 9. Dancing Thurs., Fri., Sat. at 10.*

Port Lucaya Marketplace has become one of the liveliest places to be after dark, with live entertainment and calypso music at Count Basie Square, which is bordered by three popular hangouts, The Corner Bar, Kaptain Kenny's Rum Runners, and The Pub at Port Lucaya. ⊠ *Sea Horse Rd., no phone.* ☉ *Daily from 10.*

Yellowbird Showroom has one of Grand Bahama's best "native" shows, with calypso, limbo, and fire dancers. ⊠ *Castaways Resort,* ☎ *242/ 352–6682.* ☉ *Wed.–Mon. from 8.*

OUTDOOR ACTIVITIES AND SPORTS

Banana Boating

Ocean Motion (⊠ Lucaya, ☎ 242/373–3923) lets you ride the banana for 10 minutes for $10. A favorite for the kids, this ride involves straddling a huge rubber banana and bumping along behind a motorboat.

Boating and Fishing

Charters

Boat charters cost about $300 a half day, $600 all day. Bahamian law limits the catching of game fish to six dolphinfish, kingfish, or wahoo per person per day.

Reef Tours (⊠ Bayside, Port Lucaya Marketplace, ☎ 242/373–5880) offers sportfishing on four custom boats; equipment is provided free. All vessels are licensed, inspected, and insured. Trips run from 8:30 to 12:30 and from 1 to 5, weather permitting; full-day trips are also available. Glass-bottom-boat tours, snorkling trips, and booze cruises are also available. Reservations are essential.

Running Mon Marina (⊠ Kelly Ct., Freeport, ☎ 242/352–6834) has daily half- and full-day deep-sea fishing charters. Equipment is included, as is free pickup and return to and from all Freeport hotels. Reservations are essential.

Marinas

Deep Water Cuy Club (⊠ Off eastern coast of Grand Bahama Island, ☎ 242/359–4831) has slips for boats of guests, for its small dive operation, and for bonefishing charters.

Lucayan Marina Village (⊠ Midshipman Rd., Port Lucaya, ☎ 242/ 373–8888) has complimentary ferry service to Port Lucaya; the marina has 150 slips, a fuel dock, pool, and bar.

Port Lucaya Marina (⊠ Bayside, Port Lucaya Marketplace, ☎ 242/373– 9090) offers a broad range of water sports and has 100 slips for vessels up to 170 ft. If you arrive in your own boat, you're permitted courtesy docking here while you shop or dine at the Port Lucaya Marketplace.

Running Mon Marina (⊠ Kelly Ct., Freeport, ☎ 242/352–6834) has 66 slips and serves as the base for a deep-sea fishing fleet. Marina facilities include gas and diesel fuel service, boatyard and on-site mechanics, a 40-ton travel lift (the only one on the island), water and power hookups, marina store, laundry facilities, showers, and rest rooms. The boatyard operates Monday–Friday from 7 AM to 6 PM and on Saturday from 7 to noon. The marina is open daily from 7 to 7.

Xanadu Marina and Beach Resort (⊠ Dundee Bay Dr., Freeport, ☏ 242/352–3811) has 400 ft of dockage plus 77 slips and provides dockside valet service.

Bowling

Sea Surf Lanes (⊠ Queen's Hwy., Freeport, ☏ 242/352–5784) has eight lanes and a snack shop.

Fitness Centers

Bahamas Princess Resort & Casino (⊠ W. Sunrise Hwy., Freeport, ☏ 242/352–6721) has an independently owned small fitness area open to guests and nonguests, with a Universal gym, bicycles, aerobics and jazz classes, a sauna, massages, and facials.

Olympic Fitness Center (⊠ Coral Beach Hotel, Lucaya, ☏ 242/373–8181) has Universal machines, weights, and aerobic classes. The fee is $5 per day, $15 per week.

YMCA Scandinavian Fitness Centre (⊠ E. Atlantic Dr. and Settler's Way, Freeport, ☏ 242/352–7074) offers weights, machines, and aerobics classes.

Golf

The three championship golf courses (two are at the Bahamas Princess Resort & Casino) and one nine-hole course are a major attraction on Grand Bahama Island. Annual events at the Lucaya Golf & Country Club include European Golf Weeks, Caribbean Golf Championships, and the Lucaya Golf & Country Club Waterford Crystal Pro-Am. The Bahamas Princess Resort & Casino hosts the Bogey Bash Golf Tournament and the Nat Moore Invitational Golf Tournament.

Bahamas Princess Resort & Casino has two 18-hole par-72 championship courses: the 6,750-yard Ruby, designed by Joe Lee, and the 6,679-yard Emerald, designed by Dick Wilson. A pro shop is also available. ⊠ W. Sunrise Hwy., Freeport, ☏ 242/352–9661. ⚄ Guests $65, nonguests $77 (shared electric cart included). Club rental $25 and $35.

Fortune Hills Golf & Country Club is a nine-hole, par-36, 3,453-yard course—a Dick Wilson and Joe Lee design—with a restaurant, a bar, and a pro shop. ⊠ E. Sunrise Hwy., Lucaya, ☏ 242/373–4500. ⚄ 9 holes $35, 18 holes $51 (shared cart included). Club rental, 9 holes $10, 18 holes $15.

Lucaya Golf & Country Club, designed in 1962 by Dick Wilson, is a dramatic 6,824-yard, par-72, 18-hole course. The 18th hole has a double lake and cascading waterfalls. There's a cocktail lounge, the Arawak Restaurant (☞ Dining, above), and a pro shop. A shared electric cart is included in the rates. ⊠ Lucaya Beach, ☏ 242/373–1066. ⚄ Guests $60; nonguests $76. Club rental $20.

Horseback Riding

Pinetree Stables runs trail and beach rides Tuesday–Sunday five times a day; all trail rides are accompanied by an experienced guide. Visitors have a choice of English or western saddles. Private lessons, including jumping and dressage, can be arranged. ⊠ Beachway Dr., Freeport, ☏ 242/373–3600. ⚄ 1½-hr beach ride $45.

Parasailing

Ocean Motion (✉ Lucaya Beach, ☎ 242/373–3923) offers five- to seven-minute parasailing rides for $30.

Paradise Watersports (✉ Xanadu Beach, Freeport, ☎ 242/352–3887) has parasailing tow boats and offers eight-minute flights for $30.

Reef Tours Ltd. (✉ Bayside, Port Lucaya Marketplace, ☎ 242/373–5880) offers parasailing from a stationary raft. It's about $30 per flight (you can have your flight captured on video for an extra charge).

Scuba Diving

Grand Bahama Island has some fascinating dive sites near the West End. An extensive reef system runs along the edge of the Little Bahama Bank from Mantinilla Shoals down through Memory Rock, Wood Cay, Rock Cay, and Indian Cay. Sea gardens, caves, and colorful reefs rim the bank all the way from the West End to Freeport-Lucaya and beyond. Some of the main dive sites around the island include *Theo's Wreck,* a 230-ft steel freighter that was sunk in 1982 near Freeport; **Angel's Camp,** a reef about 1¼ mi off Lucayan Beach, offering a scattering of small coral heads surrounding one large head; **Pygmy Caves** (in the same area as Angel's Camp), formed by overgrown ledges that cut into the reef; **Zoo Hole,** west of Lucaya, with huge caverns at 75 ft containing various types of marine life; and **Indian Cay Light,** off West End, featuring several reefs that form a vast sea garden. Grand Bahama Island is also home of UNEXSO, considered one of the finest diving schools in the world.

Caribbean Divers (✉ Bell Channel Inn, opposite Port Lucaya, ☎ 242/373–9111) offer guided tours, instruction, and equipment rental.

UNEXSO (Underwater Explorers Society) (✉ Box F 2433, Bayside, Port Lucaya Marketplace, ☎ 242/373–1244, 954/351–9889, or 800/992–3483), a world-renowned scuba-diving facility, provides full equipment for rental, 15 guides, and seven boats, as well as NAUI and PADI certification. Underwater cameras are available for rent, or you can have a dive videotaped for you for $35. A standard three-dive package costs $99; a 20-dive package is $499. Special underwater destinations include Shark Junction and Ben's Cavern. UNEXSO and its sister company, Dolphin Experience, are known for their work with Atlantic bottle-nosed dolphins. ☞ Exploring, *above*.

Xanadu Undersea Adventures (✉ Xanadu Beach Resort, ☎ 242/352–3811 or 800/327–8150) offers a resort course for $79; shark dives for $62 and night dives for $47 are also available.

Sea Kayaking

Kayak Nature Tours (✉ Queen's Cove, Freeport, ☎ 242/373–2485) is an eight-hour voyage through the shallow seas along Grand Bahama's north shore. Spot blue heron, crabs, fish, and other marine life as you paddle silently through mangrove creeks. A picnic lunch is served on a deserted island. Trips last from about 8 to 5. The cost is $75, with lunch and round-trip transportation from your hotel included.

Snorkeling

Aside from dive shops, a number of tour operators offer snorkeling trips to nearby reefs.

Pat & Diane (✉ Lucaya, ☎ 242/373–8681) take snorkelers to a shallow reef three times a day on 1¾-hour cruises for $25. Evening cruises are also $25.

Tennis

The island has more than 50 courts, many lighted for night play. All courts are hard surface unless otherwise noted.

Princess Country Club has nine courts, with five of them lighted for night play. ✉ *W. Sunrise Hwy., Freeport,* ☎ *242/352–6721.* ☏ *$10 per hr for guests, $12 per hr for non-guests.*

Silver Sands Hotel has two courts. ✉ *Royal Palm Way, Lucaya,* ☎ *242/ 373–5700.* ☏ *Guests free, nonguests $6 per hr.*

Xanadu Beach Resort has three clay courts. ✉ *Sunken Treasure Dr., Freeport,* ☎ *242/352–6782.* ☏ *Guests free, nonguests $5 per hr.*

Waterskiing

Paradise Watersports (✉ Xanadu Beach, Freeport, ☎ 242/352–2887) lets you ski the waves for about 1½ mi, which costs $20; a half-hour lesson is available for $40.

Windsurfing

Ocean Motion (✉ Lucaya Beach, ☎ 242/373–3923) rents Windsurfers for $20 per hour; lessons cost $15 per hour.

SHOPPING

In the hundreds of stores, shops, and boutiques in the International Bazaar in Freeport and at the Port Lucaya Marketplace, you can find duty-free goods costing up to 40% less than what you might pay back home. You'll have to use your own judgment in considering more precious items such as Mexican silver or Chinese jade. Don't try to haggle with shopkeepers, except at the straw markets. At the several perfume shops in the Bazaar and at Port Lucaya, fragrances can often be purchased at a sweet-smelling 30% below U.S. prices. The straw market at Port Lucaya is in wooden stalls at the east end of the Port Lucaya Complex, where vendors expect you to bargain for straw goods, T-shirts, and souvenirs.

Shops in Freeport and Lucaya are open Monday–Saturday from 10 to 6. Stores may stay open later in Port Lucaya.

Markets and Arcades

Goombay Park Arts & Crafts (✉ Behind International Bazaar, no phone) is a straw market consisting of dozens of brightly painted booths resembling little wooden houses.

International Arcade (✉ Connects the International Bazaar and the Princess Casino, no phone) has its own collection of smart shops, primarily branches of stores found at the adjacent International Bazaar, including Colombian Emeralds International, the Leather Shop, and Parfum de Paris.

International Bazaar (⊠ W. Sunrise Hwy. and E. Mall Dr., ☎ 242/352–2828) should be your first stop for the best bargains on fine imported goods, exotic items, and international fashions. This 10-acre complex consists of an array of shops displaying imports from 25 different countries.

Port Lucaya Marketplace (⊠ Sea Horse Dr., ☎ 242/373–8446) has about 100 boutiques and restaurants housed in 12 quaint pastel-color buildings in an attractive harborside setting. Free entertainment is provided by local musicians, who often perform at the bandstand in the afternoons and evenings.

Regent Centre (⊠ Explorers Way, between E. Mall Dr. and W. Mall Dr., no phone) will satisfy your shopping fever with its 60 stores in three mall buildings. This is where local people do their shopping, but you'll also find branches of shops that sell mainly duty-free items, such as the Leather Shop and B. H. L. Duty-Free Liquor Supermarket.

Specialty Shops

Antiques
Old Curiosity Shop (⊠ International Bazaar, ☎ 242/352–8008) carries old English clocks, lithographs, brass, and silver objets d'art.

China and Crystal
Island Galleria (⊠ International Bazaar and Port Lucaya Marketplace, ☎ 242/352–8194 and 242/373–8404) carries china and crystal by Waterford, Wedgwood, Aynsley, Swarovski, and Coalport.

Lladro Gallery (⊠ International Bazaar, ☎ 242/352–2660), an island gallery shop, specializes in Lladro figurines and Swarovski and Waterford crystal.

Midnight Sun (⊠ International Arcade, ☎ 242/352–9515) is the place to go for gift items by Royal Worcester, Stratton, Daum, and Lalique; you can also purchase Hummel figurines.

Cigars
The Bahamas certainly hasn't missed the cigar trend of the '90s. In fact, some fine stogies are sold here. Beware though, it's illegal to bring Cuban cigars into the United States.

Bahamas Best (⊠ International Bazaar, ☎ 242/352–4848) carries souvenirs and T-shirts, but also has a good supply of Cuban, Honduran, Jamaican, and Dominican cigars.

Cigars Etc. (⊠ International Bazaar, ☎ 242/351–6229) is a chic boutique that stocks a wide range of cigars from Cuba, Honduras, Nicaragua, Dominican Republic, and elsewhere, plus tobacco accessories and collectibles.

The Smoker's Cafe (⊠ International Bazaar, ☎ 242/351–6899) sells only Cuban cigars and also specializes in Cuban coffee and cigar accessories.

Smoker's World (⊠ International Bazaar, ☎ 242/351–6899) is a tiny shop that specializes in only Cuban cigars.

Fashion
Androsia House (⊠ Port Lucaya Marketplace, ☎ 242/373–8384) sells brightly colored batik fabrics and fashions handmade on the island of Andros.

Caribbean Cargo (⊠ International Bazaar, ☎ 242/352–2929) has a good selection of swimwear and beachwear, including Reef sandals.

Gemini (⊠ International Bazaar, ☏ 242/352–4809) specializes in shoes and clothing.

Jewelry and Watches

Colombian (⊠ International Bazaar and Port Lucaya Marketplace, ☏ 242/352–5380) purveys a line of Colombia's famed emeralds.

Colombian Emeralds International (⊠ International Bazaar, International Arcade, and Port Lucaya Marketplace, ☏ 242/352–5464) is *the* place to find diamonds, rubies, sapphires, and gold jewelry; the best brands in watches, including Tissot, Omega, and Citizen, are also available here. The exterior of the stylish shop is decorated with the plaster faces of Aztec gods.

Leather Goods

Gucci Boutique (⊠ International Bazaar, ☏ 242/352–4580) patterns its leather creations with its highly recognizable logo. Roman columns and statues of warriors make for a unique shopping experience.

Leather Shop (⊠ International Bazaar and International Arcade, ☏ 242/352–5491) sells HCL, Vitello, Land, and Fendi handbags, shoes, and briefcases.

Unusual Centre (⊠ International Bazaar, ☏ 242/352–3994) carries eelskin leather, peacock feather goods, and fine fashion jewelry.

Perfumes

Les Parisiens Perfumes (⊠ International Bazaar, ☏ 242/352–5380) stocks Giorgio products and the latest scents from Paris.

Oasis (⊠ International Arcade, International Bazaar, and Port Lucaya Marketplace, ☏ 242/352–5923) is a complete pharmacy with a selection of French perfumes; it also sells cosmetics.

Parfum de Paris (⊠ International Arcade, International Bazaar, and Port Lucaya Marketplace, ☏ 242/352–8164) offers the most comprehensive range of French fragrances on the island.

Perfume Factory (⊠ International Bazaar, ☏ 242/352–9391) sells a large variety of perfumes, lotions, and colognes by Fragrance of the Bahamas. A product called Guanahani was created to commemorate the 500th anniversary of Christopher Columbus's first landfall in the New World. Pink Pearl actually contains conch pearls, and Sand cologne for men has a small amount of island sand in each bottle. You can also create your own scent, name, and register it.

Miscellaneous

Intercity Records (⊠ International Bazaar and Port Lucaya Marketplace, ☏ 242/352–8820) is the place to buy records, tapes, and CDs of that Junkanoo, reggae, and soca music that served as a soundtrack for your vacation. Tapes cost $8–$10 and CDs are $20 each, which are not bargain prices, but island music is less easy to find back home.

Photo Specialist (⊠ Port Lucaya Marketplace, ☏ 242/373–7858) carries an extensive range of photo and video equipment and repairs cameras.

Souvenirs of Paradise (⊠ International Bazaar, ☏ 242/352–1790) sells the usual souvenir items with Bahamian appeal.

UNEXSO Dive Shop (⊠ UNEXSO, Port Lucaya Marketplace, ☏ 242/373–1244) sells everything water-related, from swimsuits to state-of-the-art dive equipment to computers.

Ye Olde Pirate Bottle House (⊠ Port Lucaya Marketplace, ☏ 242/373–2000) is a well-stocked souvenir shop, and the adjoining museum, dedicated to the history of bottles, is worth the $3 admission. On display are 250 bottles, some dating back to the 15th century.

GRAND BAHAMA ISLAND A TO Z

Arriving and Departing

By Plane

Freeport International Airport (☎ 242/352–6020) is just off Grand Bahama Highway, about six minutes from downtown Freeport and about 10 minutes from Port Lucaya.

American Eagle (☎ 800/433–7300) serves Freeport from Miami, with American Airlines connections from many U.S. cities. **Bahamasair** (☎ 242/352–8341 or 800/222–4262) serves Freeport International Airport with flights from Fort Lauderdale and Miami, as well as via Nassau. **Comair** (☎ 800/354–9822) serves Freeport daily from Fort Lauderdale as Delta's international partner airline. **Delta** (☎ 800/221–1212) serves Freeport from Orlando only. **Laker Airways** (☎ 305/653–9471) provides charter service from Fort Lauderdale, Chicago, Hartford, Cleveland, Cincinnati, Richmond, and Raleigh/Durham.

BETWEEN THE AIRPORT AND HOTELS
No bus service is available between the airport and hotels. Metered taxis meet all incoming flights, and rides cost about $8 to Freeport; $12 to Lucaya.

By Ship

Freeport is the port of call for numerous cruise lines, including Carnival Cruise Lines, Celebrity Cruises, Discovery Cruises, Dolphin & Majesty Cruise Line, Premier Cruise Lines, and Sea Escape Cruise Lines (☞ Cruise Travel *in* the Gold Guide).

BETWEEN THE HARBOR AND FREEPORT
Taxis meet all cruise ships. With six to eight passengers per cab, drivers charge $3 per person to the International Bazaar, and $4 per person to Port Lucaya. Individual passengers are charged by meter; the trips cost about $10 and $12, respectively.

Getting Around

By Bicycle

Flat Grand Bahama is perfect for bicycling, with its broad avenues and long, straight stretches of highway. Wear sunblock, carry a bottle of water, and look left. Bicycle rentals are inexpensive, $10–$15 a day. Try **Castaways Resort** (✉ W. Mall Dr. and International Bazaar, ☎ 242/352–6682), **Princess Country Club** (✉ W. Sunrise Hwy. and The Mall S, ☎ 242/352–6721), and **Princess Tower** (✉ W. Sunrise Hwy., ☎ 242/352–9661). **Club Fortuna Beach Resort** (✉ Churchill Beach, ☎ 242/373–4000) has bicycles available for free use by guests.

By Bus

Buses are an inexpensive way to travel the 4 or 5 mi between downtown Freeport and Port Lucaya Marketplace. Many privately owned buses travel around downtown Freeport and Lucaya for a fare of 75¢.

By Car

If you plan to drive around the island, it's cheaper to rent a car than to hire a taxi. Automobiles, jeeps, and vans can be rented at the Freeport International Airport; cars run $35–$80 per day; gas is about $2.50 a gallon. Car-rental companies include **Avis Rent-A-Car** (☎ 242/352–7666) with cars at $77 and vans at $135; **Bahama Buggies** (☎ 242/352–8750) is across from the International Bazzar; their bright pink and teal open jeeps cost $50 for 8 hours and $65 per day; **Dollar Rent-A-Car** (☎ 242/352–9325) has cars for $55 and $80; **Thrifty** (☎ 242/352–9308) rents cars beginning at $47; and **Star Rent-A-Car** (☎ 242/352–5953) rents cars for $35, jeeps for $55, and vans for $75 per day.

By Scooter

Grand Bahama's flat terrain and straight, well-paved roads make for good scooter riding. Rentals run about $35–$40 a day. Helmets are required and provided. Contact **Princess Country Club** (✉ W. Sunrise Hwy. and The Mall S, ☎ 242/352–6721) and **Princess Tower** (✉ W. Sunrise Hwy., ☎ 242/352–9661). Cruise-ship passengers can also rent motor scooters in the Freeport Harbour area.

By Taxi

Limos are commonly used as taxis in Grand Bahama—what a way to arrive at the casino! Fares are fixed by the government at $2 for the first ¼ mi and 30¢ for each additional ¼ mi regardless of whether the taxi is a regular-size cab, van, or stretch limo. Taxi companies in Freeport include:

Freeport Taxi Co., Ltd. (✉ Logwood Rd., ☎ 242/352–6666), and **G. B. Taxi Union** (✉ Freeport International Airport, ☎ 242/352–7101).

Opening and Closing Times

Banks are generally open Monday–Thursday 9:30–3 and Friday 9:30–5. Some of the major banks on the island include Bank of the Bahamas, Bank of Nova Scotia, Barclays Bank, and Royal Bank of Canada.

Shops are usually open Monday–Saturday 10–6, although they sometimes close earlier on Thursday, Friday, and Saturday. Straw markets and pharmacies are open on Sunday.

Contacts and Resources

Emergencies

Ambulance (☎ 242/352–2689 or 242/352–6735).

Bahama Air Sea Rescue (☎ 242/352–2628).

Fire Department (☎ 242/352–8888).

Hospital. The government-operated Rand Memorial Hospital (✉ E. Atlantic Dr., ☎ 242/352–6735) has 74 beds.

Police (☎ 919).

Guided Tours

Tours can be booked through the tour desk in your hotel lobby, at tourist information booths, or by calling one of the tour operators listed below.

AIR TOURS

You can take short airplane flights around Grand Bahama, to Nassau, or to some of the nearby Out Islands on **Taino Air** (✉ Freeport, ☎ 242/352–8885).

EXCURSIONS

A Grand Bahama day trip will take you to the major attractions on the island at a cost of $12 to $18 per person for an approximate three-hour tour. A glass-bottom-boat tour, which visits offshore reefs and sea gardens, starts at $20. If you're interested in a trip to the Garden of the Groves, expect to pay about $10. A tour of the historic West End costs $16.

For evening entertainment, a dinner cruise will cost around $40. Night-club tours are about $20.

You can even take a day trip to New Providence Island that includes round-trip air transportation, a sightseeing tour of Nassau, a visit to Paradise Island, and shopping on Bay Street. Such a package will cost about $175.

The following tour operators on Grand Bahama offer a combination of the tours described above, and several of them have desks in major hotels (all mailing addresses are for Freeport):

Bahamas Travel Agency (⊠ Box F 3778, ☎ 242/352–3141), **Bain's Travel Service** (⊠ Box F 42045, ☎ 242/352–3861 or 800/372–6963), **Executive Tours** (⊠ Box F 40837, ☎ 242/352–8858), **H. Forbes Charter & Tours** (⊠ Box F 41315, ☎ 242/352–9311), **Reef Tours Ltd.** (⊠ Box F 12609, ☎ 242/373–5880), **Best Island Travel** (⊠ Box F 40869, ☎ 242/352–4811), and **Sunworld Travel and Tours** (⊠ Box F 42631, ☎ 242/352–3717).

SPECIAL-INTEREST TOURS

East End Adventures. This land-and-sea guided ecotour includes a trip to the Lucayan National Park and a jeep ride along pristine beaches and through dense pine forests to Sweeting's Cay. Snorkeling, catch-and-release fishing, and a speedboat ride are included. A Bahamian lunch is served on a nearby island called Lightbourne's Cay. ⊠ *Freeport,* ☎ *242/373–6662.* *Daylong tours $110.* ☉ *Trips depart at 8 AM and return at 6 PM.*

Kayak Nature Tours. All-day eco-excursions are offered through pristine wilderness by kayak (of course), van, and on foot. The tour includes two hours of kayaking through Grand Bahamas' mangrove environment for a look at bird and marine habitats, a guided nature hike through Lucayan National Park and its caves, swimming and snorkeling on Gold Rock beach, and a full picnic lunch. Air-conditioned transport is provided to and from your hotel. ⊠ *Queen's Cove, Freeport,* ☎ *242/373–2485.* *Daylong tour $75.* ☉ *Hotel pickup 8–8:30 AM and return 5–5:30 PM.*

Seaworld Explorer. If you don't want to go too far underwater, this semisubmarine does not submerge. You descend into the hull of the boat and observe sea life in air-conditioned comfort from a vantage point 5 ft below the surface. The vessel departs from Port Lucaya and travels to Treasure Reef. ⊠ *Bayside, Port Lucaya Marina, Port Lucaya,* ☎ *242/373–7863.* *1½-hr voyage $33.* ☉ *Daily trips at 10, 11:30, 1:30, and 3.*

Visitor Information

Grand Bahama Island Tourism Board (☎ 242/352–8356, 𝐅𝐀𝐗 242/352–7840) has its main office and a separate tourist information center near the entrance to the International Bazaar in Freeport. Branch offices are located at the Freeport International Airport (☎ 242/352–2052), and Port Lucaya (☎ 242/373–8988) at the southeast entrance to the Port Lucaya Marketplace. Ask about Bahamahosts, specially trained tour guides who will talk to you about island history and culture and pass on their individual and imaginative knowledge of Bahamian folklore. Tourist offices are open weekdays, 9 to 5 (the airport office is also open weekends).

4 The Out Islands

To escape the crowds and the glittering modernity of New Providence and Grand Bahama, get yourself on a boat or plane to one of the Out Islands, where a slower-paced way of life prevails. Wander quiet beaches and narrow, sand-strewn streets, or lunch in a village where fishermen's tidy homes are painted in soft pastel shades and shrouded in brilliantly colored vegetation.

BONUS MILES MAKE GREAT SOUVENIRS.

Earn Miles With Your MCI Card.

Take the MCI Card along on this trip and start earning miles for the next one. You'll earn frequent flyer miles on all your calls and save with the low rates you've come to expect from MCI. Before you know it, you'll be on your way to some other international destination.

Sign up for MCI by calling
1-800-FLY-FREE

Earn Frequent Flyer Miles.

Is this a great time, or what? :-)

Easy To Call Home.

1. To use your MCI Card, just dial the WorldPhone access number of the country you're calling from.
2. Dial or give the operator your MCI Card number.
3. Dial or give the number you're calling.

American Samoa	633-2MCI (633-2624)
# Antigua	1-800-888-8000
(Available from public card phones only)	#2
# Argentina (CC)	0-800-5-1002
# Aruba ÷	800-888-8
# Bahamas	1-800-888-8000
# Barbados	1-800-888-8000
# Belize	557 from hotels
	815 from pay phones
# Bermuda ÷	1-800-888-8000
# Bolivia ♦ (CC)	0-800-2222
# Brazil (CC)	000-8012
# British Virgin Islands ÷	1-800-888-8000
# Cayman Islands	1-800-888-8000
# Chile (CC)	
To call using CTC ■	800-207-300
To call using ENTEL ■	800-360-180
# Colombia (CC) ♦	980-16-0001
Collect Access in Spanish	980-16-1000
# Costa Rica ♦	0000-012-2222
# Dominica	1-800-888-8000
# Dominican Republic (CC) ÷	1-800-888-8000
Collect Access in Spanish	1121
# Ecuador (CC) :	999-170
El Salvador	800-1767
# Grenada ÷	1-800-888-8000
Guatemala (CC) ♦	9999-189
Guyana	177
# Haiti ÷ Collect Access	193
Collect Access in French/Creole	190
Honduras ÷	8000-122
# Jamaica ÷ Collect Access	1-800-888-8000
(From Special Hotels only)	873
From payphones	★2
# Mexico (CC)	
Avantel	01-800-021-8000
Telmex ▲	001-800-674-7000
Mexico Access in Spanish	01-800-021-1000
# Netherlands Antilles (CC) ÷	001-800-888-8000
Nicaragua (CC)	166
(Outside of Managua, dial 02 first)	
Collect Access in Spanish from any public payphone	★2
# Panama	108
Military Bases	2810-108
# Paraguay ÷	00-812-800
# Peru	0-800-500-10
# Puerto Rico (CC)	1-800-888-8000
# St. Lucia ÷	1-800-888-8000
# Trinidad & Tobago ÷	1-800-888-8000
# Turks & Caicos ÷	1-800-888-8000
# Uruguay	000-412
# U.S. Virgin Islands (CC)	1-800-888-8000
# Venezuela (CC) ÷ ♦	800-1114-0

You've read the book. Now book the trip.

© 1998 Preview Travel Inc. CST #2022036-40

For all the best deals on flights, hotels, rental cars, and vacation packages, book them online at www.previewtravel.com. Then click on our Destination Guides featuring content from Fodor's and more. You'll find hotels, restaurants, attractions, and things to do around the globe. There are even interactive maps, videos, and weather forecasts. You'll have everything you need to make your vacation exactly what you want it to be. All it takes is a trip online.

Travel on Your Terms™
www.previewtravel.com
aol keyword: previewtravel

preview
travel SM

THE QUIET, SIMPLER WAY OF LIFE of the Bahama Out Islands, sometimes referred to as the Family Islands, is startlingly different from the fast-paced glitz and glitter of Nassau and Freeport. On the dozen or so islands outside of New Providence and Grand Bahama that are equipped to handle tourists, you leave the sophisticated nightclubs, casinos, bazaars, and shopping malls behind. If you love the outdoors, however, you'll be in fine shape: Virtually all the Out Islands have good to excellent fishing, boating, and diving, and you'll often have endless stretches of beach all to yourself. For the most part, you won't find hotels that provide the costly creature comforts taken for granted in Nassau and Freeport—although this is changing with the development of luxury resorts like Pink Sands on Harbour Island and Club Med–Columbus Isle on San Salvador. Accommodations in the Out Islands are generally modest lodges, rustic cottages, and small inns with balustraded balconies—many without telephones and TV (inquire when making reservations if these are important to you). Making a phone call to friends back home, or receiving one, will often require a trip to the local BaTelCo (Bahamas Telecommunications Corporation) telephone station. Another modern convenience you'll have to do without—in fact, one that many are happy to do without—is the ATM cash-machine. At press time, not a single one existed on the Out Islands (although a Marsh Harbour bank has plans to add a machine). Cash advances on credit cards are the only method of replenishing spending money.

Updated by
Jenner Bishop

Along with the utter lack of stress on an Out Islands holiday, you'll find largely unspoiled environments. Roughing it in Inagua, for example, is a small price to pay for the glorious spectacle of 60,000 pink flamingos taking off into the bright blue sky. And a day of sightseeing can mean little more than a stroll down narrow, sand-strewn streets in fishing villages, past small, pastel-color homes where orange, pink, and bright-red bougainvillea spill over the walls. Meals, even those served in hotels, most always incorporate local specialties, from conch and freshly-caught fish to chicken with peas 'n' rice. Island taverns are tiny and usually noisy with chatter, and you can make friends with locals over a beer and a game of pool or darts much more quickly than you would in the average stateside cocktail lounge. Nightlife may involve listening to a piano player or a small village combo in a clubhouse bar, or joining the crowds at a local disco playing everything from R&B to calypso.

The Out Islands were once mostly the domain of yachters and private plane owners; the tourist who discovered a hideaway on Andros, Eleuthera, or in the Exumas would cherish it and return year after year to find the same faces as before. But the islands are slowly becoming more and more popular, largely because of increased airline activity. Most islands are served from Nassau or Florida daily; others may only have a couple of incoming and outgoing flights a week. If you want to sample an Out Island without feeling completely cut off, choose a slightly busier spot that is closer to the mainland United States, such as Bimini, Eleuthera, or Great Abaco Island. If you go farther away from the mainland, to a place like Cat Island or San Salvador, you'll feel much more like you're getting away from it all.

Pleasures and Pastimes

Dining

For the most part, hotels in the Out Islands serve a combination of Bahamian, Continental, and American cuisines. Restaurants are often family-run and focus on homestyle dishes. You'll notice that there is little variety from one local dining spot to the next. It is each cook's special flair that creates a loyal following. You'll find fish, especially grouper, on almost every menu; the Bahamian specialty is boiled fish with tomatoes and spices. You usually can't go wrong with conch or lobster either. Side dishes are generally peas 'n' rice, potato salad, and coleslaw—often all three in the same meal.

Because much of the food is imported, eating out in the Bahamas is expensive, even on the less developed islands. Entrées will run anywhere from $10 to $30 per person and drinks aren't cheap. A service charge of 15% is virtually always added to your bill. Lobster, which is found all over the islands, costs the same as an imported New York strip steak.

CATEGORY	COST*
$$$$	over $35
$$$	$25–$35
$$	$15–$25
$	under $15

per person, excluding drinks and service

Lodging

The small hotels of the Out Islands are mostly owner-operated, which ensures a personal touch. Some accommodations use an honor bar system—mix your own and sign for it—so you really feel at home. Many hotels specialize in fishing or diving and offer packages which may include airfare, lodging, meals, and a number of fishing or diving trips. There are also self-contained resorts, which have their own sports facilities. When you make a reservation, find out if the hotel has any special packages. Also, if a hotel doesn't offer certain activities on its property—fishing, snorkeling, diving—it will most likely make such arrangements for you. Be sure to inquire when making reservations.

Although accommodations may be small and out of the way, don't expect your Out Island vacation to be inexpensive. The islanders have to import almost everything; produce and other goods coming by mail boat can arrive spoiled or broken. This means $7 hamburgers and gasoline at $3 per gallon—for residents and for you. A pack of cigarettes will run you more than $5—here's your chance to quit! Still, it's hard to put a price on the total escape these resorts offer. What would you pay for a powdery pink beach that stretches for miles with no footprints but your own? Or water so clear that snorkeling makes you feel like you're flying? Or a seafood dinner harvested the same day? You might not have an in-room phone, TV, or air-conditioning, but you may find that those conveniences aren't so important in paradise.

The Out Island Promotion Board can also help you find a house to rent. Properties of all sizes and prices are available, and monthly rentals can be as much as one-third less than combined weekly rates. Linens, cookware, and utilities are usually included. Sometimes a part-time cook, fishing or diving trips, and airport pickups are also part of the package.

The peak season is mid-December to mid-April. After that, room rates tend to drop by as much as a third. Price categories that follow apply to all of the Out Islands hotels. An 8% tax is added to your hotel bill, representing resort and government levies. Most hotels add a 10% gratuity for maid service, and a 3%–6% surcharge may be added to credit-card payments by some resorts. Ask about taxes, surcharges, and service charges when making your reservation—it can add over 20% to your bill.

CATEGORY	COST*
$$$$	over $200
$$$	$150–$200
$$	$100–$150
$	under $100

*All prices are for a double room in high season, excluding tax and service charges.

THE ABACOS

The Abacos, a boomerang-shape cluster of cays in the northeastern Bahamas, stretch from tiny Walker's Cay in the north to Hole-in-the-Wall, more than 130 mi to the southwest. Many of these cays are very small, providing exquisitely desolate settings for private picnics. The Abacos have their fair share of lagoons, tranquil bays and inlets, and pine forests where wild boar roam, but they also are home to the third-largest community in the Bahamas, the commercial center of Marsh Harbour, with all the amenities of a small town, including shops, restaurants, and hotels. The two main islands, Great Abaco and Little Abaco, are fringed on their windward shore by an emerald necklace of cays that forms a barrier reef against the broad Atlantic.

The Abacos' calm, naturally protected waters, long admired for their beauty, have helped the area become the sailing capital of the Bahamas. The islands' resorts are particularly popular with yachting and fishing enthusiasts because of the fine boating facilities available, among them the Treasure Cay Marina, the Boat Harbour Marina at Marsh Harbour, and Walker's Cay Club Marina. Man-O-War Cay remains the boatbuilding center for the Bahamas; its residents turn out traditionally crafted wood dinghies as well as high-tech crafts made of fiberglass. The Abacos play host annually to internationally famous regattas and to a half dozen game-fish tournaments. Outside of the resorts, the oceanside villages of Hope Town and New Plymouth also appeal to tourists for their charming New England ambience.

The Abacos' first settlers, New England Loyalists, arrived in 1783. Other families soon followed from Virginia and the Carolinas, bringing with them their plantation lifestyle and their slaves. These early arrivals tried to make a living from farming, but the Abacos' land was resistant to the growing of crops. Next, many settlers turned to the sea for sustenance; some of them started fishing, while others took advantage of the occasional wreck of passing ships.

At the end of the 18th century Bahamian waters weren't charted, and lighthouses wouldn't be built in the area until 1836. The wreckers of the Abacos worked at night, shining misleading lights to lure ships to destruction onto rocks and shoals—and then seizing the ships' cargo. Of course, not all these wrecks were caused by unscrupulous islanders; some ships were lost in storms and foundered on hidden reefs as they passed through the Bahamas. Nevertheless, by fair means or foul, wrecking remained a thriving industry in the Abacos until the mid-1800s.

The notorious deeds of the wreckers have long faded into history and legend. Today, about 10,000 residents live peacefully in the Abacos. Many of these enterprising, friendly people are seafarers, earning an honest living as boatbuilders, fishermen, and fishing guides. Because the Abacos are one of the most visited destinations in the Out Islands, an increasing number of residents work in the tourist industry.

Numbers in the margin correspond to points of interest on the Abacos map.

Great Abaco Island

❶ Most visitors to the Abacos make their first stop on the east coast of Great Abaco Island at **Marsh Harbour,** the third-largest city in the Bahamas and the commercial center of the Abacos. Besides having its own airport, Marsh Harbour is considered by boaters to be one of the easiest harbors to enter; it has several full-service marinas, such as the 170-slip Boat Harbour Marina and the 75-slip Conch Inn Marina.

Stock up on groceries and supplies here on the way to other islands. The downtown area has several well-equipped supermarkets and department and hardware stores. There are also banks, gas stations, and a few good, moderately priced restaurants. Most of the gift shops are on the main street, which has the island's only traffic light.

On a hilltop overlooking Marsh Harbour stands **Seaview Castle,** built by "Doctor" Evans Cottman (d. 1976), a high-school biology teacher from Madison, Indiana, who became the islands' official "unqualified practitioner" in the 1940s (i.e., he wasn't really a doctor, but he played one in the Bahamas). Cottman wrote of his experiences in a fascinating book called *Out Island Doctor.* Today, the yellow-and-white painted castle houses an outdoor café and gift shop (☞ Castle Cafe, *below*).

❷ About 30 mi south of Marsh Harbor lies the small, eclectic artist's colony of **Little Harbour.** The centerpiece is sculptor **Pete Johnston's Foundary,** out of which he casts magnificent life-like bronze sculptures from the ages-old wax-mold method. Alas! As in all art, somedays the muse is absent—your visit could be enchanting or downright sleepy. No trip to Little Harbour would be complete without a stop at Gilligan's Island-esque **Pete's Pub,** which has an Abacos-wide reputation for its laid-back attitude and decor.

About 20 mi south of Marsh Harbour is the little settlement of **Cherokee Sound** (pop. 165), whose inhabitants mostly make their living crawfishing. The deserted Atlantic beaches and serene salt marshes in this area are breathtaking.

❸ **Sandy Point,** a rustic fishing village with a lovely beach that attracts shell collectors, is just over 50 mi southwest of Marsh Harbour. There are no communities to visit south of Sandy Point, but a major navigational lighthouse stands at **Hole-in-the-Wall,** on the southern tip of Great Abaco (it's not open to visitors).

❹ A rugged winding road leads off the Great Abaco Highway, about 40 mi south of Marsh Harbour, passing through the dense pine woodlands of the **Bahamas National Trust Sanctuary,** a reserve for the endangered Bahamian parrot (your best chance of seeing the bird is at dawn). More than 100 other species have been sighted in this area.

Dining and Lodging

$$$ ✕ **Mangoes.** This busy spot near the harbor is known for its spicy coconut shrimp, cracked conch, and pork tenderloin in mango sauce. Gourmands will appreciate innovative daily specials, such as grilled wahoo marinated in garlic and rosemary, served with sautéed leeks and anchovy sauce. ⊠ *East Bay St., Marsh Harbour,* ☎ *242/367–2366. AE, MC, V. Closed Sun.*

$$$ ✕ **Sapodilly's.** If the colorful bi-level patios don't grab your eye— Sapodilly's wooden beams are painted lime-green, hot pink, and bright yellow—just follow your nose toward savory smells of this restaurant's flavorful dishes, which include conch fritters, a grilled fresh catch-of-the-

The Abacos

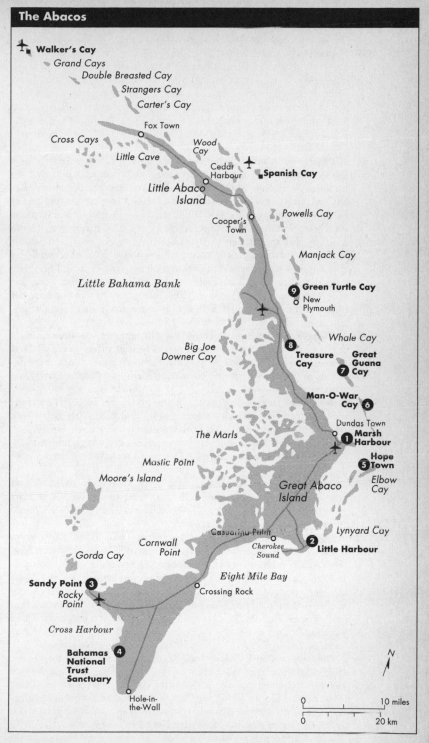

Walker's Cay
Grand Cays
Double Breasted Cay
Strangers Cay
Carter's Cay
Cross Cays
Fox Town
Wood Cay
Little Cave
Cedar Harbour
Spanish Cay
Little Abaco Island
Cooper's Town
Powells Cay
Manjack Cay
Little Bahama Bank
Green Turtle Cay
New Plymouth
Whale Cay
Big Joe Downer Cay
Treasure Cay
Great Guana Cay
Man-O-War Cay
The Marls
Dundas Town
Marsh Harbour
Mastic Point
Hope Town
Moore's Island
Elbow Cay
Great Abaco Island
Casuarina Point
Lynyard Cay
Cornwall Point
Cherokee Sound
Little Harbour
Gorda Cay
Eight Mile Bay
Sandy Point
Rocky Point
Crossing Rock
Cross Harbour
Bahamas National Trust Sanctuary
Hole-in-the-Wall

0   10 miles
0   20 km

day, and the best burger in Marsh Harbor, topped with blue cheese, bacon, and mushrooms. There is live music Friday nights. ⊠ *Queen Elizabeth Dr., Marsh Harbour,* ☎ *242/367–3498. AE, MC, V. No lunch Mon.*

$$$ ✕ **Wally's.** Across the road from the water in a pink two-story build-
★   ing resembling a small mansion, this is one of the Bahamas' best look-
ing—and popular—restaurants. Inside are Haitian-style paintings and
white wicker chairs on terra-cotta tiles. The menu includes wild Abaco
boar, turtle sautéed in onions and mushrooms, as well as grilled wahoo,
tuna, and duck breast—and key lime pie. Open for lunch and dinner.
⊠ *East Bay St., Marsh Harbour,* ☎ *242/367–2074. AE, D, MC, V.
Closed Sun.–Mon.*

$$ ✕ **Different of Abaco.** Owner Nettie Symonette's famous bush tea—a
spicy concoction made from twelve local plants served up in icy blue
tin mugs—is outshined only by her fabulous anecdotes. Screened, Bahamian push-out windows and handsome hunter-green seating accent
the spacious, airy dining room. While there's no set menu, you can count
on delectable fare—Nettie's scrambled eggs are a divine start to the
morning, and the kitchen's conch chowder, fresh catches, and peas 'n
rice are the real thing. Stop to read the wooden pillars and walls on
which guests have penned poems and praises to Nettie and her Heritage Bonefishing Club (☞ Fishing, *below*). If you've rented a car, this
spot is well worth the 25-minute drive south from Marsh Harbour (14
mi). A taxi ride here costs $70. Call by noon for dinner reservations.
⊠ *Casuarina Point,* ☎ *242/366–2150. MC, V.*

$$ ✕ **Flippers.** Coconut grouper and rack of lamb are the heavy hitters
at this bistro, but definitely choose owner Marcia Albury's spicy, baked
mac-n-cheese as your side dish! A loyal following turns out for the de-
licious soups, chowders, and curries. ⊠ *Memorial Plaza, Marsh Har-
bour,* ☎ *242/367–4657. AE, MC, V. No dinner Sun.*

$$ ✕ **Jib Room.** Harbor-view patio dining under this large yellow-and-
white-striped tent includes popular BBQ nights, serving baby-back
ribs Wednesdays, seafood on Fridays, and New York strip steak Sundays. The lunch menu is strictly casual eats—hot wings, conch burgers, fish nuggets, and nachos. ⊠ *Pelican Shores, Marsh Harbour,* ☎
242/367–2700. MC, V. Closed Tues.

$–$$ ✕ **Mother Merle's Fishnet.** Famous for Merle's special fried chicken and
conch fritters, this unpretentious dining room just outside Marsh Harbour is almost always busy. ⊠ *Dundas Town,* ☎ *242/367–2770. No
credit cards. Closed Wed. No lunch.*

$ ✕ **Castle Cafe.** This yellow-and-white castle was built as the hilltop dream
home of local hero Evans "Out Island Doctor" Cottman. Now a family-run cafe, it has a quaint, European feel and the island's most picturesque patio, on which to savor a cappuccino, milkshake, or "Castle
Creeper" cocktail. Count on fresh homemade soup and tasty sand-
wiches—check the board for more ambitious specials like escargot in
garlic butter. Wednesday's Happy Hour (5–7 PM) is a magic chance to
watch dusk melt over the cove below. ⊠ *Seaview Castle, Marsh Harbour,* ☎ *242/367–2315. MC, V. Closed weekends. No dinner.*

$ ✕ **George-the-Conch-Salad-Man.** Keep your ears pricked for distant
megaphone warblings that are mostly unintelligible, save for the two
key words: "conch salad." A colorful local character, George, drives
up and down Queen's Highway in a dilapidated pick-up truck, grafit-
tied with world's-best-conch-salad propaganda—the odds are good you'll
agree. ⊠ *Queen's Hwy., Marsh Harbour. No credit cards.*

$ ✕ **Island Bakery.** It's a close race between this Marsh Harbour bak-
ery and its main competitor, Flour House, so visiting sweet tooths may
just have to taste-test cinnamon rolls from both! The Bahamian bread
loafs are delicious. ⊠ *Don McKay Blvd., Marsh Harbour,* ☎ *242/367–
2129. No credit cards. Closed Sun.*

$ ✕ **Lee's Diner & Flour House Bakery.** Checked tablecloths liven up this modest bakery, where lunches include sumptuous slices of quiche, open-face coconut-shrimp sandwiches, and deli-meat or seafood subs on fresh-baked bread. Daily specials range from Bahamian chicken souse to curried mutton. ⊠ *Behind Memorial Plaza, Marsh Harbour,* ☎ *242/ 367–4233. No credit cards. Closed Sun. No dinner.*

$$$$ ✕🏨 **Great Abaco Beach Resort & Boat Harbour.** Sit in an Adirondack chair and gaze upon the Sea of Abaco from your balcony at this resort with all oceanfront rooms. The aesthetics improved with an extensive 1997 rennovation—spacious rooms have natural-stone tile floors and antique-white wicker furnishings set against salmon or rich blue walls. Bold, artistic textiles, marble wet bars, and in-room satellite TVs round out the spiffed-up accomodations. If you need more space, pick one of the fancier two-bedroom, two-bath villas, with a thoroughly modern kitchen, living room, and dining area. Besides offering complimentary windsurfing and kayaking, the resort's full-service dive shop will arrange fishing charters and boat rentals. Of course, you can just nurse your cool drink poolside, delivered from a thatched hut or swim-up Pool Bar. ⊠ *Box AB 20511, Marsh Harbour, Abaco,* ☎ *242/ 367–2158 or 800/468–4799,* 𝐅𝐀𝐗 *242/367–2819. 52 rooms and 6 villas. Restaurant, 2 bars, lounge, refrigerators, 2 pools, 2 tennis courts, dive shop, dock, windsurfing, boating, fishing, mountain bikes, coin laundry. AE, D, MC, V.*

$$$ 🏨 **Abaco Towns by the Sea.** Consider these beachfront or ocean-view condos if you need family accommodations: units have a master bedroom, a room with two twin beds, a living room with pull-out sleeper couch, and a fully equipped kitchen with dishwasher. The place could use a face-lift to transform the circa 1970-suburban-condo feel, and definitely avoid the "garden" rooms, which are dark and cramped. The condos are run by a homeowner's association rather than a hotel, which means the maid service is weekly and guests are expected to leave all dishes washed and take trash out to the dumpster. ⊠ *Box AB 20486, Marsh Harbour, Abaco,* ☎ *242/367–2227 or 800/322–7757,* 𝐅𝐀𝐗 *406/ 257–8575. 64 condos. Restaurant, bar, in-room safes, pool, 2 tennis courts, Ping-Pong, beach, fishing, coin laundry. AE, D, MC, V. EP.*

$$–$$$ 🏨 **Different of Abaco.** Imagine a serene getaway that embraces the area's
★ natural habitat, with wild boar, peacocks, heron, and flamingos peacefully coexisting with the guests. This ecotourism resort is the home of the premier bonefishing club on the island (☞ Heritage Bonefishing Club, *in* Outdoor Activities and Sports, *below*) and is owner Nettie Symonette's labor of love. Her eye for design and color is reflected throughout the property. Stay in one of the airy, colonial-style rooms at the Seashell Beach Club, with wooden floors, vaulted open-beamed ceilings, wall sconces, handcrafted furniture, and muted natural fabrics—you can pop out your front door for a dip in the pool or out your back door to the tranquil row of beachside hammocks. Nettie labors to preserve Bahamian culture with a number of on-site exhibits, including a circa 1500 Lucayan village of 14 *caneyas* (thatched huts), which are also available as accomodations. Canoes are available gratis for exploring the environs. The inn will provide your transport to and from the airport and one round-trip transfer to and from Marsh Harbour. Otherwise, it's a $70 cab fare into town. ⊠ *Casuarina Point (⊠ Box AB 20092, Marsh Harbour),* ☎ *242/366–2150 or 242/327–7921,* 𝐅𝐀𝐗 *242/327–8152. 28 rooms. Bar, dining room, pool, lake, outdoor hot tub, beach, snorkeling, boating, fishing, bicycles, billards, coin laundry. MC, V. FAP.*

$$ 🏨 **Island Breezes.** With a few simple but attractive rooms, this orange-and-white, one-story hostelry provides every amenity at a bargain rate. Slatted-wood ceilings, platform beds, ceiling fans, and satellite TV are in all rooms. ⊠ *Next door to Conch Inn Marina, Box AB 20453, Marsh Harbour, Abaco,* ☎ 242/367–3776, ℻ 242/367–4179. *8 rooms. Air-conditioning, fans, kitchenettes. MC, V. EP.*

$$ 🏨 **Lofty Fig Villas.** These six spacious villas are desirably located near the harbor, adjacent to restaurants, marinas, bars, and a dive shop. The villa kitchens are fully equipped and the supermarket is about a 10-minute walk. For families or groups on a budget, this is a good option. ⊠ *Across from Mangoes Restaurant, Box AB 20437, Marsh Harbour, Abaco,* ☎ ℻ 242/367–2681. *6 villas. Air-conditioning, pool. MC, V. EP.*

$ 🏨 **Conch Inn Resort & Marina.** This low-key marina hotel between the ferry dock and the town center is Marsh Harbour's best choice for budget travelers. Each simple, clean room at this motelish property has white-tile floors, white-rattan furniture, and color-splashed bedspreads. All rooms have cable TV and a phone. The full-service 75-slip marina is one of the best and busiest in Marsh Harbour and is the Bahamas' headquarters for the first-class Moorings yacht charter service; small beaches are within walking distance. The ferry to Great Guana Cay leaves from the inn. ⊠ *Box AB 20469, Marsh Harbour, Abaco,* ☎ 242/367–4000, ℻ 242/367–4004. *9 rooms. Restaurant, bar, pool, dive shop, docks, coin laundry. MC, V. EP.*

Outdoor Activities and Sports

BICYCLING

Look for the row of blue mountain bikes at the Great Abaco Beach Resort, where **Sea Horse Boat Rentals** (☎ 242/367–2513) keeps a rental fleet. Available daily, bikes rent for $10 the first 24 hours, $5 each additional day. A blue-and-yellow hut across from the Conch Inn, **R&L Rent-a-Ride** (☎ 242/367–2744) rents bicycles for $2/hour, $5/half day, $8/full day, or $35/week. They're closed Saturdays and have limited Sunday hours.

BOATING

CHARTERS. Sailboats can be chartered by the week or longer, with or without crew. **The Moorings** (☎ 242/367–4000 or 800/535–7289) is at the Conch Inn Resort & Marina in Marsh Harbour. This is the Bahamas' division of one of the foremost yacht-charter agencies in the world, which provides every service needed for yachters—from provisions to professional captains.

MARINAS. In Marsh Harbour, **Boat Harbour Marina** (☎ 242/367–2158) has 172 fully protected slips and a slew of amenities. **Conch Inn Marina** (☎ 242/367–4000) has 75 slips and is the home of The Moorings charters. **Marsh Harbour Marina** (☎ 242/367–2700) has 60 slips.

RENTALS. Renting a boat to tour the Abacos is a must, especially if you're staying on the outer cays. Powerboats, from 18-ft Boston whalers to 26-ft Paramounts, can be rented on a daily, three-day, or weekly basis. Daily rates run from $75 to $135, three-day rates from $210 to $270, and weekly rates from $400 to $800. Reserving your boat in advance is recommended, and remember that rates don't include fuel. In Marsh Harbor, try **Rich's Boat Rentals** (☎ 242/367–2742), **Sea Horse Boat Rentals** (☎ 242/367–2513), or **Rainbow Rentals** (☎ 242/367–4602). Catamaran fans should contact **Laysue Rentals** (☎ 242/367–2513).

EVENTS

Several sporting events are held annually in the Abacos. The **Boat Harbour Billfish Championship** is held in June. July brings the weeklong **Regatta Time in Abaco,** a series of five races, accompanied by nightly parties and entertainment. To participate, write to Regatta Time in Abaco (⊠ Box 428, Marsh Harbour, Abaco), or contact David Ralph (☎ 242/

367–2677, FAX 242/367–3677). November hosts the **All Abaco Regatta** (☎ 242/366–2198 or 242/367–2343), featuring Native Bahamian sloop boats. For information about any events on the Abacos, call Marsh Harbour's **Abaco Tourist Office** (☎ 242/367–3067) or the **Out Island Promotion Board** (☎ 954/359–8099 or 800/688–4752).

FISHING

You can find bonefish in the flats, yellowtail on the reefs, or marlin in the deep of the Abacos. The **Heritage Bonefishing Club** (☎ 242/366–2150) lures the hook, line, and sinker crowd to Casuarina Point at Different of Abaco—an angler's paradise. For deep-sea fishing or billfishing, **Capt. Creswell Archer** (☎ 242/367–4000 or 242/367–2787) will spend a half day or full day out on his sportfishing vessel with you. **Abaco Delight Guide Services** (☎ 242/367–4426) provides Skipper James's tutelage in the challenges of spearfishing.

SCUBA DIVING AND SNORKELING

Pelican Cays National Park at Marsh Harbour is a main dive site. Snorkelers will want to visit Mermaid Beach, just off Pelican Shores Road in Marsh Harbour, where live reefs and green moray eels make for some of the Abacos' best snorkeling. **Dive Abaco** (☎ 242/367–2787 or 800/247–5338) and **Great Abaco Beach** (☎ 242/367–2158), both in Marsh Harbour, rent scuba and snorkeling equipment and have daily reef and wreck dives. (☞ Scuba Diving *in* the other Abacos island sections, *below*). **Rainbow Rentals** (☎ 242/367–4602) and **Sea Horse Boat Rentals** (☎ 242/367–2513) rent snorkeling gear.

TENNIS

Abaco Towns by the Sea (☎ 800/332–7757) and **Great Abaco Beach Resort** (☎ 242/367–2158) both open their courts to visitors.

WINDSURFING

Windsurfing is offered at the **Great Abaco Beach Resort** (☎ 242/367–2158).

Shopping

At Marsh Harbour's traffic light, look for the blue-and-white-striped awnings of **Abaco Treasures** (☎ 242/367–3460), purveyors of fine china, crystal, perfumes, and gifts.

Barefoot Gifts (✉ Queen's Hwy., Marsh Harbour, ☎ 242/367–3596) is your best bet for hats, sandals, tropical jewelry, and souvenir sportswear.

Cultural Illusions (✉ Memorial Plaza, Marsh Harbour, ☎ 242/367–4648) sells memorable Bahamian creations—Androsia clothing and fabric, stained glass, and handmade keepsakes like wooden bowls crafted by local artisan Steven Knowles.

John Bull (✉ Queen's Hwy., Marsh Harbour, ☎ 242/367–2473), near the harbor, is a branch of a leading Nassau shop and sells watches and perfumes.

Johnston Studios Art Gallery (✉ Little Harbour, ☎ 242/367–2720), 45 minutes south of Marsh Harbor, displays original bronzes by the Johnstons, as well as a collection of prints and gifts.

Juliette Gallery (✉ Queen Elizabeth Dr., Marsh Harbour, ☎ 242/367–4551) has Bahamian art, sculpture, stained glass, and handmade furniture.

Little Switzerland (✉ Queen Elizabeth Dr., Marsh Harbour, ☎ 242/367–3191) sells watches, perfumes, and designer cosmetics—it's at the entrance to the Great Abaco Beach Resort.

Elbow Cay

⑤ The charming village of **Hope Town,** where most of the families among its 300-some residents have lived for generations, lies southeast of Marsh Harbour, on Elbow Cay. A 20-minute ferry ride from Marsh Harbour arrives here several times a day (☞ *see* Abacos A to Z). You'll find few cars and other pesky trappings of modern life here. In fact, most residents remember well the day the island first got telephone service—back in 1988! Before that, everyone called each other the way many still do here and in other Out Islands: by VHF, the party line for boaters.

This laid-back community enthusiastically welcomes visitors. Upon arrival in Hope Town you'll first see a much-photographed Bahamas landmark, a 120-ft-tall, peppermint-stripe lighthouse, built in 1838. The light's construction was delayed for several years by acts of vandalism by residents afraid of it ending their profitable wrecking practice. Today, the Hope Town lighthouse is one of the last three hand-turned, kerosene-fueled beacons in the Bahamas. Weekdays 10–4 the lighthouse keeper will welcome you at the top for a superb view of the sea and the nearby cays.

For an interesting walking or bicycle tour of Hope Town follow the two narrow lanes that circle the village and harbor. The saltbox cottages—painted in brilliant blues, purples, pinks, and yellows—with their white picket fences, flowering gardens, and porches and sills decorated with conch shells, will remind you of a New England seaside community—Bahamian style. You may want to stop at the **Wyannie Malone Historical Museum** (no phone) on Queen's Highway, the main street. It contains memorabilia and photographs of Hope Town. Admission is free; hours vary. Many of the descendants of Mrs. Malone, who settled here with her children in 1875, still live on Elbow Cay.

Smack in the center of town lies an old, turquoise municipal building with offices clearly labeled "Commissioner," "Post Office," and "Visitor Information." Forget about the first two—they've long since relocated—but Hope Town's **Visitor Information** "office" is a cement room containing a few well-papered bulletin boards on which everything from current happenings to restaurant menus are posted. Poking around the building's ground floor, you'll also find the quirky and charming **Dolphin Exhibit,** where local school children and marine-life scholars have cooperatively posted the "Get to Know Your Local Dolphins" key, a dorsal-fin guide to a few favorites of the some 85 bottlenose dolphins residing in the Sea of Abaco.

There are several churches in this tiny town. On Sunday mornings, you'll hear sermons floating through open windows. Don't be surprised if while wandering the streets, you come across an alfresco Catholic service in the dockside park. Residents joke that the priest has to stand in the hot sun while the congregation enjoys the shade of sprawling trees "so he won't talk so long."

Dining and Lodging

$$$ ✕ **Abaco Inn.** Enjoy a Bahamian omelet for breakfast (served like a tostada, with fresh seafood and herbs piled on top), sherry-spiked conch chowder for lunch, or a dinner of Angus-beef filet mignon and Bahamian lobster tail, known as the "Reef & Beef." For dessert, crème brûlée is the house specialty. The indoor decor is somewhat hodge-podge—mismatched seating, a metal fish sculpture here, a wooden airplane propellor there—but it's hard to knock any dining room that has two fireplaces. Call for free van service. ✉ *Hope Town,* ☎ *242/366–0133. AE, D, MC, V.*

$$$ ✕ **Club Soleil.** Overlooking the inn's marina, this spacious, wood-beamed dining room serves up fresh seafood dishes, home-baked bread, and Bahamian peas 'n' rice on cheery tropical-print cloths. People come from all over for Club Soleil's Champagne Sunday Brunch—definitely make reservations. Open for breakfast and dinner. ⊠ *Club Soleil Resort, Hope Town, Elbow Cay,* ☎ *242/366–0003. MC, V. Closed Mon. No dinner Sun.*

$$$ ✕ **Harbour's Edge.** This bar-restaurant is Hope Town's premier hangout. Try tender conch burgers, grilled grouper, or lobster salad for lunch and dinner, or chose from the daily specials board. On Sundays, the Edge serves authentic Bahamian breakfasts. You can also rent bikes here for $8 a day and cue up on the island's only pool table. Live bands occasionally play on weekends. ⊠ *Hope Town, Elbow Cay,* ☎ *242/ 366–0292. MC, V. Closed Tues.*

$$$ ✕ **Hope Town Harbour Lodge.** Creamy lobster fettuccine is one of the most popular dishes, but grouper spring rolls with mustard-chutney sauce and sizzling plates of fresh-fish fajitas are among the creative Bahamian–style dishes. The dining room has an intimate, island-elegant ambience—with dark-stained walls, large windows, rattan chairs, and lively shell- and fish-print cloths—but a meal savored from the cozy terrace is the romantic's choice, with elevated views of the harbor and rungs of twinkling lights that wind up the coconut trees. After your meal, order an apertif from the Wrackers Bar and mosey into the lounge, where checkers, backgammon, and a collection of magazines await you. ⊠ *Hope Town, Elbow Cay,* ☎ *242/366–0095. Reservations essential. MC, V. No dinner Mon.*

$$ ✕ **Rudy's Place.** Rudy's, set charismatically in a renovated house, is a favorite among locals. Rave reviews go to the crawfish baked with Parmesan cheese. Complimentary pickup is available. ⊠ *Hope Town, Elbow Cay,* ☎ *242/366–0062. MC, V. Closed Sun.*

$ ✕ **Cap'n Jack's.** There's a handful of booths and a small bar, but the majority of seating at this casual eatery is out on the dock-patio under the large pink-and-white-striped awning. The menu ranges from mac-n-cheese to turtle burgers to Cornish hens. Cap'n Jack's serves three meals a day and has live music Wednesday and Friday nights. ⊠ *Hope Town, Elbow Cay,* ☎ *242/366–0247. Reservations essential. MC, V.*

$ ✕ **Munchies.** This casual snack bar is the place for a late-night bite, as well as daily lunch and dinner specials, which include conch fritters, fish or turkey burgers, and peas 'n' rice. ⊠ *Hope Town, Elbow Cay,* ☎ *242/366–0423. No credit cards. No dinner Sun.*

$$$$ ▥ **Turtle Hill Vacation Villas.** About a mile outside Hope Town, this attractive cluster of four two-bedroom villas is Hope Town's latest (1997) lodging addition. Bougainvillea- and hibiscus-lined walkways encircle the central swimming pool, overlooked by each of the unit's generous latticework private patios. Inside, villas are tastefully furnished with light-wood paneling, tile floors, and rattan furnishings, as well as sleeper sofas. Large kitchens have dark green marble counters and a variety of appliances, including microwaves. Cassette players, satellite TV, and VCRs are also included. The lovely beach is a short two-minute walk, and each villa comes with a golf cart for jaunts into town. Choose an upper villa for distant views of the sea. ⊠ *Off Queens Hwy. between Hope Town and White Sound, Hope Town,* ☎ FAX *242/366–0557. 4 villas. Pool, air-conditioning, fans, in-room VCRs, beach. AE, D, MC, V. Closed Sept.*

$–$$$$ ▥ **Elbow Cay Properties.** Besides being the most cost-efficient way to stay on Elbow Cay, a private house or villa for a week or more is also one of the most comfortable. Many of the houses and villas for rent are on the water, with a dock or a sandy beach right out front. Owners Jane Patterson and Carrie Cash will find you a place to match your wishes and budget. They can also arrange boat and bike rentals, and set you up with a golf cart—perfect for negotiating Hope Town's very narrow lanes. ⊠ *Hope Town,* ☎ ℻ 242/366–0035. *34 houses and villas. No credit cards.*

$$$ ⊞ **Hope Town Hideaways.** Across the harbor from Hope Town village
★ is the ideal vacation spot for those who really want seclusion—virtually the only way to get here is by boat. The owners, Abaco native Chris Thompson and his wife, Peggy, who is American, create a warm, relaxing atmosphere. The property's 11-acre grounds are planted with peppers, bananas, avocados, and passion fruit, as well as wild orchids and other exotic flowers. The clean, modern villas have airy cathedral ceilings, large kitchens stocked with an impressive collection of wares, and french doors opening onto decks with harbor views—each of these two-bedroom units is cleanly decorated with festive prints, light woods, and ceiling fans. The patio area in front of the villas has a grill, and you're minutes away by boat from a choice of local restaurants—the Hideaways will provide your dinghy for traversing the harbor. Peggy can also rent you a private villa or house just about anywhere else on Elbow Cay, as her company manages most properties. ⊠ *Hope Town, Abaco,* ☎ *242/ 366–0224 or 800/688–4752,* ℻ *242/366–0434. 4 villas, 1 one-bedroom cottage. Air-conditioning, fans, in-room VCRs. AE, MC, V. EP.*

$$–$$$ ⊞ **Sea Spray Resort and Villas.** Consider this resort if you're planning to catch any waves in Hope Town, as the villas are just off Garbanzo Beach, a favorite with surfers. The villas have full kitchens, outdoor grills, and decks; each is spacious and clean, although the interiors could use some color coordination and snazzing up. Some improvements to decor have been made. Sunfish sailboats are available free; motorboats, bikes, and snorkeling gear are available to rent. The gift store on site sells everything from charcoal to surfboard wax. They've recently added a restaurant with a European-trained gourmet chef and a 70-slip marina. ⊠ *South-end, White Sound, Elbow Cay, Abaco,* ☎ *242/ 366–0065,* ℻ *242/366–0383. 7 villas. Restaurant, outdoor lounge, air-conditioning, pool, dock, snorkeling, surfing, boating, fishing. AE, MC, V. EP, MAP.*

$$ ⊞ **Abaco Inn.** About 2 mi south of Hope Town, this beachfront resort overlooks both the ocean and bay and caters to singles and couples. The cozy villas—six ocean- and six harbor-view—have simple, comfortable furnishings, and individual hammocks for dozing. The two suite units, with sunrise and sunset water views from two opposite decks, are the best accomodations. There are no phones or TVs in the rooms, but satellite TV is installed in the bar—and the lounge has live music a couple of nights a week. A weathered gazebo faces the ocean, and a thatched solarium on the beach is available for nude sunbathing. After your complimentary pickup in Hope Town, you'll probably want to rent your own boat so you can zoom into town or to one of the smaller islets around Elbow Cay; you can tie up at the resort. Bicycles (available gratis to guests) are another option for getting into town. Excellent reefs for snorkeling and diving are nearby. ⊠ *Hope Town,* ☎ *242/ 366–0133 or 800/468–8799,* ℻ *242/366–0113. 12 rooms. Restaurant, bar, lounge, pool, beach, boating, fishing, baby-sitting, coin laundry. AE, D, MC, V. EP, MAP.*

$$ ⊞ **Club Soleil Resort and Marina.** This Spanish-style resort has an idyllic location in a grove of coconut palms, bougainvillea, and hibiscus, just across the harbor from Hope Town and a short walk from secluded beaches on the ocean side of Elbow Cay. The modern rooms have cedar closets, tile floors, and private balconies. Rooms are without phones, but do have TVs with VCRs; videos are available in town. Using local driftwood and other beach finds, the Dutch owner has created tasteful works of art for each room. The pool is steps from the bar and popular restaurant (☞ *above*), where windows overlooking the water give the feeling of being on a ship. The hosts are happy to help arrange boat rentals, diving, fishing, sailing, or touring. ⊠ *Hope Town,* ☎ *242/366–0003 or 800/626–5690,* FAX *242/366–0254. 6 rooms. Bar, dining room, in-room VCRs, pool, dock. MC, V. EP, MAP.*

$$ 🏨 **Hope Town Harbour Lodge.** Choose one of the clean, newly decorated cottage rooms—six are clustered around the pool and two are on the ocean—as the main lodge's harbor-view rooms are rather lifeless and could use some sprucing up. Most rooms have air-conditioning, and none have phones or TVs to distract you. Snorkelers will note that the lodge's beach has a live coral reef 25 feet from the shore; snorkel gear is available for $8/day. The hotel has its own dock, and can arrange for boating, kayaking, fishing, or diving. ⊠ *Hope Town,* ☎ *242/366–0095 or 800/316–7844,* FAX *242/366–0286. 18 rooms, 1 3-bedroom house. 2 restaurants, 2 bars, lounge, refrigerators, pool, beach, dock, laundry service. MC, V. EP.*

Outdoor Activities and Sports

BOATING

CHARTERS. Sail Abaco (☎ 242/366–0172) offers half- or full-day captained charters on catamaran yachts. Full-day trips are $300 for up to six passengers.

MARINAS. Club Soleil (☎ 242/366–0003) has 14 slips, **Sea Spray Resort** (☎ 242/366–0065) has 24 slips, and **Hope Town Hideaways** (☎ 242/366–0224) has 12 slips.

RENTALS. Creative Native (☎ 242/366–0309) rents 13-ft dinghys for $75/day and kayaks for $30/day. **Island Marine** (☎ 242/366–0282) has 17- to 22-ft boats available for rent from $80 to $105 a day. **Sea Horse Boat Rentals** (☎ 242/367–2513) has Bimini-top boats from 18-ft Privateers to 22-ft Boston Whalers at their Hope Town location. **Dave's Dive Shop and Boat Rentals** (☎ 242/366–0029) will deliver your boat to your accomodations.

FISHING

Seagull Charters (☎ 242/366–0266) sets up guided deep-sea excursions with Captain Robert Lowe, who has over 30 years' experience in the local waters. **Wild Pigeon Charters** (☎ 242/366–0461) offers bonefishing, reef fishing, and bottom fishing with Abaco bonefishing champion, "Bonefish Dundee."

SCUBA DIVING AND SNORKELING

Dave's Dive Shop and Boat Rentals (☎ 242/366–0029) offers 2-tank dives for $65 and resort dives for beginners. They also rent gear to snorkeling fans heading out for Sandy Cay.

SURFING

Creative Native Surf Shop (☎ 242/366–0309) rents long and short surfboards and body boards; open weekdays 10 AM–2 PM.

WINDSURFING

Sea Spray Resort (☎ 242/366–0065) attracts windsurfers to the choice waters just off Garbanzo Beach.

Shopping

Island Gallery (☎ 242/366–0354) sells wind chimes, sandals, resort wear, jewelry, and island music.

Man-O-War Cay

❻ Many of Man-O-War Cay's residents are named Albury, descendants of early Loyalist settlers who started the tradition of handcrafting boats more than two centuries ago. They remain proud of their heritage and continue to build fiberglass boats today. This shipwrighting center of the Abacos lies south of Green Turtle and Great Guana cays, an easy 45-minute ride from Marsh Harbour by water taxi or aboard a small rented outboard dinghy. Man-O-War Cay also has a 26-slip marina.

A mile north of the island, you can dive to the wreck of the USS *Adirondack,* which sank after hitting a reef in 1862; it lies among a host of cannons in 20 ft of water. The cay is also a marvelous place to walk. Two main roads, Queen's Highway and Sea Road, are often shaded with arching sea grape trees interspersed with palms and pines. The island is secluded, but it has kept up to date with satellite television and full phone service. There are three churches, which most of the 300 residents faithfully attend, and a one-room schoolhouse. No liquor is sold here, but you're welcome to bring your own. Restaurants post their daily specials on "The Pole" in the center of town.

Dining and Lodging

$$ ✕ **Man-O-War Marina Pavillion.** Try the grouper fingers here or, if it's Friday or Saturday, the BBQ steak, chicken, or ribs. ⊠ *Waterfront,* ☎ *242/365–6185. No credit cards. Closed Sun.*

$–$$ ✕ **Ena's Place.** Stop in this joint when you want great conch burgers and coconut or pumpkin pie. ⊠ *Waterfront, Man-O-War Cay,* ☎ *242/365–6187. No credit cards. Closed Sun.*

$$$ ⌂ **Schooner's Landing.** This small, Mediterranean-style resort with just four two-bedroom town-house condos is perched on a rocky promontory overlooking a long, isolated beach. Rooms are airy with wicker furniture and ceramic tile floors. There's no restaurant, but within walking distance is almost everything on the cay, including restaurants. There's also a barbecue and wet bar in the gazebo, and nearby grocery stores deliver. Manager Brenda Sawyer knows the island well; dinner with her at Ena's or the Pavillion is a good way to learn the ropes. ⊠ *Man-O-War Cay, Abaco,* ☎ *242/365–6072,* FAX *242/365–6285. 4 condominiums. Air-conditioning, in-room VCRs, beach, boating, fishing, laundry service. AE, MC, V (8% surcharge). EP.*

Outdoor Activities and Sports

BOATING

Man-O-War Marina (☎ 242/365–6008) has 26 slips.

SCUBA DIVING

Man-O-War Dive Shop (⊠ Man-O-War Marina, ☎ 242/365–6013) organizes trips and rents tanks.

Shopping

Albury's Sail Shop (☎ 242/365–6014) is popular with boaters, who stock up on colorful canvas duffle bags, briefcases, jackets, hats, and purses.
Caribbean Closet (☎ 242/365–6384) sells clothing and resortwear.
Island Treasures (☎ 242/365–6072) has a wide selection of T-shirts, souvenirs, and Abaco-made ceramics.

Great Guana Cay

❼ You'll be welcomed to Great Guana Cay, a narrow island off Marsh Harbour, by a hand-lettered sign that claims IT'S BETTER IN THE BAHAMAS, BUT . . . IT'S GOODER IN GUANA. If you love beautiful empty beaches and grassy dunes, you'll agree. Great Guana Cay is 7 mi long, and has only 120 residents. The cries of roosters are about the loudest sound you'll hear in the drowsy village, and cars are absent from the narrow palm-lined roads that are bordered by clapboard cottages with picket fences.

Dining and Lodging

$–$$$ ✕ **Nipper's Beach Bar & Grill.** With one of the most awesome ocean views in the islands, this set of brightly striped, split-level gazebos is the party-hearty spot on Great Guana Cay. Lunch is mostly burgers and sandwiches. The Sunday night boar roasts and Wednesday night bonfires and fireworks on the beach are not to be missed. Nurse a "Nipper Tripper"—a concoction of 5 rums and 2 juices. ⊠ *Great Guana Cay,* ☎ *242/365–5143. AE, D, MC, V.*

$$$ ✕🏨 **Guana Beach Resort and Marina.** After you're met at the dock by a staff-member bearing your rum-spiked Guana Grabber, settle into your room and get used to the rhythm of total relaxation—hammocks sway gently in the palm grove; tiny waves lap against the cove's shore. The hottest action might be a board game played on an umbrella-covered poolside table, or a rousing match of the "ring game" in the resort's bar. The resort has its own small beach with thatched shelters, but a 10-minute walk through town leads to a spectacular stretch of sand that runs the 7-mi length of the island and provides more than enough opportunities for snorkeling and shelling. The resort offers bicycles and Sunfish sailboats for exploring, and will arrange for deep-sea, bottom, and bonefishing excursions. Choose one of the newer beachfront rooms, with attractive hibiscis-print bedspreads, rattan furnishings, and stonework accents. The palm grove rooms have kitchenettes, but could use a bit of a face-lift. ⊠ *Box AB 20474, Marsh Harbour, Abaco,* ☎ *242/365–5133 or 800/227–3366,* 🖷 *242/365–5134 or 954/423–9733. 7 villas, 7 rooms. Bar, dining room, air-conditioning, pool, beach, dock, snorkeling, boating, bicycles, baby-sitting. MC, V. EP, MAP.*

Treasure Cay

❽ Running through large pine forests that are still home to wild horses and boars, the wide, paved Sherben A. Boothe Highway leads north from Marsh Harbour for 20 mi to Treasure Cay, which is technically not an island but a large peninsula connected to Great Abaco by a narrow spit of land. Here you'll find a small community of mostly winter residents, a 3,000-acre farm that grows winter vegetables and fruit for export, and a spectacular 3½-mi-long stretch of pearly white sand.

Treasure Cay is a large-scale real estate development project. The centerpiece is the Treasure Cay Resort and Marina, with its Dick Wilson–designed golf course and 150-slip marina. Unlike the rest of the Abacos, Treasure Cay completely lacks a sense of history or community—those seeking local color and an authentic Bahamian experience will find Treasure Cay rather sterile. Fortunately, historic Elbow Cay, Man-O-War Cay, and Green Turtle Cay are all easily accessible by boat.

The commercial center of Treasure Cay consists of two rows of shops near the resort with a post office, laundromat, ice-cream parlor, a couple of grocery stores, and the BaTelCo. You'll also find car-, scooter-, or bicycle-rental offices here. North of the shops, the tiny Treasure Cay **Community Center** houses a small library, open Mondays, Wednesdays, and Fridays from 3 to 5 PM.

Dining and Lodging

$$ ✕ **Touch of Class.** Ten minutes north of Treasure Cay, this highly recommended spot serves delicious Bahamian cuisine. Call about the free shuttle bus. ⊠ *Queen's Hwy. at Treasure Cay Rd.,* ☎ *242/365–8195. No credit cards.*

$ ✕ **Cafe La Florence.** Stop into this bakery for a hot cup of joe and a cinnamon roll, or a slice of quiche. Adjacent, Florence's blue ice-cream parlor is your answer for treats à la mode. ⊠ *Treasure Cay,* ☎ *242/367–2570. No credit cards. Closed Sun.*

$$-$$$ ×⊞ **Treasure Cay Resort and Marina.** Hotel room and town house–style accommodations form a long pastel row along the water's edge of this resort's 150-slip marina. Rooms come in various configurations, some with mini-refrigerators, microwaves, and small dining counters. Every room is equipped with satellite TV, but no rooms have phones. Request one of the handsome bi-level suites that was renovated in 1998, where vaulted ceilings, pine headboards and armoires, full modern kitchens, and washer-dryer combos are standard, and loft bedrooms have generous-sized master baths. The orange-upholstered Spinnaker restaurant is 1970s-esque, serves three meals a day (including delectably sweet johnny cake squares), and will prepare the day's fresh catch to order (try it cajun-style "blackened"). The resort has the Out Islands' only 18-hole championship golf course, as well as six tennis courts. ⊠ *On marina (⊠ 2301 S. Federal Hwy., Fort Lauderdale, FL 33316),* ☎ *242/365–8578, 954/ 525–7711, or 800/327–1584 for reservations,* FAX *954/525–1699. 64 rooms, 32 suites. Restaurant, 2 bars, dining room, lounge, air-conditioning, pool, 18-hole golf course, 6 tennis courts, beach, diving, dock, snorkeling, windsurfing, boating, fishing, baby-sitting. AE, MC, V.*

$$$$ ⊞ **Treasure Houses.** Set around a courtyard of interconnected swimming pools, footbridges, and burbling waterfalls, seven octagon-shaped houses perch on stilts for lovely beach views. Each two-bedroom guest house has airy, exposed-beam ceilings, plush carpeting, rattan and bamboo furniture, and muted tropical-print textiles. Bedrooms open onto narrow private patios. Queen-size sleeper sofas, cable TV, and fully equipped kitchens are also standard. Tour the cay with the two gratis bicycles that accompany each unit—Treasure Houses are 1 mi from the main resort (☞ *below*) and stores—or rent a golf cart. Use of the laundry machines is complimentary. ⊠ *On marina, Treasure Cay (⊠ 2301 S. Federal Hwy., Fort Lauderdale, FL 33316),* ☎ *242/365– 8535, 954/525–7711, or 800/327–1584 for reservations,* FAX *954/ 525–1699. 7 2-bedroom houses. 6 pools, air-conditioning, beach, snorkeling, laundry. AE, MC, V. EP, MAP.*

Outdoor Activities and Sports

BICYCLING

Wendell's Bicycle Rentals (☎ 242/365–8687) rents bikes for $4/half day, $6/day, $35/week.

BOATING

C &C Boat Rentals (☎ 242/365–8582) rents boats by the day, three days, or week. A 20-ft Wellcraft rents for $85/day; a 25-ft Nova rents for $135/day. Snorkel equipment is included with boat rental. **J. I. C. Boat Rentals** (☎ 242/365–8465) rents 20 to 24-ft Anglers from $90 to $150 a day; three-day and weekly rates are also available. Try to reserve your boat at least a week in advance.

EVENTS

The Treasure Cay leg of the **Bahamas Billfish Championship** is held in May, as is the annual **Treasure Cay International Billfish Tournament.** The **CABO Sportfishers Challenge** takes pleace in June. Call **Treasure Cay Services** (☎ 954/525–7711 or 800/327–1584) for information.

FISHING

Arrange for local deep-sea or bonefishing fishing guides through **Treasure Cay Resort and Marina** (☎ 242/365–8250).

GOLF

A half mile from the **Treasure Cay Resort and Marina** (☎ 242/365–8535) is the property's par-72 course designed by Dick Wilson, with no tee times necessary and carts available. A driving range, putting green, and a small pro shop are also on site.

SCUBA DIVING AND SNORKELING

No Name Cay and Whale Cay are popular marine life sites. The 1865 wreck of the steamship freighter **San Jacinto** also affords scenic diving and chances to feed the resident green moray eel. **Divers Down** (☎ 242/365–8465) rents equipment and takes divers and snorkelers out to a variety of sites. **C & C** (☎ 242/365–8582) offers dive trips and a $55 "Snorkel & Island" trip, which includes reef snorkeling and a beach cookout.

TENNIS

Treasure Cay Resort and Marina (☎ 242/365–8535) has six of the best courses in the Abacos, and four are lighted for night play. Fees are $14 per hour for the hard courts and $16 per hour for the clay courts; rackets rent for $4.

WINDSURFING

Windsurfers are available for rent at the **Treasure Cay Resort and Marina** (☎ 242/365–8250).

Shopping

Treasure Cay is home to **Abaco Ceramics** (☎ 242/365–8489), featuring their signature white clay pottery with blue fish designs.

Green Turtle Cay

A 10-minute ferry ride from a dock on Treasure Cay will take you to Green Turtle Cay. The tiny island is steeped in Loyalist history, and is surrounded by several deep bays, sounds, and a nearly continuous strip of fine ocean beach. An easy way to explore the entire island is by small outboard dinghy or Boston whaler, which can be rented by the hour or the day at most resorts and marinas.

New Plymouth, which was first settled in 1783, is the main community on Green Turtle. Most of its approximately 550 residents eke out a living by diving for conch or exporting lobster and fish through the Abaco Seafood Company. Narrow streets flanked by wild-growing flora (such as amaryllis, hibiscus, and poinciana), wind between rows of weatherbeaten New England–style white clapboard cottages with shutters trimmed in bright colors. During the Civil War, New Plymouth provided a port of safety for Confederate blockade runners. One Union ship, the USS *Adirondack,* was pursuing a gunrunner and wrecked on a reef in 1862 at nearby Man O War Cay. One of the ship's cannons now sits at the town harbor.

If your accomodations aren't in New Plymouth proper, you'll need transportation into town. Many hotels provide an ocassional shuttle, and there is one taxi on Green Turtle Cay, but most people travel via golf cart or rental boat.

New Plymouth's most frequently visited attraction is the **Albert Lowe Museum** on the main thoroughfare, Parliament Street. The Bahamas' oldest historical museum, it's dedicated to a model shipbuilder and direct descendant of the island's original European-American settlers. You can learn island history through local memorabilia from the 1700s, Lowe's model schooners, and old photographs, including one of the aftermath of the 1932 hurricane that nearly flattened New Plymouth. Also on display paintings by acclaimed artist Alton Lowe, Albert's son. ⊠ *Parliament St.,* ☎ *242/365–4094.* ☎ *$3.* ☉ *Mon.–Sat. 9–11:45 and 1–4.*

Just a few blocks from here, on Victoria Street, is **Miss Emily's Blue Bee Bar** (☎ 242/365–4181), which stands next to a jail whose door is hanging on its hinges—it hasn't been used in recent history. Fans of the drink

Goombay Smash will be sorry to hear that bar's owner, Mrs. Emily Cooper, passed away in 1997, but daughter Violet continues serving up Emily's famous concoction of rum, pineapple juice, and apricot brandy. Mementos of customers—business cards, expired credit cards, T-shirts—and Junkanoo masks cover the walls.

The past is also present in the **Memorial Sculpture Garden,** across the street from New Plymouth Inn—note that it is laid out in the pattern of the British flag. Immortalized in busts perched on pedestals are local residents who have made important contributions to the Bahamas. Plaques detail the accomplishments of British Loyalists, who came to the Abacos from New England and the Carolinas, their descendants, and the descendants of those brought as slaves, such as Jeanne I. Thompson, a contemporary playwright and the country's second woman to practice law.

Dining and Lodging

$–$$ ✕ **Islands Deli & Bake Shoppe.** This spot serves grub like jalapeño poppers, T-bone steaks, and baby back ribs. Save room for one of the many creative desserts made with candy bars. Islands serves breakfast, lunch, and dinner. ⊠ *Parliament St.,* ☎ *242/365–4082. No credit cards.*

$–$$ ✕ **Laura's Kitchen.** There's not much of a view from the pink-and-white-curtained windows, and the chrome hotel ballroom–style chairs are covered in clear plastic, but this simple, two-room eatery makes for a tasty, inexpensive lunch or dinner. Complimentary transportation is provided to and from your hotel—call by 5 PM to arrange it. Final score: ambience 2, conch burger 10. ⊠ *Across from Shellhut, on King St.,* ☎ *242/365–4287. MC, V (4% surcharge).*

$ ✕ **The Wrecking Tree.** The wooden deck of this casual restaurant was built around the wrecking tree, a place where 19th-century wrecking vessels brought their salvage. Come here for hearty breakfasts or lunches of cracked conch or fish 'n' chips. Dinners may include curried mutton or (upon request) turtle steak. ⊠ *Bay St.,* ☎ *242/365–4263. No credit cards. No lunch Sun.*

$ ✕ **Ole B's Ice Cream.** A checkerboard floor and red-upholstered chrome stools decorate this soda fountain. If you're not in the mood for a float or sundae, go for a fruit smoothie. The few red and white booths are popular spots for sandwiches and a variety of salads. Weekends are Pizza Nights—call in your order by 4 PM and mention if you'll be enjoying your pie here or elsewhere. ⊠ *Bay St.,* ☎ *242/365–4409. No credit cards. Closed Sun.*

$$$ ✕🏠 **Green Turtle Club.** Cheerful yellow cottages and buildings are
★ scattered amid lush trees and shrubs at this inn, where the vibe is simultaneously refined and easygoing. Villa accomodations are available, but choose one of the rooms—some of the most handsomely appointed in all the Out Islands—with their mahogany Queen Anne–style furniture, gleaming hardwood floors, Oriental rugs, and tasteful indigo-and-white print spreads. Breakfasts and lunches are served under the vaulted roof of a terra-cotta–tiled veranda, but it's the lively dinner seating under the harbor-view dining room's chandeliers that makes the inn come alive, with guests feasting on sumptuous cuisine and recounting the day spent snorkeling off Manjack Cay or touring the island on the club's 1920s-designed *Abaco Queen.* After indulging in one of Julie's desserts—don't miss the peanut butter pie—migrate into the Tipsy Turtle Bar. Wallpapered in $1 bills, the tavern's action can range from live music to a backgammon game in front of the fire. The resort has a 32-slip marina. ⊠ *North end of White Sound (*⊠ *Box AB 22792, Green Turtle Cay, Abaco),* ☎ *242/365–4271 or 800/688–4752,* 📠 *242/365–4272. 24 rooms, 2 suites, 8 villas. Restaurant, bar, dining room, lounge, air-conditioning, fans, refrigerators, in-room VCRs,*

pool, exercise room, beach, dive shop, dock, snorkeling, boating, fishing, piano, coin laundry. AE, MC, V. EP, MAP.

$$–$$$ ✕ 🔟 **Bluff House Beach Hotel.** The highest hill in the Abaco chain is home to this romantic hideaway, which has sweeping views of the sheltered harbor. Accommodations come in a variety of configurations, including rooms, suites, villas, and one studio with a kitchenette. Split-level town-house suites with ocean views are the best—these comfortable, spacious rooms have wood paneling, tropical-style wicker furniture, carpet with parquet-inlay floors, and double doors opening onto balconies with expansive ocean vistas. It's an antidote to city life here—no phones, TVs, or locks on doors. Sets of steps and tiered wooden walkways lead to the main building, where the cocktail lounge feels like a homey living room and a French door–lined dining room serves complimentary wine with excellent Bahamian and American fare by candlelight. Don't miss Bluff House's Thursday night BBQ (lobster, ribs, chicken, etc.) and beach bonfire, with live Junkanoo entertainment. Snorkeling equipment is also complimentary. Charters are available for bonefishing and deep-sea fishing, snorkeling, picnicking, and diving. ✉ *Between Abaco Sea and White Sound (✉ Box AB 22886, Green Turtle Cay, Abaco),* ☎ *242/365–4247,* FAX *242/365–4248. 13 rooms, 4 suites, 1 studio with kitchen, 4 villas. Bar, dining room, lounge, air-conditioning, refrigerators, pool, tennis court, beach, dock, snorkeling, boating, fishing, laundry service. AE, D, MC, V. EP, MAP.*

$$ ✕ 🔟 **New Plymouth Inn.** This charming, two-story historic hostelry with white balconies is in the center of New Plymouth. Built in 1830, it was a French mercantile exchange, a warehouse (in which shipwreckers stored their plunder), and a private residence before it opened as a hotel in 1946. Present owner Wally Davies built the charming patio pool and expanded the tropical gardens. Cozy, carefully restored rooms have solid chests and chairs, quilts on the canopy beds, and private terra-cotta–tiled baths. Upstairs, the top room contains a queen-size bed and two twins, and has one of the loveliest views of the sea and of the village rooftops. The restaurant is popular with local residents and visitors alike, so you'll need to make a reservation. ✉ *Parliament St., Green Turtle Cay,* ☎ *242/365–4161 or 800/688–4752,* FAX *242/365–4138. 9 rooms. Bar, dining room, lounge, air-conditioning, fans, pool. MC, V. MAP.*

$$$–$$$$ 🔟 **Linton's Cottages.** On a rise overlooking an isolated beach, these two cottages attract families, groups of friends, and couples looking for escape. Each has two comfortable bedrooms, a screened-in porch, a combination living-and-dining room, and a fully equipped kitchen. When you aren't fishing, snorkeling, scuba diving, waterskiing, sailing, windsurfing, shell-hunting, or using the barbecue, you can relax in hammocks. You can arrange to have someone prepare meals. Boats are available for rent, and ask about fishing and diving guides. ✉ ✉ *South Loyalist Road, Green Turtle Cay (✉ Box 158601, Nashville, TN 37215),* ☎ *615/269–5682,* FAX *615/353–1882. 2 cottages, fans, kitchens, bicycles. No credit cards.*

$$$ 🔟 **Coco Bay Cottages.** Sandwiched between one beach on the Atlantic and another calmer sandy stretch on the bay, these homey cottages (three with two bedrooms and one with three) have water views. Attractively furnished, they come complete with telephones (a rare commodity), modern kitchens, and linens. Snorkeling and diving are excellent around the reef that protects the Atlantic beach. The bay, where sunset views are fabulous, is prime territory for shell-collecting and bonefishing. ✉ *North of New Plymouth Green Turtle Cay,* ☎ *242/365–5464 or 800/752–0166,* FAX *242/365–5465. 4 cottages. Kitchens, snorkeling. MC, V.*

$$$ ▣ **Sand Dollar Luxury Condos.** This two-story, pink building has Victorian touches, including a portico and generous-sized balconies with filigree accents. Fully equipped kitchens are large and serviceable, and the condos—in the heart of New Plymouth—are a stone's throw from a grocery store. Bicycles and a 14-ft boat are also included gratis with your stay. Choose one of the upstairs units—either "Sunrise" or "Sunset"—for eastward bay views or western views of the village and distant Sea of Abaco. These condos require a four-night minimum stay. ⊠ *Parliament St., New Plymouth (⊠ Box AB 22786, Green Turtle Cay),* ☎ *242/365–4221,* FAX *242/365–4046. 2 2-bedroom condos. Air-conditioning, dock, bicycles, shops. AE, MC, V. EP.*

Nightlife

Nightlife on the Out Islands is virtually nonexistent, but the place to go in New Plymouth is the **Rooster's Rest** (☎ 242/365–4066), a pub and restaurant perched in a bright red building. On weekends, the joint shakes until the wee hours. Try to catch the reggae-calypso sounds of local band, the **Gully Roosters**—check with **Green Turtle Club** (☎ 242/365–4271) and **Bluff House Beach Hotel** (☎ 242/365–4247) to find out where they're playing. Shooting a game of pool in the back room of **Miss Emily's Blue Bee Bar** (☎ 242/365–4181) is always a good bet, too.

Outdoor Activities and Sports

BICYCLING

Curtis Bike Rentals (☎ 242/365–4128) is open Mondays through Saturdays. **D&P Rentals** (☎ 242/365–4125) also rents bikes on Green Turtle Cay.

BOATING

MARINAS. Green Turtle Club (☎ 242/365–4271) has 32 slips. The **Bluff House** (☎ 242/365–4247) hopes to have a new marina facility in 1999.

RENTALS. Donny's Boat Rentals (☎ 242/365–4119) rents boats ranging from 14-ft Whalers to 23-ft Makos. **Dame's Rentals** (☎ 242/365–4205) has 17- and 22-ft boats. If you're unable to rent a vessel on Green Turtle Cay, consider procuring one in nearby Treasure Cay.

EVENTS

The **Green Turtle Yacht Club Fishing Tournament** is held in May. In the beginning of July, the **Bahamas Cup** boat race circumnavigates Green Turtle Cay. Call the **Abaco Tourist Office** (☎ 242/367–3067) or **Out Island Promotion Board** (☎ 954/359–8099 or 800/688–4752) for information.

FISHING

Ronnie Sawyer (☎ 242/365–4070) is one of the Bahamas' premier bonefishing guides. Call **Joe Sawyer** (☎ 242/365–4173) for a morning of reef-fishing in his 29-ft boat.

SCUBA DIVING AND SNORKELING

Brendal's Dive Shop (☎ 242/365–4411) is the longtime favorite with Green Turtle Cay visitors—don't miss the chance to hand-feed large grouper. **Green Turtle Club Divers** (☎ 242/365–4271) has a full-service dive shop on at the hotel, and offers a 15% discount to divers and snorkelers staying there.

Rent your snorkel gear at one of the dive shops, and call **Lincoln Jones** (☎ 242/365–4223), known affectionately as "the Daniel Boone of the Bahamas," for an unforgettable snorkeling adventure and lunch of fresh conch or lobster on a deserted beach.

TENNIS

Bluff House (☎ 242/365–4247) has one court.

Shopping

Annexed to the Plymouth Rock Cafe, **Ocean Blue Gallery** (✉ Parliament St., ☎ 242/365–4234) is a two-room gallery containing paintings, sculptures, and other works by over 50 local artists.

The **Sand Dollar Shoppe** (☎ 242/365–4221) sells upscale souvenir items and handcrafted Abaco Gold jewelry.

Sid's Grocery (☎ 242/365–4055) has a sizeable collection of books on local Bahamian subjects—great for souvenirs or for replenishing your stock of reading material.

Just off Bay Street, **Vert's Model Ship Shop** (no phone) features Vert Lowe's handcrafted two-mast schooners and sloops. Model prices range anywhere from $100 to $1200. If Vert's shop door is locked, knock at the white house with bright pink shutters.

Spanish Cay

With handsome beaches and one resort, this 200-acre island gives you the impression that you've escaped the rest of the world.

Dining and Lodging

$$$$ ✕⊞ **Inn at Spanish Cay.** For 40 years this was the preserve of billionaire Clint Murchinson, former owner of the Dallas Cowboys, and his "rich and famous" friends. Now the house and beautifully landscaped grounds are open to well-heeled guests who reside in one- or two-bedroom apartments or villa suites with private gardens. Rental golf carts and bicycles are available for exploring the island's five beaches and 7 mi of shoreline. There's a 70-slip full-service marina with fishing and diving on nearby reefs, and rental boats for sojourns to the uninhabited islands around Spanish Cay. Two restaurants cater to guests' whims—in fact, the chef will fish with you, then prepare your catch. Private pilots and charter flights can fly directly into Spanish Cay's 5,000-ft runway. ✉ Box 882, Cooperstown, Abaco, ☎ 242/365–0083 or 888/722–6474, FAX 242/365–0083. 5 villa suites, 7 apartments. 2 restaurants, 2 bars, air-conditioning, fans, 4 tennis courts, beaches, dock, snorkeling, boating, fishing, bicycles. MC, V. FP.

Tennis

Inn at Spanish Cay (☎ 242/365–0083) has four lighted courts.

Walker's Cay

Fishing enthusiasts have been returning to this privately owned islet for years, and the lone hotel caters to anglers and divers. With few of the wispy casuarina trees that abound on most Out Islands, Walker's Cay sprouts more of the gnarled, thick-trunked trees more common in cooler regions. Walker's Cay isn't known for its beaches—most visitors sail off to sandy shores on neighboring islands.

Dining and Lodging

$$–$$$ ✕⊞ **Walker's Cay Hotel and Marina.** A self-contained resort on the northernmost island of the Bahamas, this 100-acre island is served by its own airline out of Fort Lauderdale. The waters around here are renowned for their spectacular fishing opportunities, and the complex is a favorite with the yachters and fishermen who flock to the Annual Billfish Tournament held here in April. Rooms are cheerfully decorated with tropical-style rattan furniture and have private patios. Sportsmen gather at the Lobster Trap restaurant to swap fish stories. Diving options include an exciting shark dive, cavernous coral reefs, and sunken tugboats. ✉ 700 S.W. 34th St., Fort Lauderdale, FL 33315, ☎ 954/

359–1400 or 800/925–5377, FAX 954/359–1414. 62 rooms, 3 villas. 2 restaurants, 2 bars, lounge, air-conditioning, pool, saltwater pool, 2 tennis courts, dive shop, dock, boating, fishing, laundry service. AE, DC, MC, V. EP, MAP.

Outdoor Activities and Sports

BOATING

Walker's Cay Hotel and Marina (☎ 954/359–1400) has a full-service 75-slip marina and some of the best yachting facilities in the Bahamas.

EVENTS

May brings the **Bertram/Hatteras Shoot-out Tournament,** the Kentucky Derby for boats, and the **Walker's Cay Billfish Tournament.** Call the **Out Island Promotion Board** (☎ 954/359–8099 or 800/688–4752) for information.

SCUBA DIVING

All the diving off the cay can be booked either through the hotel or through **Neal Watson's Undersea Adventures** (☎ 800/327–8150). The living reefs here grow atop a fossil coral reef that forms a limestone buttress. The Shark Rodeo dive allows you to safely float among 100-plus Blacktip and Caribbean Reef sharks as they feed.

Abacos A to Z

Arriving and Departing

BY MAIL BOAT

From Potter's Cay, Nassau, the M/V *Mia Dean* sails Tuesday to Green Turtle Cay, Hope Town, Marsh Harbour, and Turtle Cay; it arrives back in Nassau on Thursday. The fare is $45, and the trip takes 12 hours. The M/V *Champion II* departs Nassau on Tuesday, calls on Wednesday at Sandy Point, Moore's Island, and Bullock Harbour, returning to Nassau on Thursday; the fare is $30. Schedules are subject to change due to weather conditions or occasional dry-docking. For details, call the **Dockmaster's office** (☎ 242/393–1064) at Potter's Cay.

BY PLANE

The Abacos have two public airports: at Treasure Cay and Marsh Harbour on Great Abaco Island.

Air Sunshine (☎ 242/367–2800 in Marsh Harbour, 242/365–8900 in Treasure Cay, 954/434–8900, or 800/327–8900) flies from Fort Lauderdale to both airports. **American Eagle** (☎ 242/367–2231 or 800/433–7300) has two daily flights to Marsh Harbour from Miami. **Bahamasair** (☎ 242/367–2095 in Marsh Harbour, 242/365–8601 in Treasure Cay, or 800/222–4262) flies from Nassau to Marsh Harbour three times daily, and from Nassau to Treasure Cay twice daily. Direct international flights depart Palm Beach into Marsh Harbour six days a week. **Cherokee Air** (☎ 242/367–2089 or 242/367–2613) is the charter-plane service of choice for island-hopping to or from the Abacos. **Continental Connection** (☎ 242/367–3415 in Marsh Harbour, 242/365–8615 in Treasure Cay, or 800/231–0856) flies into both Marsh Harbour and Treasure Cay from seven different Florida locations. **Island Express** (☎ 242/367–3597 in Marsh Harbour, 242/365–8697 in Treasure Cay, or 954/359–0380) flies daily from Fort Lauderdale into both public airports. **Twin Air** (☎ 954/359–8266) has scheduled flights to Treasure Cay from Fort Lauderdale and flies to other parts of the Abacos by charter. **US Airways Express** (☎ 242/365–8686 or 800/622–1015) flies into both public airports from Orlando and Palm Beach.

Getting Around

BY BOAT

Because Abaco is made up of so many islands, many agree that a small boat is the easiest way to get around and allows the freedom to explore uninhabited areas and secluded beaches. When traveling during high season, remember to reserve your boat at least a week in advance. It's advisable to check with your hotel, too, before renting a boat; they can either make arrangements for you or recommend the most convenient agent.

Rich's Boat Rentals (☎ 242/367–2742), **Sea Horse Boat Rentals** (☎ 242/367–2513), and **Laysue Rentals** (☎ 242/367–4414) are all in Marsh Harbour.

If you fly into Treasure Cay, **C & C Boat Rentals** (☎ 242/365–8582) and **J.I.C. Boat Rentals** (☎ 242/365–8465) rent boats by the day, three-days, or week.

BY CAR

Although you can explore the main city of the Abacos, Marsh Harbour on Great Abaco Island, on foot, you will need a car to see the rest of Great Abaco and the other main island, Little Abaco. In Marsh Harbour, you can rent automobiles from **H & L Car Rentals** (✉ Shell Gas Station, ☎ 242/367–2854), **Reliable Car Rentals** (☎ 242/367–3015), and **A & P Rentals** (☎ 242/367 2655). At Treasure Cay Airport, **Corniche Car Rentals** (☎ 242/365–8623) has a large rental fleet. Rentals are expensive at about $70 a day and up; weekly rentals are cheaper. It's easiest to have your hotel make your arrangements.

BY FERRY

Albury's Ferry Service (☎ 242/367–3147 or 242/365–6010) leaves Marsh Harbour for the 20-minute ride to Hope Town daily at 10:30 AM and 4 PM and, additionally, at 12:15 PM on Monday, Thursday, and Saturday; ferries make the return trip at 8 AM and 1:30 PM every day and also at 11:30 AM on Monday, Thursday, and Saturday. If you take the 4 PM ferry, you must stay overnight. A same-day round-trip costs $12; one-way costs $8. For $30, Albury's will sell you a coupon for three round-trips on regularly-scheduled boats, good for two weeks from date of purchase. Albury's also provides service between Marsh Harbour and Man-O-War Cay or Guana Cay. Note on ferry protocol: in these friendly parts, it's customary to lend a hand to fellow passengers loading and unloading their various boxes, bags, etc.

Green Turtle Cay Ferry (☎ 242/365–4032) leaves the Treasure Cay airport dock at 10:30, 2:30, and 4:15, and returns from Green Turtle Cay at 8, 1:30, and 3; one-way fares are $8.

BY GOLF CART

In Hope Town, try **Hope Town Cart Rentals** (☎ 242/366–0064) or **Island Cart Rentals** (☎ 242/366–0448), where carts rent for $35/day and $210/week . **D&P Rentals** (☎ 242/365–4125) rents carts on Green Turtle Cay.

On Treasure Cay, **Cash's Resort Carts** (☎ 242/365–8465), **Blue Marlin Rentals** (☎ 242/365–8687), and **Chris Carts** (☎ 242/365–8053) all rent golf carts by the half day, day, week, or month.

BY TAXI

Taxi services meet arriving planes at the airports to take you to your hotel or to the dock, where you can take a water taxi to neighboring islands such as Green Turtle Cay or Elbow Cay. Hotels will arrange for taxis to take you on short trips and back to the airport. A combination taxi–water-taxi ride from Treasure Cay Airport to Green Turtle Cay

BOATING IN THE ABACOS

THE ABACOS PROVIDE SUPERB cruising grounds. Marinas and services for yachtsmen range from rugged and rustic to high-tech facilities, mostly the latter. Walker's Cay at the top of the Abacos is about 55 mi northeast of West End at the tip of Grand Bahama Island, and it's also a 55-mi crossing from Palm Beach. Many cruising yachtsmen coming from the north opt for the 110-mi route from Florida's Fort Pierce–Vero Beach area to Walker's Cay.

Walker's Cay and its neighbor, Grand Cay, represent the contrasts in facilities available. Walker's Cay has a high-class, 75-slip, full-service marina, a 2,500-ft paved airstrip, and extravagant hotel comforts. Grand Cay is a ramshackle settlement of about 200 people and four times that many dogs of mixed breed, called Bahamian potcakes. Yachtsmen will find the anchorage off the community dock adequate. Double anchors are advised to handle the harbor's tidal current.

Heading south from Walker's Cay and Grand Cay, you will pass (and maybe want to explore by dinghy) a clutch of tiny cays and islets, such as Double Breasted Cays, Roder Rocks, Barracuda Rocks, Miss Romer Cay, Little Sale Cay, and Great Sale Cay. Great Sale Harbour provides excellent shelter. Snorkeling in the shallows along the mangroves, you might spot manta rays and eagle rays, sand sharks, and perhaps a school of small barracuda. Other small islands in the area are Carter Cay, Moraine Cay, Umbrella Cay, Guineaman Cay, Pensacola and Allen's cays (which are now virtually one island since a hurricane filled in the gap between them), and the Hawksbill Cays. Most offer varying degrees of lee anchorage. Fox Town, due south of Hawksbill Cay on the western tip of Little Abaco, is the first refueling stop for powerboats traveling east from West End.

A narrow causeway joins Little Abaco to Great Abaco, where the largest community at the north end is Cooper's Town. Stock up here on groceries, hardware, marine parts, liquor, and beer. There's also a coin laundry, a telephone station, a few restaurants, bakeries, and a resident doctor. Green Turtle Cay has excellent yachting facilities at White Sound to the north and Black Sound to the south. The Green Turtle Club dominates the northern end of White Sound, while Bluff House, halfway up the sound, has docks on the inside and a dinghy dock below the club on the bank side.

South of New Plymouth on Great Abaco's mainland stands the Treasure Cay Hotel Resort and Marina with one of the finest and longest beaches in the area. A New England–style charmer lies a little to the south: Man-O-War Cay, a boatbuilding settlement. This island, with the 26-slip Man-O-War Marina, is devoid of cars, beer, liquor, and women in skimpy bikinis.

The most photogenic lighthouse in the Bahamas sits atop Elbow Cay, signaling the harbor opening to Hope Town. Boats also make their way to two less-developed neighboring islands: Guana Cay, with a 22-slip marina, and Spanish Cay, with a 70-slip full-service marina.

Back on Great Abaco is Marsh Harbour, largest settlement in the Abacos, which has plenty of facilities. These include the modern (and growing) 172-slip Boat Harbour Marina, a full-service operation on the east side of the island. Marinas on the other side of town include the 75-slip Conch Inn Marina, the 60-slip Marsh Harbour Marina, and smaller facilities.

costs $13. The ride from Marsh Harbour Airport to Hope Town on Elbow Cay costs $11. Fares are generally $1.50 per mile.

Opening and Closing Times

Banks, located at Marsh Harbour and Treasure Cay on Great Abaco Island, New Plymouth on Green Turtle Cay, Hope Town on Elbow Cay, and on Man-O-War Cay, are generally open Monday–Thursday 9–1, Friday 9–5.

Contacts and Resources

EMERGENCIES

Police or fire (☎ 919). The **Marsh Harbour Clinic** (☎ 242/367–2510) has a resident doctor and a nurse. A few areas in the Abacos still do not have direct long-distance dialing, and emergencies have to be reported to the hotel management. BaTelCo (the Bahamas Telecommunications Corporation) has a system of microwave relay stations in the Abacos that provides direct-dial connections to the outside world without going through an operator.

GUIDED TOURS

Papa-Tango Tours (☎ 242/367–3753) depart daily from Marsh Harbour's Boat Harbour Marina for daylong trips that include touring the islands, shopping, fishing, shelling, and snorkeling. In Green Turtle Cay, **Green Turtle Club** (☎ 242/365–4271) offers an "Abaco Aventure" tour of nearby historic islands. From Treasure Cay, board the **Sunset Splash Mermaid Cruise** (☎ 242/365–8475) for daily glass-bottom boat trips or a sunset "booze cruise."

VISITOR INFORMATION

Visit, call, or write Marsh Harbour's **Abaco Tourist Office** (✉ Box AB20663, Marsh Harbour, Abaco, ☎ 242/367–3067, FAX 242/367–3068).

ANDROS

Andros, the largest of the Bahamian islands (100 mi long and 40 mi wide), is the least explored of them all, a place serrated by channels and tiny inlets with such names as North Bight, Middle Bight, and South Bight. Although not frequently visited, Andros is popular with sports lovers for its excellent bonefishing and its diving opportunities. The Spaniards who came here in the 16th century called it *La Isla del Espiritu Santo*—the Island of the Holy Spirit—and it has retained its eerie mystique to this day.

In fact, the descendants of a group of Seminole Indians and runaway slaves who left the Florida Everglades in the mid-19th century settled in Andros and remained hidden from the outside world until a few decades ago. They continue to live as a tribal society. Their village, near the northern tip of the island, is called Red Bay, and they make a living by weaving straw goods. The Seminoles are credited with originating the myth of the island's legendary (and elusive) *chickcharnies*—red-eyed, bearded, green-feathered creatures with three fingers and three toes that hang upside down by their tails from pine trees. These mythical characters supposedly wait deep in the forests to wish good luck to the friendly trespasser and vent their mischief on the hostile.

Andros's western shore, which lies 30 mi west of Nassau, is utterly barren and not recommended to yachters. The island's lush green interior is covered with wild orchids and dense forests of pine and mahogany, fringed on its western edge by miles of mangrove swamp. The forests provide nesting grounds for parrots, partridges, quail, white-crowned pigeons, and whistling ducks, and hunters come to Andros from

September to March in search of game. There are only about a dozen settlements and a handful of hotels on the eastern shore.

The Andros Barrier Reef—the third-largest reef in the world—is within a mile of the east shore and runs for 140 mi. It has an enchanting variety of marine life, and is easily accessible to divers. Sheltered waters within the reef average 6 to 15 ft, but on the other side of the reef ("over the wall") lie the depths (over 6,000 ft) of the Tongue of the Ocean, which is used for testing submarines and underwater weapons by the U.S. and British navies. They operate under the acronym AUTEC (Atlantic Underwater Test and Evaluation Center), and their base is located near Andros Town.

Numbers in the margin correspond to points of interest on the Andros map.

Nicholl's Town

❿ Nicholl's Town, at the northeastern corner of Andros, is the largest village on the island, with a population of about 600. This friendly community has stores for supplies and groceries, a few hotels, a public medical clinic, a telephone station, and small restaurants that serve Bahamian fare. A few miles north of Nicholl's Town is a crescent beach and a headland known as **Morgan's Bluff**, named after the 17th-century pirate Henry Morgan, who allegedly dropped off some of his stolen loot in the area.

Dining and Lodging

$$ ✕🏨 **Conch Sound Resort Inn.** The simple, clean, and spacious rooms have brown- and beige-carpting, mahogany furniture, handmade quilts, soft cushioned chairs, and satellite TV. Bonefishing and diving can be arranged; the beach is a 10-minute walk but the hotel will provide transportation. ✉ *Box 23029, Nicholl's Town,* ☎ *242/329–2060 or 242/329–2341. 14 rooms. Restaurant, bar, air-conditioning, pool, fishing. No credit cards. EP.*

$ ✕🏨 **Green Windows Inn.** The inn's rooms are over a restaurant and bar. The beach is a 10-minute walk away and flats are nearby for bonefishing aficionados (bonefishing guides are easily arranged). The restaurant serves seafood and Bahamian fare, such as steamed fish and peas 'n' rice. ✉ *Box 23076, Rawfon St., Nicholl's Town,* ☎ *242/329–2194,* ℻ *242/329–2016. 10 rooms, 4 with bath. Restaurant, bar. AE, V. EP.*

Fresh Creek–Andros Town

Andros lures fishing enthusiasts to its fabulous bonefishing flats, and **⓫** divers can't get enough of the sprawling **Andros Barrier Reef** just offshore Fresh Creek–Andros Town. Snorkelers can explore such reefs as the Three Sisters, where visibility is clear 15 ft to the sandy floor, and jungles of elkhorn coral snake up to the surface. Divers can delve into the 60-ft-deep coral caves of the Petrified Forest, beyond which the wall slopes down to depths of 9,000 ft (☞ The Up-Close Undersea Adventures *in* Andros box, *below*).

⓬ Batik fabric called Androsia is made in **Fresh Creek.** Fresh Creek is also home to the Small Hope Bay Lodge, the area's dive resort.

⓭ About 30 mi south of Nicholl's Town on the east coast is the small hamlet of **Andros Town.** Although the only thing to see here is the airport, 5 mi inland from Andros Town is **Captain Bill's Blue Hole**—one of several on the island—a delightful freshwater spring with ropes for swinging across it. Also near Andros Town, you can commune with nature by strolling along forest paths and taking in the wild orchids.

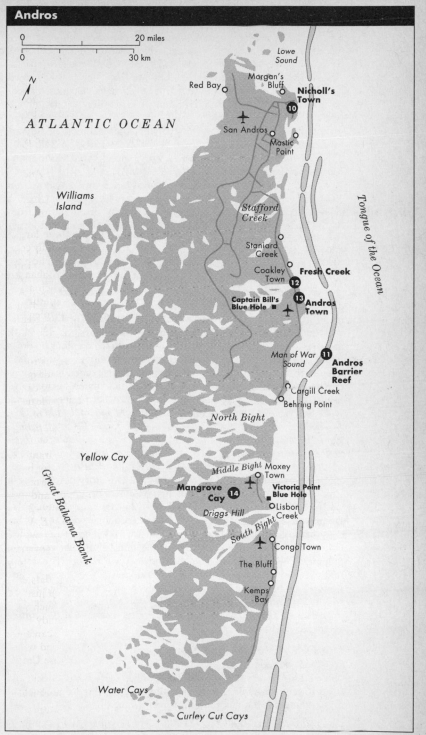

0   20 miles
0   30 km

N

ATLANTIC OCEAN

Red Bay

Morgan's Bluff

Lowe Sound

Nicholl's Town ⑩

San Andros

Mastic Point

Williams Island

Stafford Creek

Staniard Creek

Coakley Town

Fresh Creek ⑫

Captain Bill's Blue Hole ⑬ **Andros Town**

Tongue of the Ocean

Man of War Sound ⑪ **Andros Barrier Reef**

Cargill Creek

Behring Point

North Bight

Yellow Cay

Great Bahama Bank

Middle Bight Moxey Town

Mangrove Cay ⑭

Victoria Point Blue Hole

Lisbon Creek

Driggs Hill

South Bight

Congo Town

The Bluff

Kemps Bay

Water Cays

Curley Cut Cays

Dining and Lodging

$ ✕ **Hank's Place.** The chicken wire–screened porch of this local hang is a favorite for native eats or a game of dominoes. If servings here are too generous, order a "snack" plate, which consists of a main course served with fries. ⊠ *Andros Town,* ☎ *242/368–2447. No credit cards.*

$$$ ✕🖬 **Andros Lighthouse Yacht Club and Marina.** The yachting crowd favors this spot, so you're sure to meet an ever-changing parade of people in the cocktail lounge and restaurant. The luxurious rooms and villas have tropical fabrics, ceiling fans, phones, TVs, refrigerators, and private patios. Reef or bonefishing, diving, and boating are easily arranged. ⊠ *Andros Town, Andros,* ☎ *242/368–2305,* 🗚 *242/368–2300. 20 rooms. Bar, dining room, refrigerators, pool, tennis court, beach, dock, bicycles. AE, D, MC, V. EP, MAP.*

$$$ ✕🖬 **Small Hope Bay Lodge.** In the central lodge you can sprawl on
★ one of the oversized throw pillows by the fireplace, gaze out from a glass-walled alcove with views of the sea, or fix yourself a drink from the *Panacea,* a fishing dory that serves as a bar. This wonderfully casual all-inclusive property—the toast of Andros since 1960—attracts divers, snorkelers, and anglers but anyone who can appreciate the unhurried life and a good story told around the dinner table will fit right in. Meals are hearty, with a choice of seafood or meat and an extensive salad bar at lunch and dinner. Rooms, decorated with local Androsia batik prints and straw work, are in rustic, beachside cottages made of coral rock and Andros pine; none have phones or TVs. Nearly everyone snorkels; novices are trained in a few minutes and don mask and gear to explore the shallow reefs or play with the dolphins up Fresh Creek. The resort has free, introductory scuba lessons every afternoon (equipment included) and offers specialty diving excursions, such as one-on-one guided explorations of blue holes and tunnels. As for bonefishing, the hotel has customized boats and experienced guides. ⊠ *Small Hope Bay, Central Andros (*⊠ *Box 21667, Fort Lauderdale, FL 33335),* ☎ *242/368–2014 or 800/223–6961,* 🗚 *242/368–2015. 20 rooms, 1 villa. 2 bars, dining room, lounge, hot tub, massage, beach, snorkeling, windsurfing, boating, kayaks, fishing, bicycles, recreation room, library, laundry service. AE, D, MC, V. FAP, all-inclusive.*

$ ✕🖬 **Chickcharnie Hotel.** This whitewashed, two-story hotel at Fresh Creek has tiny rooms. Eleven of them have air-conditioning and a private bath; the five remaining rooms have ceiling fans and shared baths. Despite the brusque management, the inn is popular with anglers because of its cheap rates and the availability of fishing boats and guides. Guests can stock up on supplies at the mini–shopping center on premises. The hotel is 3 mi from the Andros Town airport. The restaurant overlooks the water and is quite good, serving—although quite slowly—the best Bahamian fare around; consider trying the steamed conch, crawfish, or grouper fingers. ⊠ *Fresh Creek, Andros Town, Andros,* ☎ *242/368–2025. 16 rooms, 11 with private bath. Bar, dining room. No credit cards. EP.*

Outdoor Activities and Sports

BOATING AND FISHING

Chickcharnie Hotel (☎ 242/368–2025) at Fresh Creek has a dock, and boats to rent for fishing. Rates run about $250 a day for a bonefishing skiff and $400 a day for a 25-ft reef-fishing boat.

Small Hope Bay Lodge (☎ 242/368–2014 or 800/223–6961) offers bonefishing, deep-sea fishing (wahoo, kingfish tuna), fly-fishing, reef fishing, seasonal tarpon fishing, and a "west side overnight"—a two-night camping/bone-and-tarpon fishing trip into the uninhabited western end of the island. Rates run from $175 to $275 for a half day and $300 to $480 for a full day (full-day trips include all gear and lunch).

UNDERSEA ADVENTURES IN ANDROS

ANDROS PROBABLY HAS THE largest number of dive sites in the country. With the third-longest barrier reef in the world (behind those of Australia and Belize), the island offers about 100 mi of drop-off diving into the Tongue of the Ocean. Uncounted numbers of **blue holes** are forming in the area; in some places, these constitute vast submarine networks that can extend more than 200 ft down into the coral (Fresh Creek, 40–100 ft; North Andros, 40–200+ ft; South Bight, 40–200 ft). Blue holes are named for their inky-blue aura when viewed from above and for the light-blue filtered sunlight that is visible from many feet below. Some of the holes have vast cathedral-like interior chambers with stalactites and stalagmites, offshoot tunnels, and seemingly endless corridors. Others have distinct thermoclines (temperature changes) between layers of water or are subject to tidal flow. The dramatic Fresh Creek site provides an insight into the complex Andros cave system; there isn't much coral growth but plenty of midnight parrot fish, big southern stingrays, and some blacktip sharks. Similar blue holes are found all along the barrier reef, including several at Mastic Point in the north and the ones explored and filmed off South Bight.

Undersea adventurers also have the opportunity to investigate wrecks such as the *Potomac,* a steel-hulled freighter that sank in 1952 and lies in 40 ft of water close to the Andros Beach Hotel in Nicholl's Town. And off the waters of Fresh Creek, at 70 ft, lies the 56-ft-long World War II LCM (landing craft mechanized) known only as the **Barge Wreck,** which was sunk in 1963 to create an artificial reef. Now encrusted with coral, it has become home to a group of groupers and a blizzard of tiny silverfish. There is a fish-cleaning station where miniature cleaning shrimp and yellow gobies clean grouper and rockfish by swimming into their mouths and out their gills, picking up food particles. It's excellent subject matter for close-up photography.

The split-level **Over the Wall** dive at Fresh Creek takes novices to the 80-ft ledge and experienced divers to a pre–Ice Age beach at 185 ft. The wall is covered with black coral and a wide variety of tube sponges. **Small Hope Bay Lodge** (☞ *above*) at Fresh Creek is the most venerable and best dive resort on Andros. It's a friendly, informal place where the only thing taken seriously is diving. There's a fully equipped dive center with a wide variety of specialty dives, including customized dive trips for families that include a private dive boat and dive-master. A two-tank dive at Small Hope Bay costs $55. If you're not certified, check out the lodge's morning "resort course" and be ready to explore the depths by afternoon!

Cargill Creek

Fishing—bonefishing in particular—is the principal appeal of this quiet area, with wadeable flats just 100 yards offshore. Consider renting a car if you plan to spend time back in Andros Town and Fresh Creek; the taxi fare is $40 one way. Bonefishing packages run about $300 a day.

Dining and Lodging

$$$$ ✕🖬 **Andros Island Bonefishing Club.** This is a down-home, few-frills kind of place. Hardcore bonefishing is the name of the game and guests have access to 100 sq mi of lightly fished flats—80–85% of the anglers are return guests. Owner Captain Rupert Leadon is the personality of the place—a warm, commanding presence with many a story of the elusive bonefish. Accommodations are functional, with two queen-size beds and ceiling fans; some have a refrigerator. The dining room–lounge has satellite TV, a fly-tying table, and a well-stocked bar. The club has 12 boats for guided fishing, which is part of its all-inclusive package. ⊠ ⊠ *Northeast Cargill Creek (⊠ Box 959, Wexford, PA 15090)*, ☏ *242/368–5167 or 800/245–1950. 13 rooms. Bar, dining room, lounge, fans, dock fishing. MC, V (5% surcharge. FAP.*

$$$ ✕🖬 **Cargill Creek Fishing Lodge.** Accomodations for bonefishing tend to be spare, based on the reasoning that anglers care about fish more than their rooms. This may be true, though this lodge manages to eke out some aesthetic appeal. High points are an attractive, high-ceilinged dining room—which serves very good Bahamian and Continental fare and freshly baked bread and desserts—and the intimate "Bonefish Lounge" honor bar overlooking the shimmering flats. (Let Manager Colleen know if you prefer a particular brand of liquor and she'll stock it for you.) A thatched barbecue and grill area is adjacent to the lounge patio, where day's-end relaxation takes place, replete with hors d'oeuvres. ⊠ *Southeast Cargill Creek (⊠ Box N-1882, Nassau)*, ☏ *242/368–5129, ℻ 242/ 368–5046. 11 rooms, 2 cottages. Bar, dining room, pool, fishing. AE, MC, V (5% surcharge) . FAP. Closed July–Sept.*

Mangrove Cay

⑭ Remote and undeveloped, Mangrove Cay draws anglers, divers, naturalists, and those who really want to get away from it all. Separated from the north and south parts of Andros by bights, Mangrove Cay is an 18-mi island unto itself, where electricty and a paved road weren't introduced until 1989. In Little Harbor and Moxey Town, at the northern tip of the cay, you'll likely spy porous mounds of sponge fishing–bounty piled up to dry before being shipped to Nassau to be sold. The Mangrove Cay draws anglers, divers, naturalists, and those who really want to get away from it all. Separated from the north and south parts of Andros by bights, Mangrove Cay is an 18-mi island unto itself, where electricty and a paved road weren't introduced until 1989. In Little Harbor and Moxey Town, at the northern tip of the cay, you'll likely spy porous mounds of sponge fishing–bounty piled up to dry before being shipped to Nassau to be sold. The **Victoria Point Blue Hole** is good for snorkeling and diving, and the island has a number of pristine spots that are sure to please strollers looking for birds or wild orchids.

Just across from the government dock, the pink **Traveller's Rest** (☏ 242/369–0044) is the only place in town for weekend nightlife and DJ-dancing. To the south, at Lisbon Creek, a free government ferry makes trips twice daily to South Andros, at 8 AM and 4 PM. Bonefishing devotees know that Mangrove Cay is a good base for excursions to Bigwood Cay Flat, where the pale turquoise water appears to stretch forever.

Dining and Lodging

$ ✕ **Dianne Cash's Ultimate Delight.** What's on the menu? "Nothing," says Dianne. "What do you want?" Dianne cooks three meals a day to order—just call a day in advance, to give her enough time to procure the ingredients. Ask for pork chops, lobster, conch salad, or Dianne's speciality—stuffed baked crabs. That's it: just four tables with white rattan chairs, a couple spots at the counter, and your own personal chef. ⊠ *Main Rd., Mangrove Cay,* ☎ *242/369–0430. No credit cards.*

$ ✕⊞ **Mangrove Cay Inn.** Chairs on the narrow front-patio walkway overlook the water, which you can ply with the inn's pedal boats. You can rent one of the inn's bicycles to explore the cay or just challenge a friend to one of the parlor's many board games. The restaurant is an inviting spot, with richly stained wooden walls and an attached bar with high captain's-chair stools. Try a hoagie sandwich prepared with onions and fresh green peppers for lunch, or the conch and lobster pasta in wine-butter sauce for dinner. ⊠ *General Post Office, Mangrove Cay, Andros,* ☎ *242/369–0069,* FAX *242/369–0014. 10 rooms, 2 suites. Restaurant, bar. No credit cards. EP, MAP, FAP.*

$ ✕⊞ **Seascape Inn.** These individual cottages with private decks over-
★ looking the ocean are the quaintest accomodations on Mangrove Cay. Owners Mickey and Joan McGowan have decorated each one with hand-crafted wooden furniture and original art. The elevated restaurant–dining room is the inn's meeting place; it holds the reading library, hosts locals who drop in for a drink or game of darts, and serves savory fare—steaks, chicken in white wine sauce. The Continental breakfasts are also delicious—Joan bakes an assortment of yummy muffins and killer banana bread. ⊠ *Mangrove Cay, Andros,* ☎ FAX *242/369–0342. 4 one-bedroom cottages, 1 cottage suite. Restaurant, bar, fishing, diving, bicycles. No credit cards. EP.*

Outdoor Activities and Sports

FISHING

Private bonefishing guide **Dennis Leadon** (☎ 242/368–5156) is highly recommended for leading anglers through the flats above Mangrove Cay. Contact **Moxey's** (☎ 242/369–0023) for available bonefishing guides for hire.

SCUBA DIVING AND SNORKELING

The dive shop at **Seascape Inn** (☎ 242/369–0342) offers snorkeling and diving excursions, rents equipment and dive kayaks, and organizes one night dive weekly.

South Andros–Driggs Hill

Driggs Hill, on South Andros, is a small settlement of pastel houses, a tiny church, a grocery store, and the Emerald Palms by the Sea hotel. At the Bluff settlement, near Congo Town, which has the island's third airport, skeletons of Arawak natives were found huddled together. A local resident attests that another skeleton was found—this one of a 4-ft-tall, one-eyed owl, which may have given rise to the legend of the mythical elflike *chickcharnie,*.

Dining and Lodging

$–$$$ ✕⊞ **Emerald Palms by the Sea.** For upscale resort accommodations on Andros, this property is your best bet. Rooms have wainscoting, heavy pine furnishings with carved-seashell designs, and four-poster beds with mosquito netting—plus satellite TVs in every room. Lined with French doors, the airy dining room is particularly handsome, with richly upholstered rattan chairs and a lattice-work ceiling. Bahamian and international cuisine are served here, and you might feast on eggs Benedict for breakfast or chicken breast stuffed with lobster and conch for dinner. ⊠ *Box 800, Driggs Hill, Andros,* ☏ *242/369–2661,* FAX *242/369–2667. 18 rooms, 2 suites. Dining room, pool, tennis court, snorkeling, boating, fishing, bicycles, car rental. AE, MC, V. EP, MAP.*

Outdoor Activities and Sports

FISHING

Jolly Boy Enterprises (☏ 242/369–2767 or 242/369–2696) provides boats and guides for bonefishing, reef fishing, or deep sea fishing.

SCUBA DIVING AND SNORKELING

Gibco's Diving (☏ 242/369–2560) takes snorkelers and divers out off the South Andros coast, but expects that they bring their own mask, fins, and wet suit.

Andros A to Z

Arriving and Departing

BY MAIL BOAT

From Potter's Cay Dock in Nassau, the M/V *Lisa J II* sails to Morgan's Bluff, Mastic Point, and Nicholl's Town in the north of the island every Wednesday, returning to Nassau the following Tuesday. The trip takes five hours and costs $30. The M/V *Lady D* leaves Nassau on Tuesdays for Fresh Creek (with stops at Spaniard Creek, Blanket Sound, and Bowne Sound) and returns to Nassau on Sunday. The trip takes 5½ hours and the fare is $30. The M/V *Mangrove Cay Express* leaves Nassau on Wednesday evenings for Lisbon Creek, and returns on Monday afternoons; the trip takes 5½ hours and costs $30. The M/V *Captain Moxey* leaves Nassau on Mondays and calls at Kemps Bay, Long Bay Cays, and the Bluff on South Andros. It returns to Nassau on Wednesday. The trip takes 7½ hours; the fare is $30. Schedules are subject to change due to weather conditions or occasional dry-docking. For more information, contact the **Dockmaster's office** (☏ 242/393–1064) at Potter's Cay.

BY PLANE

Andros has four airports: **San Andros** in the north (☏ 242/329–4224), **Andros Town** in Central Andros (☏ 242/368–2030), the **Mangrove Cay** airport (☏ 242/369–0083 or 242/369–2640), and **Congo Town** in South Andros (☏ 242/369–0083 or 242/369–2640). Check with your hotel for the proper airport.

Bahamasair (☏ 242/339–4415 or 800/222–4262) has two daily flights (except Wednesdays) from Nassau to San Andros, Andros Town, and Congo Town. Flights to Mangrove Cay leave once a day, except Tuesdays and Wednesdays. **Congo Air** (☏ 242/377–8329) flies from Nassau to Mangrove Cay and Congo Town. **Island Express** (☏ 954/359–0380) flies from Fort Lauderdale to all four airports. **Lynx Air International** (☏ 888/596–9247) flies from Fort Lauderdale to Congo Town three days a week. **Major Air** (☏ 242/352–5778) has service from Freeport to all four airports. **Small Hope Bay Lodge** (☏ 242/368–2014 or 800/223–6961) offers flight service from Fort Lauderdale to Andros Town for a minimum of two passengers and can be chartered for island-hopping.

Getting Around

Andros has no tour operators, and cabdrivers will charge around $80 to $120 for a half-day tour of the island. Most visitors opt to get around by bicycle.

BY BICYCLE

Bicycles are available at **Andros Lighthouse Yacht Club and Marina** (⊠ Andros Town, ☎ 242/368–2305), **Chickcharnie Hotel** (⊠ Andros Town, ☎ 242/368–2025), **Small Hope Bay Lodge** (⊠ Fresh Creek, ☎ 242/368–2014), **Mangrove Cay Inn** (⊠ Mangrove Cay, ☎ 242/369–0069), and **Seascape Inn** (⊠ Mangrove Cay, ☎ 242/369–0342.

BY CAR

If you need a rental car, your best bet is to have your hotel make arrangements. There are no rental cars on Mangrove Cay.

BY FERRY

A free government ferry makes the under-half-hour trip between Mangrove Cay and South Andros twice daily. It departs South Andros at 8 AM and 4 PM, and departs Mangrove Cay at 8:30 PM and 4:30 PM. Call the **Commissioner's Office** (☎ 242/369–0331) for more information.

BY TAXI

Taxis meet incoming planes at the airports, and they can also be arranged through the hotels. Rates are around $1.50 a mile.

Opening and Closing Times

The **Canadian Imperial Bank of Commerce** (☎ 242/329–2382), in San Andros, is open Wednesday from 10:30 to 2:30.

Contacts and Resources

EMERGENCIES

Police: North Andros (☎ 919); Central Andros (☎ 242/368–2626); South Andros (☎ 242/329–4733). **Medical Clinics:** North Andros (☎ 242/329–2239); Mangrove Cay (☎ 242/369–0089); South Andros (☎ 242/369–4620).

Telephone service is available only through the front desk at Andros hotels, so emergencies should be reported to the management. A doctor lives in San Andros. Medical clinics are located at Mastic Point, Nicholl's Town, and Lowe Sound, each with a resident nurse. A health center at Fresh Creek has both a doctor and a nurse. A clinic at Mangrove Cay has a nurse.

THE BERRY ISLANDS

The Berry Islands consist of two dozen–plus small cays stretching in a curve like a new moon north of Andros and New Providence Island. Although a few of the islands are privately owned, most of them are uninhabited—except by rare birds using the territory as their nesting grounds, or by visiting yachters dropping anchor in secluded havens. The Berry Islands start in the north at Great Stirrup Cay, where a lighthouse guides passing ships, and they end in the south at Chub Cay, only 35 mi north of Nassau.

Most of the islands' 700 residents live on Great Harbour Cay, which is 10 mi long and 1½ mi wide. Its main settlement, Bullock's Harbour, has a couple of small restaurants and a grocery store. The Great Harbour Cay resort, a few miles away from Bullock's Harbour, was developed in the early 1970s; it is geared toward fishing enthusiasts. Both Chub and Great Harbour cays are close to the Tongue of the Ocean, where big game fish roam.

The Berry Islands appear just north of Andros Island on the Baha¹ map at the front of this guide.

Chub Cay

Dining and Lodging

$$–$$$ ✕🏨 **Chub Cay Club.** This once-private resort opened its facilities to the public in 1994. The huge marina can handle more than 96 oceangoing craft and offers charter boats with guides for big-game and flat fishing, the main pursuits here. The cay claims itself as the "fish bowl" of the Bahamas, and that also means great diving. The resort's rooms overlook the ocean or are clustered next to an oversize freshwater pool; villas are on the horseshoe-shape beach facing west. The Harbour House Restaurant serves a good variety of Caribbean and Continental dishes. With fresh fish, conch, and lobsters arriving daily, seafood is the obvious choice. ✉ *Box 661067, Miami Springs, FL 33266,* ☎ *242/325–1490 or 800/662–8555,* 🅵🅰🆇 *242/322–5199. 16 rooms, 9 villas. Restaurant, 3 bars, dining room, grocery, air-conditioning, refrigerators, 2 pools, 2 tennis courts, beach, dive shop, dock, boating, fishing, bicycles. AE, MC, V. EP.*

Outdoor Activities and Sports

BOATING

The clarity of Bahamian waters is particularly evident when you cross the Great Bahama Bank from the Bimini area along the Berry Islands on the way to Nassau. The depth of the waters here is seldom more than 20 ft. Grass patches and an occasional coral head or flat coral patch dot the light sand bottom. Starfish abound, and you can often catch a glimpse of a gliding stingray or eagle ray. You might spot the odd turtle, and if you care to jump over the side of the boat with a mask, you might also pick up a conch or two in the grass.

SCUBA DIVING

Reefs, walls, caves, and canyons are among the nine sites surrounding this fish-abundant cay. In cooperation with Chub Cay Club, **Undersea Adventures** (☎ 242/323–2412, 800/327–8150, or 954/462–4100), run here by divemaster Bill Nelson, leads a morning two-tank dive and an afternoon one-tank dive. Night dives can also be scheduled.

Great Harbour Cay

Boating

In the upper Berry Islands, **Great Harbour Cay** (☎ 242/367–8838) has an 80-slip, full-service marina that can handle boats up to 150 ft. Accessible through an 80-ft-wide channel from the bank side, Great Harbour Cay has one of the most pristine beaches in the Bahamas running along its east side.

Dining and Lodging

$$–$$$$ ✕🏨 **Great Harbour Cay.** The resort rents out privately owned villas and town houses on a daily and weekly basis. The furnishings and layouts differ, but all units have TVs and sundecks; none have phones. Management meets you at the airport and can help you find the services of fishing guides for bonefishing, bottom fishing, and deep-sea fishing. You can find a light lunch at the Beach Club, full meals at the Wharf Restaurant on the marina, and a more expensive fish-and-seafood buffet a couple of nights weekly at the yacht club's private Tamboo Club, to which resort guests are admitted. ✉ ✉ *Bullocks Harbour, Central Great Harbour Cay (✉ 3512 N. Ocean Dr., Hollywood, FL 33019),* ☎ *242/367–8838, 954/921–9084, or 800/343–7256,* 🅵🅰🆇 *242/367–8115 or 954/921–1044. 15 villas, 6 town houses. 3 restaurants, bar, air-conditioning, 9-hole golf course, beach, dock, snorkeling, boating, fishing, bicycles. AE, MC, V. EP.*

Berry Islands A to Z

Arriving and Departing

BY MAIL BOAT

M/V *Champion II* leaves Potter's Cay, Nassau, every Thursday for the Berry Islands. For schedules and specific destinations, call the **Dockmaster's office** (☎ 242/393–1064) at Potter's Cay.

BY PLANE

Both Great Harbour Cay and Chub Cay resorts provide transportation from the airport for their guests.

Island Express (☎ 954/359–0380) has charters from Fort Lauderdale to Chub Cay and Great Harbour Cay. **Tropical Diversions Air** (☎ 954/921–9084 or 800/343–7256) flies to Great Harbour Cay from Fort Lauderdale.

Getting Around

Happy People's (☎ 242/367–8117) has rental bikes, Jeeps, and boats available for exploring the island.

Contacts and Resources

EMERGENCIES

Police (✉ Bullock's Harbour, Great Harbour Cay, ☎ 242/367–8344). **Great Harbour Cay Medical Clinic** (☎ 242/367–8400).

THE BIMINIS

The Biminis have long been known as the big-game-fishing capital of the Bahamas. The nearest Bahamian islands to the U.S. mainland, they consist of a handful of islands and cays just 50 mi east of Miami, across the Gulf Stream that sweeps the area's western shores. Most visitors spend their time on North Bimini. Throughout the year, more than a dozen billfish tournaments draw anglers to the Gulf Stream and the Great Bahama Bank from the United States, Canada, Britain, and the rest of Europe. Marinas such as Weech's Bimini Dock, the Bimini Big Game Fishing Club, and Bimini's Blue Water, all on the eastern side of skinny North Bimini, provide more than 150 slips for oceangoing craft, many of them belonging to weekend visitors who make the short trip from Florida ports. The western side of North Bimini, along Queen's Highway, is one long stretch of beautiful beach.

All the hotels, restaurants, churches, and stores in the Biminis are along North Bimini's King's and Queen's highways, which run parallel to each other. Everything on North Bimini, where most of the islands' 1,600 inhabitants reside, is so close together you do not need a car to get around. Sparsely populated South Bimini, separated from its big brother by a narrow ocean passage, is where Juan Ponce de León allegedly looked for the Fountain of Youth in 1513. Tourists are sometimes still approached by locals offering to show them the exact site of the Fountain of Youth, which is supposedly close to South Bimini's little airstrip.

Ernest Hemingway did battle with his share of game fish around North Bimini, which he visited for the first time in 1935 from his home in Key West. He made frequent visits here, where he wrote much of *To Have and Have Not* and *Islands in the Stream*. He is remembered in the area as a picaresque hero, not only for his graphic descriptions of his fishing exploits, but for his drinking and brawling, including a fistfight he had with his brother Leicester on the Bimini dock.

Other notables lured to the island have included Howard Hughes and Richard Nixon. The most rooted American to the Biminis was entrepreneur Michael Lerner. He discovered Bimini years before Hemin

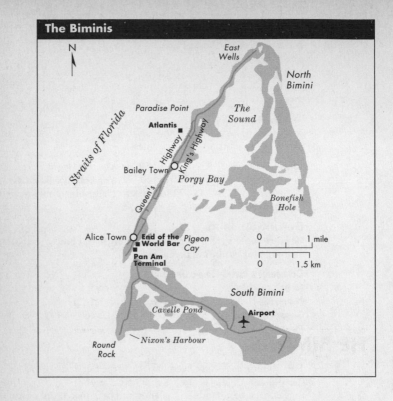

The Biminis

and is the man credited with teaching Papa how to catch giant tuna. Lerner was a great friend to the Biminis and established, among other things, the Lerner Marine Research Laboratory, which conducted research on dolphins and sharks from 1947 to 1974.

The Biminis also have a notorious history as a jumping-off place for illicit dealings; first during the Civil War, when it was a refuge for profiteers bringing in war supplies from Europe, and then during Prohibition, when it was a haven for rumrunners. Today things are pretty quiet—rumrunners have been replaced with fishermen and Floridians. Spring break brings lots of students who cruise over from Fort Lauderdale for wild nights at what was Papa Hemingway's favorite watering hole, the Compleat Angler. Uncharacteristic of the rest of the Out Islands, summer is Bimini's busy season.

Alice Town

The main community of the Biminis, Alice Town, is at the southern end of North Bimini; here, Pam Am Airbridge's seaplanes splash down in the harbor, lumber up a ramp, and park on the other side of King's Highway. Near the Pan Am seaplane landing area's customs and immigration office are the Art Deco ruins of Bimini's first hotel, the **Bimini Bay Rod and Gun Club,** a resort and casino that was built in the early 1920s and destroyed by a hurricane in 1926.

The **Compleat Angler Hotel** (⊠ King's Hwy., ☎ 242/347–3122) was Ernest Hemingway's hideaway in the '30s, and the Hemingway legend is perpetuated with a room full of memorabilia related to the writer, including pictures of Hemingway with gigantic fish and framed excerpts from his writings, most of them concerning battles with sharks. A photo of Cuban fisherman Angelmo Hernández, the supposed model for the hero of *The Old Man and the Sea,* also hangs in the bar.

The late Ossie Brown, who ran this hotel until 1995, claimed a Cuban man walked into the hotel some years ago, said he was Hernández's grandson, and handed over the photograph. More recently the Angler was in the news as the place where Gary Hart destroyed his hopes for the 1988 Democratic presidential nomination. He and Donna Rice were photographed in full color whooping it up on the bandstand in the bar of the hotel; the infamous picture now hangs in a place of honor.

The back door of the small, noisy **End of the World Bar** is always open to the harbor. This place—with a sandy floor and visitors' graffiti, business cards, and other surprises on every inch of wall, ceiling, and bar space—is a good spot to meet some local folk over a beer and a backgammon board. In the late '60s, the bar became a hangout of the late New York congressman Adam Clayton Powell, who retreated to North Bimini while Congress investigated his alleged misdemeanors; among other guests, Powell entertained American reporters, who knew they could find him here, ready to dispense flowery quotes. A marble plaque in his honor is displayed in the bar, and an annual Bimini fishing tournament is named in his memory. The bar is 100 yards from the Bimini Bay Rod and Gun Club ruins, on your right as you walk north on King's Highway (cars that meet head-on have to slow down so they can scrape past each other). ⊠ *King's Hwy., no phone.* ⊙ *Daily 9 AM–3 AM.*

Dining and Lodging

$–$$ ✕ **Red Lion.** Venture through twin doors emblazoned with the red tudor lions for fresh seafood and native dishes. There's a view out the back sliding-glass doors onto a small bay between the marinas. ⊠ *King's Hwy.,* ☎ *242/347–3259. No credit cards.*

$ ✕ **Capt. Bob's.** Try the Bimini bread French toast or fish and eggs at this popular breakfast spot. ⊠ *King's Hwy.,* ☎ *242/347–3260. No credit cards. Closed Sun.*

$ ✕ **CJ's Deli.** Grab an orange stool at the counter for a sausage and egg breakfast, or a lunch of the best cracked conch on the island—try it with either tartar sauce or ketchup. CJ's isn't open for dinner but does serve "late-night snacks." ⊠ *King's Hwy.,* ☎ *242/347–3295. No credit cards. No dinner.*

$$$–$$$$ ✕⌷ **Bimini Big Game Fishing Club and Hotel.** This is a favorite choice
★ among fishing and yachting types who take advantage of the full-service 75-slip marina. If you're here to fish, you might prefer a spacious cottage, where you can easily prepare a lucky catch on an outdoor grill. Although all interiors are pleasant and comfortable—with teal accents and combination carpet-and-tile floors—and every room has a TV, second-floor rooms have the decent views. The club's Gulfstream restaurant is the most upscale dining on the island, with cuisine ranging from escargot to T-bone steaks. If you plan to stay here during one of the major fishing tournaments, reserve well in advance. ⊠ *King's Hwy. at pink wall, Box 699, Alice Town,* ☎ *242/347–3391 or 800/737–1007,* ℻ *242/347–3392. 33 rooms, 2 suites, 12 cottages. Restaurant, 3 bars, 2 dining rooms, air-conditioning, pool, tennis court, boating, fishing, baby-sitting, laundry service. AE, MC, V. EP.*

$$–$$$ ✕⌷ **Bimini Blue Water Resort.** The Browns, a pioneer family in the islands, own this resort as well as the Compleat Angler Hotel (☞ *below.* This was one of Hemingway's Bimini hideaways. Its restaurant, the Anchorage, is believed to have been the main setting for *Islands in the Stream* and was once the home of Michael Lerner. You can still rent Marlin Cottage, where the author wrote much of the novel. The cottage, with its matching cannons in front, remains the best place on the island for watching the sunset and, on a clear evening, the reflection of Miami's lights on the water. Its smallish rooms have blue-and-white furniture, wood-paneled walls, private balconies, and TVs. The An-

chorage specializes in conch and lobster and provides a gorgeous view of the Gulf Stream. There's also a full-service marina with 32 modern slips. Although the entrance to the hotel is on King's Highway, the building sits on top of a 20-ft hill and faces Queen's Highway on the western side. ⊠ *King's Hwy. (⊠ Box 601, Alice Town),* ☎ *242/347–3166 or 800/688–4752,* ℻ *242/347–3293. 9 rooms, 1 3-bedroom cottage. Bar, dining room, pool, beach. AE, MC, V. EP.*

$–$$$$ ⌂ **Sea Crest Hotel and Marina.** This yellow, three-story hotel has simply furnished rooms with tile floors, cable TV, and balconies. Pick a room on the third floor—you'll enjoy lofty, open-beam ceilings and nice views from either side of the building—sea or marina. This motelish property is an excellent value for families, as children under age 12 stay free. The beach is a two-minute walk away. ⊠ *King's Hwy., Box 654, Alice Town, Bimini,* ☎ *242/347–3071,* ℻ *242/347–3495. 11 rooms, 1 2-bedroom suite, 1 3-bedroom suite. MC, V (5% surcharge). EP.*

$–$$ ⌂ **Weech's Bimini Dock and Bay View Rooms.** This Alice Town marina (full-service, except fuel), has pleasant but unadorned rooms with paneled walls, pastel spreads and drapes, and either two twins or a double and a twin bed; the apartment has a full kitchen and a seating area. The beach is a five-minute walk. ⊠ *½ block from Pan-Am Air Bridge, Box 613, Alice Town, Bimini,* ☎ *242/347–3028,* ℻ *242/347–3508. 5 rooms, 1 apartment. Air-conditioning, boating. No credit cards. EP.*

$ ⌂ **Compleat Angler Hotel.** This well-worn, informal, wood-sided hotel
★ dates back to the early '30s and will forever be associated with Hemingway, who often drank here after a day of stalking marlin. The place is far from posh, but these three stories of rich wood paneling exude an unforgttable sense of place and are the most charismatic accommodations on Bimini. Exterior rooms open onto the wraparound porch, which overlooks the courtyard bar and the street. The walls of the bar are plastered with fishing photographs and personalized auto-license plates. The bar is the liveliest nightspot on the island, with live music on weekends, but this can be a negative if you're trying to sleep upstairs. Guests have access to the pool and marina facilities of the Blue Water Resort (☞ *above*). ⊠ *3 blocks from Pam Am Air Bridge, King's Hwy. (⊠ Box 601, Alice Town, Bimini),* ☎ *242/347–3122,* ℻ *242/ 347–3293. 12 rooms. 3 bars, lounge, air-conditioning. AE, MC, V. EP.*

Outdoor Activities and Sports

BOATING AND FISHING

Bimini Big Game Fishing Club (☎ 242/347–3391 or 800/737–1007), a first-class, full-service 75-slip marina, charges $500 to $900 a day, and $400 for a half day of deep-sea fishing. **Bimini Blue Water Marina** (☎ 242/347–3166) charges from $700 a day, and from $400 a half day, with captain, mate, and gear included; this marina features 32 modern slips and usually hosts the annual Hemingway Billfish Tournament. **Weech's Bimini Dock** (☎ 242/347–3028), with 15 slips, has four Boston whalers, which it rents for $120 a day, and $60 a half day.

EVENTS

The Biminis host the following fishing tournaments throughout the year: the **Hemingway Championship** (February), the **Annual Bacardi Rum Billfish Tournament** (March), the **Bimini Billfish Championship** (March), the **Big Game Club Bimini Festival** (May), the **Big Five Tournament** (June), the **Hatteras and Latin Builder's Tournaments** (July), the **Bimini Native Open Tournament** and **Bacardi Family Open Tournament** (August), **Small BOAT—Bimini Open Angling Tournament** (September), and the **Wahoo Tournament** (November). In 1998, the island inaugurated an annual **Bimini Regatta,** which takes place at the end of March. For information on dates and tournament regulations, call the **Bahamas News Bureau** (☎ 800/327–7678).

SCUBA DIVING AND SAILING

The Biminis offer some excellent diving opportunities, particularly for watching marine life. The **Bimini Barge** wreck rests in 100 ft of water; **Little Caverns** is a medium-depth dive with scattered coral heads, small tunnels, and swim-throughs; **Rainbow Reef** is a shallow dive popular for fish gazing. And, of course, there's **Atlantis** (☞ *below*). Dive packages are available with most Bimini hotels.

Bimini Undersea (☎ 242/347–3089 or 800/348–4644) charges $39 for a one-tank dive, $69 for a two-tank, and $89 for three dives. It also rents and sells snorkel gear and arranges trips for $25 per person, including mask, snorkel, and fins. Excellent snorkeling is available mere steps from the beach. Afternoon excursions to frolic with a delightful pod of Atlantic spotted dolphins are offered for $79.

Shopping

Upstairs in the Burns House Building, the **Gateway Gallery** (✉ King's Hwy., ☎ 242/347–3131) sells Bahamian-made jewelry, crafts, and paintings in a variety of price ranges.

Elsewhere on North Bimini

Toward the north end of King's Highway, there are a couple of bars, grocery shops, clothing stores, a group of colorful straw market stalls, and women sitting by the side of the road selling mouthwatering Bimini bread (it is sold warm, soft, and sweet). The northwestern part of the island bears the ruins of an unrealized luxury development that was to include a marina, private homes, and a hotel. The developers ran out of money and abandoned the project, leaving the frames of a half-dozen homes looking out on an untrampled, shell-strewn beach.

Atlantis, this curious rock formation under about 20 ft of water, 500 yds off shore at Bimini Bay, is shaped like a backward letter J, some 600-ft long at the longest end. It's the shorter 300-ft extension that piques the interest of scientists and visitors alike—the precision patchwork of large, curved-edge stones form a perfect rectangle measuring about 30 ft across; a few of the stones are 16 ft square. It is purported to be the found "lost city" predicted by Edgar Cayce (1877–1945), a psychic with an interest in prehistorical civilizations. Archaeologists estimate the formation to be between 5,000 and 10,000 years old. Carvings in the rock appear to some scientists to resemble a network of highways. Skeptics have pooh-poohed the theory, conjecturing that they are merely turtle pens built considerably more recently.

Most of the island's residents live in **Bailey Town** in small, pastel-color concrete houses, a higgledy-piggledy combination of different shapes and sizes. Here you'll find the attractive **Wesley Methodist Church,** built in 1858, with a bell tower on the roof. Bailey Town lies on Queen's Highway north of the Bimini Blue Water Resort.

OFF THE **HEALING HOLE** – Locals recommend a trip here for curing what ails
BEATEN PATH you—gout and rheumatism are among the supposedly treatable afflictions. Ask your hotel to arrange a trip out to this natural clearing in the mangrove flats of North Bimini; you can take a leap of faith into the water and, if nothing else, enjoy a refreshing dip.

Biminis A to Z

Arriving and Departing

BY MAIL BOAT

M/V *Bimini Mack* sails from Potter's Cay, Nassau, to Cat Cay and Bimini on a varying schedule. The trip takes 12 hours and costs $45 one-way. For information, call the **Dockmaster's office** (☎ 242/393–1064) at Potter's Cay.

Pan Am Airbridge (☎ 800/424–2557 or 800/359–7262) has several 25-minute flights daily into Alice Town, North Bimini, from Miami's terminal at Watson Island on the MacArthur Causeway, and from Fort Lauderdale (40 minutes). If you've just arrived at Miami International Airport, the taxi ride (about $10) to the Watson Island terminal across from the Port of Miami will take about the same time it takes to get to North Bimini. North Bimini is also served from Pan Am's base in Nassau–Paradise Island (☎ 242/363–1687). Pan Am uses amphibians, with takeoffs and landings on water. Baggage allowance is 30 pounds per passenger.

If you don't have heavy luggage, you might decide to walk to your hotel from the seaplane terminal in Alice Town, the main settlement on North Bimini. The Bimini Bus Company meets planes and takes incoming passengers to Alice Town in 12-passenger vans. The cost is $3. A $5 taxi-and-ferry ride takes visitors from the South Bimini airport to Alice Town.

Getting Around

BY BICYCLE
Bimini Undersea (☎ 242/347–3089) rents bikes for $5 per hour or $20 per day.

BY BUS
The **Bimini Bus Company** has minibuses available for a tour of the island. Arrangements can be made through your hotel.

BY CAR
Visitors do not need a car on North Bimini and usually walk wherever they go; there are no car-rental agencies.

BY GOLF CART
Rental golf carts are available at the Sea Crest Hotel Marina from **Capt. Pat's** (☎ 242/347–3477) for $75 a day or $20 for the first hour and $10 for each additional hour, or at the Compleat Angler from **Compleat Golf Cart Rentals** (☎ 242/347–3122) for $20 for the first hour and $10 for each additional hour.

Opening and Closing Times

The **Royal Bank of Canada** (☎ 242/347–3030) is open Monday and Friday from 9 to 3, and Tuesday through Thursday from 9 to 1. Note that most stores are closed on Sunday.

Contacts and Resources

EMERGENCIES
Police and fire (☎ 919). **North Bimini Medical Clinic** (☎ 242/347–3210) has a resident doctor and a nurse.

TELEPHONES
Pay phones are scattered along King's Highway. If you have trouble placing your call, the office of the Bimini Big Game Resort will place a call for you for about $2.50.

VISITOR INFORMATION
The **Biminis Tourist Office** (✉ Government Bldg., Alice Town, ☎ 242/347–3529, FAX 242/347–3530) is open weekdays from 9 to 5:30, and also has a booth at the straw market. The building it occupies was the site of the Lerner Marine Laboratory.

CAT ISLAND

Cat Island is 130 mi southeast of Nassau and is a close neighbor of San Salvador, the reputed landing place of Christopher Columbus—although many Cat Islanders maintain that Columbus landed here instead, and that Cat Island was once known as San Salvador. Chatting with other residents, you might find some who knew or are related to native son Sidney Poitier, who left as a youth before becoming the famed movie actor and director.

The island was named after a frequent notorious visitor, Arthur Catt, a piratical contemporary of Edward "Blackbeard" Teach. Slender Cat Island is about 80 mi long, boot-shaped, with high cliffs and dense forest. Its shores are ringed with mile upon mile of exquisite, untrampled beaches, edged with casuarina trees. Some of the original inhabitants' descendants, who migrated long ago to New York, Detroit, and Miami, are slowly returning here; large, new homes have started to appear throughout the island. The population is about 2,000.

Residents fish, farm, and live a peaceful existence. The biggest event of the year remains the Annual Cat Island Regatta in August, which draws yachters to this faraway island.

Numbers in the margin correspond to points of interest on the Cat Island map.

Arthur's Town and Bennett's Harbour

⑮ **Arthur's Town**'s claim to fame is that it was the boyhood home of actor Sidney Poitier, who has written about growing up here in his autobiography; his parents and relatives were farmers. The village has a BaTelCo station, a few stores, and Pat Rolle's **Cookie House Bakery** (☎ 242/354–2027)—a lunch or dinner spot, and an island anecdote. If you drive south from Arthur's Town, which is nearly at the island's northernmost tip, the winding road passes through small villages and bays where fishing boats are tied up.

⑯ One of the island's oldest settlements of small, weather-beaten houses, **Bennett's Harbour,** is some 15 mi south of Arthur's Town; at the Bluff, you can see bread baked daily in whitewashed ovens beside many of the homes.

New Bight

⑰ The settlement of New Bight, where you'll find a small grocery store, a bakery, and the Bridge Inn, is near the New Bight (also called "The Bight") airport, and just south of Fernandez Bay Village. The Village is actually a resort on a long, curved bay and is the lodging for most Cat Island visitors. Between the airport and the town is the small, blue **First and Last Chance Bar,** run by Iva Thompson. This is a good place to have a beer with the locals, play dominoes, and check out Miss Iva's straw work, which is some of the best in the Bahamas. New Bight is also the home of the **Sailing Club** (☎ 242/342–3054), a bar and restaurant specializing in fish, conch, and mutton; on Saturday nights, a local DJ keeps locals and a few tourists dancing until about 1 AM.

⑱ At the top of 206-ft Mt. Alvernia, the **Hermitage** is the final resting place of the extraordinary Father Jerome. Above the tomb's entrance, carved in stone, is the epitaph BLESSED ARE THE DEAD WHO DIE IN THE LORD and inside, past the wooden gate that hangs on its hinges, his body lies interred. He died in 1956 at the age of 80, and was buried, supposedly with his arms outstretched, the pose resembling Christ's crucifixion.

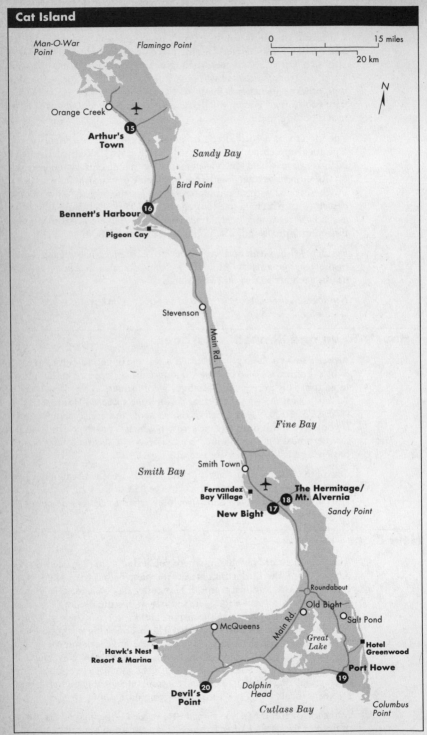

Man-O-War
Point

Flamingo Point

0   15 miles

0   20 km

N

Orange Creek

15

**Arthur's
Town**

Sandy Bay

Bird Point

Bennett's Harbour **16**

Pigeon Cay

Stevenson

Main Rd.

Fine Bay

Smith Town

Smith Bay

Fernandez
Bay Village

**The Hermitage/
Mt. Alvernia**

18

New Bight **17**

Sandy Point

Roundabout

McQueens

Old Bight

Salt Pond

Main Rd.

Great
Lake

**Hotel
Greenwood**

Hawk's Nest
Resort & Marina

Port Howe

**Devil's
Point** **20**

Dolphin
Head

19

Columbus
Point

Cutlass Bay

Father Jerome, born John Hawes, had traveled the world, and eventually settled in the Bahamas. An Anglican who converted to Roman Catholicism, he built two churches, St. Paul's and St. Peter's, on Bahamas' Long Island, as well as the St. Augustine Monastery in Nassau. He retired to Cat Island to live out his last dozen years as a hermit, and his final, supreme act of religious dedication was to carve the steps up to the top of Mt. Alvernia. Along the way, he also carved the 14 Stations of the Cross, representing events from the Passion of Christ, and, at the summit, he built a child-size abbey with a small chapel, a conical bell tower, and living quarters comprising three closet-size rooms.

The pilgrimage to the Hermitage begins next to the commissioner's office at New Bight, at a dirt path that leads to the foot of Mt. Alvernia. Try not to miss the slightly laborious experience of climbing to the top. The Hermitage provides a perfect, inspired place to pause for quiet contemplation; it also has glorious views of the ocean on both sides of the island. A caretaker sees to it that someone clears the weeds around the tomb, which islanders regard as a shrine, and lights a candle in Father Jerome's memory.

Dining and Lodging

$$$$ ✕🏠 **Fernandez Bay Village.** Tony and Pam Armbrister run this resort
★ just north of New Bight. Brick-and-stone villas are spread along a stunning white-sand beach; each accommodates four to six persons and has a kitchen (there's a handy grocery store at the resort), a terrace facing the sea, and a private garden with a shower. Only one phone is available on the property, at the front desk. The dinner menu relies on fresh fish and local vegetables; excellent, buffet-style meals are often served on the beach patio, though a comfortable, mahogany-beamed dining room is also used. Canoes and kayaks are free to use, and captained 23-ft boats can be hired by the hour. Nightlife here usually involves conversation around a bonfire or stargazing from the moonlighted beach. Donna, the ebullient manager, can be counted on to try to accommodate your every whim. ✉ *1 mi west of airport (1507 S. University Dr., Suite A, Plantation, FL 33324)*, ☎ *242/342–3043, 954/474–4821, or 800/940–1905*, ℻ *954/474–4864. 5 villas, 6 1-bedroom cottages. Bar, dining room, beach, snorkeling, boating, waterskiing, fishing, bicycles, laundry service. AE. MAP with cottages only, EP.*

$–$$ ✕🏠 **Bridge Inn.** This motel-style property, run by Cat Islanders Mr. and Mrs. Russell (with the help of their large family), is about 300 yards from a beach, and a more isolated one is about a mile down a back road. The wood-paneled, high-ceilinged rooms have private baths and cable TV. The hotel's dining room serves hot breakfasts, from french toast to conch and grits, and can prepare picnic lunches; popular dinner dishes are conch salad, native mutton, and a grouper, crab, and rice entree. Rooms with air-conditioning cost extra. ✉ *New Bight,* ☎ *242/342–3013 or 800/688–4752,* ℻ *242/342–3041. 12 rooms. Bar, dining room, beach, snorkeling, boating, bikes, billiards, baby-sitting. MC, V. EP, MAP, FAP.*

Port Howe

⑲ At the conch shell–lined traffic roundabout, head east out toward Port Howe, believed by many to be Cat Island's oldest settlement. Nearby, you'll see the ruins of the **Deveaux Mansion,** a stark, two-story, whitewashed building overrun with wild vegetation. Once it was a grand house on a cotton plantation, home of Col. Andrew Deveaux of the U.S. Navy, who gained thousands of acres of Cat Island property as reward for his daring raid that recaptured Nassau from the Spaniards in 1783. Just beyond the mansion ruin is the entrance road to the Greenwood Beach Resort, which sits on an 8-mi stretch of practically untouched velvet-sand beach.

Dining and Lodging

$$ ✕▣ **Greenwood Beach Resort.** This isolated resort is about 45 min-
★ utes from the airport. Rooms are cheerfully decorated with colorful fish stencils. The large clubhouse, with its purple-and-white walls and vivid tropical paintings, is the center of activity. You can relax at the attractive sand-and-shells-under-glass bar, in the small library and lounge, or on the large stone veranda that overlooks the ocean. Depending on the number of diners, dinner is served family-style at a shared table or at cluster of tables in the main lodge. ✉ *Port Howe, Cat Island,* ☎ *242/342–3053 or 800/688–4752,* ℻ *242/342–3053. 20 rooms. Bar, dining room, fans, pool, beach, dive shop, snorkeling, boating, fishing, bicycles, laundry service. AE, MC, V (4% surcharge). MAP, FAP.*

Scuba Diving and Snorkeling

Cat Island Dive Center (✉ Greenwood Beach Resort, Port Howe, ☎ 242/342–3053) is the island's premier dive facility, with a 30-ft dive boat and great snorkeling just a few minutes offshore. Beginners can take the $80 crash course, and seasoned divers will enjoy the spectacular wall-diving opportunities. Snorkelers can rent gear from the dive shop and take ½-day specialized snorkeling trips. Bubble watchers are also rented for $15.

Devil's Point

㉒ The small village of Devil's Point, with its pastel-color, thatch-roof houses, lies about 10 mi west of Columbus Point. Beachcombers will find great shelling on the pristine beach. You'll also find the ruins of the **Richman Hill–Newfield plantation,** which once stretched from the lake to the ocean.

Dining and Lodging

$$ ✕▣ **Hawk's Nest Resort & Marina.** At the southwestern tip of Cat Island, this small waterfront resort, just yards from a long sandy beach, has its own runway and an eight-slip marina. The patios of the guest rooms, the dining room, and the lounge overlook the ocean. With cheerful peach walls and bright bedspreads, rooms have either one king-size or two queen-size beds. For dinner, the Bahamian fried chicken is a crowd pleaser—it's marinated in lime juice and red peppers, fried, and then steamed with onions and more peppers. Families who like feeling at home should consider renting the two-bedroom house next to a beach that is known for its multitude of shells. ✉ *Devil's Point, Cat Island,* ☎ ℻ *242/357–7257 or* ☎ *800/688–4752. 10 rooms, 2-bedroom house. Bar, dining room, air-conditioning, in-room VCRs, beach, dive shop, snorkeling, boating, fishing, bicycles. MC, V. MAP.*

Cat Island A to Z

Arriving and Departing

BY MAIL BOAT

The *North Cat Island Special* leaves Potter's Cay, Nassau, every Wednesday for Bennett's Harbour and Arthur's Town, returning on Saturday. The trip takes 14 hours and costs $40 one-way. M/V *Sea Hauler* leaves Potter's Cay on Tuesday for Smith Bay and New Bight, returning on Sunday. The trip is 7 hours long; the fare is $40. For information, call the **Dockmaster's office** (☎ 242/393–1064) at Potter's Cay.

BY PLANE
Air Sunshine (☎ 954/435–8900 or 800/327–8900) flies into New Bight from Fort Lauderdale. From Nassau, **Bahamasair** (☎ 242/339–4415 or 800/222–4262) flies into Arthur's Town or New Bight Airport in the center of Cat Island twice weekly. **Island Express** (☎ 954/359–0380) has service into New Bight from Fort Lauderdale.

Several hotels also offer their own charter flights from Nassau: **Fernandez Bay Village** (☎ 800/940–1905), **Greenwood Beach Resort** (☎ 242/342–3053), and **Hawk's Nest Resort & Marina** (☎ 800/688–4752).

There are no taxis on Cat Island. Resort owners make arrangements beforehand with guests to pick them up at the airport. If you miss your ride, just ask around the parking lot for a lift; anyone going in your direction (there's only one road) will be happy to drop you off.

Getting Around

BY CAR
The **New Bight Service Station** (☎ 242/342–3014) and **Candy's Market** (☎ 242/342–3011) rent cars and can pick you up from New Bight airport; rates depend on the number of days you're renting.

Contacts and Resources

EMERGENCIES
Cat Island has three **medical clinics**—at Smith Bay, Old Bight, and Arthur's Town. There are few telephones on the island, but the front desk of your hotel will be able to contact the nearest clinic in case of an emergency.

CROOKED AND ACKLINS ISLANDS

Historians of the Bahamas tell us that as Columbus sailed down the lee of Crooked Island and its southern neighbor, Acklins Island (the two are separated by a short water passage), he was riveted by the aroma of native herbs wafting out to his ship. Soon after, Crooked Island, which lies 225 mi southeast of Nassau, became known as one of the "fragrant islands." The first known settlers didn't arrive until the late 18th century, when Loyalists brought their slaves from the United States and established cotton plantations. It was a doomed venture because of the island's poor soil, and those who stayed made a living of sorts by farming and fishing. A salt and sponge industry flourished for a while on Fortune Island, south of Crooked Island, but the place is now a ghost town. Today the 400-plus inhabitants who live on Crooked and Acklins islands continue to eke out an existence by farming and fishing. The islands are best known to travelers for splendid tarpon and bonefishing, but not much else. They are about as remote as populated islands in the Bahamas get. Much of the islands still does not have power, and many residents rely on generators for electricity. Phone service, where available, often goes out for weeks at a time.

Although the plantations have long crumbled, two relics of those days are preserved by the Bahamas National Trust on the northern part of Crooked Island, which overlooks the Crooked Island Passage separating the cay from Long Island. Old Spanish guns have been discovered at one ruin, **Marine Farm,** which may have been used as a fortification.

Crooked Island is 30 mi long and surrounded by 45 mi of barrier reefs that are great for diving. They slope from 4 to 50 ft, then plunge to 3,600 ft in the Crooked Island Passage, once one of the most important sea roads for ships following the southerly route from the West Indies to the Old World. The one-room airport is on **Colonel Hill,** where you get an uninterrupted view of the region all the way to the narrow passage between Crooked Island and Acklins Island. There are two landmark lighthouses. The sparkling white **Bird Rock Lighthouse** (built in 1872) in the north once guarded the Crooked Island Passage. The rotating flash from its 115-ft tower still welcomes pilots and sailors to the Pittstown Point Landings resort, currently the only suitable lodging on the islands. The **Castle Island** lighthouse (built in 1867), at the southern tip of Acklins Island, formerly served as a beacon for pirates who used to retreat there after attacking ships.

Crooked and Acklins islands appear southeast of Andros Island on the Bahamas map at the front of this guide.

Dining and Lodging

$$ ✕🏠 **Pittstown Point Landings.** This completely isolated all-inclusive property on the north end of the island has miles of open beach on its doorstep, which should delight sun worshipers au naturel. The majority of guests arrive by private plane on the resort's own 2,300-ft landing strip (however, the main Colonel Hill Airport is only 15 mi away). The main office is in a mid-18th-century building that housed the first post office in the Bahamas. The modern, large, airy rooms are pleasantly furnished and have oversize windows with views of Bird Rock lighthouse. The dining room, Ozzie's Café, serves Bahamian cuisine and is happy to cater to individual tastes. Diving, bonefishing, and deep-sea fishing can be arranged with local outfitters. ⊠ *238-A Airport Rd., Statesville, NC 28677,* ☎ *242/344–2507 or 800/752–2322,* ℻ *704/881–0771. 12 rooms. Bar, dining room, lounge, fans, shuffleboard, volleyball beach, snorkeling, fishing, bicycles. AE, MC, V. EP, FAP.*

Crooked and Acklins Islands A to Z

Arriving and Departing

BY MAIL BOAT

M/V *Lady Mathilda* sails from Potter's Cay in Nassau to Acklins Island, Crooked Island, Inagua, and Mayaguana. The boat leaves Nassau once a week on a varying schedule; call the **Dockmaster's office** (☎ 242/393–1064) in Potter's Cay for schedule information; the fare is $65–$70, depending on your destination. A government ferry service between Crooked Island and Acklins Island operates daily 9–4.

BY PLANE

Bahamasair (☎ 800/222–4262) flies from Nassau to Crooked and Acklins islands twice a week. Airports are in Colonel Hill, Crooked Island, and at Spring Point on Acklins Island. Pittstown Point Landings can pick up its guests flying into Colonel Hill by prior arrangement.

Contacts and Resources

EMERGENCIES

Police (☎ 242/344–2599) and **Commissioner** (☎ 242/344–2197) on Crooked Island.

The two government medical clinics on Acklins Island are at Spring Point and Chesters Bay. Crooked Island's clinic is at Landrail Point. The resident doctor and nurse for the area live in Spring Point. Nurses are also available at Colonel Hill on Crooked Island, and Masons Bay on Acklins. You can contact these medical professionals through your hotel.

ELEUTHERA

Eleuthera is considered by many Out Islands aficionados to be one of the most enjoyable destinations in the Bahamas. Its appealing features include miles and miles of unspoiled beach, green forests, rolling hills, and rich, red soil in the north that produces pineapples and a variety of vegetables. Eleutheran residents, who live in boldly colored houses adorned with bougainvillea, welcome visitors warmly; most will be happy to let you know where to find bargains at a little tucked-away straw market or recommend the best restaurant on the island for conch chowder. The famous strip of pink-sand beach at Harbour Island gets more attention, but the eastern shore of Eleuthera, from remote James Point to Governor's Harbour, is also pink sand.

Shaped like a praying mantis, Eleuthera is 110 mi long and mostly less than 2 mi wide. It lies 200 mi southeast of Florida and 60 mi east of Nassau. The island was named by a group from Britain who came here seeking religious freedom in 1648. Led by William Sayle, a former governor of Bermuda, the group took the name of the island from the Greek word for freedom. The Eleutheran Adventurers, as they called themselves, gave the Bahamas its first written constitution, which called for the establishment of a republic.

The Eleutheran Adventurers landed first on the middle of the island, close to what is now called Governor's Harbour. After quarreling among themselves, the group split up, and Sayle led one faction around the northern tip of the island by boat. This group was shipwrecked and took refuge at Preacher's Cave, where an altar-shaped rock formation makes it easy to imagine where the castaways held their religious services. The cave, and the crude altar at which they worshiped, is still in existence, close to North Eleuthera.

Later in 1648, Sayle journeyed to the United States to seek help in settling his colony, but the people he left behind began to leave the island. By 1650, most of them had left for New England, leaving only a few of the original Adventurers to trade with passing ships in salt and *brasiletto* wood. Around 1666, Sayle returned to the Bahamas, this time to what is now called New Providence, which was ideally situated for shipping routes. Eleuthera was "revisited" at the end of the Revolutionary War by Loyalists who fled America with their slaves. The new settlers constructed colonial-style homes that still stand, and they started a shipbuilding industry. Today the population of Eleuthera—and of Harbour Island and Spanish Wells, which lie offshore in the north—totals more than 10,500 and consists of descendants of the original Adventurers, Loyalists, and the Loyalists' slaves. It is the second-largest population of the Out Islands.

Numbers in the margin correspond to points of interest on the Eleuthera map.

Rock Sound

㉑ One of Eleuthera's largest settlements, the village of Rock Sound has a small airport serving the southern part of the island. **Front Street,** the main thoroughfare, runs along the seashore, where fishing boats are tied up. If you walk down the street, you'll eventually come to the pretty, whitewashed **St. Luke's Anglican Church,** a contrast to the deep blue and green houses nearby, with their colorful gardens full of poinsettia, hibiscus, and marigolds. If you pass the church on a Sunday, you'll surely hear fervent hymn-singing through the open windows. Rock Sound has the island's largest supermarket shopping center, where locals stock up on groceries and supplies. Buy fresh fruit—citrus in the winter and luscious papayas and avocados in the spring and summer—from **Rock Sound Farms** (no phone), or one of the town's other roadside fruit vendors.

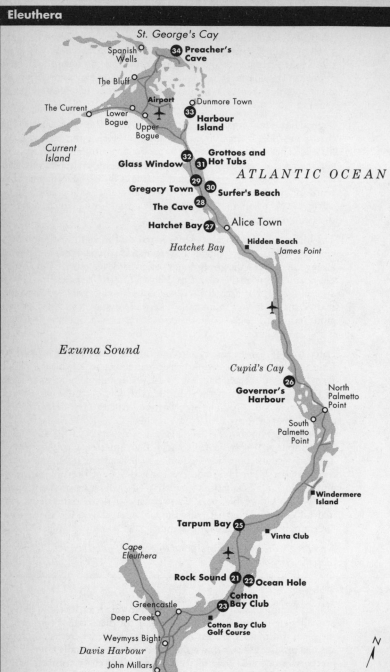

St. George's Cay

Spanish
Wells

The Bluff

34 **Preacher's
Cave**

Airport

Dunmore Town

The Current

Lower
Bogue

33 **Harbour
Island**

Upper
Bogue

Current
Island

32 **Grottoes and
Hot Tubs**

Glass Window **31**

ATLANTIC OCEAN

Gregory Town **29** **30** **Surfer's Beach**

The Cave **28**

Hatchet Bay **27** Alice Town

Hatchet Bay

Hidden Beach
James Point

Exuma Sound

Cupid's Cay

26

**Governor's
Harbour**

North
Palmetto
Point

South
Palmetto
Point

Windermere
Island

Tarpum Bay **25**

Vinta Club

Cape
Eleuthera

Rock Sound **21** **22** **Ocean Hole**

**Cotton
Bay Club**

Greencastle

23

Deep Creek

Cotton Bay Club
Golf Course

Weymyss Bight

Davis Harbour

John Millars

0   10 miles

0   15 km

**Bannerman
Town** **24**

㉒ **Ocean Hole,** a large inland saltwater lake a mile southeast of Rock Sound, is connected by tunnels to the sea. Steps have been cut into the coral on the shore so visitors can climb down to the lake's edge. Bring a piece of bread or some fries and watch the fish emerge for their hors d'oeuvres, swimming their way in from the sea. The hole had been estimated to be more than 100 fathoms (600 ft) deep, but, in fact, its depth was measured by a local diver at about 75 ft—he reports a couple of cars at the bottom, too.

㉓ Ten miles south of Rock Sound, the now defunct **Cotton Bay Club** hotel is where you'll find the still-operating and well-known Robert Trent Jones golf course, studded with tree groves and nestled against the sea. Cotton Bay was once an exclusive club, the domain of Pan Am's founder, Juan Trippe, who would fly his friends to the island on a 727 Yankee Clipper for a weekend of golf.

㉔ The tiny settlement of **Bannerman Town** (pop. 40) is at the southern tip of the island. From the north end of Eleuthera (near Preacher's Cave), it is about a three-hour drive down the Queen's Highway. The beach here is gorgeous, and on a clear day you can see the highest point in the Bahamas, Mt. Alvernia (elevation 206 ft), on distant Cat Island. The town lies about 30 mi from the Cotton Bay Club (☞ *above*), past the quiet, little fishing villages of **Wemyss Bight** (named after Lord Gordon Wemyss, a 17th-century Scottish slave owner) and **John Millars** (pop. 15), barely touched over the years.

Dining

$$–$$$ ✕ **Sammy's Place.** This reasonable (and spotless) stop, owned by Sammy Culmer and managed mainly by his personable daughter Margarita, serves conch fritters, fried chicken and fish, and peas 'n' rice. ✉ *Albury Lane, Rock Sound,* ☎ *212/334–2121. No credit cards.*

Outdoor Activities and Sports

GOLF

Robert Trent Jones Jr. Course (✉ Cotton Bay Club, Rock Sound, ☎ 242/334–6156), an 18-hole, 7,068-yard, par-72 course, is now open to the public. The club has caddies, but no carts. Greens fees are $70, club rental is $150.

SCUBA DIVING

South Eleuthera Divers–Tim Riley (✉ Rock Sound, ☎ 242/334–2221) is the only dive operation in the southern part of the island. This full-service outfit offers diving to the seldom-visited reefs and wrecks off Rock Sound and Cape Eleuthera. Arrange your diving as far in advance as possible, as Tim holds down a couple other jobs as well.

Shopping

The **Almond Tree** (☎ 242/334–2385) is a mint green house with hibiscus-painted shutters. Inside, the quaint gift shop has a collection of handmade gifts, jewelry, and straw work.

Goombay Gifts (✉ Fish St., ☎ 242/334–2191), owned by Janice and Michael Knowles, is the place to shop for shell necklaces, straw work, and souvenirs.

Tarpum Bay

㉕ Waterfront Tarpum Bay is one of Eleuthera's loveliest settlements, with hilly roads flanked by weather-beaten homes with colored shutters and goats roaming the streets. The town is the site of a small artists' colony. One of the island's more unusual characters—a self-proclaimed mystic and prodigious painter named G. MacMillan Hughes—lives here. A bearded, ponytailed Scots-Irish expatriate, he resides in a stone castle from the top of which pennants fly. He uses mediums such as paint, color photocopy, and collage in his surreal works. Behind a monumental, sculpted front gate, triangular steps lead to his **Castle Art Gallery** (✉ Lord St., ☎ 242/334–4091). The gallery is open daily 9:30 to 5. Just south of the village of Tarpum Bay is **Flanders Art Studio** (☎ 242/334–4187), where Mal Flanders sells watercolors and canvases of local scenes, as well as driftwood paintings. The studio is open Monday through Saturday 9 to 5.

Dining and Lodging

$ ✕⊞ **Hilton's Haven.** Not to be confused with the well-known U.S. hotel chain, this Hilton is an unassuming 10-room motel across the road from a beach and just around the corner from that unique attraction, the MacMillan Hughes Gallery and Castle. This tidy, unpretentious place is run by a matronly local nurse named Mary Hilton. Rooms have private baths and patios; downstairs they are fitted with air-conditioning, upstairs you'll find ceiling fans. Ms. Hilton serves good home cooking in her small restaurant. The hotel is a two-minute walk from the beach and about 8 mi from the Rock Sound Airport. ✉ *Tarpum Bay, Eleuthera,* ☎ *242/334–4231 or 800/688–4752,* Ⅲ *242/334–4020. 10 rooms, 1 apartment. Bar, dining room. No credit cards. EP, MAP.*

Shopping

You can stock up on groceries, souvenirs, and the like at **Tarpum Bay Shopping Center** (☎ 242/334–4022).

En Route Snorkelers and divers will want to spend some time at **Gaulding's Cay** beach, north of Tarpum Bay. Swim out to the tiny island off shore to witness a concentration of sun anenomes—as if someone had laid carpet—so spectacular it dazzled even Jacques Cousteau's biologists. Gaulding's Cay is also a nice 1,500-ft shelling stretch for beachcombers. Just north of Gaulding's Cay, distinguished **Windermere Island** is the site of vacation homes to the rich and famous, including members of the British Royal family. Don't plan on any drive-by ogling of these million dollar homes—the security gate prevents sightseers from passing.

Governor's Harbour

㉖ Governor's Harbour, also known as Colebrooke Town, is where the intrepid Eleuthera Adventurers landed. The drive between Governor's Harbour and Rock Sound is about 35 minutes. If you're here when the mail boats M/V *Bahama Daybreak III* and M/V *Eleuthera Express* chug in, you'll be treated to the sight of residents from around the island unloading mattresses, lumber, mail, stacks of vegetables, and other household necessities. You might also see the same Eleutherans loading their own vegetables and pineapples for export to Nassau. While they're here, they'll stop in at their mailboxes at the small post office in the town's pink government building.

If you're cooking during your stay, consider that the Governor's Harbour waterfront is a great place to procure fresh fish and conch. The town is also home to the island's only movie theater, with one screen that usually alternates between two releases.

Dining and Lodging

$–$$ ✕ **Mate & Jenny's.** A few miles south of Governor's Harbour, this neighborhood restaurant specializes in pizza—try one topped with conch. Sandwiches, Bahamian specialites, and ice-cream sundaes are also served. The walls are painted with tropical sunset scenes and decorated with photos, and the jukebox and pool table add to the joint's local color. ✉ *South Palmetto Point,* ☎ *242/332–1504. MC, V accepted for bills over $40. Closed Tues. No lunch Sun.*

$$–$$$ ✕▥ **Club Med Eleuthera.** Certainly, this is the only place on Eleuthera where you can join a circus workshop and swing on a trapeze! This large, all-inclusive resort is oriented toward very young families; there are programs for kids—from 12 months to 12 years—where they can learn to dive, sail, and even join the circus. Other offerings include sailing, waterskiing, and snorkeling. Social life revolves around the main complex, which houses a dining room, an open-air cocktail lounge, a dance floor, a theater, a disco, and a boutique. The guest rooms are sparsely decorated in white and pastels; none have TVs or phones. A distinctive carefree Bahamian ambience peremeates the place. The resort is 9 mi south of Governor's Harbour Airport, and the Club Med Marina is a 10-minute shuttle ride away. If you're staying elsewhere, but want to enjoy the extravagant Club Med buffet-style meals, call for information. ✉ *Box EL 25080, Governor's Harbour, Eleuthera,* ☎ *242/332–2270 or 800/258–2633,* FAX *242/332–2855. 284 rooms. 3 restaurants, 2 bars, pool, air-conditioning, 8 tennis courts, aerobics, volleyball, beach, snorkeling, boating, cabaret, fishing, children's program. AF, MC, V. All-inclusive.*

$$ ✕▥ **Buccaneer Club.** On a hillside overlooking the town and the harbor, this former home has been transformed into a family-run inn. Bougainvillea, hibiscus, and coconut palms flourish on the grounds. The modern guest rooms, with two double beds and full baths, are decorated with brightly painted furniture. On the top floor of this three-story building, you'll find the most spacious of the rooms, which also has a wonderful view of Governor's Harbour and the water. The beach is a leisurely 10-minute stroll away, and the harbor, where you can also swim, is within shouting distance. ✉ *Box 86, Governor's Harbour, Eleuthera,* ☎ *242/332–2000,* FAX *242/332–2888. 5 rooms. Restaurant, bar, pool, shop. MC, V. EP.*

$$ ✕▥ **Unique Village.** This resort, just south of Governor's Harbour near North Palmetto Point, has large, tile-floor rooms. Besides these handsome rooms, it's the round restaurant, with its pagoda-style natural wood ceiling, wraparound covered deck, and wonderful view of the beach, that makes this village unique—try the chateaubriand for two with a caesar salad, or any of the seafood specialties. The small bar has satellite TV, high captain's chairs, and views from second-story windows. ✉ *Box EL 25187, Governor's Harbour, Eleuthera,* ☎ *242/332–1830,* FAX *242/332–1838. 10 rooms, 4 villas. Restaurant, bar, air-conditioning, snorkeling, fishing. MC, V. EP, MAP, FAP.*

$$–$$$ ▥ **Palmetto Shores Vacation Villas.** These spacious, south-facing villas on the bay are an attractive option for families, couples, or groups. They come with one, two, or three bedrooms—able to sleep up to six people—a large kitchen, lounges, and TVs. The villas have tile floors throughout and offer all the comforts of home, with easy strolls to beaches, a small restaurant, and shopping at a general store. ✉ *South Palmetto Point, Box EL 25131, Governor's Harbour, Eleuthera,* ☎ FAX *242/332–1305. 15 villas. Air-conditioning, 2 tennis courts, dock, snorkeling, boating, fishing, bicycles, car rentals. V. EP.*

$$ ▥ **Laughing Bird Apartments.** English architect Dan Davies and his wife Jean, a nurse, own four apartments on an acre of land at the water's edge. The Davies furnish linens, crockery, and the first gallon of drinking water; you buy the rest. This is a quiet place, where relaxing and fishing are the name of the game. With a little effort, you can arrange for a variety of water sports or tour the island by rental car. Four restaurants are within walking distance, or you can stock your kitchen from local stores. ✉ *Box EL 25076, Governor's Harbour, Eleuthera,* ☎ *242/332–2012,* FAX *242/332–2358. 4 apartments. Air-conditioning, kitchens, tennis court, beach, fishing. D, MC, V. EP.*

Snorkeling

Heading north on Queen's Highway out of Governor's Harbour, Airport Beach lies on the island's Atlantic side, opposite the North Eleuthera airport. Stop to appreciate this impressive 7-mi stretch of pink sand, which has good snorkeling at its north end.

If you've got four-wheel drive, take the road east at the settlement of James Cistern to reach James Point, with another beautiful beach, snorkeling opportunities, and 3- to 10-ft waves for surfers. About 4 mi north of James Cistern on the Atlantic side, take the rough-hewn steps down to Hidden Beach, a sandy little hideaway sheltered by a rock-formation canopy and affording maximum privacy. It's also a great spot for novice snorkelers.

Hatchet Bay and Environs

㉗ Hatchet Bay has mid-Eleuthera's only marina. Be sure to notice the names of the town's side roads, which have such colorful designations as Lazy Road, Happy Hill Road, and Smile Lane. Just south of town, the Rainbow Inn and Restaurant is the hub of activity for this stretch of Eleuthera.

㉘ North of Hatchet Bay, lies **The Cave,** a subterranean, bat-populated tunnel, complete with stalagmites and stalactites, which was supposedly once used by pirates to hide their loot. An underground path leads for over a mile to the sea, ending in a lofty, cathedral-like cavern; within its depths fish swim in total darkness. The adventurous may wish to explore this area with a flashlight (follow the length of guide string along the cavern's floor), but it's best to inquire first at one of the local stores or the Rainbow Inn for a guide. To find The Cave, drive north from Hatchet Bay and watch for the vine-covered silo on the north side of Queen's Highway, take the left turn soon thereffer, marked by a white stripe down the center of Queen's Highway. En route to The Cave, Sweeting's Pond is surrounded by all sorts of local myths—from Loch Ness–esque inhabitants to tales of a submerged plane wreckage.

Dining and Lodging

$$ ✕🏨 **Rainbow Inn.** This beloved institution's immaculate, generously
★ sized cabins dot the inn's beachfront grounds. You won't find rattan furniture and white tile floors—instead dark-wood interiors with modern furniture and wooden dressers bring to mind a cozy ski-cabin. All have large private porches and microwaves. Co-owner Charlie Moore is an island expert and great resource for planning your day trips around Eleuthera. The restaurant ($$–$$$) is one of the island's best, with a classy, but no-fuss atmosphere and exhibition windows that face gorgeous sunsets. It's not uncommon for islanders to drive great distances for a meal here, especially for rib nights (Wednesdays) and steak nights (Fridays). Also famous are the Bahamian steamed fish and minced lobster, thick chowders, and spicy boiled fish. The Nautical Bar, hung with authentic ships wheels salvaged from wrecks, drips with local color. On Wednesday and Friday nights, you'll usually find a Bahamian folk singer strumming away. Nurse those Goombay Smashes on the screened dining porch for as long as you like, co-owner "Krabby" Ken won't be bashful about letting you know when it's time to leave— if he picks up your candle, blows it out, and sets it back down in front of you, you're outta there. ✉ 2½ *mi south of Hatchet Bay (Box EL 25053, Governor's Harbour, Eleuthera),* ☎ ℻ 242/335–0294 *or* ☎ *800/688–0047. 4 apartments, 2 2-bedroom villas, 1 3-bedroom villa. Restaurant, bar, air-conditioning, fans, kitchenettes, saltwater pool, tennis court, fishing, bicycles. MC, V. EP, MAP.*

Gregory Town and Environs

㉙ Gregory Town sits on top of a cliff, though many of its charming pastel homes are actually down in a gully. The town's annual **Pineapple Festival** begins on the Thursday evening of the Bahamian Labor Day weekend, at the beginning of June. With live music, juicy-ripe pineapple (served every possible way), and settlement-wide merriment continuing into the wee hours, this is Gregory Town's most lively happening.

㉚ Gregory Town's claim to fame lies about 2½ mi south of town, where **Surfer's Beach,** a site of the 1960's "Beach Bum" culture, still packs wave-catchers from December to May. If you don't have a jeep, you can walk the ¾ mi to this Atlantic-side beach—follow rough-and-bumpy Ocean Boulevard at Eleuthera Island Shores just south of town.

㉛ If you're too lulled by the ebb and flow of lapping waves and prefer your shores crashing with dramatic, tall-white sprays, perhaps a visit to Eleuthera's **Grottoes and Hot Tubs** will revive you. The sun warms these tidal pools, making them a markedly more temperate soak than the sometimes-chilly ocean. On most days, refreshing sprays and rivulets tumble into the tubs, but on some it can turn dangerous; if the waves are crashing over the top of the cove's centerpiece mesa, pick another day to stop here. If you're driving from Gregory Town, the entrance is approximately 5 mi north, marked by two thin tree stumps on the right (Atlantic) side of the Queen's Highway. If you reach the one-lane Glass Window bridge, you've gone too far.

㉜ At a very narrow point of the island a few miles north of Gregory Town, you'll find a place where a slender concrete bridge links two sea-battered bluffs that separate the Governor's Harbour and North Eleuthera districts. Sailors going south in the waters between New Providence and Eleuthera supposedly named this area the **Glass Window** because they could see through the narrow cavity to the Atlantic on the other side. Stop to watch the northeasterly deep-azure Atlantic swirl together under the bridge with the southwesterly turquoise Great Bahama Bank, producing a brilliant aquamarine froth. Artist Winslow Homer found the site stunning, too—he painted *Glass Window* in 1885. It's thought that the bridge was a natural span until the early 1900s when rough currents finally washed it away. A 1991 storm lifted up the just-completed two-lane bridge, setting it down some 7 feet to the south, which accounts for the now-one-lane scaffold's zig.

Dining and Lodging

$–$$ ✕ **Elvina's Bar-Restaurant-Washeteria.** Shoot some pool, enjoy some down-home Bahamian cuisine, and wash those traveling clothes! Walls are covered with license plates and bumper stickers, and the surfboards hanging from the ceiling have been stowed there by surfer-regulars. Elvina's husband, known around these parts as "Chicken Ed," is from Louisiana and the jambalaya here is the real thing.⊠ *Governor's Harbour,* ☎ *242/335–5032. No credit cards.*

$$ ✕🏨 **Cove-Eleuthera.** This seaside inn sits on 30 secluded acres. There's a tiny, sandy cove for swimming, and superb snorkeling is just a few flipper beats from shore—in fact, this is a great spot for the water-wary to learn! The hotel also has a lovely freshwater pool; the patio that surrounds it is ideal for breakfast or cocktails, or simply relaxing poolside, listening to the ocean's waves lapping at low, rocky promontories. Rooms are clustered in quadraplex configurations and have tile floors, high slanted ceilings, and white rattan furnishings. The window-lined restaurant—popular for sunset viewing—is immense, serving three moderately priced meals a day (picnic lunches are available) with a dinner menu that varies nightly. Government-standardized taxi-fare charts refer to this inn as Pineapple Cove—as most locals do also. ⊠ *3 mi south of Glass Window bridge and 2 mi north of Gregory Town (106 S. Cortez Dr., Circle L, Margate, FL33068),* ☎ *242/335–5142, 954/974–3913, or 800/552–5960,* FAX *242/335–5338. 27 rooms. Bar, dining room, lounge, pool, 2 tennis courts, snorkeling, boating, fishing, bicycles. AE, MC, V. EP, MAP.*

$ ✕⊡ **Cambridge Villas.** This two-story motel is a favorite with surfers on a budget because it's cheap and clean. The complex surrounds a patio area with worn chairs and a large (though unkempt) saltwater pool. Budget travelers may not mind, but the unfinished cement structure at the rear of the hotel is downright unsightly. The dining room serves good Bahamian food, including conch chowder and broiled grouper. Adjacent, the bar has satellite TV and is popular with locals and visitors. The motel, 20 mi from the North Eleuthera Airport and 22 mi from the Governor's Harbour Airport, shuttles guests either to lovely swimming 1½ mi away or to the surfing beach. ⊠ *Box 1548, Gregory Town, Eleuthera,* ☎ *242/335–5080, 800/688–4752, or 242/ 335–5308. 18 rooms. Bar, dining room, refrigerators, saltwater pool. AE, MC, V. EP, MAP.*

Nightlife

The debonair **Dr. Seabreeze** strums his acoustic guitar singing native songs that are nothing short of precious oral history. He plays Wednesday and Friday nights at the Rainbow Inn (☞ *above*), Thursday nights at Unique Village (☞ *above*), and Saturday nights at The Cove–Eleuthera (☞ *above*).

Outdoor Activities and Sports

FISHING

Capt. Gregory Thompson (☎ 242/335–5357 or 242/335–5369) will take you out for a half- ($400) or full- ($600) day of deep sea fishing. Prices include from one to six persons on the Captain's 32-ft Stamas Sport Fish vessel.

SURFING

In Gregory Town, stop by **Rebecca's** (☎ 242/335–5436) general store and crafts shop, where local surf-guru "Ponytail Pete" stocks a few supplies and posts a chalkboard listing surf conditions and tidal reports.

TENNIS

Cove-Eleuthera (☎ 242/335–5142) has two courts; guests of the resort play free, but visitors must pay a fee.

Shopping

Island Made Shop (☎ 242/335–5369), run by Pam and Greg Thompson, is a good place to shop for Bahamian arts and crafts, including Androsia batik (made on Andros island), driftwood paintings, Abaco ceramics, and prints.

Harbour Island

㉝   Harbour Island has often been called the prettiest of the Out Islands due to its 3 mi of powdery sand beach, tinted pink by powdered shells and coral, and its colorful colonial clapboard houses edged by picket fences and tropical flowers. The residents have long called it Briland, their faster way of pronouncing "Harbour Island." Although taxis, golf carts, and bikes are available, you can explore the island without too much exertion. Within its 2 sq mi are tucked some of the Bahamas' most attractive small hotels, each strikingly distinct. At several that are perched on a bluff above the shore, you can fall asleep with the windows open and listen to the waves lapping the beach. You reach Harbour Island via a five-minute ferry ride from the North Eleuthera dock; fares are $8 per person, $4 per person in a boat of 2 or more, plus an extra dollar to be dropped off at the private docks of Valentine's or Romora Bay Club.

Old trees line the narrow streets of **Dunmore Town,** named after the 18th-century royal governor of the Bahamas, Lord Dunmore, who built a summer home here and laid out the town; the community was once second in the country to Nassau in terms of its prosperity. It's the only town on Harbour Island and you can take in all its attractions during a 20-minute stroll. Stop first at the **Harbour Island Tourist Office** (☎ 242/333–2621), in the yellow building opposite the ferry dock; get a map and ask about current events. Across the street is a row of straw-work stands, including Dorothea's, Pat's, and Sarah's, where you'll find straw bags, hats, accessories, T-shirts, and tourist tchotchkes. On Dunmore Street, you can visit the oldest Anglican church in the Bahamas, **St. John's,** built in 1768, and the distinguished 1848 **Wesley Methodist Church**; both hold services. **Loyalist Cottage,** one of the original settlers' homes (ca. 1797), has also survived. Many other old houses, with gingerbread trim and picket fences, have amusing names such as "Beside the Point," "The Grapevine," and "Up Yonder." Offshore lies a long coral reef, which protects the beach and has excellent snorkeling; you can see multicolored fish and a few old wrecks.

Dining and Lodging
Note that most Harbour Island hotels are closed from September through late October or early November.

$$$$ ✕ **Pink Sands.** The chic fare coming out of the kitchen is a fusion of Caribbean, Bahamian, and Asian culinary style. Lunch is served daily at the ocean-view Blue Bar from 11:30–4, it's usually packed and the service can be slow, so shoot for an early or late arrival. The prix fixe dinner ($65) is served on a two-level patio enclosed by lush vegetation. A lively Junkanoo BBQ buffet takes place Saturday nights at the Blue Bar ($45). ⊠ *Chapel St., Dunmore Town,* ☎ *242/333–2030. Dinner reservations essential. AE, V.*

$$$$ ✕ **Romora Bay Club.** This hotel's alfresco "Sloppy Joe" bar—infinitely classier than the name suggests—is the best place to enjoy cocktail and views of the Harbour Island sunset. Arrive with plenty of time to secure your seat on the deck. Make reservations for fine post-dusk dining in the hotel's intimate Ludo's dining room, where Continental cuisine is prepared expertly. ⊠ *South end of Dunmore St., Dunmore Town,* ☎ *242/333–2325. Reservations essential. AE, MC, V.*

$$$$ ✕ **Runaway Hill Club.** To get a table for dinner you'll need to make reservations in the morning—if you can get them. Dishes are superb—such as carrot and orange bisque, shrimp scampi, and artfully seasoned fish—and the hosts of this small inn could hardly be more personable. ⊠ *Dunmore Town,* ☎ *242/333–2150. AE, MC, V. Closed Sun.*

$$–$$$ ✕ **Harbour Lounge.** This pink building with white shutters is across from the government dock. Arrive early if you want good seats for watching the sunset over cocktails on the front porch. The lunch and dinner fare is excellent—try the smoked dolphinfish with garlic pita chips. ⊠ *Dunmore Town,* ☎ *242/333–2031. MC, V. Closed Mon.*

$$ ✕ **Miss Mae Tea Room & Fine Things.** If shopping for international imports at Fine Things works up your appetite, head into the Tea Room for breakfast—perhaps French toast or an omelet—or lunch—maybe spinach soup and quiche—in the sunny garden out back. ⊠ *Dunmore Town,* ☎ *242/333–2002. No credit cards.*

$–$$ ✕ **Ma Ruby's.** This is perhaps the best—certainly the friendliest—bite in town. Owner and chef Ma Ruby fix up savory Bahamian delights, from breakfasts of grits, eggs, and johnnycakes to hearty dinners of lobster, spareribs, and fresh grouper. Dinners are accompanied by two vegetables and a potato (baked or mashed), but leave room for Ma Ruby's home-baked coconut tarts, key lime pie, or native pound cake. Vegetarians rejoice: there's always an entrée just for you, plus one of the tastiest garden salads in the islands. ⊠ *South end of Colebrook St., Dunmore Town,* ☏ *242/333–2161. AE, MC, V.*

$ ✕ **Angela's Starfish.** In a turquoise house on top of a hill off Dunmore
★ Street, Angela's is the local favorite for cracked conch, grouper fingers, pork chops, and peas 'n' rice. Hearty breakfasts are also served. ⊠ *Dunmore Town,* ☏ *242/333–2253. No credit cards.*

$ ✕ **Dunmore Deli.** Under a green-and-white-striped awning shading a wooden deck, this deli serves up gourmet alfresco breakfasts and lunches at charming bistro tables. ⊠ *Dunmore Town,* ☏ *242/333–2644. Closed Sun. No credit cards.*

$ ✕ **PJ's Restaurant.** This low-key spot, with four stained-wooden tables, quaint blue curtains, and a few hanging plants has locals streaming in for ham-and-cheese sandwiches on hearty Bahamian-bread buns and pork chop dinners. "Pizza pans" are also popular. P.S., PJ isn't the owner's name; it stands for her children, "precious jewels." ⊠ *Barrack at Munning's St., Dunmore Town,* ☏ *242/333–2835. Closed Sun. No credit cards.*

$ ✕ **Seaview Takeaway.** Right at the foot of the ferry dock, this blue snack stand is renowned for its cracked conch and cheeseburgers. ⊠ *Dunmore Town,* ☏ *242/333–2542. Closed Sun. No dinner. No credit cards.*

$$$$ ✕🏠 **Dunmore Beach Club.** With a reputation for being formal and exclusionary, Dunmore Beach is trying to tone down its image with a more relaxed approach; yet men must wear jackets (neckties are now optional) to dinner and women need dress accordingly. Furthermore, the management prefers guests who either have already stayed at this club or are friends of those who have. The Dunmore is proud of its guest to staff ratio (almost one-to-one) and the length of service of its employees (10 years is not considered a long time here). Rooms are comfortable with white and pastel accents, rattan, tile floors, handmade quilts, but no phones or TVs. The clubhouse, where you'll find the ocean-view honor bar, is decorated with rattan and chintz furniture, pale green and peach walls, jalousie windows, tan carpet, and hanging plants and knickknacks. The restaurant serves a four course international menu at 8 PM (virtually always for guests only). ⊠ *Box EL 27122, Harbour Island, Eleuthera,* ☏ *242/333–2200,* 𝖥𝖠𝖷 *242/333–2429. 12 units in 6 cottages. Bar, dining room, tennis court. MC, V. FAP.*

$$$$ ✕🏠 **Ocean View.** Martha Stewart would feel at home here in the ca-
★ sual elegance of gingham checks, floral prints, and vivid colors. The stunning guest rooms are individually decorated with antique pieces, including armoires, side tables, and chests from southern France, original etchings and paintings, and intricate tile floors. The three largest rooms are upstairs, off the living-dining room, which has a cozy sitting area by a fireplace. Though guest rooms on the lower level are tiny, they are beautifully done in contrasting color schemes; all have cedar closets and a shared patio facing the ocean, which licks the pink-sand beach below. On the sprawling upper patio, a giant chessboard with huge chess pieces overlooks the water. In the bar, walls are hung with weathered musical instruments (wind and string), as well as the colorful Haitian-inspired paintings of Amos Ferguson, probably the Bahamas' best-known artist. Canadian owner Pip Simmons vows that Ocean View will never have TVs or phones in rooms. Trained in France and Switzerland, she is the head chef; she and her Bahamian staff whip up such artful dishes as puff pastry filled with spinach, cream of celery soup, beef tenderloin in béarnaise sauce, and pastries with home-made vanilla ice cream or mango sorbet. If you are not staying here,

you must make dinner reservations by 9 AM. ⊠ *Box 134, Harbour Island, Eleuthera,* ☎ *242/333–2276. 9 rooms. Bar, dining room, beach. AE, MC, V. EP, MAP.*

$$$ ✕⊡ **Coral Sands Hotel.** Sharon King has run this easygoing, two-story ★ resort since 1968 with her former movie-actor husband, Brett King (whom you may have caught in such films as *Flying Leathernecks* with John Wayne or *Payment on Demand* with Bette Davis). The hotel is the most reasonably priced on Harbour Island's spectacular 3-mi-long pink beach, and has 14 hilly acres descending into the heart of Dunmore Town. Although the architecture appears a tad dated compared with surrounding hotels, the high number of loyal guests attests to the warm atmosphere and charm. Upstairs rooms are reached by attractive, curving steps and have access to expansive patios. Rooms in the lower building all have small private balconies. Breakfasts are served on the large, covered balcony, through the open arches of which breathtaking views of the ocean can be devoured. Bahamian and American dinners are presented by the fireplace of the romantic Mediterranean Cafe and luncheon at the casual Beach Bar Lounge and Sundeck (high above the rosy sand); picnics to other islands can be arranged. The Yellowbird Bar offers guitar music; a game room has cable TV, a pool table, and card tables. ⊠ *Harbour Island, Eleuthera,* ☎ *242/333–2350, 242/ 333–2320, or 800/468–2799,* FAX *242/333–2368. 23 rooms, 8 suites, 2 villas. 2 bars, dining room, tennis court, diving, snorkeling, boating, fishing. AE, MC, V. EP, MAP.*

$$–$$$ ✕⊡ **Valentine's Yacht Club.** Island-hopping yachters like to tie up at Valentine's modern, fully equipped 39-slip marina. The club hosts the North Eleuthera Regatta on Columbus Day, but it's a great place anytime for a drink and a conch burger in the shaded dock restaurant. There's always a lot of activity, with anglers and divers coming and going. Valentine's has a complete dive shop, offering a variety of dives, including trips to Current Cut, where divers can coast through a bevy of sea life without moving a fin; and to Sink Hole and Bat Cavern, an introduction to the spooky pleasures of cave diving. Resort guests enjoy good Bahamian cooking and motel-style rooms. Valentine's provides a shuttle from its harbor side of the island over to the pink-sand beach, and will arrange excursions for both bone- and deep-sea fishing. ⊠ *Northeast Harbour Island, ¼ mi from Dunmore Town, Box 1, Harbour Island, Eleuthera,* ☎ *242/333–2142 or 800/323–5655,* FAX *242/333–2135. 21 rooms. 2 restaurants, 2 bars, air-conditioning, pool, tennis court, diving, dive shop, fishing, bicycles. AE, MC, V. EP, MAP.*

$–$$ ✕⊡ **Tingum Village.** If you're on a budget, the clean and simple Tingum Village may be just your ticket. On the south end of town and a short walk from the famous pink-sand beach of Harbour Island, the servicable rooms here have white-tile floors, wood ceilings, ceiling fans, and comfortable, functional furnishings. Hammocks are strung between palms. Ma Ruby's Restaurant (☞ *above*) serves Bahamian food on a breezy covered patio three times daily. ⊠ *Next to the Harbour Island Library, Harbour Island, Eleuthera,* ☎ FAX *242/333–2161. 12 rooms, 1 3-bedroom cottage. Restaurant, bar, air-conditioning. MC, V. EP, MAP.*

$$$$ ⊡ **Pink Sands.** This is the hippest hostelry in the Out Islands, if not ★ the entire country, right down to the choice of ambient music—a joyful mix of Caribbean, western and southern African, and Brazilian sounds. Island Records founder and hotel entrepreneur Chris Blackwell has spared no expense since he bought Pink Sands following 1992's Hurricane Andrew and transformed it into a boutique resort of handsome cottages with white, stepped roofs. Some guests rent golf carts to get around the lush, expansive property, while others manage on foot. Cottages come in studio, one-, and two-bedroom configurations and are positioned for maximum privacy. Each has a kitchenette

with a wet bar, stocked minibar, toaster, coffeemaker, and spacious bath
with beautiful Italian tiles. Walls and ceilings are painted in pastels that
highlight the rough marble floors and creative Adirondack–meets–Art
Deco furnishings; colorful African-print bedspreads, throw pillows, chair
cushions, and lamp shades add to the fun but tasteful decor. All units
come with a phone, CD player, and collection of CDs. On the sands
just below the Blue Bar, where lunches are served, comfortable teak
chaises and thatched cabanas provide beach relaxation for sun- and
shade-seekers alike. The "main house" has a gorgeous entertainment
center–library, a bar lighted by a suspended string of cobalt blue–shaded
spotlights, an attractive exercise studio, a small boutique, and a dining space (for inclement weather). The main dining area (☞ *above*)
serves alfresco on terraced levels above the main house; long pants are
required for dinner. The Pink Sands seems to lack nothing; however,
some complain that the ultratrendy attitude here takes away from
local color. ⊠ *Box 87, Harbour Island, Eleuthera,* ☏ *242/333–2030
or 800/688–7678,* ⅏ *242/333–2060. 26 rooms in 18 cottages. Restaurant, 2 bars, dining room, in-room safes, minibars, pool, 3 tennis
courts, exercise room, beach, snorkeling. AE, MC, V. MAP.*

$$$$ 🏨 **Runaway Hill Club.** A flight of stairs leads down to Harbour Island's
★   fabled beach from this intimate hotel perched on a bluff. Once a private residence, this place maintains a homey ambience. The original
rooms are individually decorated; most face the sea to catch the cool
breezes (Room 2 is especially nice); the rest overlook the gardens. The
newer hilltop villa building has larger, more uniform rooms with a colorful patchwork quilts, bookshelves with an array of titles, and electronic safes. A small pool and deck hover over the beach. The restaurant
here is highly regarded island-wide(☞ *above*); each morning you'll find
the daily prix fixe menu handwritten and displayed on an antique brass
music stand in the front hall. Hosts Carol and Roger Becht and their
staff quickly make vacationers feel like old friends. They are always
happy to help arrange water sports and other activities and to fill visitors in on the island's (mainly weekend) nightlife scene. It's not unusual for people to book their stay for the following year as they check
out. Children are not permitted at Runaway Hill Club. ⊠ *Box EL 27031,
Harbour Island, Eleuthera,* ☏ *242/333–2150,* ⅏ *242/333–2420. 10
rooms. Bar, dining room, lounge, pool, beach. AE, MC, V. EP, MAP.*

Nightlife

Enjoy a brew on the wraparound patio of **Gusty's** (☏ 242/333–2165),
on the northern point of Harbour Island. This lively hot spot has sand
floors, a few tables covered in orange-batiked cloths, and patrons
shooting pool, playing the ring game, or watching sports on satellite
TV. Jimmy Buffet once played an inpromptu free concert here.

Enter through the marinelife-muraled hallway at **Seagrapes** (⊠ Cole-
brook and Gibson Sts., ☏ 242/333–2439) to a large nightclub with
a raised stage that's home to the local Funk Gang band. If you need a
break from the often-crowded dance floor, shoot a game of pool or
take a table upstairs along a mezzanine lined with colorful Junkanoo
headdresses.

Valentine's Yacht Club & Marina (☏ 242/333–2142) is particularly lively
on weekend nights. The waterfront Reach Grill and the second-story
Reach Up deck make wonderful vantage points for sunset watching
or imbibing.

Vic-Hum Club (⊠ Barrack St., ☏ 242/333–2161) occasionally hosts
live Bahamian bands in a room decorated with classic record album
covers; otherwise, you'll hear a variety of recorded music, from calypso
to American pop and R&B.

Outdoor Activities and Sports
BOATING AND FISHING
There are abundant spots around the island to bonefish (at a cost of around $75 a half day), bottom fish ($75 a half day), reef fish ($20 an hour), and deep-sea fish ($250–$600 a full day). And there is great bonefishing right off Dunmore Town at Girl Bay. The Harbour Island Tourist Office (☞ Eleuthera A to Z, *below*) can arrange bone- and bottom-fishing trips and excursions, as can all the major hotels.

Ross' Garage (☎ 242/333–2122) rents boats. **Valentine's Yacht Club** (☎ 242/333–2142) can arrange various types of fishing and has small boats for rent. **Big Red Rentals** (☎ 242/333–2045) offers Boston whalers (from 13 to 21 ft) and banana-boat rides.

SCUBA DIVING AND SNORKELING
Current Cut, the narrow passage between North Eleuthera and Current Island, is loaded with marine life and provides a roller-coaster ride on the tides. **Devil's Backbone,** in North Eleuthera, offers a tricky reef area with a nearly infinite number of dive sites and a large number of wrecks. **Fox Divers** (☎ 242/333–2323) rents scuba equipment and offers instruction, certification, dive packages, and daily dive trips. **Valentine's Dive Center** (☎ 242/333–2309) rents and sells equipment and provides all levels of instruction, certification, dive packages, and daily group and custom dives. **Big Red Rentals** (☎ 242/333–2045) rents snorkeling equipment and offers snorkeling excursions.

Shopping
Briland's Ambrosia (☎ 242/333–2342) has a good selection of bathing suits, bags, and other items made from the bright batik fabric created on the island of Andros.

Miss Mae Tea Room & Fine Things (☎ 242/333-2276) has been known to stock everything from leggings and sarongs in an array of bold colors to jewelry, exquisite stationery and journals, and even gourmet pasta and olive oil.

After the top-notch restoration of his great great grandfather's house, proprietor Charles Carey opened the tasteful **Princess Street Gallery** (☎ 242/333–2788), featuring fine art by locals and artists who spend part of the year on Harbour Island.

Sugar Mill (☎ 242/333–2173) sells prints by local artists, Bahamian coin jewelry, picture frames decorated with shells from Eleuthera, and wooden puzzles from the nearby island of Spanish Wells, along with multihued sarongs from Indonesia, ceramics from Italy, and Haitian steel-drum cutout wall hangings.

North Eleuthera
㉞ Preacher's Cave. At the tip of the island, this cave is where the Eleutheran Adventurers took refuge and held services when their ship hit a reef more than three centuries ago. You can see inside the cave, with its original stone altar. The last 2 mi of the road to Preacher's Cave are rough, but passable—if you go slowly.

Spanish Wells
Off the northern tip of Eleuthera lies St. George's Cay, the site of Spanish Wells. The Spaniards used this as a safe harbor in the 17th century while they transferred their riches from the New World to the Old; supposedly they dug wells from which they drew water during their frequent visits. Today water comes from the mainland. Unfortunately, 1992's Hurricane Andrew devastated some of Spanish Wells's

landmarks, but most now have been rebuilt. Residents live on the eastern end of the island in clapboard houses that look as if they've been transported from a New England fishing village. Tourists have little to do but hang out on the beach, dive, and dine on fresh seafood at **Jack's Out Back** (☎ 242/333–4219). Descendants of the Eleutheran Adventurers continue to sail these waters and bring back to shore fish and lobster (most of the Bahamas' langoustes are caught in these waters), which are prepared and boxed for export in a factory at the dock. So lucrative is the trade in crawfish that the 700 inhabitants may be the most prosperous Out Islanders in the Bahamas. Those who don't fish here grow tomatoes, onions, and the inevitable pineapples. You reach Spanish Wells by taking a five-minute ferry ride ($5–$9, depending on your stop) from the North Eleuthera dock.

Eleuthera A to Z

Arriving and Departing

BY MAIL BOAT

The following mail boats leave from Nassau at Potter's Cay; for schedules, contact the **Dockmaster's office** (☎ 242/393–1064) at Potter's Cay, Nassau.

M/V *Current Pride* sails to The Current, Lower Bogue, and Upper Bogue on Thursday, returning Tuesday. M/V *Bahamas Daybreak III* leaves on Monday for South Eleuthera, stopping at Rock Sound, and returns on Tuesday; it then leaves Thursday from Nassau for The Bluff and Harbour Island, returning on Sunday. The *Eleuthera Express* sails for Governor's Harbour and Spanish Wells on Monday and Thursday, returning to Nassau on Tuesday and Sunday, respectively. The *Captain Fox* departs for Hatchet Bay and Harbour Island on Friday, returning on Wednesday. The fare is $20 for all Eleutheran destinations.

BY PLANE

Eleuthera has three airports: at **North Eleuthera** (☎ 242/335–1242); at **Governor's Harbour** (☎ 242/332–2321), near the center of the island; and at **Rock Sound** (☎ 242/334–2177), in the southern part of the island. Because Eleuthera's resorts are scattered throughout the island, you'll need to find out in advance which airport is appropriate. If you're staying in Harbour Island or Spanish Wells, for example, your destination will be North Eleuthera Airport, and you'll take a taxi and ferry trip from there. For Club Med Eleuthera, you will fly to Governor's Harbour. Make sure you head for the airport closest to your hotel.

American Eagle (☎ 800/433–7300) has daily flights to Governor's Harbour from Miami. **Bahamasair** (☎ 800/222–4262) has daily service from Nassau and Miami to all three airports. **Cherokee Air** (☎ 242/367–2089 or 242/367–2613)), is a charter on-demand service based in Marsh Harbour. It flies all over the Bahamas and serves Palm Beach and Fort Lauderdale as well. **Continental Connection** (☎ 800/231–0856) has daily flights to North Eleuthera from Miami and Fort Lauderdale. **Major Air** (☎ 242/352–5778) has service from Freeport to all three Eleuthera airports. **Twin Air** (☎ 954/359–8266) flies from Fort Lauderdale three times a week to Governor's Harbour and Rock Sound and four times a week to North Eleuthera. **US Airways Express** (☎ 800/622–1015) flies daily from Fort Lauderdale to Governor's Harbour and North Eleuthera.

Taxis wait for incoming flights at all three airports and can also be found at most resorts. If you land at North Eleuthera and need to get to Harbour Island, off the north coast of Eleuthera, take a taxi ($4) to the ferry dock on Eleuthera, a water taxi ($4) to Harbour Island, and, on the other side, another taxi ($3 to Coral Sands, for example). You follow a similar procedure to get to Spanish Wells, which is also off the north shore of Eleuthera. Taxi service from Governor's Harbour Airport to the Cove-Eleuthera is $42 for two people; the fare to Rainbow Inn is $24. The taxi stand phone number at Governor's Harbour is 242/332–2568.

Getting Around

Harbour Island is easily explorable on foot—it only takes 30 minutes to walk the length of the island—though you'll be wise to rent a golf cart if you're staying for a few days. Visiting the main sites of Eleuthera will require renting a car. North to south is about a three-hour drive. Governor's Harbour, which lies approximately at the midpoint of the long, skinny island, is a 40-minute drive from Glass Window in the north, and a 35-minute drive from Rock Sound in the south.

BY BICYCLE OR SCOOTER

Big Red Rentals (⊠ Harbour Island, ☎ 242/333–2045) provides scooters and bicycles. **Michael's Cycles** (⊠ Harbour Island, ☎ 242/333–2384) rents bikes and mopeds.

BY CAR

Your hotel will be the least-complicated bet for arranging a car rental and can usually have a vehicle delivered to you at the airport. Request four-wheel drive if you plan to visit Preacher's Cave or Surfer's Beach.

Johnson's Rentals (☎ 242/332–2226), **Arthur Nixon** (☎ 242/332–1006 or 242/332–2568), **Hilton's Car Rentals** (☎ 242/335–6241 or 242/332–2568), and **Cecil Cooper** (☎ 242/359–7007 or 242/332–2568) all rent cars from Governor's Harbour—call to discuss delivery of your automobile.

In Rock Sound, **Dingle Motor Service** (☎ 242/334–2031) rents cars. **Barerra's** (⊠ Harbour Island, ☎ 242/333–2361) has minivans.

BY GOLF CART

If you're not much for walking, there are several golf cart rental companies on Harbour Island. Carts rent for about $50/day; definitely negotiate if you'll be renting for longer.

Golf carts are available from: **Big Red Rentals** (☎ 242/333–2045), **Dunmore Rentals** (☎ 242/333–2372), **Grant's** (☎ 242/333–2157), **Johnson's Garage** (☎ 242/333–2376), **Karotio's Eagles Rentals** (☎ 242/333–2750), **Ross' Garage** (☎ 242/333–2122), and **Sunshine Carts** (☎ 242/333–2509).

BY TAXI

To explore the island, you'd best rent a car, which is cheaper than hiring a taxi, unless having a driver who can double as your tour guide is worth the expense. Taxis are available through your hotel.

Opening and Closing Times

Barclays Bank has offices in Governor's Harbour and Rock Sound, and is open Monday through Thursday from 9:30 to 3, Fridays until 5.

Royal Bank of Canada, in Harbour Island, Governor's Harbour, and Spanish Wells, is open weekdays from 9:30 to 3, Mondays and Thursdays until 5.

Scotia Bank, in North Eleuthera, open weekdays from 9:30 to 3, Mondays and Thursdays until 5.

Contacts and Resources

EMERGENCIES

Police: Governor's Harbour (☎ 242/332–2111), Rock Sound (☎ 242/334–2244), Harbour Island (☎ 242/333–2111), and Spanish Wells (☎ 242/333–4030).

Medical Clinics: Harbour Island (☎ 242/333–2227), Governor's Harbour (☎ 242/332–2001 or 242/332–2774), Spanish Wells (☎ 242/333–4064), and Rock Sound (☎ 242/334–2226).

GUIDED TOURS

Arthur Nixon (☎ 242/332–2568 or 242/332–1006) is probably the most knowledgeable authority on Eleuthera. His presentation will make you want to stand up and applaud.

VISITOR INFORMATION

Contact the **Eleuthera Tourist Office** (☎ 242/332–2142, ⨎ 242/332–2480) or the **Harbour Island Tourist Office** (✉ Bay St., ☎ 242/333–2621, ⨎ 242/333–2622).

THE EXUMAS

On the Exumas, you'll still find wild cotton, leftover from plantations established by Loyalists after the Revolutionary War, and breadfruit trees, which a local preacher bought from Captain William Bligh in the late 18th century. The islands are now known as the onion capital of the Bahamas, although many of the 3,600-odd residents earn a living by fishing as well as farming. Your first impression of the people of the Exumas may be that almost all of them have the surname Rolle. Lord John Rolle, who imported the first cotton seeds to these islands, had more than 300 slaves, to whom he bequeathed not only his name but also the 2,300 acres of land that were bestowed on him by the British government in the late 18th century. This land has been passed on to each new generation and can never be sold to outsiders.

The Exumas begin less than 35 mi southeast of Nassau and stretch south for about 90 mi, flanked by the Great Bahama Bank and Exuma Sound. They are made up largely of some 365 fragmented little cays. The two main islands, Great Exuma and Little Exuma, lie in the south, connected by a bridge. The islands' capital, George Town, on Great Exuma, is the site of one of the Bahamas' most prestigious and popular sailing events, the Out Islands Regatta, in which locally built wooden workboats compete. During the winter, George Town's Elizabeth Harbour is a haven of yachts; the surrounding waters are legendary for their desolate islands, coves, bays, and harbors.

The Exumas certainly offer their share of impressive characters. One of them, Gloria Patience, who is in her early eighties and lives south of George Town, is known as the Shark Lady because she used to go out regularly in her 13-ft Boston whaler and catch sharks with a 150-ft-long hand line. Hundreds of makos, hammerheads, and lemon sharks have met their match with Ms. Patience, whose family came from Ireland and Scotland. Still making good use of various shark parts, she drills holes in their teeth and vertebrae to create pendants, necklaces, and earrings, and turns their jawbones into wall hangings, all of which she sells to visitors from **Patience House,** her home–museum–gift shop in the tiny settlement known as The Ferry. Coming from George Town, she's a few hundred yards beyond the one-lane "The Ferry" bridge—there's no sign, but her white house is on the left, with a narrow, gravel driveway and lush front yard. Knock on any door in The Ferry and someone will gladly direct you. Across from the Exuma Market in George Town, "Mom" drives her delectable breads and pastries in daily from Williams Town and couldn't be more gracious. **Mom's Bakery** is the white van parked on the side of the road. Stop to savor a coconut turnover and her company.

Numbers in the margin correspond to points of interest on the Exumas map.

Little Exuma and Great Exuma

③ The old village of **Williams Town** lies at the southern tip of Little Exuma Island. Wild cotton still grows out in these parts, en route to the **Hermitage,** a former plantation house with ruins of slave cottages nearby.

③ Five miles south of George Town lies **Rolle Town,** a typical Exuma village—without the tourist trappings. Residents grow onions, mangoes, bananas, and other crops.

③ Although **George Town** is the island's hive of activity, it's still on the no-need-for-a-traffic-light scale. The most imposing structure here is in the town center—the white-pillared, sandy pink, colonial-style **Government Administration Building,** modeled on Nassau's Government House and containing the commissioner's office, police headquarters, courts, and a jail. Atop a hill across from the government building is the whitewashed **St. Andrew's Anglican Church** (originally built around 1802 and rebuilt in 1991), whose blue doors welcome many locals every Sunday. Behind the church is the small Lake Victoria. A leisurely stroll around town will take you past a straw market and a few shops. You can buy fruit and vegetables and bargain with fishermen for some of the day's catch at the **Government Wharf,** where the mail boat comes in. The wharf is close to **Regatta Point** (☎ 242/336–2206), an attractive guest house named after the annual Out Islands Regatta that curls around Kidd Cove, where the 18th-century pirate Captain Kidd supposedly tied up.

③ Just over a mile off the George Town shore lies **Stocking Island.** The 7-mi-long island has only seven inhabitants, a gorgeous stretch of white beach rich in seashells, and plenty of good snorkeling sites. Jacques Cousteau's team is said to have traveled a length of some 1,700 ft into **Mystery Cave,** a blue hole grotto beneath the island at a depth of 70 ft. Club Peace &Plenty's ferry runs over to Stocking Island twice daily, at 10 AM and 1 PM and charges $8 for non-guests. Near the Stocking Island pier, Peace & Plenty Beach Club rents a variety of watersports gear, provides changing rooms (with plumbing), and operates a lunch spot where Dora's "heavenly burgers and dreamful dogs" are the eats of choice. To enjoy the setting sun from Stocking Island, Higgins Landing (☞ Dining and Lodging, *below*) serves sumptuous gourmet dinners in an intimate setting with antiques and romantic kerosene lamplight; a ride aboard their dinner ferry—a classic 1957 lobster boat—is included with your prix fixe meal.

③ From the top of **Mt. Thompson,** rising from the beach, there is a pleasing view of the **Three Sisters Rocks** jutting above the water just offshore. During your walks, you may glimpse a flock of roaming peacocks on Great Exuma. Originally, a peacock and a peahen were brought to the island as pets by a man named Shorty Johnson, but when he left to work in Nassau, he abandoned the birds, who gradually proliferated into a colony. Some locals hunt these birds because they eat crops, but they are difficult to catch. Mt. Thompson is about 12 mi north of George Town, past Moss Town.

④ The town of **Rolleville** sits on a hill above a harbor, 20 mi north of George Town. Its old slave quarters have been transformed into livable cottages. The town's most prominent citizen, Kermit Rolle, runs the **Hilltop Tavern** (☎ 242/336–6038), a seafood restaurant and bar guarded by an ancient cannon.

Dining and Lodging

$$ ✕ **Eddie's Edgewater.** The specialty at this popular spot is turtle steak,
★ but the menu also offers low fat steamed chicken (call ahead, or wait

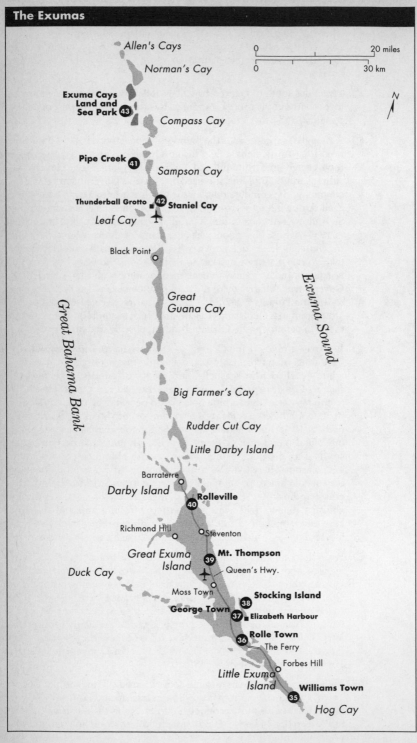

Allen's Cays

Norman's Cay

Exuma Cays Land and Sea Park (43)

Compass Cay

Pipe Creek (41)

Sampson Cay

Thunderball Grotto (42) **Staniel Cay**

Leaf Cay

Black Point

Great Guana Cay

Exuma Sound

Great Bahama Bank

Big Farmer's Cay

Rudder Cut Cay

Little Darby Island

Barraterre

Darby Island (40) **Rolleville**

Richmond Hill   Steventon

Great Exuma Island (39) **Mt. Thompson**

Duck Cay   Queen's Hwy.

Moss Town

Stocking Island

(38)

George Town (37) **Elizabeth Harbour**

Rolle Town (36)

The Ferry

Forbes Hill

Little Exuma Island   **Williams Town**

(35)

Hog Cay

0 ———————— 20 miles
0 ———————— 30 km

N

the 40 minutes preparation time). Don't miss the rake 'n' scrape band on Mondays—rakes and saws serve as instruments. ⊠ *Charlotte St., George Town,* ☎ *242/336–2050. MC, V. Closed Sun.*

$–$$ ✕ **Iva Bowe's Central Highway Inn.** About 10 mi from George Town, close to the airport, this casual lunch and dinner spot has an island-wide reputation for the best native food. Grace one of those fish-shaped straw placemats with one of the delectable shrimp dishes—coconut beer shrimp, spicy Cajun shrimp, or scampi, all for around $10. ⊠ *Queen's Hwy.,* ☎ *242/345–7014. No credit cards. Closed Sun.*

$–$$ ✕ **Tino's Restaurant and Sports Lounge.** The owner of this tiny local gathering spot and eatery doesn't close his doors until the last person leaves, which can be in the wee hours of the morning. The cracked conch, heaping portions of peas 'n' rice, and conch fritters are all good choices. The sports-themed bar has a pool table and satellite TV. ⊠ *Queens Hwy., next to Belltelco office, George Town,* ☎ *242/336–2838. No credit cards.*

$ ✕ **Big D's Conch Spot #2.** Near the government dock, look for this striped, octagonal thatched hut and enjoy a mouthwatering bowl of fresh conch salad prepared before your very eyes. ⊠ *Government Dock, George Town, no phone. Closed Sun., Tues., Thurs., Sat. No credit cards.*

$ ✕ **Ruth's Deli.** Grab a lunchtime seat at the yellow counter and enjoy a sandwich or burger here. The service is far from speedy, but you can use the time to catch up on the outside world via Ruth's satellite TV. ⊠ *Charlotte St., George Town,* ☎ *242/336–2596. No credit cards. Closed Sun.*

$ ✕ **Towne Café.** George Town's bakery serves breakfast—consider trying the stew fish or chicken souse—and lunch—seafood sandwiches with three sides, or grilled fish. Towne Café is open until 5 PM. ⊠ *Marshall Complex, George Town,* ☎ *242/336–2194. No credit cards. Closed Sun.*

$$$$ ✕🏠 **Peace & Plenty Bonefish Lodge.** The swankest bonefishing lodge
★ in the Out Islands is on a peninsula 10 mi south of George Town. Dark wood and handsome hunter-green accents lend a gentleman's-club feel to the bar and dining room, where photos of anglers and their catches grace the walls alongside signed jerseys from Mickey Mantle and Duke Snider. Upstairs, the "private lodge" has a fly-tying table, card table, satellite TV, small reading and video libraries, and an honor bar. The large rooms have dark-green rattan furnishings, louvered wooden doors, and private balconies overlooking the water. "Reel" adventurers will find contemplative, restful spots on the large deck, upstairs veranda, or in a hammock on the sandy point that juts out beyond the lodge's fish pond. There's a free ferry to Stocking Island and a shuttle-van runs between George Town and Peace & Plenty's Beach Inn (☞ *below*). In the dining room, Chef Les prepares hearty fare—from 16-ounce New York strip steaks to vegetarian dishes. ⊠ *Box EX 29173, George Town,* ☎ *242/345–5555,* FAX *242/345–5556. 8 rooms. Restaurant, 2 bars, air-conditioning, fans, snorkeling, fishing, bicycles. MC, V. MAP.*

$$$–$$$$ ✕🏠 **Hotel Higgins Landing.** This refined haven is the only resort on
★ luscious, undeveloped Stocking Island. Owners Carol and Dave Higgins are naturalists at heart, managing to create a place that's heralded both for its casual elegance and its environmentally respectful design: Higgins Landing is 100% solar powered (don't worry, everything still works when its overcast!). The post-and-beam cottages have screen windows with dark-green shutters and private, spacious decks with turquoise ocean views. The immaculate interiors have antique furnishings, queen-size beds, ceiling fans, and cool, saltillo-tile floors and

folksy Americana decor. At the water's edge, with views of Elizabeth Harbor, the bar acts as an alfresco living room by day, with guests playing checkers or darts, or reading from the hotel's library. The grounds are alive with colorful blossoms as well as egrets, hummingbirds, osprey, and herons, and the teeming marine life ranges from green sea turtles and eagle rays to the occasional porpoise. Walkers should borrow one of Carol's maps of the island's barefoot trails, and snorkelers will want to explore the offshore reefs. A Sunfish, Hobie Cat, pedalboat, or rowing dinghy are available, and you can dock your own rental boat here. Rates include a full breakfast, and a prix fixe dinner that's served by candlelight on china. Nonguests may dine Thursday through Sunday, but must make reservations early, as intimate dinners here are limited to 14 people. The most popular lunch for guests is a gourmet picnic box to go. Children under 18 are not permitted during the winter season, although family arrangements can be worked out in summer. ✉ *Box EX 29146, George Town, Exuma,* ☎ *242/336–2460,* 𝔽𝔸𝕏 *242/357–0008. 5 cottages. Restaurant, bar, beach, dock, snorkeling, boating, fishing, library. D, MC, V. No smoking. MAP, FAP.*

$$$ ✕🖵 **Club Peace & Plenty.** The granddaddy of Exuma's omnipresent Peace & Plenty empire, this pink, two-story hotel is near the heart of George Town. With a mast facing the calm Exuma Sound and the resort's crest tiled into the shallow end, the ship's bow-shape pool takes center stage. The cheerful rooms have satellite TVs and private balconies—most overlooking the pool, with ocean views in the periphery, though a handful of the rooms have full ocean vistas. In high season, the hotel is known for its Saturday night parties on the pool patio, where Lermon "Doc" Rolle has been holding court at the bar since the '70s. The indoor bar, which was once a slave kitchen, attracts locals and a yachting crowd, especially during the Out Islands Regatta; its walls are decorated appropriately with ships' name boards, anchors, rudders, and assorted lights. You can take the free ferry twice a day to the beach just across the water on Stocking Island. The hotel's restaurant serves some of the best dishes in town—dine on the terrace (the ambience inside is a bit flat). ✉ *Box 29055, George Town, Exuma,* ☎ *242/336–2551 or 800/525–2210,* 𝔽𝔸𝕏 *242/336–2093. 35 rooms. 2 bars, dining room, pool, beach, diving, boating, dock fishing. AE, MC, V. EP, MAP.*

$$$ ✕🖵 **Coconut Cove Hotel.** This intimate hotel exudes the gracious hospitality of owners Pam Predmore and Tom Chimento. Social activity revolves around the thatched gazebo bar, where guests can enjoy expansive views of the tranquil bay with a specialty drink of Bartender "Fuzz," while perched atop bar stools in the pool's shallow end or on terra firma. The Paradise Suite has its own private terrace hot tub, a king-size bed, walk-in closet, TV-VCR, and an immense bathroom replete with a black-marble Jacuzzi bathtub. Other rooms have queen-size beds, tile floors, TVs, remote-control air-conditioning, and good views from private terraces. Bathrobes and fresh-daily floral arrangements are nice touches in the rooms. A new cottage efficiency includes a kitchenette. Top-notch fare at Coconut Cove includes Angus beef, fresh pastas, and gourmet pizzas served outside on the deck or inside by the fireplace. ✉ *Box EX 29299, George Town, Exuma,* ☎ *242/336–2659 or 800/688–475,* 𝔽𝔸𝕏 *242/336–2658. 12 rooms, 1 cottage. Restaurant, bar, air-conditioning, minibars, pool, diving, fishing, laundry service. MC, V. EP.*

$$$ ✕🖵 **Peace & Plenty Beach Inn.** This 16-room resort on 300 ft of beach is a mile west of its big brother, the Club Peace & Plenty (☞ *above*), and a shuttle runs between the two four times daily. The units' floors and walkways are tiled in white, have simple tropical-print accents, and French doors opening onto private patios or balconies that overlook the freshwater pool and ocean. Once in the dining room, marvel at the

tiered cathedral ceiling of rich-stained pine and feast on blackened mahi-mahi, New York–cut Angus steak, or the delicious chicken breast Alfredo with sundried tomatoes baked in a crispy puff dough; reservations are required. Manager Charlie Pflueger is a charmer bar-none and a wonderful source of island lore. ✉ *Box 29055, George Town, Exuma,* ☎ *242/336–2250 or 800/525–2210,* FAX *242/336–2253. 16 rooms. Restaurant, 2 bars, refrigerators, pool, fishing. AE, MC, V. EP, MAP.*

$$ 🏨 **Regatta Point.** Soft pink with hunter-green shutters, this handsome two-story guest house overlooks Kidd Cove from its own petite island. Connected to George Town by a short causeway, the property is only a five-minute walk from town, but out of the fray enough to have a secret hideaway's charm. In addition to a picturesque view of the yachts in Elizabeth Harbour, large vaulted-ceilinged rooms have truly pleasing interiors and porches well designed to catch the cool, incoming trade winds. For families or those seeking maximum privacy, a cottage unit with sweeping views sits next to the main house. The hotel has no restaurant, but units come with modern kitchens, and maid service is included. Sunfish and bicycles are available gratis to guests. ✉ *Box 29006, Regatta Point across from George Town, Exuma,* ☎ *242/ 336–2206 or 800/688–0309,* FAX *242/336–2046. 1 one-bedroom unit, 1 2-bedroom unit, 3 suites, 1 cottage. Fans, beach, dock, boating, fishing, bicycles, laundry service. MC, V. EP.*

$–$$ 🏨 **Palms at Three Sisters Beach Resort.** A spectacular 1,200-ft stretch of white beach is the main attraction of this two-story, exterior corridor hotel. Rooms have satellite TV and private patios or balconies with wonderful views of the ocean, but the interiors are lackluster and could use some sprucing up. Downstairs rooms have air-conditioning, while upstairs ceiling fans keep the air moving—specify your preference when making a reservation. The resort is only 3 mi north of the airport but feels quite isolated; van service into George Town is provided to guests twice daily (or as required) for a nominal fee. The restaurant serves three meals a day. ✉ *Box 29215, George Town, Exuma,* ☎ *242/358–4040,* FAX *242/358–4043. 12 rooms, 2 cottages. Restaurant, bar, tennis, snorkeling, laundry service. MC, V. EP.*

$ 🏨 **Two Turtles Inn.** Location and price are the main draws—although these carpeted rooms are clean and air-conditioned, don't be surprised if your room is a hodgepodge of clashing (and worn) spreads, drapes, and upholsteries. A few efficiency units provide stove/sink/refrigerator combinations, but there's a restaurant and courtyard barbecue parties if you don't want to cook. Steer clear of the cottage unit, it's dingy and cramped. The inn is across the street from the village green and the straw market, with George Town's friendly thoroughfare a stone's throw away. The closest beach is a 10-minute ferry ride to Stocking Island. ✉ *Box 29251, George Town, Exuma,* ☎ *242/336–2545,* FAX *242/336– 2528. 11 rooms. Bar, dining room, air-conditioning. AE, MC, V. EP.*

Nightlife

On Mondays, head to **Eddie's Edgewater** (☎ 242/336–2050) for the rousing rake 'n' scrape band. **Two Turtles Inn** has barbecues in the lively patio courtyard and happy hours at the tables and benches surrounding the central license plate–decorated bar. A few miles north of George Town, the **Whale Tail** (no phone) splashes with live native music on Saturday nights. In season, **Club Peace & Plenty's** (☎ 242/336–2551) poolside bashes keep Bahamians and vacationers on the dance floor Wednesday and Saturday nights.

Outdoor Activities and Sports

BOATING

Renting a boat provides for unforgettable explorations of the cays near George Town and beyond. A number of area hotels allow guests to tie up rental boats at their docks. For those who want to take a water jaunt through Stocking Island's hurricane holes, paddleboats and Sunfish sailboats are ideal options. **Exuma Dive Centre** (☎ 242/336–2390) rents 17-ft Polar Craft boats with Bimini tops for $75 a day and $375 a week. **Exuma Fantasea** (☎ 242/336–3483) has a fleet of 17- and 18-ft Boston Whalers with small dive platforms.

On Stocking Island **Peace & Plenty Beach Club** (☎ 242/336–2551) rents paddleboats ($15/half day) and Sunfish sailboats ($20/half day).

EVENTS

Annual New Year's Day Cruising Regatta is held in January at the Staniel Cay Yacht Club (☞ *below*), with international yachts taking part in a series of races. At the beginning of March, the **Cruiser's Regatta** hosts visiting boats for a week of races, cookouts, and partying in George Town. **Out Islands Regatta** is the most important yachting event of the year in the Bahamas; it takes place in April. Commencing in Elizabeth Harbour in George Town, island-made wooden sailing boats compete for trophies; onshore, the town is a three-day riot of Junkanoo parades, Goombay music, arts and crafts fairs, and continuous merriment.

FISHING

Most hotels can arrange for local guides, and a list is available from the **Exuma Tourist Office** (☎ 242/336-2430). **Exuma Dive Centre** (☎ 242/336–2390) rents fly- and deep-sea fishing rods. **Shadow Pleasure Tours** (☎ 242/336–2968) will take you out for a day of deep-sea fishing. **Reno Rolle** (☎ 242/345–5003) is a highly recommended bonefishing guide, as are any of the guides from **Peace & Plenty Bonefish Lodge** (☎ 242/345–5555).

SCUBA DIVING

Angel Fish Blue Hole is a popular dive spot from George Town. **Stocking Island Mystery Cave** is full of mesmerizing schools of colorful fish, but is for experienced divers only. **Exuma Dive Centre** (☎ 242/336–2390) offers a 50% discount on rental equipment when you take one of their dive trips, which start at $50. **Exuma Fantasea** (☎ 242/336–3483 or 800/760–0700) specializes in eco-diving to protect and preserve the marine environment.

SNORKELING

On Stocking Island, **Peace & Plenty Beach Club** rents snorkel gear for $10 a day, and viewboards by the hour; take their ferry over to the island (☞ Exploring, *above*). **Exuma Dive Centre** (☎ 242/336–2390) and **Exuma Fantasea** (☎ 242/336–3483) rent equipment and offer snorkeling trips.

TENNIS

Near the airport, **The Palms at Three Sisters Beach Resort** (☎ 242/358-4040) has one court and grants privileges to nonguests for $10/hr.

WINDSURFING

On Stocking Island, **Peace & Plenty Beach Club** (☎ 242/336–2551) rents windsurfers for $15 per half day and $30 per full day.

Shopping

In the Exumas, George Town is the place to shop. **Exuma Market** (✉ Across from Scotia Bank, George Town, ☎ 242/336–2033) is the island's largest grocery; boaters tie up at the skiff docks in the rear, on Victoria Lake.

N & D Ice-Cream and Vegetable Stand (✉ Queen's Hwy., ☎ 242/336–2236) can help cool you off while you shop for fresh produce.

Peace & Plenty Boutique (⊠ Opposite Club Peace & Plenty, ☎ 242/ 336–2551) has a good selection of Androsia shirts and dresses.

Sandpiper Boutique (⊠ Queen's Hwy., ☎ 242/336–2084) has upscale souvenirs, from high-quality cards and books to batik clothing and art.

Cays of the Exumas

A band of cays—with names like Rudder Cut, Big Farmer's, Great Guana, and Leaf—stretches north from Great Exuma.

㊶ Boaters will want to explore the waterways known as **Pipe Creek,** a winding passage through the tiny islands between Staniel and Compass cays. There are great spots for shelling, snorkeling, diving, and bonefishing. The **Samson Cay Yacht Club** (☎ 242/355–2034), at the creek's halfway point, is a good place for lunch or dinner.

㊷ **Staniel Cay** is a favorite destination of yachters and makes the perfect home base for visiting the Exuma Cays Land and Sea Park. The island has an airstrip, two hotels, and one paved road. Virtually everything is within walking distance. Oddly enough, as you stroll past brightly painted houses and sandy shores, you are as likely to see a satellite dish as a woman pulling a bucket of water from a roadside well. At one of three grocery stores, boat owners can replenish their supplies. The friendly village also has a small red-roof church, a post office, and a straw vendor.

Just across the water from the Staniel Cay Yacht Club is one of the Bahamas' most unforgettable attractions: **Thunderball Grotto,** a beautiful marine cave that snorkelers (at low tide) and experienced scuba divers can explore. In the central cavern, shimmering shafts of sunlight pour through holes in the soaring ceiling and illuminate the glass-clear water. You'll see right away why this cave was chosen as an exotic setting for such movies as 007's *Thunderball* and *Never Say Never,* and the mermaid tale, *Splash.*

Above Staniel Cay, near the northern end of the Exumas, lies the 176-sq-mi **Exuma Cays Land and Sea Park,** which spans 22 mi between ㊸ Conch Cut and Wax Cay Cut. You must charter a small boat or seaplane to reach the park, which has more than 20 mi of petite cays. Hawksbill Cay and Warderick Wells (both with remains of 18th-century Loyalist settlements), as well as Hall's Pond have marked hiking trails. At Shroud Cay, jump into "Camp Driftwood," where the strong current creates a natural whirlpool that whips you around a rocky outcropping to a powdery beach. Part of the Bahamas National Trust, the park appeals to divers, who appreciate the vast underworld of limestone, reefs, drop-offs, blue holes of freshwater springs, caves, and a multitude of exotic marine life, including one of the most impressive stands of rare pillar coral in the Bahamas. Strict laws prohibit fishing and taking coral, plants, or even shells away as souvenirs. A list of park rules is available at the headquarters on Warderick Wells. Stay tuned: a real-estate developer currently has plans to encroach upon the area, although locals are organizing to preserve the land as a sanctuary.

North of the park is **Norman's Cay,** a beautiful, now-abandoned island with 10 mi of rarely trodden white beaches, which attract an occasional yachter. It was once the private domain of convicted Colombian drug smuggler Carlos Lehder, whose planes left from there for drop-offs in Florida. It's now owned by the Bahamian government. **Allan's Cays** are at the northernmost tip of the Exumas and are home to the rare, protected Bahamian iguana.

Dining and Lodging

$$ ✕🏠 **Staniel Cay Yacht Club.** Sunsets are particularly dramatic from this small group of cottages perched on stilts along a rocky bank. Once upon a time, this club drew luminaries such as Malcolm Forbes and Robert Mitchum; it has now settled into a low-key getaway for yachters and escapists. The cottages' pièces de résistance are broad ocean vistas, which you can drink in from the comfort of your bed or from a chaise lounge on your good-sized, private balcony. While these individual studios may be a tad cozy, they are well thought-out, with smart shelving nooks and considerate touches like full-size coffeemakers with a supply of both regular and decaf brews; matching tab curtains and berber carpet give these units a modern feel. The "Other Boat" cottage sleeps four and has an upstairs master bedroom with a table and chairs on the unit's large, screened sunporch. The cuisine is noteworthy here, deliciously prepared and always served with fresh vegetables. Take a tour of the cay in one of the club's golf carts. ✉ *Stanley Cay (✉ 2233 S. Andrews Ave., Fort Lauderdale, FL 33316),* ☎ *242/355–2024 or 954/467–8920,* 🖷 *954/ 522–3248 or 242/355–2044. 4 one-bedroom cottages, 1 2-bedroom cottage, 1 3-bedroom cottage. Restaurant, bar, air-conditioning, ceiling fans, boating, fishing, piano. AE, MC, V. MAP.*

$ ✕🏠 **Happy People Marina.** You may find this casual hotel a bit isolated if you're not interested in yachting. The property is close to Staniel Cay, but it's a long way from the George Town social scene. A local band, however, plays at the Royal Entertainer Lounge, and a small restaurant serves Bahamian meals. The simple motel-style rooms are on the beach; some have private baths. ✉ *Staniel Cay,* ☎ *242/355– 2008. 8 rooms, 1 2-bedroom apartment. Restaurant, bar, dining room, air-conditioning, dock. No credit cards. EP.*

Nightlife

The island has two nightspots, the **Royal Entertainer Lounge** (✉ Happy People Marina, ☎ 242/355–2008), where live bands perform on special occasions, and the newer **Club Thunderball** (✉ East of Thunderball Grotto, ☎ 242/355–2012); this sports bar and dance club, built on a bluff overlooking the water, serves lunch and has Friday evening barbecues and a mooring; it is run by a local pilot.

Outdoor Activities and Sports

BOATING AND FISHING

Staniel Cay Yacht Club (☎ 242/355–2024) rents 13-ft whalers and arranges for fishing guides.

SCUBA DIVING AND SNORKELING

Staniel Cay Yacht Club (☎ 242/355–2024) fills tanks from its compressor and expects its new, full dive shop to open by October 1998. Call ahead, or plan to bring your own scuba gear. You can also rent masks and fins for snorkeling. **Pink Pearl Market** (☎ 242/355–2040) sells snorkel equipment and is open Monday through Saturday. **Exuma Cays Land and Sea Park** and **Thunderball Grotto** (☞ *above*) are excellent snorkeling sites.

Exumas A to Z

Arriving and Departing

BY MAIL BOAT

M/V *Grand Master* travels from Nassau to George Town on Tuesday and returns to Nassau on Friday. Travel time is 12 hours and fares range from $35 to $40 depending on your destination. M/V *Ettienne & Cephas* leaves Nassau on Tuesday for Staniel Cay, Farmers Cay, Black Point, and Baraterre, returning to Nassau on Saturday. The full trip takes 21 hours;

call for fares to specific destinations. For further information contact the **Dockmaster's office** (☎ 242/393–1064) at Potter's Cay, Nassau.

BY PLANE

Exuma International Airport, 9 mi from George Town, is the official airport for the Exumas, and the official port of entry. It's also one of the tidiest airports in the Bahamas. Taxis wait at the airport for incoming flights. The cost of a ride from the airport to George Town is about $22 for two. Staniel Cay, near the top of the chain, has a 3,000-ft airstrip that accepts charter flights and private planes, but you must clear customs at the Andros, Nassau, or Exuma airport first.

Air Sunshine (☎ 954/435–8900 or 800/327–8900) flies into George Town four days a week, with planes leaving from Fort Lauderdale, St. Petersburg, and Sarasota. **American Eagle** (☎ 800/433–7300) has daily service from Miami. **Bahamasair** (☎ 800/222–4262) has daily flights from Nassau and twice-weekly flights from Miami to George Town. **Island Express** (☎ 954/359–0380) flies from Fort Lauderdale to George Town and Staniel Cay. **Lynx Air International** (☎ 888/596–9247) flies from Fort Lauderdale to George Town. **Stella Maris** (☎ 954/359–8236, 242/336–2106, or 800/426–0466) is available for charter flights to or from the Exumas.

Getting Around

You can stay in George Town proper and enjoy touring Great Exuma by car, but if you want a closer look at any of the hundreds of nearby, deserted Exuma cays, you'll appreciate the greater freedom of a boat. If you want to go to Staniel Cay, through Pipe Creek, or to the Exuma Cays Land and Sea Park, water passage via the Exuma Sound or Great Bahama Bank is the only route.

BY BICYCLE

In George Town, **N & D Ice-Cream and Vegetable Stand** rents bicycles for $10/day. In George Town's Scotia Bank building, **Thompson's Rentals** (☎ 242/336–2442) has bicycles. Contact **Chamberlain Rentals** (☎ 242/355–2020) if you want to pedal around Staniel Cay.

BY BOAT

To reach Stocking Island from George Town, the **Club Peace & Plenty Ferry** (☎ 242/336–2551) leaves from the hotel's dock twice daily at 10 AM and 1:00 PM; the ferry departs from the Stocking Island dock at 10:30 AM and 1:30PM. The fare is $8 round-trip for non–Peace & Plenty guests. For more information on boat rentals in the Exumas, *see* Boating *in* Outdoor Activities and Sports sections, *above*.

BY CAR

In George Town, you can rent an automobile through: **Thompson's Rentals** (☎ 242/336–2442) or **Sam Grey Enterprises** (☎ 242/336–2101). **Two Turtles Inn** (☎ 242/336–2545) rents jeeps. Hotels also can arrange car rentals.

BY GOLF CART

Staniel Cay Yacht Club (☎ 242/355–2024) rents golf carts for exploring Staniel Cay.

BY SCOOTER

In George Town, **Exuma Dive Centre** (☎ 242/336–2390) rents motor scooters for $40 a day.

BY TAXI

Your George Town hotel will arrange for a taxi if you wish to go exploring or need to return to the airport. You can also call **Kermit Rolle** (☎ 242/345–6038) or the **Luther Rolle Taxi Service** (☎ 242/345–5003).

Opening and Closing Times

The **Bank of Nova Scotia** in George Town is open weekdays 9:30–3.

Contacts and Resources

EMERGENCIES

George Town: **Police** (☎ 919 or 242/336–2666), **Medical Clinic** (☎ 242/336–2220).

Staniel Cay: **Police** (☎ 242/355–2042), **St. Luke's Medical Clinic** (☎ 242/355–2010).

GUIDED TOURS

Kermit Rolle (☎ 242/345–6038) will take you on an informative, enjoyable tour of Little and Great Exuma. From George Town, **Captain Cole** (☎ 242/345–0074) arranges overnight trips up to the Exuma Cays Land and Sea Park.

VISITOR INFORMATION

The **Exuma Tourist Office** (☎ 242/336–2430, FAX 242/336–2431) is in George Town across the street from St. Andrew's Anglican Church.

INAGUA

Great Inagua, the third-largest island in the Bahamas, is 25 mi wide and 45 mi long. The terrain is mostly flat and covered with scrub. The island's unusual climate of little rainfall and continual trade winds created rich salt ponds, which have brought prosperity to the island over the years. The Morton Salt Company harvests a million tons of salt annually at its Matthew Town factory. About 25% of Inaguans earn their living by working for the company. Inagua is best known not for its salt, however, but for the huge flocks of shy pink flamingos that reside in the island's vast national park and on the property belonging to the salt company. In addition to the famous flamingos, the island is home to one of the largest populations of the rare Bahamian parrot, as well as to herons, egrets, owls, cormorants, and over a hundred other species of birds.

While the birds have moved in wholeheartedly, the island remains virtually undiscovered by outsiders. Avid bird-watchers make up the majority of the tourists who undertake the long trip to this most southerly of the Out Islands, about 300 mi southeast of Nassau and 50 mi off the coast of Cuba. Lack of exposure means, on the one hand, that people are still friendly and curious about each new face in town—you won't feel like just another tourist—and since crowds and traffic are nonexistent, there's nothing to bother you but the rather persistent mosquito population (be sure to bring strong insect repellent). On the other hand, tourist facilities are very few and far between. The only inhabited settlement on Inagua is Matthew Town, a small, dusty grid of workers' homes and essential services. The four "hotels" are functional at best. There's no official visitor information office (although Great Inagua Tours is very helpful), and if you're a beach lover, Inagua is not for you. While there are a couple of small swimming areas near Matthew Town and a few longer stretches farther north, no perfect combination of hotel and beach has yet been built. However, the virgin reefs off the island have caused a stir among intrepid divers who bring in their own equipment. The buzz is that Inagua could become a hot dive destination. Great Inagua Tours may open a scuba operation, so divers, stay tuned.

Great Inagua Island appears in the southeast corner of the Bahamas map at the front of this guide.

Matthew Town

About 1,000 people live on Inagua, whose capital, Matthew Town, is on the west coast. The "town" is about a block long. There's the large pink, run-down government building (housing the commissioner's office, post office, and customs office), a power plant, a grocery and liquor store, Morton's Main House (a guest house), the After Work Bar, the bank, and the small Kiwanis park that comes complete with a bench for sunset-gazing. Most houses here have the ubiquitous, huge satellite dishes prominently displayed. It is rumored that a lot of the money for these, and the houses they are attached to, came from the heady drug-smuggling days of the 1980s. Today, a U.S. Coast Guard helicopter base at the airport has pretty much put an end to that gold rush.

The **Erickson Museum and Library** is a welcome part of the community, particularly the surprisingly well-stocked and equipped library. The Morton company built the complex in the former home of the Erickson family, who came to Inagua in 1934 to run the Morton company. The museum displays the history of the island, to which the company is inextricably tied. ⊠ *Gregory St., on the northern edge of town across from the police station,* ☎ *242/339–1863.* ⌨ *Free.* ☉ *Weekdays 3–6:30, Sat. 9–6:30.*

The desire to marvel over the salt process entices few visitors to Inagua, but the **Morton Salt Company** (☎ 242/339–1300) is omnipresent on the island: It has over 2,000 acres of crystallizing ponds and over 34,000 acres of reservoirs. Over a million tons of salt are produced every year for such industrial uses as salting icy streets. (They produce more when the Northeast has a bad winter!) Even if you decide not to tour the facility, you'll be able to see the mountains of salt glistening in the sun from the plane. In an unusual case of industry assisting its environment, the crystallizers provide a feeding ground for the flamingos. As the water evaporates, the concentration of brine shrimp in the ponds increases, and the flamingos feed on these animals. Tours are available.

Dining and Lodging

$–$$ ✕ **Cozy Corner.** Cheerful and loud, this lunch spot has a pool table and a large seating area with a bar—stop in for a chat with locals over a beer and cheeseburger. ⊠ *Matthew Town, Inagua,* ☎ *242/339–1440. No credit cards*

$$ ✕🏨 **Crystal Beach View.** About half a mile from the airport, this one-story stone structure is on a coral-stone stretch of coastline where the grounds are strewn with detritus. It is the largest hotel in town, but is in need of some significant sprucing up, though the rooms are adequate. There *is* a honeymoon suite with a tub in the middle of the room and a king-size bed on a raised platform (consider other honeymoon locales before this one!). The island's sole pool is filled with salt water only when the hotel is fairly full—a major disappointment for off-peak guests and a hazard when empty. The lobby lounge is a friendly place to watch TV and chat with other guests, as is the bar in the Crystal Ruins restaurant ($–$$). This eatery serves breakfast, lunch, and dinner, with a focus on Bahamian cuisine. ⊠ *Gregory St., Matthew Town,* ☎ *242/339–1550,* 𝐅𝐀𝐗 *242/339–1670. 13 rooms. Restaurant, bar, lobby lounge, air-conditioning, pool, beauty salon. No credit cards. EP.*

$$$ 🏨 **Sunset Apartments.** These apartments are under eternal construc-
★ tion right along the water on the southern side of Matthew Town. Two units are open; the other two are slated for finishing in fall 1998. These cement units have white walls and modern Caribbean-style, terracotta–tile floors, and rattan furniture; they also have small terraces, a picnic area, and a gas grill. About a five-minute walk away is a small,

secluded beach called the Swimming Hole. This is by far your best bet for accommodations on Inagua. ⊠ *(c/o Ezzard Cartwright, Matthew Town, Inagua),* ☎ *242/339–1362. 2 apartments. Fans, kitchenettes, boating. No credit cards.*

$ ⊞ **Main House.** The Morton Salt Company operates this small, simple guest house. There are two floors; the air-conditioned rooms on the second floor share a sitting area with couches and a telephone. Rooms are spotless and spacious with dark-wood furnishings, Masonite paneled walls, and floral-print drapes and spreads. Room 6 is the largest. All rooms have TVs, which are all tuned to whatever station the master satellite tuner is on. (You have to find the Main House mistress to change stations. The hospital next door is also on the same system, so there's competition for requests.) The green-and-white hotel is right in Matthew Town, behind the grocery store and directly across the street from the island's noisy power plant. But it's cheap and clean. ⊠ *Matthew Town, Inagua,* ☎ *242/339–1267. 5 rooms. No credit cards. EP.*

$ ⊞ **Walkine's Guest House.** Eleanor and Kirk Walkine operate this basic, split-level stone guest house just south of the center of Matthew Town. There are no dining facilities, but Topps Restaurant is a half-mile away. ⊠ *Gregory Street south, across from beach, Matthew Town, Inagua,* ☎ *242/339–1612. 5 rooms, 3 with private bath. Air-conditioning. No credit cards.*

Elsewhere on the Island

In addition to the salt ponds on the island, birds and other wildlife also reside in the **Bahamas National Trust** reserve, which spreads over 287 sq mi and occupies most of the western half of the island. Nature lovers, ornithologists, and photographers are drawn to the area and to Lake Windsor (a 12-mi-long brackish body of water in the center of the island) to view the spectacle of more than 60,000 flamingos feeding, mating, or flying (although you will rarely see all those birds together in the same place). When planning your trip, keep in mind that flamingo mating season is October–February, and the nesting season is March–April. Flamingos live on Inagua year-round, but the greatest concentrations come at these times. If you visit right after hatching, the scrambling flocks of fuzzy, gray baby flamingos are very entertaining—they can't fly until they're older. You don't have to tour the Trust property to see flamingos, but there are camping facilities on the grounds, and wardens will give guided tours. Arrangements can be made through your hotel or by calling Great Inagua Tours (☞ Contacts and Resources *in* Inagua A to Z, *below*).

From **Southwest Point,** a mile or so south of the capital, you can see the coast of Cuba on a clear day, just over 50 mi west, from atop the lighthouse (built in 1870 after a huge number of shipwrecks on offshore reefs). This is one of the last four hand-operated kerosene lighthouses in the Bahamas—be sure to sign the guest book after your climb.

Villa Rental

A four-bedroom cottage in a completely secluded area out toward the northwest point of the island rents for about $150 per day (negotiable depending on the length of stay). The cottage sits right on the beach and has a patio for sunset viewing. There's a fully equipped kitchen, dining area, an outdoor shower in addition to the indoor bath, and a private strip of beach with a section cleared of rocks for swimming. The cottage is not elegant, but it is completely private. Be warned however: If there has been a recent rain, mosquitoes will be fierce; be sure to ask about them when booking. Call Larry Ingraham at **Great Inagua Tours** (☎ 242/339–1862) with inquiries.

Inagua A to Z

Arriving and Departing

M/V *Lady Mathilda* makes weekly trips from Nassau to Matthew Town, also stopping at Crooked Island, Acklins Island, and Mayaguana. M/V *Abilin* goes to Long Island, and then on to Matthew Town; the boat departs Nassau on Tuesday. For information on specific schedules and fares, contact the **Dockmaster's office** (☎ 242/393–1064) at Potter's Cay, Nassau.

Bahamasair (☎ 242/339–4415 or 800/222–4262) has flights on Monday, Wednesday, and Friday from Nassau to Matthew Town Airport. Taxis sometimes meet incoming flights. It's best to make prior arrangements with your hotel to be picked up.

Getting Around

The **Pour More Bar** (☎ 242/339–1232) and the **Crystal Beach View Hotel** (☎ 242/339–1550) rent bikes for exploring.

Inagua Trading Ltd. (☎ 242/339–1330) has several cars for rent by the day.

If you need a taxi for anything, ask your hotel to make arrangements, or call 242/339–1284 and ask for Rocky.

Opening and Closing Times

The **Bank of the Bahamas** (☎ 242/339–1815) in Matthew Town is open Monday through Thursday 9:30 to 2 and Friday 9:30 to 5:30.

Contacts and Resources

Police (☎ 242/339–1263).

Hospital (☎ 242/339–1249).

Great Inagua Tours (☎ 242/339–1862, FAX 242/339–1204) is a full-service information and sightseeing operation run by Larry and Marianne Ingraham. The company specializes in ecotourism and organizes bird-watching and wildlife-viewing excursions, but Larry can arrange anything from a flamingo tour or a bonefishing trip to car rental and accommodations. He is an invaluable source of information and assistance for planning and executing your visit.

LONG ISLAND

Never more than 4 mi wide, Long Island, one of Columbus's stopping-off places, lives up to its name; its Queen's Highway runs for close to 80 mi, through some 35 villages and farming towns where you'll always find a little straw market beckoning. One of the island's 4,500 residents once nicknamed the highway Rhythm Road, a reference perhaps to the many potholes that used to make driving it a syncopated ride. The government has finally completed construction, and Queen's Highway is now paved and smooth. The scenery on the way changes from shelving beaches and shallow bays on the west coast to rugged headlands that drop suddenly to the sea on the east coast. The southern end of the island has sea cliffs unique to the Bahamas.

Numbers in the margin correspond to points of interest on the Long Island map.

Cape Santa Maria and Stella Maris

㊹ Columbus named the island's northern tip, **Cape Santa Maria,** in honor of one of his ships. The area has truly stunning beaches—among the best in the country—and is the home of the elegant Cape Santa Maria Beach Resort.

Take a side trip on the unpaved road out to **Columbus Cove,** 1½ mi north of the Cape Santa Maria resort. Here are the monument and plaque that commemorate Columbus's landing, as well as tremendous views of the protected harbor he sailed into. Divers can explore the wreck of a ship, the M/V *Comberbach,* which lies just off the headland. The Stella Maris Resort sunk the leaky 103-ft freighter in 1985 to create an artificial reef and an excellent dive site nearly 100 ft under. The road to the cove is too rough for most vehicles, but it happens to be a fine walk. An easier way to reach the Cove is by boat.

㊺ **Stella Maris** means the Star of the Sea, and it's home to the all-encompassing Stella Maris Resort Club, along with its airport. In a world of its own, the resort has a marina, yacht club, and tiny shopping complex, with a bank, a post office, and a general store.

At nearby **Shark Reef,** divers can safely watch groups of a dozen sharks at a time being fed fish by a scuba master. Stella Maris lies about 12 mi south of Cape Santa Maria, off Queen's Highway past the ruins of the 19th-century **Adderley's Plantation.** Long Island was another Bahamian island where fleeing Loyalists attempted, with little success, to grow cotton. You can still see parts of the plantation's three buildings up to roof level; the remains of two other plantations, **Dunmore's** and **Gray's,** are also on the island.

Dining and Lodging

$ ✕ **Barbie's Ice Cream Restaurant and Bar.** Between Stella Maris and Cape Santa Maria, this casual spot serves sandwiches and burgers for lunch, and native Bahamian dinner specials—and, of course, ice cream. ⊠ *Queen's Hwy., Glintons,* ☎ *242/338–5009. No credit cards.*

$$$–$$$$ ✕🏨 **Cape Santa Maria Beach Resort.** This peaceful luxury resort has
★ nine colonial-style cottages spread along a gorgeous, 4-mi stretch of velvety white-sand beach. Spacious, one- and two-bedroom units contain marble-tile floors, two queen-size beds, elegant rattan furniture (including a writing desk and dresser), pastel linens and walls—but no TVs or phones. Dressing rooms have a well-lighted mirror and plenty of counter space, plus a separate, colorfully tiled room for the tub and toilet. Each unit also has its own large, fully furnished screened porch, which allows guests to enjoy beach views sans mosquitoes. Meals include both North American and Bahamian fare. By the fall of 1998, a new common building with a lobby, gear-rental office, and restaurant should be completed. The hotel attracts fishing enthusiasts—and can provide deep-sea, reef, and bonefishing excursions aboard one of its many boats. ⊠ *(Oak Bay Marine Group, 1327 Beach Dr., Victoria, BC V8S 2N4),* ☎ *242/338–5273 or 800/663–7090,* ℻ *242/338–6013 or 250/598–1361. 8 one-bedroom villas, 10 2-bedroom villas. Restaurant, 2 bars, air-conditioning, snorkeling, windsurfing, waterskiing, boating, fishing, bicycles, baby-sitting, coin laundry. AE, D, MC, V. All-inclusive.*

$$–$$$$ ✕🏨 **Stella Maris Resort Club.** Sitting atop a hilly east coast ridge overlooking the ocean, this resort attracts many Germans and other Europeans. Standard rooms and one-bedroom cottages are closest to the

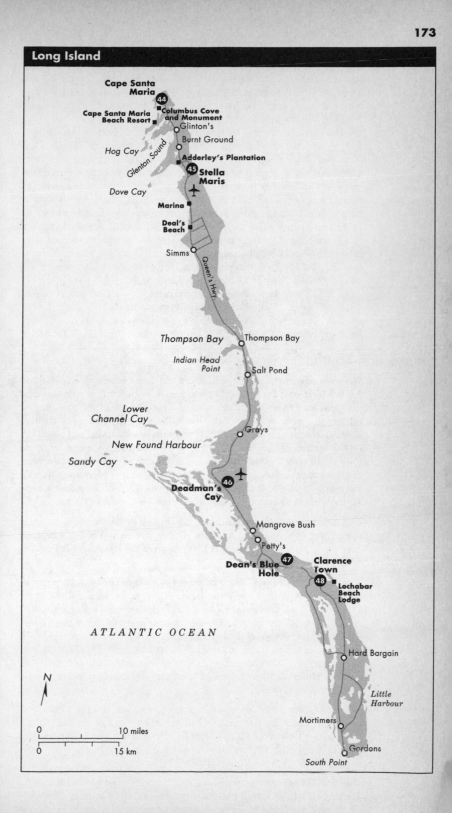

Cape Santa Maria

Cape Santa Maria Beach Resort

44

Columbus Cove and Monument

Glinton's

Burnt Ground

Hog Cay

Glenton Sound

Adderley's Plantation

45 Stella Maris

Dove Cay

Marina

Deal's Beach

Simms

Queen's Hwy.

Thompson Bay

Thompson Bay

Indian Head Point

Salt Pond

Lower Channel Cay

New Found Harbour

Grays

Sandy Cay

46

Deadman's Cay

Mangrove Bush

Petty's

Dean's Blue Hole

47

Clarence Town

48

Lochabar Beach Lodge

Hard Bargain

Little Harbour

Mortimers

Gordons

South Point

ATLANTIC OCEAN

N

0   10 miles

0   15 km

clubhouse and have tropical decor, with rattan furniture and tile floors. The resort also has two-, three-, and four-bedroom villas and bunga- lows, some with private pools. The clubhouse contains the dining room, bar, TV lounge, and gift shop. You can swim in three freshwa- ter pools or explore east coast beach coves with excellent snorkeling. Although diving and fishing are the most popular pursuits here, you can also take advantage of free snorkeling trips, glass-bottom boat cruises, Sunfish sailing, and bicycles. The club takes divers to Dean's Blue Hole and Shark Reef, as well as to a variety of wrecks on Conception Island, for world-class wall diving. Overnight trips can be arranged on the resort's 65-ft dive boat, which sleeps 14 people. In addition, Stella Maris has its own cabana preserve on Cape Santa Maria with a stun- ning beach; a shuttle goes there daily. The weekly "Out Island Cave Party" on Monday is a night of buffet BBQ, music, and dancing, set in a huge cavern on the property, and on Wednesdays there's a rum punch party and BBQ. The restaurant serves Bahamian and Continental cuisine. ⊠ *1100 Lee Wagener Blvd., No. 354, Fort Lauderdale, FL 33315;* ☎ *242/336–2051, 954/359–8236, or 800/426–0466,* ℻ *954/ 359–8238. 20 rooms, 12 one-bedroom cottages, 7 2-bedroom cottages, 4 beach houses. Bar, dining room, lounge, air-conditioning, kitch- enettes, refrigerators, 3 pools, Ping-Pong, dive shop, snorkeling, boat- ing, waterskiing, fishing, bicycles, laundry service. AE, MC, V. EP, MAP.*

Simms and South

Simms is one of the oldest settlements on Long Island, 8 mi south of Stella Maris past little pastel-color houses. Some of these abodes dis- play emblems to ward off evil spirits, an indication of the presence of Obeah, the superstitious voodoolike culture found on many of the Ba- hamian islands. There are a couple of quirky eats to be had roadside on this stretch of Queen's Highway. On the east side of the road, look for a small conch salad stand that's intermittantly open and prepares the snack right before your eyes. Immediately south of Simms, you may see rising smoke and tables out in the front yard of **Jeraldine's Jerk Pit** (no phone). These tasty eats are delectable.

The annual Long Island Regatta is held in **Salt Pond** every May among competing Bahamian-made boats. The regatta is the island's biggest event, and attracts contestants from all over the islands. Salt Pond is 10 mi south of Simms.

㊶ The town of **Deadman's Cay** is home for most of the island's popula- tion. Here you'll find a few shops, churches, and schools. Just east of Deadman's Cay, **Cartwright's Cave** has stalactites and stalagmites and eventually leads to the sea. The cave has apparently never been com- pletely explored, though Indian drawings were found on one wall. For guided cave tours, contact Leonard Cartwright (☎ 242/337–0235). There are several other caves, supposedly pirate-haunted, around Simms, Millers, and Salt Pond; a local should be able to point you in the right direction.

Between Deadman's Cay and Clarence Town, just past the settlement of Petty's, watch for the pink and white pillars that line the turnoff for **㊷** **Dean's Blue Hole.** At 660 ft, it's thought to be the second deepest blue hole in the world. Curious divers will want to contact the dive shop at Stella Maris (☎ 242/338–2050).

㊸ **Clarence Town** is the setting for Long Island's most celebrated land- marks, **St. Paul's Church** (Anglican) and **St. Peter's Church** (Catholic). They were both built by Father Jerome, a priest who is buried in a tomb in the Hermitage atop Cat Island's Mt. Alvernia. As an Anglican named John Hawes he constructed St. Paul's; later, after converting to Catholicism, he built St. Peter's. The architecture of the two churches is similar to that of the missions established by the Spaniards in California in the late 18th century. Clarence Town is the most picturesque settlement on Long Island, with a harbor and dock and the government headquarters in addition to the two churches. The town finally received electricity in 1997, but many residents still await telephones.

Dining and Lodging

$$ ✕ **Thompson Bay Inn.** Near Salt Pond, look for this bright yellow, local eatery, serving up Bahamian favorites such as boil fish, cracked conch, and peas 'n' rice. Be sure to call ahead for reservations. ✉ *Queen's Hwy., Thompson Bay,* ☎ *242/338–0052. Reservations essential. No credit cards.*

$ ✕ **The Forest.** Just south of Clarence Town, this bright pink restaurant serves spicy wings and potato skins, as well as cracked conch, barbecued chicken, and grouper fingers. Enjoy a drink at the bar—made of sea shells embedded in glossy resin—a game of pool, and, on Friday nights, live bands and dancing. ✉ *Queen's Hwy., Miley's,* ☎ *242/337–3287. No credit cards.*

$ ✕ **Kooters.** Grab a seat on the deck at this casual, immaculate spot for a lovely view of Mangrove Bush point and a conch burger or club sandwich with homemade fries. Daily specials range from ribs to seafood. Save room for one of the many flavors of ice cream. ✉ *Queen's Hwy., Mangrove Bush,* ☎ *242/337–0340. No credit cards. Closed Sun.*

$ 🏠 **Lochabar Beach Lodge.** This mellow, picturesque getaway is the best place to stay on southern Long Island. Owners Dick and Dawn Meehan have constructed two 600-sq-ft guest studios overlooking a dramatic blue hole, that exude thoughtful, casual charm. Designed to catch the tradewinds, double wooden doors open to views of the water and perpetual breezes. There are dinette islands with stools, although you can also eat alfresco on your deck. Dawn will take you into town to stock up on groceries at the beginning of your stay, but if you're not into cooking, the lodge has a meal plan with the Forest (☞ *above*)— $11 per person, per day, for lunch and dinner. At low tide, you can stroll the cove's entire beach, and round the point into Clarence Town. Your hosts will gladly arrange for a car rental and bonefishing excursions. ✉ *1 mi south of Clarence Town at Big Blue Hole, Box N-30330, Clarence Town,* ☎ FAX *242/337–3123 or* ☎ *242/337–0331. 2 rooms. Fans, kitchenettes, snorkeling, fishing. No credit cards. EP, FAP.*

Nightlife

On the north end of Long Island, **Potcakes** (✉ At the Stella Maris marina, ☎ 242/336–2106) is an attractive bar, open every night except Tuesdays. There's sure to be a congregation of boths locals and visitors shooting pool, watching satellite TV, or enjoying the expansive ocean view from the patio. Twice a month, the live reggae sounds of Nu Image get the dance floor hopping. Just south of Clarence Town, **The Forest** (✉ Queen's Hwy., Miley's, ☎ 242/337–3287), has dancing Friday nights.

Shopping

Wild Tamarind (✉ About ½ mi east of Queen's Hwy., Petty's, ☎ 242/337–0262) is Denis Knight's ceramics studio. Stop in for a lovely bowl, vase, or sculpture, but call first in case he's out fishing.

Long Island A to Z

Arriving and Departing

BY MAIL BOAT

M/V *Abilin* makes a weekly trip from Nassau to Clarence Town, on the south end of the island. The boat leaves Nassau on Tuesday; the trip takes 18 hours and the fare is $45. The M/V *Sherice M* leaves Nassau on a varying schedule with stops in Salt Pond, Deadman's Cay, and Seymour's. The travel time is 15 hours; fare is $45. For more information contact the **Dockmaster's office** (☎ 242/393–1064) at Potter's Cay, Nassau.

BY PLANE

If you're a guest at Cape Santa Maria or Stella Maris, fly into the Stella Maris airport. Use the Deadman's Cay airport if you're staying in Clarence Town. Landing at the wrong airport will mean a $120 cab ride.

Bahamasair (☎ 242/339–4415 or 800/222–4262) flies nearly daily from Nassau to Stella Maris and Deadman's Cay. **Island Express** (☎ 954/359–0380) flies from Fort Lauderdale to the Stella Maris airport Thursday–Sunday. **Stella Maris** (☎ 954/359–8236, 242/336–2106, or 800/426–0466) has charter flights from Exuma and Nassau to Stella Maris. Taxis meet incoming flights. The fare to the resort from the airport is $4.

Getting Around

BY CAR

Taylor's Rentals (☎ 242/338–7001) rents high-quality cars for the most reasonable rates on the island. Hotels will also arrange for guests' automobile rental.

BY SCOOTER

Taylor's Rentals (☎ 242/338–7001) has scooters available for $46 per day, $30 per half day.

Opening and Closing Times

At the Stella Maris resort, the **Bank of Nova Scotia** (☎ 242/338–2002) is open Tuesday and Thursday 10–2; farther south, the Deadman's Cay branch is open Monday–Thursday 9–1 and Friday 9–5. **Royal Bank of Canada** has a branch in Grays, and another on Deadman's Cay; hours for both branches are Monday–Thursday 9–1 and Friday 9–5.

Contacts and Resources

EMERGENCIES

Police: Clarence Town (☎ 231); Deadman's Cay (☎ 242/337–0444); Simms (☎ 242/338–8555).

SAN SALVADOR

On October 12, 1492, Christopher Columbus disturbed the lives of the peaceful Lucayan Indians by landing on the island of Guanahani, which he named San Salvador. He knelt on the beach and claimed the land for Spain. (Though findings of a computerized study published in a 1986 *National Geographic* article, point to Samana Cay, 60 mi southeast, as the exact point of the weary explorer's landing.) Three monuments on the 7-by-12-mi island commemorate Columbus's arrival, and the 500th-anniversary celebration of the event was officially focused here in 1992.

A 17th-century pirate named George Watling, who frequently sought shelter on the island, changed San Salvador's name to Watling's Island. The Bahamas government switched the name back to San Salvador in 1926.

Numbers in the margin correspond to points of interest on the San Salvador map.

Fernandez Bay to Riding Rock Point

In 1492, the inspiring sight that greeted Christopher Columbus by moonlight at 2 AM was a terrain of gleaming beaches and far-reaching forest. The peripatetic traveler and his crews—"men from Heaven," the locals called them—steered the *Niña, Pinta,* and *Santa María* warily

49 among the coral reefs and anchored, so it is recorded, in **Fernandez Bay.** A cross erected in 1956 by Columbus scholar Ruth C. Durlacher Wolper Malvin stands at his approximate landing spot. Ms. Malvin's **New World Museum** (no phone), near North Victoria Hill on the east coast, contains artifacts from the era of the Lucayans. Admission to the museum is free; it's open by appointment (your hotel can make arrangements). An underwater monument marks the place where the *Santa María* anchored. Nearby, another monument commemorates the passage of the Olympic flame on its journey from Greece to Mexico City in 1968.

Fernandez Bay is close to what is now the main community of **Cockburn Town,** mid-island on the western shore. Queen's Highway encircles the island from Cockburn Town, where the weekly mail boat docks. This small village's narrow streets contain two churches, a commissioner's office, a police station, a courthouse, a library, a clinic, a drugstore, and a telephone station.

50 Columbus first spotted and recorded **Riding Rock Point.** The area now serves as the home for the Riding Rock Inn, a popular resort for divers. Just north of the point is the island's other resort, the Club Med–Columbus Isle, set at the foot of a 2-mi-long, gorgeous beach. Riding Rock Point is about a mile north of Cockburn Town.

Dining and Lodging

$$$$ ✕🏨 **Club Med–Columbus Isle.** This 80-acre village opened in 1992 and
★ is billed as the most luxurious of all the Club Med resorts, with state-of-the-art dive facilities, elegant rooms, and a long stretch of private beach. German-born interior designer Gisela Trigano has used sun, moon, and stars motifs throughout the resort representing that which guided Columbus to the New World. Most of the decorations were imported from Asia, Africa, and South America, including feathered Brazilian headdresses, Indian birdcages, 18th-century Pakistani pillars, Thai rice-paper flowers, Vietnamese jars, and carved doors from Mali. Hundreds of palm trees from Miami enhance the sparse landscape and protect the beach from erosion. The buildings are painted brilliant blues, greens, yellows, pinks, and purples. All rooms have patios or balconies, a walk-in closet, TV, telephone, and are brightly fitted with crisp turquoise spreads, white walls, tile floors, and handcrafted furniture and art. Bathrooms have plenty of mirrors and counter space and excellent water pressure in the tiled shower. Guided bike tours introduce vacationers to island life beyond the resort. Unlike some Club Meds, this one caters primarily to upscale couples, and the atmosphere is more low-key than at most. More than 40 pristine dive sites are a half hour from shore. The dive facilities include three custom-made 45-ft catamarans and a decompression chamber. ⊠ *3 mi north of Riding Rock Point (⊠ 40 W. 57th St., New York, NY 10019),* ☎ *242/331–2000 or 800/258–2633,* FAX *242/331–2222. 260 rooms. 3 restaurants, lounge, refrigerators, pool, beauty salon, massage, 9 tennis courts, exercise room, diving, bicycles, nightclub, theater, laundry service, car rental. AE, MC, V.*

$$ ✕🏨 **Riding Rock Inn.** This motel-style resort attracts divers with three dives per day to excellent offshore reefs and a drop-off wall teeming with life. It's also the only place to stay on San Salvador where you can avoid the relentless enthusiasm of the Club Med staff. The inn's

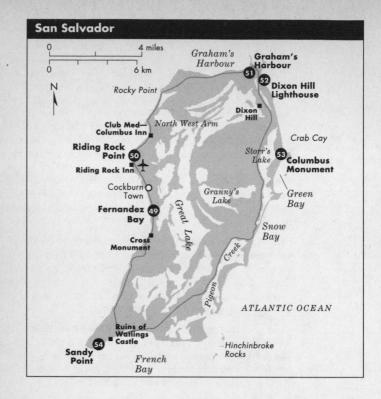

San Salvador

(map labels) Graham's Harbour · Graham's Harbour · Dixon Hill Lighthouse · Rocky Point · Dixon Hill · Crab Cay · Club Med—Columbus Inn · North West Arm · Storr's Lake · Columbus Monument · Riding Rock Point · Riding Rock Inn · Green Bay · Cockburn Town · Granny's Lake · Great Lake · Fernandez Bay · Snow Bay · Cross Monument · Pigeon Creek · ATLANTIC OCEAN · Ruins of Watlings Castle · Sandy Point · Hinchinbroke Rocks · French Bay · 0 4 miles · 0 6 km · N

three buildings house rooms facing either the ocean or the freshwater pool. Standard rooms are painted off-white, with wooden furniture and redwood patios. Deluxe modern oceanfront rooms (recommended) have tile floors, wicker furniture, telephones, and cable TV. The restaurant serves Bahamian dishes as well as such American favorites as hearty pancake breakfasts. ⊠ *Riding Rock Point (⊠ 1170 Lee Wagener Blvd., Suite 103, Fort Lauderdale, FL 33315), ☎ 954/359–8353 or 800/272–1492, ℻ 954/359–8254. 42 rooms, 2 villas. Restaurant, bar, air-conditioning, refrigerators, pool, tennis court, dive center, fishing, bicycles. MC, V (5% surcharge). EP, FAP.*

Outdoor Activities and Sports

Club Med (☎ 242/331–2000) has dive boats and a decompression chamber. In addition, there are nine tennis courts, sailing, and windsurfing, among other sports.

Riding Rock Inn (☎ 800/272–1492) is affiliated with Guanahani Dive Ltd., which uses mostly buoyed sites to avoid any damage to the marine environment by dropping anchor. It also offers resort and certification courses, and a modern underwater photographic facility. They rent all kinds of camera gear and do slide shows of divers' work. Riding Rock also rents bicycles and snorkel gear and will arrange fishing trips ($400 for a half day and $600 for a full day). The waters hold tuna, blue marlin, and in the winter, wahoo.

Around San Salvador

⑤ Columbus describes **Graham's Harbour** in his diaries as large enough "to hold all the ships of Christendom." A complex of buildings near the harbor houses the **Bahamian Field Station**, a biological and geological research institution that attracts scientists and students from all over the world.

52 A couple of miles south of Graham's Harbour stands **Dixon Hill Lighthouse.** Built around 1856, it is still hand-operated, and the light from its small kerosene lamp beams out to sea every 15 seconds to a maximum distance of 19 mi, depending on visibility. The lighthouse keeper must continually wind the apparatus that projects the light. A climb to the top of the 160-ft landmark offers a fabulous view of the island, which includes a series of inland lakes. The keeper is present 24 hours a day. Knock on his door and he'll take you up to the top and explain the machinery. Drop $1 in the box when you sign the guest book on the way out.

53 No road leads to the **Columbus Monument** on Crab Cay. You have to make your way along a bushy path. This initial tribute to the explorer was erected by the *Chicago Herald* newspaper in 1892, far from the presumed site of Columbus's landing. A series of little villages winds south of here for several miles, such as Holiday Track and Polly Hill, that once contained plantations.

54 **Sandy Point** anchors the southwestern end of the island, overlooking French Bay. Here, on a hill, you'll find the **ruins of Watling's Castle,** named after the 17th-century pirate. The ruins are more likely the remains of a Loyalist plantation house than a castle from buccaneering days. You can walk from Queen's Highway up the hill to see what is left of the ruins, which are now engulfed in vegetation.

San Salvador A to Z

Arriving and Departing
BY MAIL BOAT

M/V *Lady Francis,* out of Nassau, leaves Tuesday for San Salvador and Rum Cay. The long trip takes 18 hours, for a fare of $40. For information on specific schedules and fares, contact the **Dockmaster's office** (☎ 242/393–1064) at Potter's Cay, Nassau.

BY PLANE

Taxis meet planes at Cockburn Town Airport. Club Med meets all guests at the airport (your account is charged $10 for the three-minute transfer). Riding Rock provides complimentary transportation for guests.

Air Sunshine (☎ 954/434–8900 or 800/327–8900) flies from Fort Lauderdale into Cockburn Town. **Bahamasair** (☎ 242/339–4415 or 800/222–4262) flies into Cockburn Town from Nassau and also offers direct service from Miami three days a week. **Riding Rock Inn** (☎ 954/359–8353 or 800/272–1492) has charter flights every Saturday from Fort Lauderdale.

Getting Around
Riding Rock Inn (☎ 954/359–8353 or 800/272–1492) rents cars for $85 a day and bicycles for $8 a day.

Contacts and Resources
EMERGENCIES

Police (☎ 218); **Medical Clinic** (☎ 207).

OUT ISLANDS A TO Z

Contacts and Resources

Emergencies
There are health centers and clinics scattered throughout the islands, but in the event of emergency illnesses or accidents requiring fast transportation to the United States, **Air Medical Services** (☎ 800/443–

0013) provides aero-medical services out of Fort Lauderdale International Airport. Its 14 aircraft are equipped with sophisticated medical equipment and a trained staff of doctors, nurses, and paramedics.

Guided Tours

Adventure Vacations (✉ 10612 Beaver Dam Rd., Hunt Valley, MD 21030, ☎ 800/638–9040), **Bahamas Travel Network** (✉ 1047 S.E. 17th St., Fort Lauderdale, FL 33316, ☎ 954/467–1133 or 800/513–5535), **Caribbean Trends** (✉ 110 E. Broward Blvd., Box 1525, Fort Lauderdale, FL 33301, ☎ 954/522–1440 or 800/221–6666, FAX 954/357–4687), **Changes in L'Attitudes** (✉ 4986 113th Ave. N, Clearwater, FL 34620, ☎ 813/573–3536 or 800/282–8272), **Ibis Tours** (✉ 5798 Sunpoint Circle, Boynton Beach, FL 33437, ☎ 800/525–9411 or for kayak tours).

For captained yacht charters, contact **The Moorings** (☎ 242/367–4000 or 800/535–7289) in Marsh Harbour. This is the Bahamas' division of one of the foremost yacht-charter agencies in the world, which provides every service needed for yachters—from provisions to professional captains. **Swift Yacht Charters** (✉ 209 S. Main St., Sherborn, MA 01770, ☎ 800/866–8340) also has yacht charters.

Americanada (✉ 139 Sauve O, Montréal, Québec H3L LY4, ☎ 514/384–6431) and **Holiday House** (✉ 110 Richmond St. E, Suite 304, Toronto, Ontario M5C 1P1, ☎ 416/364–2433).

Visitor Information

The **Bahama Out Islands Promotion Board** (✉ 1100 Lee Wagener Blvd., No. 204, Fort Lauderdale, FL 33315, ☎ 954/359–8099 or 800/688–4752) has a fantastic staff that provides extra-mile information about lodging, travel, and activities in the islands and can book reservations at many of the hotels. On request, the board will send color brochures about island resorts.

The Bahamas Ministry of Tourism's **Bahamas Tourist Office** (✉ Box N-3701, Market Plaza, Bay St., Nassau, Bahamas, ☎ 242/322–7500 can assist with travel plans and information; see Visitor Information in the Gold Guide for the list of branch offices in the United States, Canada, and the U.K.

5 Turks and Caicos Islands

Descending into the warm sea, the diver is supported like a balloon suspended in space. Weightless and floating free, she sways with the whim of gentle currents. Beneath her, a turquoise parrot fish pecks at a coral wall that's painted with muted indigos, lavenders, yellows, and pinks. The diver delicately places her pinky finger on a pink-tipped sea anemone; it clings playfully, not wanting to let go. She gently pulls her hand away and then swims off to explore more of this world of grace and color.

Updated by
JoAnn
Milivojevic

SCUBA DIVERS and beach aficionados have long known about the Turks and Caicos (pronounced *kay*-kos). To them, this British Crown colony of more than 40 islands and small cays (only eight of which are inhabited) is a gem that offers priceless stretches of sand and offshore reefs that are rich in marine life. Situated in an archipelago that trails off the arch of the Bahamas, the Turks and Caicos lies 575 mi southeast of Miami and about 90 mi north of Haiti. The total landmass of these two groups of islands is 193 square mi; the total population is some 12,350.

The Turks Islands include Grand Turk, which is the capital and seat of government, and Salt Cay, with a population of about 200. It is claimed that Columbus's first landfall was on Grand Turk. Legend also has it that these islands were named by early settlers who thought the scarlet blossoms on the local cactus resembled the Turkish fez.

Approximately 22 mi west of Grand Turk, across the 7,000-ft-deep Christopher Columbus Passage, is the Caicos group: South, East, West, Middle, and North Caicos and Providenciales (nicknamed Provo). South Caicos, Middle Caicos, North Caicos, and Provo are the only inhabited islands in this group; Pine Cay and Parrot Cay are the only inhabited cays. "Caicos" is derived from *cayos,* the Spanish word for cay, and is believed to mean, appropriately, "string of islands."

Around 1678, Bermudians began to rake salt from the flats on these islands, returning to Bermuda to sell their crop. Despite French and Spanish attacks and pirate raids, the Bermudians persisted and established a trade that became the bedrock of the Bermudian economy. In 1766 Andrew Symmers settled here to hold the islands for England. Later, loyalists from Georgia obtained land grants in the Caicos Islands, imported slaves, and continued the lifestyle of the pre–Civil War American South.

Today, the Turks and Caicos are known for their booming banking and insurance institutions, which lure investors from the United States and beyond. The government has also devised a long-term plan to promote tourism. Provo, in particular, is well on its way to becoming a Caribbean destination as well as an offshore financial center. Mass tourism, however, is not in the cards; government guidelines promote a "quality, not quantity" policy, including conservation awareness and firm restrictions on building heights and casino construction. And, without a port for cruise ships, the islands remain uncrowded and peaceful.

THE TURKS

Grand Turk

Bermudian colonial architecture abounds on this string bean of an island (just 6 mi long and 1 mi wide). Buildings have walled-in courtyards to keep wandering donkeys from nibbling on the foliage. The island caters to divers, and it's no wonder: the Wall, a perpendicular slice of vertical coral mountain, is a quick swim out from many lodges. In fact, divers will usually spend their surface interval time comfortably on shore rather than confined to a boat.

Exploring Grand Turk

Pristine beaches with vistas of turquoise waters, small local settlements, historic ruins, and native flora and fauna are among the sights to see on Grand Turk. Keep an eye out for fruit-bearing trees like lime, papaya, and custard apple. Birds to look for include the great blue heron, the woodstar hummingbird, and the squawking Cuban crow. Fewer than 4,000 people live on Grand Turk, a 7½-square-mi island, and it's hard to get lost as there aren't many roads. Given the light traffic, you may prefer to explore on a motor scooter.

Numbers in the margin correspond to points of interest on the Turks and Caicos Islands map.

❶ **Cockburn Town.** The buildings in this, the colony's capital and seat of government, reflect the 19th-century Bermudian style of architecture. The narrow streets are lined with low stone walls and old street lamps, now powered by electricity. Horses and cattle wander around as if they own the place, and the occasional donkey cart clatters by, carrying a load of water or freight. In one of the oldest stone buildings in the Turks and Caicos, the **Turks & Caicos National Museum** houses the Molasses Reef wreck of 1513, the earliest shipwreck discovered in the Americas. The natural-history exhibits include artifacts left by Taino, African, North American, Bermudian, French, and Latin American settlers. An impressive addition to the museum is the coral reef and sea-life exhibit, faithfully modeled on a popular dive site just off the island. ⊠ *Duke St., Cockburn Town,* ☎ *649/946–2160.* ⊡ *$5.* ⊙ *Mon.–Tues. and Thurs.–Fri. 9–4, Wed. 9–6, Sat. 10–1.*

Beaches

There are more than 230 mi of beaches in the Turks and Caicos Islands, ranging from secluded coves to miles-long stretches. Most beaches are soft coralline sand. Tiny cays offer complete isolation for nude sunbathing and skinny-dipping. Many are accessible only by boat. **Governor's Beach,** a long white strip on the west coast of Grand Turk, is one of the nicest beaches on this island; it's very long and wide, offering you plenty of sparkling, powder-soft sand on which to stroll.

Dining

Like everything else on these islands, dining out is a very laid-back affair, which is not to say that it's cheap. Because of the high cost of importing all edibles, the price of a meal is usually higher than in the United States. Reservations are generally not required, and dress is casual.

CATEGORY	COST*
$$$	over $25
$$	$15–$25
$	under $15

*per person for a three-course meal, excluding drinks, service, and 7% sales tax

AMERICAN

$$ ✕ **Sandpiper.** Candles flicker on the Sandpiper's terrace, which is set beside a flower-filled courtyard at the Sitting Pretty Hotel (☞ Lodging, *below*). The leisurely pace here creates a relaxing setting to experience such blackboard specialties as lobster, filet mignon, seafood platter, or pork chops with applesauce. ⊠ *Duke St., Cockburn Town,* ☎ *649/946–2232. AE, D, MC, V.*

$$ ✕ **Secret Garden.** Menu highlights at the Salt Raker Inn's (☞ Lodging, *below*) restaurant, include a seafood platter, grilled lobster tail, pork chops, and roast leg of lamb. For dessert, try the tasty apple pie. The Sunday dinner and sing-along are popular. The outdoor garden is beautifully landscaped with hibiscus, bougainvillea, palms, and tropical plants; sea nets, glass balls and local paintings round out the decor. ⊠ *Duke St., Cockburn Town,* ☎ *649/946–2260. AE, D, MC, V.*

CARIBBEAN

$ ✕ **Pepper Pot.** Beachside on Front Street is a little blue shack where Peanuts Butterfield makes her famous spicy conch fritters. ✉ *Front St., Cockburn Town, no phone. No credit cards.*

ECLECTIC

$–$$$ ✕ **Turk's Head Inn.** The menu changes daily at the lively restaurant in the Turk's Head Inn (☞ *Lodging, below*), touted by many residents as the best on the island. Some staples include escargots, pâté, and a handful of other delectables, including local grouper fingers perfectly fried for fish-and-chips. Look for lobster, quiche, steaks, and homemade soups on the blackboard menu. You may not want to leave after your meal—come nightfall, the inn's bar is abuzz with local gossip and mirthful chatter. ✉ *Duke St., Cockburn Town,* ☎ 649/946–2466. AE, MC, V.

SEAFOOD

$ ✕ **Regal Begal.** Drop by this popular local eatery for local specialties such as cracked conch, minced lobster, and fish-and-chips. The atmosphere is casual and the decor unmemorable, but the portions are large and the prices easy on your wallet. ✉ *Hospital Rd., Cockburn Town,* ☎ 649/946–2274. *No credit cards.*

$ ✕ **Water's Edge.** Relaxed waterfront dining awaits you at this pleasantly rustic eatery. The limited menu covers the basics with a twist—from barbecued grouper to a fresh seafood crepe. A kids' menu is also available. The food is authentic and filling, and the view at sunset breathtaking, but the irresistible homemade pies are enough to justify a visit. ✉ *Duke St., Cockburn Town,* ☎ 649/946–1680. *MC, V. Closed Mon.*

Lodging

Throughout the islands, accommodations range from small (sometimes non-air-conditioned) inns to splashy resorts to the ultimate-in-luxury hotels. Most of the medium and large hotels offer a choice of EP and MAP. People who don't rent a car or scooter tend to eat at their hotels, making MAP a better option.

Another option that's popular, particularly with families, is renting a self-contained villa or private home; contact the **Ministry of Tourism** (☎ 649/946–2321) three to six months in advance for more information. Please note that the government hotel tax does not apply to guest houses with fewer than four rooms. Because of the popularity of scuba diving on all the islands, virtually all the hotels offer dive packages. Dive packagers offering air-hotel-dive packages include **Dive Provo** (☎ 800/234–7768) and **Undersea Adventures** (☎ 800/234–7768).

CATEGORY	COST*
$$$$	over $250
$$$	$170–$250
$$	$110–$170
$	under $110

All prices are for a standard double room in winter, excluding 8% tax and 10%–15% service charge.

$$ ▥ **Arawak Inn and Beach Club.** These yellow, condo-style accommodations have private bedrooms, tiled baths, kitchens, and living rooms with sofa beds. With so much space, you and your children (those under 12 stay free) will probably love it here. The complex is steps away from a fabulous white-sand beach, and the management offers free shuttle service into town daily. Don't feel like cooking? The restaurant serves up delicious Caribbean meals. The hotel offers dive packages through a shop just a two-minute walk down the main street. ✉ *Near White*

Sands Beach (Box 190), Cockburn Town, ☎ *649/946–2277 or 888/ 332–3113 (reservations service),* FAX *649/946–2279. 15 units. Restaurant, bar, air-conditioning, pool, horseback riding. MC, V.*

$$ 🏨 **Guanahani Beach Hotel.** Sun worshipers take note: this hotel owns one of Grand Turk's finest stretches. The palm-tree-lined property is also popular with honeymooners, so you may find an air of romance. The rooms all have ocean views, pale ceramic tile floors, full baths, two double beds, and primary-color Caribbean-print spreads and curtains. You can rent a crewed 35-ft yacht for day trips or moonlight rides, and dive packages are available through a dive shop, just steps away. ✉ *Box 178, Cockburn Town,* ☎ *649/946–2135 or 800/725–2822,* FAX *649/946–1460. 16 rooms. Restaurant, 2 bars, pool. MC, V.*

$$ 🏨 **Salt Raker Inn.** Across the street from the beach, this galleried house was the home of a Bermudian shipwright 180 years ago. What the guest quarters lack in elegance they make up for in cleanliness and comfort. Each has tile floors, air-conditioning, and a mini-refrigerator. Ask for one of the three garden rooms, which have screened porches, or opt for a suite and an ocean view. (Note that dive packages are available.) The fare at the Secret Garden (☞ Dining, *above*) is straightforward; you can even get a piece of apple pie. ✉ *Duke St. (Box 1), Cockburn Town,* ☎ *649/946–2260,* FAX *649/946–2817.* ✉ *U.K. reservations: 44 Birchington Rd., London NW6 4LJ,* ☎ *0171/328–6474. 10 rooms, 2 suites. Restaurant, bar, air-conditioning, bicycles. AE, D, MC, V. EP.*

$$ 🏨 **Sitting Pretty Hotel.** Cockburn Town's main drag halves this hotel.
★ On one side, comfortable, lodge-style rooms and balconied suites with kitchens run along a white sand beach. Beachfront rooms have bamboo furniture, colorful Haitian art, and tidy baths. On the other side of the street are rooms that ooze island charm, as well as a pool, and a garden. The Sandpiper (☞ Dining, *above*) is a good place for a steak or lobster dinner. ✉ *Duke St. (Box 42), Cockburn Town,* ☎ *649/946– 2232,* FAX *649/946–2877. 40 rooms, 2 suites. 2 restaurants, 2 bars, air-conditioning, room service, pool, dive shop, windsurfing, boating, bicycles, shop, baby-sitting, travel services. AE, MC, V. EP, MAP.*

$$ 🏨 **Turk's Head Inn.** Built in 1850 by a prosperous salt miner, this building has served as the American consulate and as the governor's guest house (Queen Elizabeth reportedly took a room here on her last visit). Under new ownership as of 1997, many renovations are promised including restoring antique bedroom furniture. Rooms are currently done in peaches or limes and have mini-refrigerators and coffeemakers. An assortment of expats have made this place their stomping ground—the bar and restaurant (☞ Dining, *above*) bustle at night. In the front courtyard, an oversize hammock is the perfect place from which to admire the well-tended garden. The beach is only a few strides away, and dive packages are available. ✉ *Duke St. (Box 58), Cockburn Town,* ☎ *649/946–2466,* FAX *649/946–2825. 7 rooms, 1 apartment. Restaurant, bar, air-conditioning. AE, MC, V.*

$–$$ 🏨 **Coral Reef Beach Club.** One- and two-bedroom units here have full kitchens, air-conditioning, and contemporary furnishings. A stay here puts you just a short drive from town and just steps from the beach. ✉ *Near The Ridge (Box 10),* ☎ *649/946–2055,* FAX *649/946–2911. 18 units. Restaurant, bar, air-conditioning, pool, hot tub, tennis court, health club, shop. AE, MC, V. EP, MAP.*

Nightlife

On Grand Turk, a fun crowd gathers at **Turk's Head Inn** (✉ Duke St., ☎ 649/946–2466) almost every night. There's folk and pop music at the **Salt Raker Inn** (✉ Duke St., ☎ 649/946–2260) on Wednesday and Sunday nights. On weekends and holidays, head over to the **Nookie Hill Club** (✉ Nookie Hill, no phone) for dancing.

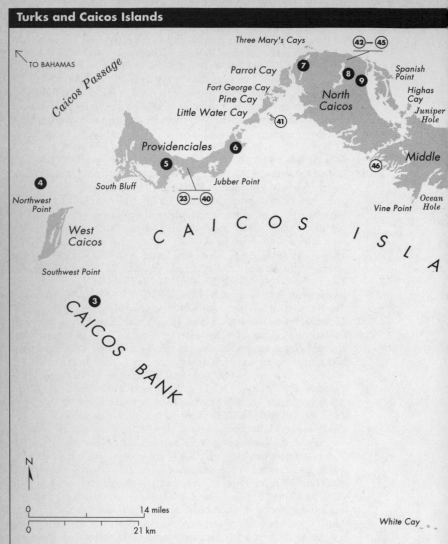

Exploring

Balfour Town, **2**
Cockburn
Harbour, **11**
Cockburn Town, **1**
Conch Bar Caves, **10**
Downtown Provo, **5**
Flamingo Pond, **8**
Island Sea Center, **6**
Kew, **9**

Molasses Reef, **3**
Northwest Reef, **4**
Sandy Point, **7**

Dining

Alfred's Place, **32**
Anacaona, **24**
Banana Boat, **39**
Caicos Cafe, **38**
Dora's, **33**
Fast Eddie's, **36**
Gecko Grille, **27**
Hey, José, **40**
Pepper Pot, **18**

Pub on the Bay, **37**
Regal Begal, **19**
Sandpiper, **15**
Secret Garden, **14**
The Terrace, **35**
Top O' the Cove
Gourmet
Delicatessen, **34**
Turk's Head Inn, **16**
Water's Edge, **20**

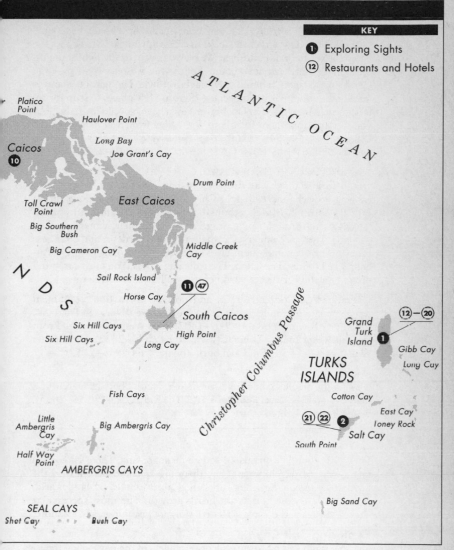

ATLANTIC OCEAN

Platico Point

Haulover Point

Long Bay

Joe Grant's Cay

Caicos ❿

Drum Point

Toll Crawl Point

East Caicos

Big Southern Bush

Big Cameron Cay

Middle Creek Cay

N D S

Sail Rock Island

Horse Cay

❶❶ ㊼

Six Hill Cays

Six Hill Cays

Long Cay

South Caicos

High Point

Christopher Columbus Passage

Grand Turk Island

⑫—⑳

❶

Gibb Cay

Long Cay

TURKS ISLANDS

Fish Cays

Cotton Cay

East Cay

Little Ambergris Cay

Big Ambergris Cay

㉑ ㉒ ❷

Ioney Rock

Salt Cay

Half Way Point

South Point

AMBERGRIS CAYS

SEAL CAYS

Big Sand Cay

Shot Cay

Bush Cay

Lodging

Arawak Inn and Beach Club, **12**

Beaches, **23**

Blue Horizons Resort, **46**

Club Caribe Beach & Harbour Hotel, **47**

Club Med Turkoise, **25**

Club Vacanze Prospect of Whitby Hotel, **42**

Coral Reef Beach Club, **17**

Erebus Inn Resort, **29**

Grace Bay Club, **24**

Guanahani Beach Hotel, **13**

JoAnne's B&B, **45**

Le Deck Hotel & Beach Club, **26**

Meridian Club, **41**

Mount Pleasant Guest House, **22**

Ocean Beach Hotel Condominiums, **43**

Ocean Club, **27**

Pelican Beach Hotel, **44**

Salt Raker Inn, **14**

Sitting Pretty Hotel, **15**

Treasure Beach Villas, **30**

Turk's Head Inn, **16**

Turquoise Reef Resort & Casino, **28**

Turtle Cove Inn, **31**

Windmills Plantation, **21**

Outdoor Activities and Sports

BICYCLING

The island's flat terrain isn't very taxing, and most roads have hard surfaces. On Duke Street in Cockburn Town, you can wheel past the beautiful Bermudian buildings. Weave your way to the lighthouse on the island's northernmost point. Follow the western road past the Coral Reef Beach Club and then back to town. Though the island is small, take water with you because there are few places to stop for refreshment. Most hotels in Cockburn Town have bicycles available, but you can also rent them for about $10 a day from **Salt Raker Inn** (⊠ Duke St., ☎ 649/946–2260), **Sea Eye Diving** (☎ 649/946–1407), and the **Sitting Pretty Hotel** (⊠ Duke St., ☎ 649/946–2232).

SCUBA DIVING AND SNORKELING

Grand Turk's famed Wall drops more than 7,000 ft and is one side of a 22-mi-wide channel called the Christopher Columbus Passage. From January through March, about 6,000 eastern Atlantic humpback whales swim through this passage en route to their winter breeding grounds. There are undersea cathedrals, coral gardens, and countless tunnels. The site names themselves are intriguing: Rolling Hill, The Anchor, The Library, The Chair, The Amazing Abyss. You must carry and present a valid certificate card before you'll be allowed to dive.

Operations that organize trips and provide instruction, equipment rentals (including underwater gear) are **Sea Eye Divers** (⊠ Duke St., Cockburn Town, ☎ FAX 649/946–1407), **Blue Water Divers** (⊠ Front St., Salt Raker Inn, Cockburn Town, ☎ 649/946–2432), and **Off the Wall Divers** (⊠ Pond St., Cockburn Town, ☎ 649/946–2159).

TENNIS

Though most folks come here for diving, landlubbers in search of a match can try the **Coral Reef Resort** (⊠ The Ridge, ☎ 649/946–2055), which has one lighted court.

Salt Cay

Only 200 people live on this 2½-square-mi dot of land. There's not much in the way of development, but there are splendid beaches on the north coast. As on the other Turks and Caicos islands, the land is arid, with mostly cactus and scrub brush growth. The most spectacular sites are beneath the waves: 10 dive sites are just minutes from shore.

Exploring Salt Cay

Salt sheds and salt ponds are silent reminders of the days when the island was a leading producer of salt. February through March, whales pass by on the way to their winter breeding grounds.

❷ **Balfour Town.** What little development there is on Salt Cay is found in this town. It's home to the Windmills Plantation hotel, the Mount Pleasant Guest House, and a few stores that sell tourist items like hand-woven baskets, T-shirts, convenience foods and beach items.

Beaches

There are superb beaches on the north coast of **Salt Cay. Big Sand Cay,** 7 mi to the south of Salt Cay, is also known for its excellent beaches.

Lodging

For general information *and* price categories, *see* Lodging *under* Grand Turk, *above.*

$$$$ **Windmills Plantation.** The attraction here is the lack of distraction: ★ no nightlife, no cruise ships, and no shopping. Owner-manager-architect Guy Lovelace and his interior designer wife, Patricia, built the hotel

as their version of a colonial-era plantation. The great house has four suites, each with a sitting area, a four-poster bed, ceiling fans, and a veranda or balcony with a sea view. All have a mix of antique English and wicker furniture. Four other rooms are housed in two adjacent buildings. Room rates for two people include snorkeling equipment, three meals, and unlimited bar drinks, wine, and beer. ⊠ *North Beach Rd.,* ☎ *649/946–6962 or 800/822–7715 (reservations service),* FAX *649/946–6930. 4 rooms or 4 suites. Restaurant, bar, pool, hiking, horseback riding, beach, snorkeling, fishing, library. AE, MC, V. EP.*

$ 🏠 **Mount Pleasant Guest House.** This simple, somewhat rustic hotel offers guests inexpensive lodging at a remote location. ⊠ *Balfour Town,* ☎ *649/946–6927 or 800/821–6670. 7 rooms, 1 with bath. Restaurant, bar, horseback riding, scuba diving, bicycles, library. MC, V.*

Scuba Diving and Snorkeling

Scuba divers can explore the *Endymion,* a recently discovered, 140-ft, wooden-hull British warship that sank in 1790. It's just off the southern point of Salt Cay. **Porpoise Divers** (⊠ Salt Cay, ☎ 649/946–6927) rents all the necessary equipment.

THE CAICOS

West Caicos

Accessible only by boat, this island is uninhabited and untamed, and there are no facilities whatsoever. A glorious white beach stretches for 1 mi along the northwest point, and the offshore diving here is among the most exotic in the islands. A wall inhabited by countless species of large marine life begins ¼ mi out. If you do tour West Caicos, take along several vats of insect repellent. It won't help much with the sharks, but it should fend off the mosquitoes and sand flies. Be advised, too, that the interior is overgrown with dense shrubs, including manchineel, whose green fruit is poisonous. Sap and even raindrops falling from the trees onto your skin can be painful.

Exploring West Caicos

❸ Molasses Reef. It is rumored to be the final resting place of the *Pinta,* which is thought to have been wrecked here in the early 1500s. Over the past few centuries numerous wrecks have occurred in the area between West Caicos and Provo, and author Peter Benchley is among the treasure seekers who have been lured to this island.

❹ Northwest Reef. The site offers great stands of elkhorn coral and acres of staghorn brambles. But it's only for experienced divers. The wall starts deep, the currents are strong, and there are sharks.

Providenciales

In the mid-18th century, so the story goes, a French ship was wrecked near here, and the survivors were washed ashore on an island they gratefully christened La Providentielle. Under the Spanish, the name was changed to Providenciales. Today, about 6,000 people live on Provo (as everybody calls it), a considerable number of whom are expatriate U.S. and Canadian businesspeople and retirees. The island's 44 square mi are by far the most developed in the Turks and Caicos.

Exploring Providenciales

❺ Downtown Provo. Near Providenciales International Airport, the downtown is really a strip mall that houses car-rental agencies, law offices, boutiques, banks, and other businesses.

⑥ **Island Sea Center.** On the northeast coast, this is the place to learn about the sea and its inhabitants. Here you'll find the **Caicos Conch Farm,** a major mariculture operation where the mollusks are farmed commercially (there are more than 2.5 million conchs in the inventory here). The farm's facilities also include a video show, a boutique, and a hands-on tank with conchs in various stages of growth. Established by the PRIDE Foundation (Protection of Reefs and Islands from Degradation and Exploitation), the **JoJo Dolphin Project** is named after a 7-ft-long male bottlenose dolphin who cruises these waters and enjoys playing with local divers. You can watch a video about JoJo and learn how to interact with him safely if you see him on one of your dives. ⊠ *Island Sea Center,* ☎ *649/946–5330;* ⊠ *Caicos Conch Farm,* ☎ *649/946–5849.* ▣ *$6.* ☉ *Mon.–Sat. 9–5.*

Beaches
A fine white-sand beach stretches 12 mi along the northeast coast of **Providenciales,** where most of the hotels are. There are also good beaches at **Sapodilla Bay.**

Dining
For general information *and* price categories, *see* Dining *under* Grand Turk, *above.*

AMERICAN

$$–$$$ ✕ **Alfred's Place.** Austrian owner Alfred Holzfeind caters to an Amer-
★   ican palate with an extensive menu that has everything from prime rib to chicken salad. The alfresco lounge is a popular watering hole for locals and tourists alike. ⊠ *Turtle Cove,* ☎ *649/946–4679. AE, D, MC, V. Closed Mon. July–Oct. No lunch weekends.*

CARIBBEAN

$–$$ ✕ **Dora's.** This popular local eatery serves island fare—turtle, shred-
ded lobster, spicy conch chowder—seven days a week, from 7 AM until the last person leaves the bar. Plastic print and lace tablecloths, hanging plants, and Haitian art add to the island ambience. Soups come with homemade bread; entrées such as fish-and-chips, conch Creole, and grilled pork chops come with a vegetable. Be sure to come early for the packed Monday- and Thursday-night all-you-can-eat $20 seafood buffets. The price includes transportation to and from your hotel. ⊠ *Leeward Hwy.,* ☎ *649/946–4558. No credit cards.*

DELI

$ ✕ **Top O' the Cove Gourmet Delicatessen.** You can walk to this tiny café on Leeward Highway from the Turtle Cove and Erebus inns (don't be put off by the location in the Napa Auto Parts plaza). Order breakfast, deli sandwiches, salads, and cool soft-swirl frozen yogurt. Top O' the Cove is open every day but Christmas and New Year's from 7 AM to 3:30 PM. ⊠ *Leeward Hwy.,* ☎ *649/946–4694. No credit cards.*

ECLECTIC

$$$ ✕ **The Terrace.** The cuisine here has a Euro-Caribbean flair, and the menu changes according to the freshest ingredients available. You can make a meal from such delicious starters as freshly baked tomato-and-goat-cheese tarts, lobster bisque, and simmered mussels. Main courses include roast rack of lamb, and fresh conch encrusted with pecans. Top it all off with a classic crème brûlée. ⊠ *Turtle Cove,* ☎ *649/946–4763. AE, MC, V. Closed Sun.*

$$–$$$ ✕ **Gecko Grille.** You can eat indoors amid tropical murals or on the garden patio at this Ocean Club restaurant (☞ Lodging, *below*). Creative fare includes almond-cracked conch with a lime *rémoulade* (a cold, mayonnaise-based sauce), and grilled pork chops marinated in papaya

juice. Portions are large, so either share or bring a hearty appetite. ⊠ *Grace Bay,* ☎ *649/946–5880. AE, MC, V.*

$–$$ ✕ **Fast Eddie's.** Plants festoon this cheerful restaurant, which is across from the airport. Broiled turtle steak, fried grouper fingers, and other island specialties are joined on the menu by old American standbys such as cheeseburgers and cherry pie. Wednesday evening there's a $20 ($10 for children) all-you-can-eat seafood buffet. Friday is prime rib and live music night. Free transportation to and from your hotel is provided. ⊠ *Airport Rd.,* ☎ *649/941–3175. MC, V.*

$–$$ ✕ **Pub on the Bay.** If beachfront dining is what you're after, it doesn't get much better than this. Located in the Blue Hill residential district, a five-minute drive from downtown Provo, this restaurant serves fried or steamed fish, oxtail stew, barbecue ribs, chicken, various sandwiches, and even turtle steak. There's no air-conditioning, so you may as well cross the street to one of three thatch-roof "huts," which stand on the beach. ⊠ *Blue Hill Rd.,* ☎ *649/941–5309. AE, MC, V.*

$ ✕ **Caicos Cafe.** There's a pervasive air of celebration in the uncovered outdoor dining area of this popular eatery. Choose from a selection of local and American cuisine, including lobster sandwiches, hamburgers, and a variety of excellent salads. ⊠ *Across from Turquoise Reef, Grace Bay,* ☎ *649/946–5278. AE, MC, V. No lunch Sun.*

FRENCH

$$–$$$ ✕ **Anacaona.** At the impressive Grace Bay Club (☞ Lodging, *below*), ★ this exquisitely designed restaurant offers a truly fine dining experience minus the tie, the air-conditioning, and the attitude. Start with a bottle of fine wine from the extensive cellar, and then enjoy a three- or four-course meal of the chef's light but flavorful cooking, which combines traditional French recipes with fresh seafood and Caribbean fruits, vegetables, and spices. Oil lamps on the tables, gently circulating ceiling fans, and the natural sounds of the breeze, ocean, birds, and tree frogs all add to the Eden-like environment. ⊠ *Grace Bay,* ☎ *649/ 946–5050. AE, MC, V.*

SEAFOOD

$$ ✕ **Banana Boat.** Buoys and other sea relics deck the walls of this brightly painted, casual restaurant on the wharf. Grilled grouper, lobster-salad sandwiches, conch fritters, and a refreshing conch salad are among the menu options. Excellent tropical drinks include the house specialty, the rum-filled Banana Breeze. ⊠ *Turtle Cove,* ☎ *649/941– 5706. AE, MC, V.*

TEX-MEX

$–$$ ✕ **Hey, José.** Frequented by locals, this restaurant claims to serve the ★ island's best margaritas. Customers also return for the tasty Tex-Mex treats: tacos, tostados, nachos, burritos, fajitas, and José's special-recipe hot chicken wings. Creative types can build their own pizzas. ⊠ *Central Sq.,* ☎ *649/946–4812, V. Closed Sun.*

Lodging

With its rolling ridges and 12-mi beach, the island is a prime target for developers. More than two decades ago a group of U.S. investors, including the DuPonts, Ludingtons, and Roosevelts, opened up this island for visitors and those seeking homesites in the Caribbean. In 1990 the island's first luxury resort, the Turquoise Reef Resort & Casino, opened as did luxurious Ocean Club, a condominium resort at Grace Bay. These were followed by the upscale Grace Bay Club resort in 1992. Competition created by the new resorts has spurred many of the older hotels to undertake much-needed renovations. For further information *and* price categories, *see* Lodging *under* Grand Turk, *above.*

$$$$ ⊞ **Beaches.** At this new member of the Sandals chain, couples are certainly still a part of the scene, but Beaches is geared toward families as well. Luxurious accommodations combined with a full range of water sports and bar service that extends to the beach make this all-inclusive resort an indulgent experience (though housekeeping can be inconsistent). The tropical landscaping is lovely and lush, as are the two large free-form lap pools (one has a swim-up bar). For even more pampering, head for the spa, which offers such services as body wraps, massages, and facials. ⊠ *Lower Bight Rd., Grace Bay,* ☎ *649/946–8000 or 800/726–3257,* FAX *649/946–8001. 200 rooms. 3 restaurants, pool, hot tub, spa, 2 tennis courts, health club, dive shop, snorkeling, surfing, windsurfing. AE, MC, V. All-inclusive.*

$$$$ ⊞ **Grace Bay Club.** Staying at this Swiss-owned, Mediterranean-style,
★ all-suites resort is a little like being the guest of honor of a very gracious host with unbeatable taste. Guest quarters, which have breathtaking views of stunning Grace Bay, are furnished with rattan and pickled wood and have such appointments as Mexican-tile floors with elegant throw rugs from Turkey and India. Although there are plenty of activities here (from diving to golf to catered picnics on surrounding islands), just letting yourself relax amid the natural beauty of this peaceful yet invigorating getaway is a major activity itself. Pamper yourself further with a French meal in the Anacaona restaurant (☞ *Dining, above).* ⊠ *Grace Bay (Box 128),* ☎ *649/946–5757 or 800/ 946–5757,* FAX *649/946–5758. 22 suites. Restaurant, bar, pool, hot tub, 2 tennis courts, beach, video games, library. AE, MC, V. EP, MAP.*

$$$–$$$$ ⊞ **Ocean Club.** This luxury resort is on a 12-mi stretch of pristine beach, a short walk from Provo's only golf course. The all-suite accommodations range from efficiency studios to deluxe quarters with an ocean view, a screened balcony, a kitchen, a dining room, and a living room. Third-floor rooms have striking cathedral ceilings, and all but efficiency units have a washer and dryer. The on-site Gecko Grille (☞ *Dining, above)* serves creative island dishes. ⊠ *Grace Bay (Box 240),* ☎ *649/ 946–5880 or 800/457–8787,* FAX *649/946–5845. 86 suites. 2 restaurants, bar, 2 pools, 18-hole golf course, tennis court, exercise room, dive shop, shops, car rental. AE, MC, V. EP.*

$$$ ⊞ **Club Med Turkoise.** This lavish resort is one of the most sumptuous of all Club Med's villages. One-, two-, and three-story bungalows line a 1-mi beach, and all the usual sybaritic pleasures are here. This club is geared toward couples, singles aged 28 and over, and divers. The package includes all the water sports and daytime activities you can handle, plus nightly entertainment. ⊠ *Grace Bay,* ☎ *649/946–5500, 800/258–2633, 212/750–1684, or 212/750–1687 in NY;* FAX *649/ 946–5501. 298 rooms. 3 restaurants, bar, snack bar, pool, 8 tennis courts, exercise room, beach, dive shop, water sports, fishing, bicycles, shop, dance club, video games, library. AE, MC, V. All-inclusive (except drinks).*

$$$ ⊞ **Le Deck Hotel & Beach Club.** This pink hostelry was built in classic
★ Bermudian style around a tropical courtyard. Its rooms and suites are clean (right down to the tile floors) and have a few basic comforts, such as color TVs and air-conditioning. Most of the folk who stay here are divers, and the atmosphere is informal and lively. ⊠ *Grace Bay (Box 144),* ☎ *649/946–5547 or 800/528–1905,* FAX *649/946–5770. 25 rooms, 2 suites. Restaurant, bar, air-conditioning, pool, beach, snorkeling, windsurfing. AE, D, MC, V. AP, EP, CP, MAP.*

$$$ ⊞ **Turquoise Reef Resort & Casino.** Oversize oceanfront rooms have
★ rattan furniture and a rich Caribbean color scheme. All rooms have a king or two double beds, a TV, and a terrace or patio. The island's only casino is here, and there's live nightly entertainment. You can also partake in daily activities that include pool volleyball and children's trea-

sure hunts. ✉ *Grace Bay (Box 205)*, ☎ *649/946–5555 or 800/992–2015*, FAX *649/946–5522. 228 rooms. 3 restaurants, 3 bars, air-conditioning, fans, room service, pool, hot tub, 2 tennis courts, exercise room, beach, dive shop, water sports, shops, casino, dance club, baby-sitting, travel services. AE, MC, V. EP, MAP.*

$$ 🏨 **Erebus Inn Resort.** The views are fabulous from this cliffside setting
★ overlooking Turtle Cove. All units have two double beds, wicker furnishings, and original island artwork, including some unique Haitian wall hangings. The higher priced cottages on the cliff are more private than the rooms in the hotel proper. The restaurant and bar, one of Provo's liveliest spots, has a menu of French and Caribbean cuisine. Five affordable restaurants are within walking distance, as arc snorkeling sites, a shopping center, and several dive operations. Frequent shuttles take you to a nearby beach. ✉ *Turtle Cove (Box 238)*, ☎ *649/946–4240 or 800/323–5655 (reservations service)*, FAX *649/946–4704. 30 rooms. Restaurant, bar, air-conditioning, 2 pools (1 saltwater), 2 tennis courts, aerobics, exercise room, baby-sitting. AE, MC, V. EP, MAP.*

$$ 🏨 **Treasure Beach Villas.** These one- and two-bedroom, modern apartments have fully equipped kitchens and ceiling fans. You may want a car or bike (Treasure Beach has rentals) to reach the grocery store or restaurants; bus service is limited. Provo's 12 mi of white sandy beach is just outside your door, and the hotel can organize fishing, snorkeling, and scuba expeditions. ✉ *The Bight*, ☎ *649/946–4325*, FAX *649/946–4108; or* ✉ *Box 8409, Hialeah, FL 33012. 8 single rooms, 10 double rooms. Pool, tennis court. AE, D, MC, V. EP.*

$ 🏨 **Turtle Cove Inn.** A marina, a free-form pool (set in a lushly landscaped area), a dive shop with equipment rentals and instruction, and lighted tennis courts attract the sporting crowd to this affordable, well-run hotel. Rooms are simple, clean, and comfortable (all have a TV, a phone, and air-conditioning; eight have mini-refrigerators). There's a free boat shuttle to the nearby beach and snorkeling reef, and dive packages are available. Turtle Cove is also within walking distance of a handful of good restaurants. ✉ *The Bight (Box 131)*, ☎ *649/946–4203 or 800/887–0477 (reservations service)*, FAX *649/946–4141. 30 rooms, 1 suite. 2 restaurants, 2 bars, air-conditioning, pool, 2 tennis courts, dive shop, bicycles. AE, MC, V. EP.*

Nightlife

Casablanca (✉ Next to Club Med, ☎ 649/946–5449) is a Monte Carlo–style nightclub with a decked-out crowd. **Disco Elite** (✉ Airport Rd., ☎ 649/946–4592) has strobe lights and an elevated dance floor. A band plays native, reggae, and contemporary music on Thursday night at the **Erebus Inn** (✉ Turtle Cove, ☎ 649/946–4240).

Le Deck (✉ Grace Bay, ☎ 649/946–5547) offers one-armed bandits every night. The **Turquoise Reef Resort** (✉ Grace Bay, ☎ 649/946–5555) has a lively lounge, where a musician plays to the mostly tourist crowd, and the island's only gambling casino, **Port Royale** (☎ 649/946–5508).

Outdoor Activities and Sports

BICYCLING

Provo has a few steep grades to conquer, but they're short, and there's little traffic. You can rent bikes at the **Island Princess** hotel (☎ 649/946–4260) at the Bight for $10 a day, through **Turtle Inn Divers** (✉ Turtle Cove Inn, ☎ 649/941–5389) for $12 a day and $60 a week, or at the **Turquoise Reef Resort & Casino** (✉ Grace Bay, ☎ 649/946–5555) for $14 a day.

BOATING AND SAILING

Sailing not your bent? Try ocean kayaking ($10 per hour for one and $15 per hour for two).

FISHING

You can rent a boat with a captain for a half or full day of sportfishing through **J&B Tours** (✉ Leward Marina, ☎ 649/946–5047) for about $300 a day. **Silver Deep** (✉ Turtle Cove Marina, ☎ 649/941–5595) will take you out for half- or full-day bonefishing or bottom-fishing, bait and tackle included. The same outfit will arrange half- or full-day deep-sea fishing trips in search of shark, marlin, kingfish, sawfish, wahoo, and tuna—with all equipment furnished. Deep-sea, bone-, and bottom fishing are also available aboard the *Sakitumi* (☎ 649/946–4065).

GOLFING

Provo Golf Club (☎ 649/946–5991) has a par-72, 18-hole, championship course that was designed by Karl Litten. It has narrow "target areas" and sandy waste areas—a formidable challenge to anyone playing from the championship tees. Fees are $90, which includes a shared electric cart. A pro shop, driving ranges, and a restaurant-bar round out the facilities.

PARASAILING

A 15-minute flight over Grace Bay is available for $45 at either **Dive Provo** (✉ Turquoise Reef Resort, Grace Bay, ☎ 649/946–5040 or 800/234–7768) or **J&B Tours** (✉ Leward Marina, ☎ 649/946–5047).

SCUBA DIVING AND SNORKELING

For excellent close-to-shore snorkeling there's a reef near the White House off Penn's Road. Diving options include any of the spectacular walls, and visibility can often exceed 100 ft. The waters are generally quite warm, though you may want a wet suit to avoid a chill on the second or third dive of the day. Dive operators include: **Aquanaut** (✉ Turtle Cove, ☎ 649/946–4048), **Art Pickering's Provo Turtle Divers** (✉ Turtle Cove Marina, ☎ 649/946–4232), **Caicos Adventures** (✉ Turtle Cove Marina, ☎ 649/946–3346), **Dive Provo** (✉ Turquoise Reef Resort, Grace Bay, ☎ 649/946–5040 or 800/234–7768), **Flamingo Divers** (✉ Turtle Cove, ☎ 649/946–4193), **J&B Tours** (✉ Leward Marina, ☎ 649/946–5047).

SEA EXCURSIONS

The *Ocean Outback* (☎ 649/946–4080), a 70-ft motor cruiser, has barbecue-and-snorkel cruises to uninhabited islands. Both the 37-ft catamaran *Beluga* (☎ 649/941–5196), $39 per half day, and the 56-ft trimaran *Tao* (☎ 649/946–5040) run sunset cruises, as well as sailing and snorkeling outings. A full-day outing on the *Tao* is $59 per person, including snorkel rental and lunch.

For $20 per person, **Dive Provo** (✉ Turquoise Reef Resort, Grace Bay, ☎ 649/946–5040 or 800/234–7768) gives two-hour glass-bottom-boat tours of the spectacular reefs. **Turtle Inn Divers** (✉ Turtle Cove Inn, ☎ 649/941–5389) offers full-day Sunday excursions for divers for $64.50 per person ($25 per person for nondivers and snorkelers). The *Turks and Caicos Aggressor* (✉ Turtle Cove Marina, ☎ 504/385–2416, FAX 504/384–0817) offers luxury six-day dive cruises.

TENNIS

Several hotels have courts. There are two lighted courts at **Turtle Cove Inn** (☎ 649/946–4203), eight courts (four lighted) at **Club Med Turkoise** (☎ 649/946–5500), two lighted courts at the **Turquoise Reef Resort** (☎ 649/946–5555), two lighted courts at the **Erebus Inn** (☎ 649/946–4240), one unlighted court at **Treasure Beach Villas** (☎ 649/946–4211), and two lighted courts at **Grace Bay Club** (☎ 649/946–5050).

Waterskiers will find the calm turquoise water ideal for long-distance runs. **Dive Provo** (⊠ Turquoise Reef Resort, Grace Bay, ☎ 649/946–5040 or 800/234–7768) charges $35 for a 15-minute run.

WINDSURFING
Rental and instruction are available at **Dive Provo** (⊠ Turquoise Reef Resort, Grace Bay, ☎ 649/946–5040 or 800/234–7768).

Shopping
New shops open every month. You'll find most stores in the five main shopping complexes: Market Place, Central Square, and Caribbean Place, all on Leeward Highway; Turtle Cove Landing, in Turtle Cove; and the newest complex, Ports of Call, in Grace Bay. Delicate baskets woven from the local top grasses and small metalworks are the only crafts native to the Turks and Caicos, and they are sold in many places.

The **Bamboo Gallery** (⊠ Market Place, ☎ 649/946–4748) sells Caribbean art, from vivid Haitian paintings to wood carvings and local metal sculptures. **Greensleeves** (⊠ Central Square, ☎ 649/946–4147) offers paintings by local artists, island-made rag rugs, baskets, jewelry, and sisal mats and bags. **Mama's Gifts** (⊠ Ports of Call, ☎ 649/941–3338) sells hand-woven and embroidered straw baskets, handbags, hats, and shell and wood jewelry. **Maison Creole** (⊠ Grace Bay, no phone) has unique Caribbean arts and crafts: painted metal sculptures, furniture, carved wood masks, canes, and bowls. **Paradise Gifts/Arts** (⊠ Central Square, ☎ 649/946–4637) has an on-site ceramics studio; you also find jewelry, T-shirts, and paintings by local artists.

At **Pelican's Pouch/Designer I** (⊠ Turtle Cove Landing, ☎ 649/946–4343) you'll find resort wear, sandals, T-shirts, perfumes, and gold jewelry on the ground floor; head upstairs for basketry, sculpture, and watercolors. **Royal Jewels** (⊠ Leeward Hwy., ☎ 649/946–4885; ⊠ Turquoise Reef Resort, Provo, ☎ 649/946–5311; ⊠ Airport, Provo, ☎ 649/946–5311) sells gold and jewelry, designer watches, and perfumes—all duty-free.

Little Water Cay

The small uninhabited cay is a protected area under the National Trust of the Turks and Caicos. On these 150 acres are two trails, a couple of small lakes, red mangrove, and an abundance of plants and trees. Boardwalks protect the ground and interpretive signs explain the habitat. The cay is home for about 2,000 rare, endangered rock iguanas. They say the iguanas are shy, but these creatures actually seem rather curious. They waddle right up to you, posing as if ready for a photo opportunity; you can usually get within a foot of them before they move.

Pine Cay

One of a chain of small cays linking North Caicos and Provo, 800-acre Pine Cay is privately owned and under development as a planned community. It's home to the Meridian Club resort—playground of jet-setters—and its 2½-mi beach is the most beautiful in the archipelago. The island has a 3,800-ft airstrip and electric carts for getting around.

Lodging
For general information *and* price categories, *see* Lodging *under* Grand Turk, *above*.

$$$$ ☷ **Meridian Club.** High rollers vacation in high style on this privately
★ owned 800-acre island. Club guests enjoy an unspoiled cay with 2½ mi of soft white sand and a 500-acre nature reserve with tropical land-

scaping, freshwater ponds, and nature trails that lure bird-watchers and botanists. A stay here is truly getting away from it all, as there are no air-conditioners, phones, or TVs. The accommodations range from spacious rooms with king-size beds (or twin beds on request) and patios to one- to four-bedroom cottage homes that range in decor and amenities from rustic to well appointed. There's also a "round room" cottage and two ocean-view atrium units that are separated by a lovely interior garden. Rooms in the main complex run $675 a night in high season and include all meals. Cottage homes start at $3,000 a week. ⊠ *Pine Cay (write to Resorts Management, ⊠ 201 1/2 E 29th St., New York, NY 10016),* ☎ *800/331–9154,* ℻ *649/946–5128. 12 rooms, 13 cottage homes. Restaurant, bar, pool, tennis court, windsurfing, boating, bicycles. No credit cards. EP, FAP.*

North Caicos

Thanks to abundant rainfall, this 41-square-mi island is the garden center of the Turks and Caicos. Bird lovers will see a large flock of flamingos here, and fisherman will find creeks full of bonefish and tarpon. Bring all your own gear; this quiet island has no water-sports shops.

Exploring North Caicos

⑧ **Flamingo Pond.** This is a nesting place for the beautiful pink birds. They tend to wander out in the middle of the pond, so bring binoculars.

⑨ **Kew.** This settlement has a small post office, a school, a church and ruins of old plantations—all set among lush tropical trees bearing limes, papayas, and custard apples. To visit Kew is to gain a better understanding of what life is like for many native islanders.

⑦ **Sandy Point.** Getting to this settlement is half the fun, as you rattle along dirt and stone-filled roads. You'll pass salt flats where you'll very likely see flamingos standing around in the shallow waters. The secluded cove here is an excellent place to snorkel.

Beaches

The beaches of North Caicos are superb for shelling and lolling, and the waters offshore present excellent opportunities for snorkeling, bonefishing, and scuba diving (there are no outfitters on the island, so you'll have to make arrangements with shops on Provo). **Three Mary's Cays** has excellent snorkeling with a friendly ancient barracuda named Old Man.

Lodging

For general information *and* price categories, *see* Lodging *under* Grand Turk, *above.*

$$ 🏨 **Club Vacanze Prospect of Whitby Hotel.** This secluded retreat is run
★ by an Italian resort chain, Club Vacanze. Miles of beach are yours for sunbathing, windsurfing, or snorkeling. Spacious guest rooms have elegant Tuscan floor tiles, pastel pink paneling (some have fragrant cedar paneling), and white stucco walls decorated with bright paintings from Santo Domingo, Dominican Republic; in true getaway fashion, rooms lack TVs and radios. The restaurant here is excellent (its cappuccino machine is a blessing for coffee lovers). ⊠ *Whitby,* ☎ *649/ 946–7119,* ℻ *649/946–7114. 28 rooms, 4 suites. Restaurant, bar, pool, air-conditioning, tennis court, dive shop, windsurfing, baby-sitting, travel services. AE, MC, V. EP, MAP.*

$$ 🏨 **Ocean Beach Hotel Condominiums.** This unpretentious place provides family-style accommodations on a 10-mi stretch of sheltered beach. The spacious units, each with a kitchenette, face the ocean. (Who needs air-conditioning when there are constant trade winds passing

through large sliding glass doors?) The hotel offers an intimate lifestyle away from the fray. ⊠ *Whitby,* ☎ *649/946–7113, 800/710–5204, or 905/336–2876 in Canada;* ℻ *649/946–7386. 10 units. Restaurant, bar, fishing, bicycles, car rental. MC, V. MAP.*

\$\$ ⊡ **Pelican Beach Hotel.** This hotel has large rooms done in pastels and dark wood trim. Ask to stay on the second floor, where rooms have high wood ceilings and fabulous ocean views. Ceiling fans and constant sea breezes keep you cool. ⊠ *Whitby,* ☎ *649/946–7112,* ℻ *649/946–7139. 14 rooms, 2 suites. Restaurant, bar, fishing. MC, V.*

\$ ⊡ **JoAnne's B&B.** This no-frills, charming bed-and-breakfast on the beach is the perfect spot for those seeking peace and quiet. Rooms are light and airy with cool, white tile floors. Two friendly dogs escort you to the sea and trot along with you as you search for shells and sunbathe on a very private stretch of beach. The owner, a former Peace Corps worker, also runs Papa Grunts, an excellent restaurant nearby. Her island stories entertain and delight. Faxing is the best way to make reservations. ⊠ *Whitby,* ☎ ℻ *649/946–7301. 3 rooms. MC, V.*

Middle Caicos

This is the largest (48 square mi) and least developed of the inhabited Turks and Caicos. Since phones are rare, the boats that dock here and the planes that land on the little airstrip provide the island's 275 residents with their connections to the outside world. **J&B Tours** offers boat trips from Provo to the mysterious Conch Bar Caves (☞ *below*).

Exploring Middle Caicos

⑩ **Conch Bar Caves.** These limestone caves have eerie underground lakes and milky-white stalactites and stalagmites. Archaeologists have discovered Arawak and Lucayan Indian artifacts in the caves and the surrounding area. It's an easy walk through the main part of the cave, but wear sturdy shoes to avoid slipping on the damp surface. You'll hear and see (and smell) some bats, but they won't bother you.

Lodging

For general information *and* price categories, *see* Lodging *under* Grand Turk, *above.*

\$\$–\$\$\$\$ ⊡ **Blue Horizon Resort.** This place offers sweet seclusion in condo-style accommodations. Units have screened-in porches, off-white tile floors, bleached wood furniture, comfortable beds, ceiling fans, and full kitchens. The slated windows open up to let in the nearly constant hillside breeze. On a spectacular cliff with a beach just down a short path, you'll feel like you're staying in your very own paradise. Fax a grocery list ahead of time, and the management will be happy to stock your refrigerator. Maid service is included in the room rate. Take a break from preparing your meals by making reservations at the café (open only January through March). Activities by request include cave exploring, fishing, and snorkeling. ⊠ *Mudjin Harbor,* ☎ *649/946–6141,* ℻ *649/946–6139. 5 cottages. Fans, kitchenettes, refrigerators. AE, MC, V.*

South Caicos

This 8½-square-mi island was once an important salt producer; today it's the heart of the fishing industry. The beaches here are small and unremarkable, but the vibrant reef is popular with divers.

Exploring South Caicos

Spiny lobster and queen conch are found in the shallow Caicos bank to the west and are harvested for export by local processing plants. The bonefishing here is some of the best in the West Indies. At the northern end of the island are fine, white-sand beaches; the south coast is great for scuba diving along the drop-off; and there's excellent snorkeling off the windward (east) coast, where large stands of elkhorn and staghorn coral shelter a variety of small tropical fish.

⓫ Cockburn Harbour. The best natural harbor in the Caicos chain is home to the South Caicos Regatta, held each year in May.

Lodging

For general information *and* price categories, *see* Lodging *under* Grand Turk, *above.*

$–$$$ ⌂ Club Caribe Beach & Harbour Hotel. Cockburn Harbour, the only natural harbor in Turks and Caicos, is the perfect setting for this hotel. In the 16 beachfront villas here you'll find studios and one-, two-, or three-bedroom apartments; they have cool tile floors and kitchenettes equipped with a mini-refrigerator and a microwave. Half the rooms don't have air-conditioning, but they get a nice breeze around the clock. The 22 harbor rooms are smaller than the others but have air-conditioning. There's a dive shop with a full-time instructor. ⊠ *Cockburn Harbour (Box 1),* ☎ *649/946–3444 or 800/722–2582,* 𝔽𝔸𝕏 *649/ 946–3446. 38 rooms. Restaurant, bar, dive shop, windsurfing, bicycles. AE, D, MC, V. EP, MAP.*

TURKS AND CAICOS ISLANDS A TO Z

Arriving and Departing

By Boat

Because of the superb diving, three live-aboard dive boats call regularly. Contact the *Aquanaut* (c/o See & Sea, ☎ 800/348–9778), the *Sea Dancer* (c/o Peter Hughes Diving, ☎ 800/932–6237), or the *Turks and Caicos Aggressor* (c/o Aggressor Fleet, ☎ 504/385–2628 or 800/ 348–2628, 𝔽𝔸𝕏 504/384–0817).

By Plane

American Airlines (☎ 800/433–7300 or 649/941–5700 in Turks and Caicos) flies daily between Miami and Provo. **Turks & Caicos Islands Airlines** (☎ 649/946–4255) is the only regularly scheduled carrier that flies between Provo, Grand Turk, and other outer Turks and Caicos islands. Many air charter services also connect the islands (☞ Guided Tours, *below*).

FROM THE AIRPORT

Taxis are available at the airports; expect to share a ride. Rates are fixed. A trip between Provo's airport and most major hotels runs about $15. On Grand Turk, a trip from the airport to Cockburn Town is about $5; from the airport to hotels outside town, $6–$11.

Getting Around

By Bus

A new public bus system on Grand Turk charges 50¢ one-way to any scheduled stop.

On Provo, shuttle buses operated by **Executive Tours** (☎ 649/946–4524) run from the hotels into town every hour, Monday–Saturday 9–6. Fares are $2 each way.

By Car

Driving here is on the left side of the road; when pulling out into traffic, remember to look to your right. Rates average $40 to $65 per day, plus a $10-per-rental-agreement government tax.

On Grand Turk, try **Dutchie's Car Rental** (☎ 649/946–2244). Agencies on Provo are **Turks & Caicos National** (☎ 649/946–4701), **Provo Rent-a-Car** (☎ 649/946–4404), **Rent a Buggy** (☎ 649/946–4158), and **Turquoise Jeep Rentals** (☎ 649/946–4910). To rent cars on South Caicos, check with your hotel manager for rates and information.

By Ferry
Ferries are available between some islands; check with local marinas. The only government ferry (☎ no phone) runs between Grand Turk and Salt Cay.

By Scooter
You can scoot around Provo by contacting **Scooter Bob's** (☎ 649/946–4684) or the **Honda Shop** (☎ 649/946–4397). On North Caicos, contact **North Caicos Scooter Rentals** (☎ 649/946–7301). Rates generally start at $25 per day for a one-seater and $40 a day for a two-seater, plus a onetime $5 government tax and gas expenses.

By Taxi
Taxis are unmetered, and rates, posted in the taxis, are regulated by the government. In Provo, call the **Provo Taxi Association** (☎ 649/946–5481) for more information.

Opening and Closing Times

Most offices and shops are open weekdays from 8 or 8:30 till 4 or 4:30. Banks are open Monday–Thursday 8:30–2:30, Friday 8:30–12:30 and 2:30–4:30.

HOLIDAYS
New Year's Day, Commonwealth Day (Mar. 10), Good Friday (Apr. 2), Easter and Easter Monday (Apr. 4–5), National Heroes Day (May 26), Queen's Birthday (June 14), National Youth Day (Sept. 26), Columbus Day (Oct. 13), International Human Rights Day (Oct. 24), Christmas, Boxing Day (Dec.26).

Contacts and Resources

Electricity
Electricity is fairly stable throughout the islands, and the current is the same as in the United States (110 volts).

Emergencies
Police: Grand Turk, ☎ 649/946–2299; North Caicos, ☎ 649/946–7116; Providenciales, ☎ 649/946–4259; South Caicos, ☎ 649/946–3299.

Hospitals: There is a 24-hour emergency room at **Grand Turk Hospital** (✉ Hospital Rd., ☎ 649/946–2333) and at **Providenciales Health-Medical Center** (✉ Leeward Hwy., ☎ 649/946–4201).

Pharmacies: Prescriptions can be filled at the **Government Clinic** (✉ Grand Turk Hospital, ☎ 649/946–2040) and at the **Providenciales Health-Medical Center** in Provo (✉ Leeward Hwy., ☎ 649/946–4201).

Scuba-Diving Accidents: A modern hyperbaric/decompression chamber is on Provo in the **Menzies Medical Centre** (✉ Leeward Hwy., ☎ 649/946–4242).

Guided Tours
A **taxi** tour of the islands costs between $25 and $30 for the first hour and $25 for each additional hour. On Provo, contact **Paradise Taxi Company** (☎ 649/941–3555). **Turtle Tours** (☎ 649/946–5585) offers a variety of bus and small-plane tours, including flights to Middle Caicos, the largest of the islands, for a visit to its mysterious caves, or to North Caicos to see the ruins of a plantation.

If you want to island-hop on your own schedule, air charters are available through **Blue Hills Aviation** (☎ 649/941–5290), **Flamingo Air Services** (☎ 649/946–2109 or 649/946–4933), and **SkyKing** (☎ 649/941–5464), all based in Provo.

Language
English is the official language of the Turks and Caicos.

Money Matters
CURRENCY
The unit of currency is the U.S. dollar.

SERVICE CHARGES, TAXES, AND TIPPING
Hotels add from 10%–15% to your bill for service and restaurants and hotels both add a 7% government tax. You'll be charged a $15 departure tax at the airport. At restaurants tip according to service; 10%–18% is common. Taxis also expect a token tip, about 10% of your fare.

Passports and Visas
U.S. citizens need some proof of citizenship, such as a birth certificate (original or certified copy), plus a photo ID or a current passport. British subjects must have a current passport. All visitors must have an ongoing or return ticket.

Precautions
Petty crime does occur here, and you're advised to leave your valuables in the hotel safe-deposit box. Bring along a can of insect repellent: The mosquitoes and no-see-ums can be vicious. If you plan to explore the uninhabited island of West Caicos, be advised that the interior is overgrown with dense shrubs that include manchineel, which has a milky, poisonous sap that can cause painful, scarring blisters.

In some hotels on Grand Turk, Salt Cay, and South Caicos signs PLEASE HELP US CONSERVE OUR PRECIOUS WATER. These islands have no water supply other than rainwater collected in cisterns, and rainfall is scant. Drink only from the decanter of fresh water your hotel provides; tap water is safe for brushing your teeth or other hygiene uses.

Telephones and Mail
The area code for the Turks and Caicos is 649 (recently changed from 809). To make calls from Turks and Caicos, dial 0 + 1 + area code + the number. You can call anywhere, anytime, through the cable and wireless system and local operators. To make local calls, dial the seven-digit number. To place credit-card calls, simply dial the 800 number of your provider. Note that calls from the islands are very expensive, and many hotels add steep surcharges for long-distance calls. Talk fast.

When writing to the Turks and Caicos Islands be sure to include the specific island as well as "Turks and Caicos, BWI" (British West Indies).

Visitor Information
For tourist information, contact the **Turks and Caicos Islands Tourist Board** (☎ 800/241–0824, tci.tourism@caribsurf.com). The **Caribbean Tourism Organization** (✉ 20 E. 46th St., New York, NY 10017, ☎ 212/682–0435) is another source of information. In the United Kingdom, contact **Morris-Kevan International Ltd.** (✉ International House, 47 Chase Side, Enfield, Middlesex EN2 6NB, ☎ 0181/367–5175).

The **Government Tourist Office** (✉ Front St., Cockburn Town, Grand Turk, ☎ 649/946–2321; ✉ Turtle Cove Landing, Provo, ☎ 649/946–4970) is open Monday–Thursday 8–4:30 and Friday 8–5.

6 Portraits of the Bahamas

In the Wake of Columbus:
A Short History of the Bahamas

In Search of Columbus

Cashing In: A Casino Gambling Primer

IN THE WAKE OF COLUMBUS:
A SHORT HISTORY OF THE BAHAMAS

YOU MIGHT CALL Christopher Columbus the first tourist to hit the Bahamas, although he was actually trying to find a route to the East Indies with his *Niña, Pinta,* and *Santa María.* Columbus is popularly believed to have made his first landfall in the New World on October 12, 1492, at San Salvador, in the southern part of the Bahamas. Researchers of the National Geographic Society, however, have come up with the theory that he may first have set foot ashore Samana Cay, some 60 mi southeast of San Salvador. The Bahamians have taken this new theory under consideration, if not too seriously; tradition dies hard in the islands, and they are hardly likely to tear down the New World landfall monument on San Salvador.

The people who met Columbus on his landing day were Arawak Indians, said to have fled from the Caribbean to the Bahamas to escape the depredations of the murderous Caribs around the turn of the 9th century. The Arawaks were a shy, gentle people who offered Columbus and his men their hospitality. He was impressed with their kindness and more than slightly intrigued by the gold ornaments they wore. But the voracious Spaniards who followed in Columbus's footsteps a few years later repaid the Indians' kindness by forcing them to work in the conquistadors' gold and silver mines in Cuba and Haiti; the Bahamas' indigenous peoples were virtually wiped out in the next 30 years, despite the fact that the Spaniards never settled their land.

In 1513 another well-known seafarer stumbled upon the western-most Bahamian islands. Juan Ponce de León had been a passenger on Columbus's second voyage, in 1493. He conquered Puerto Rico in 1508 and then began searching thirstily for the Fountain of Youth. He thought he had found it on South Bimini, but he changed his mind and moved on to visit the site of St. Augustine, on the northeast coast of Florida.

In 1629 King Charles I claimed the Bahamas for England, though his edict was not implemented until the arrival of English pilgrims in 1648. Having fled the religious repression and political dissension then rocking their country, they settled on the Bahamian island they christened Eleuthera, the Greek word for freedom. Other English immigrants followed, and in 1656 another group of pilgrims, from Bermuda, took over a Bahamian island to the west and named it New Providence because of their links with Providence, Rhode Island. By the last part of the 17th century, some 1,100 settlers were trying to eke out a living, supplemented by the cargoes they salvaged from Spanish galleons that ran aground on the reefs. Many settlers were inclined to give nature a hand by enticing these ships onto the reefs with lights.

Inevitably, the British settlers were joined by a more nefarious subset of humanity, pirates and buccaneers like Edward Teach (better known as Blackbeard, he was said to have had 14 wives), Henry Morgan, and Calico Jack Rackham. Rackham numbered among his crew two violent, cutlass-wielding female members, Anne Bonney and Mary Read, who are said to have disconcerted enemies by swinging aboard their vessels topless. Bonney and Read escaped hanging in Jamaica by feigning pregnancy.

For some 40 years until 1718, pirates in the Bahamas constantly raided the Spanish galleons that carried booty home from the New World. During this period, the Spanish government, furious at the raids, sent ships and troops to destroy the New Providence city of Charles Town, which was later rebuilt and renamed Nassau, in 1695, in honor of King William III, formerly William of Orange-Nassau.

In 1718 King George I appointed Captain Woodes Rogers the first royal governor of the Bahamas, with orders to clean up the place. Why the king chose Rogers for this particular job is unclear—his thinking may well have been that it takes a pirate to know one, for Woodes Rogers had been a privateer. But he did take control of Nassau, hanging eight pirates from trees on the site of what was to become the British Colonial Hotel. Today, a statue of the former governor stands at the hotel entrance, and the street that runs along the waterfront is named after him. Rogers also inspired the saying *Expulsis piratis, restitua commercia* (Piracy expelled, commerce restored), which remained the country's motto until Prime Minister Lynden O. Pindling replaced it with the more appropriate and optimistic Forward, Upward, Onward Together, on the occasion of independence from Britain in 1973.

Although the Bahamas enjoyed a certain measure of tranquillity, thanks to Rogers and the governors who followed him, the British colonies in America at the same time were seething with a desire for independence. The peace of the islanders' lives was to be shattered during the Revolutionary War by a raid in 1778 on Nassau by the American navy, which purloined the city's arms and ammunition without even firing a shot. Next, in 1782, the Spanish came to occupy the Bahamas until the following year. Under the Treaty of Versailles of 1783, Spain took possession of Florida, and the Bahamas reverted to British rule.

THE BAHAMAS were once again overrun, between 1784 and 1789, this time by merchants from New England and plantation owners from Virginia and the Carolinas who had been loyal to the British and were fleeing the wrath of the American revolutionaries. Seeking asylum under the British flag, the Southerners brought their families and slaves with them. Many set up new plantations in the islands, but frustrated by the islands' arid soil, they soon opted for greener pastures in the Caribbean. The slaves they left behind were set free in 1834, but many retained the names of their former masters. That is why you'll find many a Johnson, Saunders, and Thompson in the towns and villages throughout the Bahamas.

The land may have been less than fertile, but New Providence Island's almost perfect climate, marred only by the potential for hurricanes during the fall, attracted other interest. Tourism was foreseen as far back as 1861, when the legislature approved the building of the first hotel, the Royal Victoria. Though it was to reign as the grande dame of the island's hotels for more than a century, its early days saw it involved in an entirely different profit-making venture. During the U.S. Civil War, the Northern forces blockaded the main Southern ports, and the leaders of the Confederacy turned to Nassau, the closest neutral port to the south. The Royal Victoria became the headquarters of the blockade-running industry, which reaped huge profits for the British colonial government from the duties it imposed on arms supplies. (In October 1990, the Royal Victoria Hotel burned down.)

A similar bonanza, also at the expense of the United States, was to come in the 1920s, after Prohibition was signed into U.S. law in 1919. Booze brought into the Bahamas from Europe was funneled into a thirsty United States by rumrunners operating out of Nassau, Bimini, and West End, the community on Grand Bahama Island east of Palm Beach. Racing against, and often exchanging gunfire with, Coast Guard patrol boats, the rumrunners dropped off their supplies in Miami, the Florida Keys, and other Florida destinations, making their contribution to the era known as the Roaring '20s.

Even then, tourists were beginning to trickle into the Bahamas, many in opulent yachts belonging to the likes of Whitney, Vanderbilt, and Astor. In 1929 a new airline, Pan American, started to make daily flights from Miami to Nassau. The Royal Victoria, shedding its shady past, and two new hotels, the Colonial (now the British Colonial Beach Resort) and the Fort Montagu Beach, were all in full operation. Nassau even had instant communication with the outside world: A few miles northwest of the Colonial, a subterranean telegraph cable had been laid linking New Providence with Jupiter, Florida. It took no flash of inspiration to name the area Cable Beach.

One of the most colorful and enigmatic characters of the era, Sir Harry Oakes, came to Nassau in the 1930s from Canada. He built the Bahamas Country Club and the Cable Beach Golf Course, a 6,500-yard, par-72 layout; he also built Nassau's first airport in the late '30s to lure the well-heeled and to make commuting easier for the wealthy residents. Oakes Field can still be seen on the ride from Nassau International Airport to Cable Beach.

Oakes was to die in an atmosphere of eerie and mysterious intrigue. Only his good friend, the late Sir Harold Christie, a real-estate tycoon and one of the most powerful of the Bay Street Boys (as the island's wealthy merchants were called), was in the house at the time that Oakes' body was found, battered and burned. This was a period when all of the news that was fit to print was coming out of the war theaters in Europe and the Far East, but the Miami newspapers and wire services had a field day with the society murder.

Although a gruff, unlikable character, Oakes had no known enemies, but there was speculation that mob hit men from Miami had come over and taken care of him because of his unyielding opposition to the introduction of gambling casinos to the Bahamas. Finally, two detectives brought from Miami pinned the murder on Oakes's son-in-law, Count Alfred de Marigny, for whom the Canadian was known to have a strong dislike. De Marigny was tried and acquitted in an overcrowded Nassau court. Much of the detectives' research and testimony was later discredited. For many years afterward, however, the mysterious and still unsolved crime was a sore point with New Providence residents.

During World War II, New Providence also played host to a noble, if unlikely, couple. In 1936 the Duke of Windsor had forsaken the British throne in favor of "the woman I love," an American divorcée named Wallis Warfield Simpson, and the couple temporarily found a carefree life in Paris and the French Riviera. When the Nazis overran France, they fled to neutral Portugal. Secret papers revealed after the war suggest that the Germans had plans to use the duke and duchess, by kidnapping if necessary, as pawns in the German war against Britain. This would have taken the form of declaring them king and queen in exile, and seating them on the throne when Hitler's assumed victory was accomplished.

Word of the plot might have reached the ears of Britain's wartime prime minister, Winston Churchill, who encouraged King George VI, the duke's younger brother and his successor, to send the couple as far away as possible out of harm's way. In 1939 the duke had briefly returned to England, offering his services to his brother in the war effort. He was given a position of perhaps less import than he had expected, for he and Wallis suddenly found themselves in the Bahamas, with the duke as governor and commander in chief.

CHANGES in the Bahamas' political climate had to wait for the war's end. For more than 300 years, the country had been ruled by whites; members of the United Bahamian Party (UBP) were known as the Bay Street Boys, after Nassau's main business thoroughfare, because they controlled the islands' commerce. But the voice of the overwhelmingly black majority was making itself heard. In 1953 a London-educated black barrister named Lynden O. Pindling joined the opposition Progressive Liberal Party (PLP); in 1956 he was elected to Parliament.

Pindling continued to stir the growing resentment most Bahamians now had for the Bay Street Boys, and his parliamentary behavior became more and more defiant. In 1965, during one parliamentary session, he picked up the speaker's mace and threw it out the window. Because this mace has to be present and in sight at all sessions, deliberations had to be suspended; meanwhile, Pindling continued his harangue to an enthusiastic throng in the street below. Two years later, Bahamian voters threw the UBP out, and Pindling led the PLP into power.

Pindling's magnetism kept him in power through independence from Britain in 1973 (though loyalty to the mother country led the Bahamians to choose to remain within the Commonwealth of Nations, recognize Queen Elizabeth II as their sovereign, and retain a governor-general appointed by the queen). For his services to his nation, the prime minister was knighted by the queen in 1983. His deputy prime minister Clement Maynard received the same accolade in 1989.

In August 1992 there came the biggest political upset since Pindling took power in 1967. His Progressive Liberal Party was defeated in a general election by the Free National Movement party, headed by lawyer Hubert Alexander Ingraham. The 45-year-old former chairman of the PLP and Cabinet member under Pindling had been expelled from the party by Pindling in 1986 because of his outspoken comments on alleged corruption inside the government. Ingraham's continued emphasis on this issue during the 1992 campaign did much to lead to Pindling's defeat and Ingraham's taking over as prime minister. Ingraham was re-elected for another five-year term in 1996.

Residents, for the most part, are proud of their country and are actively involved in bettering their own lot—the last complete census showed about 27% of the population was attending school at one level or another. And in the spirit of their national motto—Forward, Upward, Onward Together—they graciously welcome the ever-increasing numbers of outsiders who have discovered their little piece of paradise.

— Ian Glass

IN SEARCH OF COLUMBUS

I first heard the singing toward the middle of the night, as the mail boat M.V. *Maxine* plowed southward between Eleuthera and the Exumas. The sound drifted faintly to where I lay doubled up on a bench in the main cabin with my head on a cardboard crate of pears and a copy of the *Bahama Journal* shielding my eyes from a yellow bug light.

It was a two-part chant, almost African in its rhythm. I looked down the dim corridor to the bridge, where the crewman at the wheel was singing softly in harmony with his companion on the midnight-to-four watch. The second man was shuffling back and forth, keeping time. It was a scene out of Conrad, and a reminder that this is still what transportation is like in much of the world: pitching through the waters of a dark archipelago, sleeping with your head on a box of fruit, while guys sing and dance on the bridge.

The *Maxine* was 14 hours out of Potter's Cay, Nassau, the Bahamas, on the 22-hour run to the island of San Salvador. I had long since abandoned my claustrophobic upper bunk in the boat's only passenger compartment and had stayed out on deck until dark, sprawling over a tarp that covered bags of cement, taking shallow breaths to ration the stench of diesel fuel. Finally, half soaked from the waves constantly breaching the port rail, I had retreated to the last remotely habitable place on board—the big common room with its table and benches and its clutter of

cargo for the islands. Four dozen eggs, the cartons taped together. An oscillating fan. Gallon jars of mayonnaise, their future owners' names written on the labels. Two galvanized tubs. Homemade sound equipment for the band that plays in the bar on San Salvador. My pillow of pears, consigned to Francita Gardiner of Rum Cay. Bags, boxes, crates—and, secured somehow on the opposite bench, with ears alert and bright, eager eyes, a life-size ceramic German shepherd, soon to be a boon companion to someone in a place where a real German shepherd probably would die of heat prostration. Every time I woke to shift positions during that endless night, I would glance across the cabin, and there would be the good dog, looking as if he were waiting for a biscuit.

It is altogether possible to fly from Nassau to San Salvador in an hour and a half, but I had cast my lot with the mayonnaise and the galvanized tubs because I wanted to reach the island by water. San Salvador is arguably the most famous landfall in history: In 1992 the New World and the Old celebrated (or lamented, depending on one's politics) the 500th anniversary of the arrival of the *Niña, Pinta,* and *Santa María* at this coral-gilt outcrop. Anticipation of the tourism the quincentennial would inspire is no doubt the reason why the creaking and malodorous *Maxine* was eventually replaced by a new 110-ft mail boat with air-conditioned cabins. Fruit-box pillows are finally going out of style in the Bahamas.

My plan was to retrace, by whatever transportation was available, the route Christopher Columbus followed through Bahamian waters after his landing at San Salvador on October 12, 1492. On the face of it, this seems a simple enough task: The log of the first voyage, lost in the original but substantially transcribed by the near-contemporary chronicler Bartolome de Las Casas, describes the fleet's circuitous route through the archipelago and the series of island landfalls it made. The problem is, the island names given are those that Columbus coined with each new discovery. From San Salvador he sailed to what he called "Santa María de la Concepción," then to "Fernandina," then to "Isabela," then to the southwest and out of the Bahamian archipelago on his way to Cuba. With the exception of San Salvador, which was called Watling Island until

1926, none of these islands bears its Columbus name today. And the distances, directions, and descriptions of terrain given in the surviving version of the log are just ambiguous enough, at crucial junctures, to have inspired nine major theories as to exactly which sequence of island landfalls was followed. Some of the theories are more than a bit tenuous, depending heavily on a blithe disregard of their own weak points and an amplification of everyone else's departures from the log or from common sense. You begin to wonder, after a while, if someone couldn't take the Las Casas translation and use it to prove that Columbus landed on Chincoteague and sailed into the Tidal Basin by way of Annapolis.

But two plausible theories stand out. One, championed by the late historian and Columbus biographer Admiral Samuel Eliot Morison, is based on a first landing at today's San Salvador. The other says the first landing was at Samana Cay, a smaller, uninhabited island on the eastern fringes of the chain. Samana Cay's most recent proponent has been Joseph Judge of the National Geographic Society; in 1986 he published an exhaustive defense of his position, based in part on a computer's estimation of where Columbus should have ended up after the Atlantic crossing. The jury is still out on both major theories, as it is on the less commonly held ones. It probably always will be. For the purposes of my trip, though, I had to choose one version and stick with it. On the basis of my layman's reading of the log, I decided to go with Morison.

In this version, San Salvador is San Salvador, Santa María de la Concepción is today's Rum Cay, Fernandina is Long Island, and Isabela is Crooked Island. This was the sequence I planned to follow as the *Maxine* approached San Salvador's Fernandez Bay at 9 o'clock in the morning.

This island is fairly large and very flat. It is green, with many trees and several bodies of water. There is a very large lagoon in the middle of the island and there are no mountains. It is a pleasure to gaze upon this place because it is all so green, and the weather is delightful.

— Christopher Columbus's log,
October 13, 1492

We docked at Cockburn Town, the only settlement of any size on San Salvador. Cockburn Town, population several hundred souls, was the type and model of the Bahamian Out Island communities I would see along the Columbus track over the next few days: three or four streets of cinder-block-and-stucco houses, some brightly painted; a grocery store and a bar—the Harlem Square Club, site of a big dominoes tournament that week; a post office/radiophone station; and a couple of churches. On the facade of the Catholic church, Holy Savior, there was a peeling relief portrait of Christopher Columbus.

In the late morning heat I walked the half mile of blacktop—scrub brush on one side and ocean views on the other—that separates Cockburn Town from the Riding Rock Inn.

The latter is a handful of cottages, a short block of plain but cheerful motel units, and a restaurant/bar, all right on the water; up at the bar most of the talk you hear has to do with skin diving. Divers are the principal clientele here. When I arrived, the place was securely in the hands of a California club called the Flipperdippers. At the poolside cookout just after I pulled in, the first snippet of conversation I caught was a tyro Flipperdipper asking an old hand if a basket starfish would eat until it exploded. The answer was no, and without waiting around to find out why the questioner suspected such a thing I got up for more rice and crabs. That's when the *maîtresse de barbecue* hove into my path and told me about the dance that night: "If you don't dance, you don't get breakfast."

With the assistance of a Flipperdipper or two, I earned my breakfast. The band was a Cockburn Town outfit of indeterminate numerical strength. Guitarists and conga drummers came and went, and everyone kept commenting that things were really supposed to start jumping when the Kiwanis meeting at the Harlem Square Club let out. Shortly after 10, the band did get a transfusion of new talent, all wearing white cabana shirts patterned with yellow-and-black Kiwanis emblems. They played a couple of good sets, but they did an even better job of exemplifying the phenomenon

---

Excerpted from The Log of Christopher Columbus, *by Robert H. Fuson, courtesy of International Marine Publishing,* © 1987.

scholars call the "Columbian Exchange," that cross-pollination of peoples, cultures, flora and fauna, foodstuffs, and microorganisms that followed in the wake of the admiral's fleet and has been transmogrifying the Eastern and Western hemispheres ever since. Here were six descendants of African slaves, wearing the insignia of an American fraternal organization, playing music written by a Jamaican who thought Haile Selassie was God, for a merry throng of skin-diving orthodontists from California on an island discovered by an Italian working for Spain but settled along with the rest of the archipelago by British and American planters who imported the slaves to begin with.

About all that was missing were the Lucayans, the native Bahamians extirpated by the Spaniards—who worked them to death in the mines of Hispaniola—within a generation after Columbus's arrival. It was the Lucayans' island I set off to see the following morning, by motor scooter and on foot.

The people here call this island Guanahani in their language, and their speech is very fluent, although I do not understand any of it. They are friendly and well-dispositioned people who bear no arms except for small spears, and they have no iron. I showed one my sword, and through ignorance he grabbed it by the blade and cut himself.

— October 12

The San Salvador of the Lucayans is but a memory, as they are. When Columbus arrived, there were tall trees on the island, but the planters of the late 18th and early 19th centuries deforested the place so that now virtually the only vegetation is the dense, stickery brush called "haulback." The island's interior, though, still conveys the same sense of impenetrability and desolation that it must have to the first Europeans who came here, and no doubt to the Lucayans themselves. Fishermen as well as cultivators must have stayed close to shore, except to travel from one end of San Salvador to the other by dugout canoe across a system of brackish lakes that covers nearly half of the interior. From a crude concrete-and-wood observation platform on a rise near the airport, you can take in the sprawl of these lakes and the lonely, thicketed hills (the terrain isn't all as flat as Columbus described it) that break them into crazy patterns. No one lives there; it's hard to imagine that anyone ever goes there.

I drove the scooter the length of the island's circuit road, past crescent beaches with white sand so fine it coats your feet like flour, past ruined plantation buildings, past "Ed's First and Last Bar," a homey little joint out in the sticks that would be beerless until the cases made it up from the mail boat dock, past four monuments to Columbus's landing at four different places (a fifth marker is underwater, where somebody decided his anchor hit bottom), and past the Dixon Hill Lighthouse ("Imperial Lighthouse Service"), billed as one of 10 left in the world that run on kerosene. Past, and then back again—I bullied the scooter up Dixon Hill, because you don't get to climb to the top of a lighthouse every day.

I went looking for the light keeper, but instead I found my ride to Rum Cay, according to Morison the second of Columbus's landfalls on his first voyage. It was a family of blue-water sailors—an American named Kent, his German wife, Britta, and their two-month-old baby, Luke, who had cruised to San Salvador from St. Thomas in their 32-foot sailboat. Having hitchhiked up from Cockburn Town, the baby in a shaded basket, they too were waiting for the light keeper to show up; after she did, and took us to the top, the sailing couple offered to let me hitch with them the next day on the 30-mile run to Rum Cay. I soon learned I would be in good hands: Later that day, Kent asked a local if he knew anything about Rum Cay.

"What do you want to know?" the man responded.

"What's the anchorage like in a southeast wind?"

I'd have asked where to eat, or if the Kiwanis had a band.

I made sail and saw so many islands that I could not decide where to go first . . . Finally, I looked for the largest island and decided to go there.

— October 14

Christopher Columbus left San Salvador on October 11, 1492, and later that day arrived at the island he named Santa María de la Concepción. My adopted family and I weighed anchor at Cockburn Town and sailed out of Fernandez Bay early in the morning of a bright June day, flying fish scudding around our bows and cottony trade clouds riding briskly above. Luke, already a veteran mariner, slept in his basket below. We sighted Rum Cay when we were 10 miles out from San Salvador—Columbus had a much higher mast to climb—but the distant shoreline was to loom for a long time before we could draw very close to it. The east shore and much of the south shore of Rum Cay are girded with lethal reefs, and both the charts and the *Yachtsman's Guide to the Bahamas* go to great pains to point out so precise a route to the anchorage that it might as well have been the directions to a parking space in George Town. Six other boats had negotiated the coral gauntlet that day, including one whose captain gave us half of a blackfin tuna he'd just caught. How Columbus safely pulled it off (his anchorage was at a point west of ours) is beyond imagining.

Rum Cay, which once made a living selling sea salt to Nova Scotia's cod packers, has shriveled in population until barely 60 people today inhabit its sole settlement of Port Nelson. An American, David Melville, opened a small skin-diving resort called the Rum Cay Club a mile from town a few years back: When I arrived, the place was closed for renovations. There were no Flipperdippers here—just Melville, a couple of handymen, and the locals down the road. Rum Cay was, for the moment, almost out of things to do and people to do them.

Almost, but not quite. There's always Kay's Bar, where proprietor Dolores Wilson turns out lovely baked chicken and coconut bread to wash down with the Out Islands' requisite gallons of beer and rum in an atmosphere dominated by a satellite TV, an antique space-age jukebox, turtle shells with colored lightbulbs in them, and a giant poster of Bob Marley wearing a beatific grin and knitted hat that looks like a Rasta halo. People who sailed to the Bahamas years ago have told me that Dolores was once something of a hell-raiser, but she seems to have settled into sweet grandmotherliness by now. For ethyl-powered amusement, I had to rely on an expatriate Oklahoman named Billy. Billy, whose personal style ran to the pirate-biker look, was Melville's mechanical factotum at the Rum Cay Club. His avocation, as I discovered when I took a Jeep ride with him to the other side of the island, is nonstop talking. In the space of an hour, Billy went chapter and verse on everything from his archery prowess in Oklahoma, to how he could build an ammonia-powered icehouse like the one in *The Mosquito Coast,* to his deepest feelings about the universe: "You know, I like everything and I hate everything."

"That's called having a lover's quarrel with the world," I told him, remembering Frost.

"Oh, they have a name for it now?"

I decided not to linger very long at Santa María de la Concepción, for I saw that there was no gold there and the wind freshened to a SE crosswind. I departed the island for the ship after a two hours' stay.

— October 16

It was Billy who drove me to catch a plane to Long Island—Columbus's Fernandina, his third landfall—on the following afternoon. Back on San Salvador, I'd been told that the ticket to getting off Rum Cay without waiting for the next mail boat was to "ask for Bobby with the plane." But there was no plane on the island's crushed-coral landing strip. Bobby had flown somewhere, so rather than spend another night I asked Melville to radio the Stella Maris Inn on Long Island for a plane. They sent a Cessna four-seater, which landed just as Billy was pouring me a rum-and-powdered-lemonade at his house—he insisted on this hospitable stopover, since it was a whole mile between Kay's Bar and the airstrip. Besides, his own much-loved blue plastic cup was empty.

Long Island: a day's sail from Rum Cay for the *Niña, Pinta,* and *Santa María* on October 17, 1492; 15 minutes in the Cessna. As we approached the landing strip, I looked down to see territory that looked almost like a manicured suburb compared with the trackless scrub forests of Rum Cay and San Salvador. Here were roads, trees, villas, broad beaches, swimming pools . . . in short, a modest but complete resort, and run by Germans to boot. This last fact is worthy of remark because of the concept known as "Bahamian time," best defined as a devil-may-care approach to the minute hand. Somehow, the Germans and Bahamians had arrived at a compromise: The shuttle to the beach leaves more or less on time, but you don't have to eat breakfast at 7:23 AM.

I wanted to follow Columbus up and down this island. Near its northern tip is a shallow cove outside of which he anchored while several of his men went ashore for water. If local legend can be trusted, they filled their casks at a deep natural well in the coral rock, which a Stella Maris driver showed me. He had drawn water there as a small boy, just 450 years after the Spanish expedition.

A couple of miles from the well was the cove, a harbor with "two entrances," according to the 1492 log, which the admiral sounded in his ships' boats. At least it seemed to me to be the place, and "Where Was Columbus?" is a game that anyone with a copy of the log can play. I explored the cove and, while snorkeling, was reminded of the entry for October 17: "Here the fishes are so unlike ours that it is amazing."

To reach Columbus's final Long Island anchorage, at a place called Little Harbour in a village with the pretty name of Roses, was not such an easy job. I rented a VW bug and drove south for nearly 80 miles to the tip of this 2-mile-wide island. The road passed through one little town after another, each with its neat cinder-block school and tiny Protestant church. At Roses I found a storekeeper who knew the road to Little Harbour. It ended at a dump a mile into the bush. I walked nearly another mile—had I been heading due east I would have been in the water. I wasn't going to find Little Harbour, not in this pounding sun on a trail narrowing to the width of an iguana, any more than Columbus was going to find Japan.

Columbus got farther than I did, though. He wandered southeast from Long Island to Crooked Island, then southwest to the southernmost of the Ragged Islands, where the tiny outpost called Duncan Town now stands. This was his last Bahamas anchorage before he sailed off to Cuba, Hispaniola, and immortality.

The odd thing is, Columbus had an easier time pressing ahead than I would have had. Although it's true that he was not only lost in the Caribbean but stuck in the 15th century, at least his fleet was self-contained, and one island was as good as an-

other. For me, the Cessnas were too expensive, the mail boats too infrequent, the lodgings from Long Island south, on Crooked Island and at Duncan Town, nonexistent. These places are as far away as they ever were. They are, in fact, parts of the New World that haven't really been discovered yet.

— William G. Scheller

CASHING IN: A CASINO GAMBLING PRIMER

For a short-form handbook on the rules, the plays, the odds, and the strategies for the most popular casino games—or to decide on the kind of action that's for you and suits your style—read on. You must be 18 to gamble; Bahamians and permanent residents are not permitted to indulge.

The Good Bets

The first part of any viable casino strategy is to risk the most money on wagers that present the lowest edge for the house. Blackjack, craps, video poker, and baccarat are the most advantageous to the bettor in this regard. The two types of bets at baccarat have a house advantage of a little more than 1%. The basic line bets at craps, if backed up with full odds, can be as low as ½%. Blackjack and video poker, at times, can not only put you even with the house (a true 50-50 proposition), but actually give you a slight long-term advantage.

How can a casino possibly provide you with a 50-50 or even a positive expectation at some of its games? First, because a vast number of suckers make the bad bets (those with a house advantage of 5%–35%, such as roulette, keno, and slots) day in and day out. Second, because the casino knows that very few people are aware of the opportunities to beat the odds. Third, because it takes skill—requiring study and practice—to be in a position to exploit these opportunities the casino presents. However, a mere hour or two spent learning strategies for the beatable games will put you light years ahead of the vast majority of visitors who give the gambling industry an average 12% to 15% profit margin.

Baccarat

The most "glamorous" game in the casino, baccarat (pronounced *bah*-kuh-rah) is a version of *chemin de fer,* popular in European gambling halls, and is a favorite with high rollers, because thousands of dollars are often staked on one hand. The Italian word *baccara* means "zero"; this refers to the point value of 10s and picture cards. The game is run by four pit personnel. Two dealers sit side by side in the middle of the table; they handle the winning and losing bets and keep track of each player's "commission" (explained below). The "caller" stands in the middle of the other side of the table and dictates the action. The ladderman supervises the game and acts as final judge if any disputes arise.

HOW TO PLAY

Baccarat is played with eight decks of cards dealt from a large "shoe" (or cardholder). Each player is offered a turn at handling the shoe and dealing the cards. Two two-card hands are dealt, the "player" and the "bank" hands. The player who deals the cards is called the banker, though the house, of course, banks both hands. The players bet on which hand, player or banker, will come closest to adding up to 9 (a "natural"). The cards are totaled as follows: ace through 9 retain face value, while 10s and picture cards are worth zero. If you have a hand adding up to more than 10, the number 10 is subtracted from the total. For example, if one hand contains a 10 and a 4, the hand adds up to 4. If the other holds an ace and 6, it adds up to 7. If a hand has a 7 and 9, it adds up to 6.

Depending on the two hands, the caller either declares a winner and loser (if either hand actually adds up to 8 or 9), or calls for another card for the player hand (if it totals 1, 2, 3, 4, 5, or 10). The bank hand then either stands pat or draws a card, determined by a complex series of rules depending on what the player's total is and dictated by the caller. When one or the other hand is declared a winner, the dealers go into action to pay off the winning wagers, collect the losing wagers, and add up the commission (usually 5%) that the house collects on the bank hand. Both bets have a house advantage of slightly more than 1%.

The player-dealer (or banker) continues to hold the shoe as long as the bank hand wins.

As soon as the player hand wins, the shoe moves counterclockwise around the table. Players are not required to deal; they can refuse the shoe and pass it to the next player. Because the caller dictates the action, the player responsibilities are minimal. It's not necessary to know any of the card-drawing rules, even if you're the banker.

BACCARAT STRATEGY

Making a bet at baccarat is very simple. All you have to do is place your money in either the bank, player, or tie box on the layout, which appears directly in front of where you sit at the table. If you're betting that the bank hand will win, you put your chips in the bank box; bets for the player hand go in the player box. (Only real suckers bet on the tie.) Most players bet on the bank hand when they deal, since they "represent" the bank, and to do otherwise would seem as if they were betting "against" themselves. This isn't really true, but it seems that way. In the end, playing baccarat is a simple matter of guessing whether the player or banker hand will come closest to 9, and deciding how much to bet on the outcome.

Blackjack

HOW TO PLAY

Basically, here's how it works: You play blackjack against a dealer, and whichever of you comes closest to a card total of 21 is the winner. Number cards are worth their face value, picture cards are worth 10, and aces are worth either 1 or 11. (Hands with aces in them are known as "soft" hands. Always count the ace first as an 11; if you also have a 10, your total will be 21, not 11.) If the dealer has a 17 and you have a 16, you lose. If you have an 18 against a dealer's 17, you win (even money). If both you and the dealer have a 17, it's a tie (or "push") and no money changes hands. If you go over a total of 21 (or "bust"), you lose immediately, even if the dealer also busts later in the hand. If your first two cards add up to 21 (a "natural"), you're paid 3 to 2. However, if the dealer also has a natural, it's a push. A natural beats a total of 21 achieved with more than two cards.

You're dealt two cards, either face down or face up, depending on the custom of the particular casino. The dealer also gives herself two cards, one face down and one face up (except in double-exposure blackjack, where both the dealer's cards are visible). Depending on your first two cards and the dealer's up card, you can **stand,** or refuse to take another card. You can **hit,** or take as many cards as you need until you stand or bust. You can **double down,** or double your bet and take one card. You can **split** a like pair; if you're dealt two 8s, for example, you can double your bet and play the 8s as if they're two hands. You can **buy insurance** if the dealer is showing an ace. Here you're wagering half your initial bet that the dealer *does* have a natural; if so, you lose your initial bet, but are paid 2 to 1 on the insurance (which means the whole thing is a push). You can **surrender** half your initial bet if you're holding a bad hand (known as a "stiff") such as a 15 or 16 against a high-up card like a 9 or 10.

BLACKJACK STRATEGY

Playing blackjack is not only knowing the rules—it's also knowing *how* to play. Many people devote a great deal of time to learning complicated statistical schemes. However, if you don't have the time, energy, or inclination to get that seriously involved, the following basic strategies, which cover more than half the situations you'll face, should allow you to play the game with a modicum of skill and a paucity of humiliation:

- When your hand is a stiff (a total of 12, 13, 14, 15, or 16) and the dealer shows a 2, 3, 4, 5, or 6, always stand.
- When your hand is a stiff and the dealer shows a 7, 8, 9, 10, or ace, always hit.
- When you hold 17, 18, 19, or 20, always stand.
- When you hold a 10 or 11 and the dealer shows a 2, 3, 4, 5, 6, 7, 8, or 9, always double down.
- When you hold a pair of aces or a pair of 8s, always split.
- Never buy insurance.

Craps

Craps is a dice game played at a large rectangular table with rounded corners. Up to 12 players can crowd around the table, all standing. The layout is mounted at the bottom of a surrounding "rail," which prevents the dice from being thrown off the table and provides an opposite wall against which to bounce the dice. It can require up to four pit personnel to run an action-packed, fast-paced game of craps. Two dealers handle the bets made on ei-

ther side of the layout. A "stickman" wields the long wooden "stick," curved at one end, which is used to move the dice around the table; the stickman also calls the number that's rolled and books the proposition bets made in the middle of the layout. The "boxman" sits between the two dealers and oversees the game; he settles any disputes about rules, payoffs, mistakes, and so on.

HOW TO PLAY

To play, just stand at the table wherever you can find an open space. You can start betting casino chips immediately, but you have to wait your turn to be the shooter. The dice move around the table in a clockwise fashion: The person to your right shoots before you, the one to the left after (the stickman will give you the dice at the appropriate time). It's important, when you're the "shooter," to roll the dice hard enough so they bounce off the end wall of the table; this ensures a random bounce and shows that you're not trying to control the dice with a "soft roll."

CRAPS STRATEGY

Playing craps is fairly straightforward; it's the betting that's complicated. The basic concepts are as follows: If, the first time the shooter rolls the dice, he or she turns up a 7 or 11, that's called a "natural"— an automatic win. If a 2, 3, or 12 comes up on the first throw (called the "comeout roll"), that's termed "craps"—an automatic lose. Each of the numbers 4, 5, 6, 8, 9, or 10 on a first roll is known as a "point": The shooter keeps rolling the dice until the point comes up again. If a 7 turns up before the point does, that's another loser. When either the point or a losing 7 is rolled, this is known as a "decision," which happens on average every 3.3 rolls.

But "winning" and "losing" rolls of the dice are entirely relative in this game, because there are two ways you can bet at craps: "for" the shooter or "against" the shooter. Betting for means that the shooter will "make his point" (win). Betting against means that the shooter will "seven out" (lose). (Either way, you're actually betting against the house, which books all wagers.) If you're betting "for" on the come-out, you'd place your chips on the layout's "pass line." If a 7 or 11 is rolled, you win even money. If a 2, 3, or 12 (craps) is rolled, you lose your bet. If you're betting "against" on the come-out, you place your chips in the "don't pass bar." A 7 or 11 loses, a 2, 3, or 12 wins. A shooter can bet for or against himself or herself, as well as for or against the other players.

There are also roughly two dozen wagers you can make on any single specific roll of the dice. Craps strategy books can give you the details on Come/Don't Come, Odds, Place, Buy, Big Six, Field, and Proposition bets.

Roulette

Roulette is a casino game that utilizes a perfectly balanced wheel with 38 numbers (0, 00, and 1 through 36), a small white ball, a large layout with 11 different betting options, and special "wheel chips." The layout organizes 11 different bets into six "inside bets" (the single numbers, or those closest to the dealer) and five "outside bets" (the grouped bets, or those closest to the players).

The dealer spins the wheel clockwise and the ball counterclockwise. When the ball slows, the dealer announces, "No more bets." The ball drops from the "back track" to the "bottom track," caroming off built-in brass barriers and bouncing in and out of the different cups in the wheel before settling into the cup of the winning number. Then the dealer places a marker on the number and scoops all the losing chips into her corner. Depending on how crowded the game is, the casino can count on roughly 50 spins of the wheel per hour.

HOW TO PLAY

To buy in, place your cash on the layout near the wheel. Inform the dealer of the denomination of the individual unit you intend to play (usually 25¢ or $1, but it can go up as high as $500). Know the table limits (displayed on a sign in the dealer area)—don't ask for a 25¢ denomination if the minimum is $1. The dealer gives you a stack of wheel chips of a different color from those of all the other players, and places a chip marker atop one of your wheel chips on the rim of the wheel to identify its denomination. Note that you must cash in your wheel chips at the roulette table before you leave the game. Only the dealer can verify how much they're worth.

ROULETTE STRATEGY

With **inside bets,** you can lay any number of chips (depending on the table limits) on a single number, 1 through 36 or 0 or 00.

If the number hits, your payoff is 35 to 1, for a return of $36. You could, conceivably, place a $1 chip on all 38 numbers, but the return of $36 would leave you $2 short, which divides out to 5.26%, the house advantage. If you place a chip on the line between two numbers and one of those numbers hits, you're paid 17 to 1 for a return of $18 (again, $2 short of the true odds). Betting on three numbers returns 11 to 1, four numbers returns 8 to 1, five numbers pays 6 to 1 (this is the worst bet at roulette, with a 7.89% disadvantage), and six numbers pays 5 to 1.

To place an **outside bet,** lay a chip on one of three "columns" at the lower end of the layout next to numbers 34, 35, and 36; this pays 2 to 1. A bet placed in the first 12, second 12, or third 12 boxes also pays 2 to 1. A bet on red or black, odd or even, and 1 through 18 or 19 through 36 pays off at even money, 1 to 1. If you think you can bet on red *and* black, or odd *and* even, in order to play roulette and drink for free all night, think again. The green 0 or 00, which fall outside these two basic categories, will come up on average once every 19 spins of the wheel.

Slot Machines

Around the turn of the century, Charlie Fey built the first mechanical slot in his San Francisco basement. Slot-machine technology has exploded in the past 20 years, and now there are hundreds of different models, which accept everything from pennies to specially minted $500 tokens. The major advance in the game, however, is the progressive jackpot. Banks of slots within a particular casino are connected by computer, and the jackpot total is displayed on a digital meter above the machines. Generally, the total increases by 5% of the wager. If you're playing a dollar machine, each time you pull the handle (or press the spin button), a nickel is added to the jackpot.

HOW TO PLAY

To play, insert your penny, nickel, quarter, silver dollar, or dollar token into the slot at the far right edge of the machine. Pull the handle or press the spin button, then wait for the reels to spin and stop one by one, and for the machine to determine whether you're a winner (occasionally) or a loser (the rest of the time). It's pretty simple—but because there are so many different types of machines nowadays, be sure you know exactly how the one you're playing operates.

SLOT-MACHINE STRATEGY

The house advantage on slots varies widely from machine to machine, between 3% and 25%. Casinos that advertise a 97% payback are telling you that at least one of their slot machines has a house advantage of 3%. Which one? There's really no way of knowing. Generally, $1 machines pay back at a higher percentage than quarter or nickel machines. On the other hand, machines with smaller jackpots pay back more money more frequently, meaning that you'll be playing with more of your winnings.

One of the all-time great myths about slot machines is that they're "due" for a jackpot. Slots, like roulette, craps, keno, and Big Six, are subject to the Law of Independent Trials, which means the odds are permanently and unalterably fixed. If the odds of lining up three sevens on a 25¢ slot machine have been set by the casino at 1 in 10,000, then those odds remain 1 in 10,000 whether the three 7s have been hit three times in a row or not hit for 90,000 plays. Don't waste a lot of time playing a machine that you suspect is "ready," and don't think if someone hits a jackpot on a particular machine only minutes after you've finished playing on it that it was "yours."

Video Poker

Like blackjack, video poker is a game of strategy and skill, and at select times on select machines, the player actually holds the advantage, however slight, over the house. Unlike slot machines, you can determine the exact edge of video poker machines. Like slots, however, video poker machines are often tied into a progressive meter; when the jackpot total reaches high enough, you can beat the casino at its own game. The variety of video poker machines is already large, and it's growing steadily larger. All of the different machines are played in similar fashion, but the strategies are different. This section deals only with straight-draw video poker.

HOW TO PLAY

The schedule for the payback on winning hands is posted on the machine, usually above the screen. It lists the returns for a high pair (generally jacks or better), two pair, three of a kind, a flush, full house, straight flush, four of a kind, and royal flush,

depending on the number of coins played—usually 1, 2, 3, 4, or 5. Look for machines that pay with a single coin played: one coin for "jacks or better" (meaning a pair of jacks, queens, kings, or aces; any other pair is a stiff), two coins for two pairs, three for three of a kind, six for a flush, nine for a full house, 50 for a straight flush, 100 for four of a kind, and 250 for a royal flush. This is known as a 9/6 machine—one that gives a nine-coin payback for the full house and a six-coin payback for the flush with one coin played. Other machines are known as 8/5 (8 for the full house, 5 for the flush), 7/5, and 6/5.

You want a 9/6 machine because it gives you the best odds: The return from a standard 9/6 straight-draw machine is 99.5%; you give up only half a percent to the house. An 8/5 machine returns 97.3%. On 6/5 machines, the figure drops to 95.1%, slightly less than roulette. Machines with varying paybacks are scattered throughout the casinos. In some you'll see an 8/5 machine right next to a 9/6, and someone will be blithely playing the 8/5 machine!

As with slot machines, it's always optimum to play the maximum number of coins to qualify for the jackpot. You insert five coins into the slot and press the "deal" button. Five cards appear on the screen—say, 5, J, Q, 5, 9. To hold the pair of 5s, you press the hold buttons under the first and fourth cards. The word "hold" appears underneath the two 5s. You then press the "draw" button (often the same button as "deal") and three new cards appear on the screen—say, 10, J, 5. You have three 5s; with five coins bet, the machine will give you 15 credits. Now you can press the "max bet" button: five units will be removed from your number of credits, and five new cards will appear on the screen. You repeat the hold and draw process; if you hit a winning hand, the proper payback will be added to your credits. Those who want coins rather than credit can hit the "cash out" button at any time. Some machines don't have credit counters and automatically dispense coins for a winning hand.

VIDEO-POKER STRATEGY

Like blackjack, video poker has a basic strategy that's been formulated by the computer simulation of hundreds of millions of hands. The most effective way to learn it is with a video poker computer program that deals the cards on your screen, then tutors you in how to play each hand properly. If you don't want to devote that much time to the study of video poker, memorizing these six rules will help you make the right decision for more than half the hands you'll be dealt:

- If you're dealt a completely "stiff" hand (no like cards and no picture cards), draw five new cards.
- If you're dealt a hand with no like cards but with one jack, queen, king, or ace, always hold on to the picture card; if you're dealt two different picture cards, hold both. But if you're dealt three different picture cards, only hold two (the two of the same suit, if that's an option).
- If you're dealt a pair, always hold it, no matter what the face value.
- Never hold a picture card with a pair of 2s through 10s.
- Never draw two cards to try for a straight or a flush.
- Never draw one card to try for an inside straight.

INDEX

215

X = restaurant, ⌷⌷ = hotel

Looking for a different kind of vacation?

Fodor's makes it easy with a full line of international guidebooks to suit a variety of interests—from adventure to romance to language help.

At bookstores everywhere.
www.fodors.com

WHEREVER YOU TRAVEL, *H*ELP IS NEVER FAR AWAY.

From planning your trip to providing travel assistance along the way, American Express® Travel Service Offices are always there to help.

Bahamas

Mundy Tours (R)
Suite 20, Regent Center 4
Freeport
809/352-4444

Playtours (R)
303 Shirley Street
Nassau
809/322-2931

Travel

http://www.americanexpress.com/travel